G000155137

Vanguard Books(Pvt)Ltd.
Karachi. Ph: 4944593

Auditing the
IT Environment

Auditing the IT Environment

Assessing and Measuring Risk and Control

ANDREW CHAMBERS
and GRAHAM RAND

FT

PITMAN
PUBLISHING

PITMAN PUBLISHING
128 Long Acre, London WC2E 9AN

A Division of Pearson Professional Limited

© Andrew Chambers and Graham Rand 1994

First published in Great Britain 1994

British Library Cataloguing in Publication Data
A CIP catalogue record for this book can be obtained from the British Library.

ISBN 0 273 03769 2

10 9 8 7 6 5 4 3 2

Phototypeset in Linotron Times Roman
by Northern Phototypesetting Co. Ltd., Bolton
Printed and bound in Great Britain
by Biddles Ltd., Guildford and King's Lynn

To Celia and Sybil

CONTENTS

PREFACE

This book seeks to fill a gap in the range of texts on IT security, control and audit. It applies audit risk analysis techniques to the IT environment itself. It is not a general computer auditing text as its deliberate focus is more on the various elements of contemporary IT.

The book's focus is less on the applications of IT to commercial tasks and, with the exception of two risk analysis tools which may be computerised, less on the general challenge of automating the audit through the use of audit interrogation software, electronic audit working papers and the like.

Too frequently auditors skirt round the *technology* of information processing and the essential controls over this technology. These may be formidable challenges to the uninitiated. We hope this book will give auditors confidence to get to grips with the various parts of this engine which drives modern business. We hope too that IT specialists will gain new insights into the control of IT by observing their specialism through the eyes of the auditor. Likewise, general management will find much of use about IT control within the pages of this book.

Many readers who are auditors will have some familiarity with the two risk analysis techniques which are explained and applied in this book. First is the audit risk formula method which we apply in Chapter 2 to determining the need to be audited of the component parts of IT within a business. Secondly, the control matrix approach which highlights and ranks in importance the risks within an IT activity; we introduce this technique in Chapter 3 and apply it in our consideration of strategic and operational IT areas in Chapters 4 to 27.

These risk analysis techniques are tried and tested tools which simplify the task of identifying and documenting major risks and assessing their control. Developed originally by auditors they should have a place in the toolkit of IT specialists and general management. It is not essential to utilise a computer in order to use these two risk analysis techniques but it can be done readily using any spreadsheet software. Alternatively, software is available to do this from:

Management Audit Ltd.
Water-mill, Old Bolingbroke, Lincs PE23 4EU
Tel: 01790 763350; Fax: 01790 763253

ACKNOWLEDGEMENTS

We are grateful to our many colleagues and friends who have taught us what we understand about IT control and audit, and about risk analysis techniques, and to those who have assisted us with this manuscript.

The risk analysis techniques we use have their origins in a respectable pedigree. Yet the genesis of the control matrix technique seems to us to be shrouded in the mists of time. Managers and auditors probably have always considered what might go wrong in a business and what measures might be effective to prevent such failures. Inevitably they always have had to acknowledge the differing degrees of potential effectiveness of these various measures and how this changes if they are not entirely complied with. Probably nobody can say when auditors first represented these concepts in internal control questionnaires – an early example was the book *Internal Control Standards and Related Auditing Procedures* [W. H. Kamp and J. A. Cashin, publ.: Brock and Wallston, Stamford, Connecticut, 1947]. Likewise it is probable that nobody knows when auditors and managers took the logical step of representing these issues as 'matrices' with *risks* across the top and *procedures* [perhaps controls or other measures] down the side. Most likely this was first done 'on the back of an envelope' in smoke-filled audit rooms – certainly before computer-based spreadsheets became available.

Systematically documented matrix-based approaches to control evaluation were established by the early 1970s prior to the new opportunities which spreadsheets were to offer. Many early examples featured in the book *Computer Control and Audit* [W. C. Mair, D. R. Wood and K. W. Davis, publ.: Touche Ross & Co., New York, 1972]. They showed matrices of business systems with exposures as the top axis and controls as the vertical axis. Using the cells where the columns intersected with the rows they applied a numeric scale to determining the extent to which each particular control could be expected to be relied upon to reduce or eliminate an exposure – having regard to its inherent potential as well as the extent to which it was being complied with. They also recognised that exposures vary in importance according to their type – they identified nine types on an increasing scale of importance from *Erroneous Record Keeping* through *Erroneous Management Decisions* to *Competitive Disadvantage*. An early example of academic auditing research which made use of control matrices was *Evaluating Internal Control* [J. K. Loebbecke and G. R. Zuber, *The Journal of Accountancy*, February 1980, pp 49–56] and a much earlier academic research example of evaluating internal control by attaching numeric weights was *Objective Internal Control Evaluation* [R. Gene Brown, *The Journal of Accountancy*, November 1962, pp 50–56].

David Lewington and his colleagues, including Joseph Short, at Merchant Investors in the UK applied and developed similar ideas in the early 1980s, documenting them in various places, notably *Risk Analysis for Internal Auditing* [Research Report No. 19, The Institute of Internal Auditors – UK, 1987] *vide*: Chapter 5 by David Lewington and

Chapter 4 by Andrew Chambers. In Research Report No. 19 David Lewington explained aspects of the control matrix technique which we develop in our Chapter 3, and Andrew Chambers explored the audit risk formula method which we develop in this book as Chapter 2. Both techniques were anticipated in the earlier *Risk Analysis* [Audit Occasional Papers, Number 4, The Chartered Institute of Public Finance and Accountancy, February 1986].

So far as we know it was David Lewington who first pointed out for the control matrix technique the natural mathematical way of resolving (a) a numeric score for the extent to which a control would be effective at reducing or eliminating an exposure in perfect circumstances with (b) another numeric score for the extent to which the control was being complied with. He and his colleagues also suggested that the varying degrees of importance of an exposure needed to be measured on two scales – first its *Type* (they called this its *Category*) and secondly its likely *Size*. They also suggested that it was possible to produce an overall grading for each exposure taking all these numeric measures into account.

Management Audit Ltd's software **Control.IT MINPLAN** and **Organis.IT MIDPLAN** takes several stages further the concepts which underpin these risk analysis tools. Our grateful acknowledgement to these, and others, for their published ideas.

Finally, but not least, we must thank Jackie Badley for her immense assistance in preparing the manuscript for this book and assisting us in so many other administrative ways to complete this project.

Andrew Chambers
Graham Rand

Part I

INTRODUCTION

1

AUDITING THE IT ENVIRONMENT

Many businesses win a competitive advantage through their intelligent application of information technology. The leading edge of IT is now its use in strategic
information systems. The focus has changed over the years. Initially IT was
applied to administrative and accounting systems – to replace what clerks used
to do. This is still important. Greater benefits came through applying IT to
operational matters – production, distribution and so on. On these foundations
it was possible to make IT an aid to management through the provision of
timely information and assistance with analysis and decision taking.

Now we have *strategic information systems*: these may have little or nothing
to do with management information systems. They aim to achieve a strategic
advantage in the marketplace through cost or price benefits, innovation or
differentiation targeted at customers, suppliers and competitors. Just one of a
legion of well-known examples has been the provision by an airline to travel
agents of on-line travel information services leading to an increase in market
share for the airline. It is unlikely that there is any enterprise, whether private
sector driven by the profit motive or public sector where measures of service
quality may be paramount, that does not have the opportunity to gain strategic
advantages though its use of IT. Often using IT strategically involves an
innovative exploitation of certain traditional corporate advantages. For
instance Reuters took advantage of its experience as a telex-based news-
gathering agency to move into on-line subscriber financial and other information services, toppling the established providers of that information who were
relying on traditional methods of data collection and delivery.

To gain these strategic advantages there is a need to be in the vanguard of
applying new IT developments in innovative ways. It is rarely an option to wait
until technology has established itself. So there are special risks associated with
unavoidable pioneering of IT applications. Accompanying these special risks is
a premium upon effective control of the IT environment, including control
over the strategic planning process for IT.

There is little strategic benefit from following leaders in applying IT innovatively though strategic disadvantages may be overcome through a determined effort to catch up with the leaders. It is always a moving target: no enterprise can ever consider it has reached IT nirvana. The challenges are the greater as the half life of state-of-the-art IT is ever getting shorter.

If strategic information systems are those targeted at suppliers, customers or competitors which seek to achieve their advantage by innovation, differentiation or price, there are other styles of IT application which are important in modern business. The following categorisation of IT systems is a strategic continuum, progressing through to the most advanced strategic systems. Many businesses today have not yet gone so far. Of course these categories overlap. For instance co-operative systems may have abundant strategic potential. If a business has not yet applied IT effectively to its basic administration and accounting, then it is likely to be strategically vital to attend to that requirement first.

Administrative and accounting systems – using IT to perform routine clerical tasks

Operational systems – using IT to automate the processes of the enterprise

Personal systems – making managers not just computer users but computer operators and possibly system developers

Expert systems – embedding professional expertise in IT systems as a tool for less professional personnel to use effectively

Co-operative systems – tying suppliers and customers to the business

Strategic systems – competitive advantage through imaginative application of IT.

Information and IT are amongst the key resources of the modern enterprise. It is unfortunate that economists do not regard information as one of the classic *factors of production*, and that accountants exclude the quality of the information resource from being an asset on the balance sheet. This makes it harder to persuade boards of directors to address IT strategically; even today few have main board directors of IT and many other directors are IT illiterate. Investors are left in the dark about the strength or vulnerability of the business associated with its successful investment in IT.

Of course an effectively controlled IT environment is essential not just for the strategic IT systems: it serves the administrative, accounting, operational and management information IT systems as well. Most managers and staff would be reluctant to claim that their information environment was well controlled. Many businesses have masses of *data* on paper and on magnetic media which is effectively inaccessible. From data is derived *information*. Many businesses have information way beyond the uses to which it is put. From information *analysis* is performed. Many enterprises are paralysed by too much analysis and too little *decision making* based upon that analysis:

- too much data – too little information?

- too much information – too little analysis?

- too much analysis – too little decision making?

- too much decision making – not enough control over implementation?

The premium on effective control in a fast-moving IT-dependent business world is not easy to discharge. Business IT is increasingly complex and difficult to understand. Volumes of transactions are increasing geometrically. Speeding response times is invariably a commercial imperative. Automation conceals activity and there are fewer people employed so less potential to observe, review and detect. More reliance has to be placed on automated auditing methodologies.

There is usually a cost dimension to effective control and audit – as there has always been. With margins acutely under pressure in a highly competitive market economy it is not easy for managements to justify a generous resourcing of control and audit activity. Managements will often be willing to adopt new, strategically important IT-based methods of conducting business with inherent control risks and fraud potential which would have been unthinkable as business practices a generation or two ago. Carefully designed risk analysis techniques have become essential to prioritise control and audit requirements. There has never been such a thing as 100 per cent control and the nearer one approximates to it the more costly every control increment becomes. Likewise there has never been such a thing as 100 per cent audit coverage.

2

IT AUDIT NEEDS ASSESSMENT

Scope

This chapter explains a methodical way of determining which IT activities should be audited and the audit resources which should be allocated to the audit of each of these activities. We use the expression **auditable unit** *to refer to an IT activity which may be the subject of an audit. The method described entails the identification of the considerations which should underpin this determination and the representation of these considerations in an audit risk formula. The formula is then applied to each auditable unit within the audit universe so as to generate for each an audit risk score. The intention is that, in general, audit resources should be allocated over time to each auditable unit in proportion to the size of the audit risk score. The method also provides the opportunity to assess the total amount of audit resource, or the number of auditors required to complete the programme of audits and the impact upon the audit programme if audit resources are constrained.*

For the purpose of this chapter it is assumed that the audit universe of auditable units is limited to IT activities. The chapter starts with a detailed explanation of this method of audit needs assessment where the audit universe comprises the IT environment activities which are the subject of Chapters 4 to 27 of this book, and Tables 2.2 to 2.10b relate to this explanation. The chapter moves on to provide sample suggestions for applying this approach where the audit universe is IT-based applications (Tables 2.11 to 2.13), and concludes by applying it to an audit universe comprising only of IT systems and applications which are under development (Tables 2.14 to 2.16).

Every audit and review function needs a way of determining its programme of future audits or reviews. The approach described in this chapter can be used by any group which has responsibility for conducting reviews of IT activities – for instance, a specialist IT audit group, an internal audit function or an IT quality assurance group. In this chapter we are illustrating this approach with respect to audit universes of IT-related activities. The general approach is equally applicable to determining audit need for other audit universes – such as accounting systems, contracts, operational auditing – although different considerations and different audit risk formulae would be likely to be relevant in such cases. For general applications of this method, readers may wish to refer to the companion volume in this series *Effective Internal Audits – How to Plan and Implement* [Financial Times/Pitman Publishing, 1992].

CHOOSING FACTORS FOR AN IT AUDIT RISK FORMULA

Table 2.1 is our starting point. It is a list of considerations which IT auditors have identified as possible considerations which they might bear in mind when they are making decisions about what IT activities (*auditable units*) to include within their plan of audits to be conducted and the amount of audit resource which is justified for each included audit. It is offered as a checklist for others to use by marking those considerations which appear to them to be relevant in audit planning. Before being too influenced by the suggestions in Table 2.1 it is preferable for an audit planning team to jot down on a blank sheet of paper the considerations which seem to them at the outset of the planning exercise to be pertinent, based upon their past experience, and only then to use the list given in Table 2.1 to suggest further possible considerations that they might have overlooked.

Table 2.1 has two further columns. The column titled FACTOR DESCRIPTION brackets together a number of CONSIDERATION DESCRIPTIONS so as to give them common labels. The rationale for this is that all of the considerations bracketed together under a single factor label are being regarded as being related. The implicit guidance is that for the purposes of audit planning it is likely that it will be adequate to use the single given factor in cases where the audit planning team has marked more than one associated consideration. It is the factors which are carried forward to later tables and are ultimately used in the audit risk formula to perform the audit needs assessment. Users of this chapter are not obliged to agree with this guidance and can alter the factor descriptions as they desire.

There is a general requirement to minimise the number of factors selected so that the audit risk formula does not become unwieldy to use. The more factors in the audit risk formula, the greater the data collection and maintenance task. The factors in the formula should be minimised commensurate with the requirement that the audit risk formula should produce audit risk scores which reflect reasonably accurately the relative audit need for each auditable unit.

The objective is to develop and use an audit risk formula which the audit planning team, and those to whom the team reports, are confident reflects the issues that ought to underpin their audit planning. A factor which would otherwise be included can be omitted if it always varies in proportion to another factor. As suggested, a consideration can be combined with another consideration, or a number of other considerations, to arrive at one factor only – where all the considerations relate to a single issue.

Audit universes which are highly homogeneous make for the development of more reliable formulae. An example would be an audit universe which comprised only of shops or branches. It is much easier to arrive at an applicable set of factors each of which can be scored for every auditable unit within such a universe. This does not invalidate the technique for more heterogeneous audit universes. In this chapter we suggest three different formulae for three different sub-sets of the IT auditing universe, and the audit department might have other formulae for other parts of their total audit universe. It follows that such an audit department will need a way to allocate total available audit resource between all the sub-sets of the audit universe – another formula may be used for that purpose.

The challenge we are discussing here is the challenge faced by all audit managements of heterogeneous audit universes. In allocating audit resources between auditable units they are having to weigh the factors which are relevant to one audit with the factors relevant to another audit – and so on – and the relevant factors will not be common to all audits. To simulate this planning approach in the audit risk formula method described in this chapter, our recommendation is that the audit risk formula should be designed so that not all factors have to be scored for each audit. The computation performed by the formula should be able to handle this variety, and it can do so readily, using any spreadsheet package. The text in Table 2.6 explains how the computation can be done to achieve this. At least one size, one control and one audit factor must be scored for each auditable unit being assessed. The scoring basis is discussed later in this chapter. A factor should be scored for an auditable unit if the auditor's judgement is that the factor is a relevant and necessary determinant of the quantum of audit resource justified for the audit and if the data is available to allow a reliable score to be given. This is analogous to the approach which audit management takes when using traditional, intuitive approaches to planning programmes of audits where the audit universe is highly variable.

INHERENT CONTROL AND AUDIT RISK

The final column in Table 2.1 categorises the considerations and factors according to whether they address *size, control* or *audit* criteria. Size criteria are measures of inherent risk. By analogy, if someone leaves £1,000 on a desk unattended, the size (or inherent) risk is £1,000. The control criteria are measures of probability consequent upon the quality of internal control. Using the same analogy, if there is a 50 per cent probability of theft of the unattended £1,000, we can say that *Risk = Size × Control* which in this case would be 1000 × 0.5 = 500.

In business we understand that risk is a function of *how much* (inherent risk, or size risk) × *how likely* (probability risk, or control risk). This is the natural way of assessing relative risk and it is therefore the way we use. Later in this chapter we shall see that the audit risk formula is structured as *size × control* with one further refinement. Size adjusted by control gives us a measure of commercial risk. Our objective is to develop an audit risk formula which can compute an audit risk score for each auditable unit within our audit universe such that the computed score suggests the quantum of audit resource warranted for each auditable unit. We need to concede that audit time may not always be allocated in proportion to commercial risk (size adjusted by control). There may be special audit criteria which suggest further adjustments in order to turn *commercial risk* into *audit risk*. Care must be taken not to allow the *audit* criteria to dominate in the audit risk formula: if we do so, we run the risk of allocating excessive amounts of audit time to relatively unimportant auditable units, and vice versa.

Good quality control reduces the inherent (size) risk. A complete absence of control cannot magnify the inherent risk but means that in all probability everything that is at risk will be lost. In the example we used above, the control risk was 0.5: the greatest it could have been would have been a score of 1.0. Later in this chapter we utilise this idea in the mathematical structure of the *control* part of the example audit risk formulae. We also apply the same concept to the *audit* part of the formulae.

Table 2.2 shows the considerations and factors selected from Table 2.1 for development into a particular audit risk formula to be applied to the auditable units within the IT environment. For the purpose of this example, later tables in this chapter through to Table 2.10 show these auditable units as being the IT strategic and operational activities covered in Chapters 4 to 27. Auditors planning in a different environment might have chosen different factors or have adjusted the wording. As it is the factors that are to be carried forward into the formula, the sequence of columns has been altered compared with Table 2.1. Note that four *size* factors have been selected in Table 2.2 as one of them is the consolidation of two considerations. Similarly, the audit risk formula will have eleven *control* factors and only four *audit* factors. The method described in this chapter requires that there should be at least one size factor, at least one control factor and at least one audit factor.

The *size* factor labelled 'OVERALL [MINPLAN] SIZE SCORE' and the *control* factor

'OVERALL [MINPLAN] CONTROL SCORE' need some explanation. They are overall size and control scores computable for an auditable unit, control matrices for which are given as tables at the end of Chapters 4 to 27. In each case the exposures-oriented control matrix has been used, but the objectives-oriented control matrix would not have been inappropriate depending upon the emphasis required in drawing up this audit plan. Chapter 3 explains this control matrix method and details of the **Control.IT MINPLAN** software are given in the Preface to this book.

These overall *size* and *control* scores are overall assessments of the auditable unit which are obtained as a result of detailed, well-informed auditing work. They are therefore especially dependable and consequently have been given more weight in the formula. Weighting factors are explained in the next section of this chapter. It is of course at the discretion of those who are developing the audit risk formula whether to include or not to include in the formula one or both of these overall MINPLAN measures and, if included, what weight to attribute to it. Doing so does provide an effective way of integrating audit assignment work with longer term audit planning. Conversely, the factor scores for an auditable unit and the audit risk score which they provide should be information which the audit team takes to the audit assignment of the auditable unit as it is useful intelligence to suggest to the team where the chief audit challenges are likely to be.

WEIGHTING FACTORS USING A MATRIX TECHNIQUE

The formula appears in Table 2.6; Table 2.7 is a summary of the factors within the formula. The factors have been differentially weighted so as to give more or less stress to individual factors in the determination of the resulting audit risk score for an auditable unit. The factor weights are shown above the factors in Table 2.6. This weighting has been a matter of judgement and, for a small number of factors, could have been done without any special aid. For a large number of factors it is unlikely that a reasonable weighting could be developed merely by casting one's eye along the list of factors as so many factors have to be compared against each other. For instance, to produce relative weights for the eleven control factors, fifty-five pairs of separate comparisons have to be made. Due to the structure of the formula, only factors appearing in the same part of the formula (the *size*, *control* or *audit* parts) have to be relatively weighted against each other. Tables 2.3, 2.4 and 2.5 show the application of a special matrix technique to develop the relative weights for the *size*, *control* and *audit* factors which have been used in the formula (Table 2.6).

The matrix technique for weighting factors requires the user to enter a value of the relative importance of one factor compared to another factor, and so on until every pair of factors has been compared in this way. Thus, if factor B is considered to be twice as important as factor A, a value of 2 is entered in the appropriate cell. The user works in the cells *above* the diagonal line of 'is' – the 'is' being the cells which represent the comparison of each factor with itself – and the score entered in a cell is the user's assessment of the relative importance of the factor at the top of the column with the factor represented by the row. In determining the scores to be entered, the user should regard each comparison of a pair of factors as a new comparison and should not endeavour to make the score to be given consistent mathematically with earlier data entered within the matrix: this ensures that every factor is compared genuinely with every other factor. Below the diagonal line of 'is' is another cell where the same two factors intersect, into which should be entered the reciprocal of the score entered above the diagonal line of 'is'.

When all the comparative data has been entered in this way a computation is conducted using all the data in the matrix so as to arrive at the relative factor weights which will be used in the formula. This computation is illustrated in Tables 2.3, 2.4 and 2.5. First, the columns and the rows are summed. Next, the totals of the columns are divided by the totals of the rows and a square root is taken of each of the results of these divisions. In this way, all the data in the matrix has been used, and the square roots have compensated accurately for the scaling impact of the divisions. The outcomes of the square roots indicate the relative weights which should be given to the factors in order to reflect the judgemental weights given to all the pairs of factors by the user. If several people are involved in developing this planning method, a higher degree of consensus reliability may be obtained by asking each to complete these matrices and then consolidating and averaging the results.

The computation illustrated in Tables 2.3, 2.4 and 2.5 takes account of all of the data in the matrix. This computation has the effect of averaging out any discrepancies within the data entered on the matrix which were caused by each comparison being made by the user as a fresh comparison with no intention of it being mathematically consistent with earlier comparisons made. This approach is preferable to completing the matrix so that every comparison is mathematically consistent with every other comparison: if the matrix were completed in this way the auditor's judgement would be restricted to the first few comparisons which the auditor made.

As a proof that the matrix technique is mathematically sound the latter method of matrix completion can be experimented with. If the first row of the matrix were completed initially and then the remaining rows of the matrix were completed in a way which was mathematically consistent with the proportions expressed in the first row, then the final weights would be exactly the same as the data entered in the first row of the matrix. Of course it would be pointless to use the matrix technique in this way – except to prove that the technique is mathematically valid.

DESIGNING A SCORING SCALE FOR EACH FACTOR

Table 2.8 is illustrative of the type of scaling system which might be developed for the formula given in Table 2.6. A five point scale has been used. Most size factors are usually hard and objective: for these, once the scoring scale has been set subjectively, the correct scores can often be determined by reference to the corporate data base. The control and audit factors are more frequently soft and subjective but even here fairly hard guidance can often be given to assist in determining what score on the scale should be given for a particular auditable unit.

THE AUDIT RISK INDEX

In the example developed in Tables 2.2 to 2.10b we have taken the strategic and operational IT topics covered in this book (Chapters 4 to 27). This is perhaps an uncharacteristically small audit universe of auditable units. They are listed in the audit risk index given as Table 2.9. The sequence number column of Table 2.9 has been set to cross-reference to the appropriate chapter in this book. Three descriptive columns in Table 2.9 have been left blank as they would add nothing to the reader's understanding if they had been completed.

The OVERALL [MINPLAN] SIZE SCORE (*Size* factor D) and the OVERALL [MINPLAN] CONTROL SCORE (*Control* factor E) are both computed from the *Exposures* control matrices given for all of the auditable units as tables at the end of Chapters 4 to 27, in this case rounded to the nearest whole number. Since the extent of compliance with controls has not been entered on those matrices as no audit fieldwork has yet been done to determine what these compliance (test) scores should be, Table 2.9 shows the OVERALL [MINPLAN] CONTROL SCORE in each case as '5' as it is being assumed that there is no control. This is rather untypical of a usual audit planning scenario: it has had the general effect of raising the audit risk scores for each auditable unit beyond what might sometimes be the case – especially so as this factor has been given a high weighting in the formula.

The mathematics of the formula computation should be arranged so as to handle the absence of some of the factor scores for any auditable unit without unduly distorting the resulting audit risk scores shown as a column in Table 2.9. In this example it has been possible to score every factor for each auditable unit making reference to the scoring scale given in Table 2.8 and the circumstances of the enterprise. A factor should not be scored if the data is unavailable or undependable, or if a score would be misleading, or the factor is not considered?(to be pertinent to the particular auditable unit being scored. The mathematics underpinning the formula is explained in Table 2.6, showing how this scoring flexibility can be achieved. The reader will also note from Table 2.6 that the maximum possible audit risk score which can be obtained is determined exclusively from the *Size* part of the formula since this provides a measure of inherent risk. The *Size* score is adjusted downwards by the scores for each of the *Control* part and the *Audit* part of the formula if there is a degree of control and if respectively there are special reasons to suggest scaling down the amount of audit attention given to the auditable unit. Table 2.9 gives the subsidiary scores for each of the three parts of the formula (*Size, Control* and *Audit*) as it is helpful to audit management and to the audit team conducting the audit to know why a particular overall audit risk score for an auditable unit was obtained.

Note that in the example audit universe given in Table 2.9, the maximum audit risk score obtained by an auditable unit is 43.5 and the minimum is 12.4. The theoretical maximum score is 100 but in practice no auditable unit is likely to approach this maximum. The spread of audit risk scores in Table 2.9 is sufficient to indicate the variations in audit resource which are justified to expend on each of these auditable units. For the purposes of this example it has been assumed that one point of audit risk score should equate to one auditor day (*vide* the Audit Units Needed column of Table 2.9) though this may be subject to adjustment on Tables 2.10a and 2.10b.

Tables 2.10a and 2.10b belong together and should be read together. The auditable units and their audit risk scores have been transferred from Table 2.9 to Table 2.10a. Table 2.10b gives summary data which is either standard data used, or the results of calculations making use of (a) the standard data, (b) any special non-standard values given to particular auditable units and (c) the audit risk scores of the auditable units, as follows:

Standard data applied in Tables 2.10a and 2.10b

Duration in months of standard audit cycle*
Audit units per point of audit risk score
Annual productive days by auditor level
Percentage productive time available for audits
Percentage standard audit mix by staff category*
Minimum audit duration (days)*

Non-standard values given to auditable units

(Any of the asterisked standard data (above) should be variable for a particular auditable unit, if it would be inappropriate for the standard values to apply).

Results of calculations

Total audit risk score
Auditor days per year (required)
Auditor establishment needed[1]

In summary, Table 2.10b summarises Table 2.10a showing that an establishment of just over eight auditors would be needed to complete the audit of all of the auditable units in this audit universe over a twelve month period and based on several assumptions given in these two tables. The standard assumptions have been adjusted in a few cases on Table 2.10a where it is considered, for instance, that the audit cycle should be reduced or extended for a particular audit, that the duration of the fieldwork should be non-standard or that the mix of auditors required for the audit should be non-standard. If just over eight auditors will not be available, then adjustments have to be made to the standard data or to the auditable units contained within the audit universe so as to match the requirement to the available number of auditors.

AUDIT RISK FORMULA FOR A UNIVERSE OF IT-BASED APPLICATIONS

Up to now in this chapter we have used an audit universe of activities within the IT environment to explain the methodology of developing audit risk scores and applying them to conducting an audit needs assessment, and Tables 2.2 to 2.10b accompanied that example. There is no need to explain the methodology again in applying it to preparing two other audit risk formulae. Tables 2.11 to 2.13 show a formula where the audit universe is IT applications, such as payroll, sales accounting, production control, and so on. Table 2.11 shows the selections which were made from the 'bale' of possible IT factors (Table 2.1) and, after having been weighted, Table 2.12 gives the resulting audit risk formula and Table 2.13 summarises the factors within that formula.

---

[1] The system assumes one director of the IT Audit Group is needed who will not be assigned to particular audits. The figures given for audit managers, seniors and assistants are however calculated from the standard data, the audit risk scores for the auditable units and from any special values assigned to particular auditable units.

Tables 2.14 to 2.16 do the same for an audit universe of new IT systems or applications under development.

SUBJECTIVITY, OBJECTIVITY, RELIABILITY AND INDEPENDENCE

The technique discussed and applied in this chapter might be criticised for being too subjective and for attaching numbers to judgements with the risk that they are interpreted as being scientifically objective. There is considerable subjectivity associated with selecting the appropriate factors for the formula, weighting them, designing their scoring scales and, in the case of some of the soft, subjective factors, in scoring them using the scales. The resultant audit risk scores for each of the auditable units are data which must be interpreted, and the development of the audit plan of audits to be conducted as well as the determination of the number of auditors needed are also highly judgemental. Decisions such as the length of the audit cycle and the minimum duration of the fieldwork for an audit are also highly subjective.

So not too much must be claimed for this tool. Its merits are that it provides the opportunity to formalise the audit planning process which too often is conducted very informally, hastily and intuitively. There are many features within this method which improve the opportunity to exercise judgement in a methodical and more reliable way. The method can establish the basis to be used for determining audit attention to IT activities and as such provides the opportunity to criticise it, to revisit it, to improve it and to obtain approval of top management and the audit committee of the board to its adoption. It provides an explanation for audit focus. It compels audit planners to commit themselves to planning assumptions, to record them and then to express their judgement to all of the parameters (in numeric form): there can be no doubt as to what judgements they come to.

Internal audit independence is enhanced by providing senior management and the board with the opportunity to concur with the basis to be used for audit planning. It then becomes less necessary for the plan of audits itself, developed using this method, to be approved by senior management and the board. It becomes readily apparent when senior management is endeavouring to deflect internal audit away from work in certain areas or to work in other areas which are intrinsically less important. Primarily internal audit should be independent in the sense that the most senior point to which it reports should be confident that the scope of internal audit work has not been influenced inappropriately by pressure exerted by a more junior point within the enterprise.

Table 2.1 IT 'bale' of factors

CONSIDERATIONS APPLICABLE TO:	Universes of IT Activities ("Auditable IT Units")	
CONSIDERATION DESCRIPTION	FACTOR DESCRIPTION	BRACKET
Amount of business capital at risk from this system	AMOUNT OF CAPITAL AT RISK	SIZE
Amount of business turnover subject to this new system	AMOUNT OF TURNOVER AT RISK	SIZE
Degree of potential customer sensitivity to system failure	BUSINESS PARTNER SENSITIVITY	SIZE
Degree of potential supplier sensitivity to system failure	BUSINESS PARTNER SENSITIVITY	SIZE
Nature of risk if system fails (e.g. lost info., cash, profit)	CATEGORY OF RISK	SIZE
Are staff fidelity bonded?	CONSEQUENTIAL LOSS	SIZE
Availability of insurance to cover all risks	CONSEQUENTIAL LOSS	SIZE
Likely recovery cost	CONSEQUENTIAL LOSS	SIZE
Estimated cost of the new system development	COST OF SYSTEM	SIZE
Projected system development costs	COST OF SYSTEM	SIZE
Risk of violating data protection legislation	IMPACT UPON THE BUSINESS	SIZE
Likely impact of the new system upon the total business	IMPACT UPON THE BUSINESS	SIZE
Risk of violating legal requirements	IMPACT UPON THE BUSINESS	SIZE
Degree of 'political' sensitivity	IMPACT UPON THE BUSINESS	SIZE
System nature (strategic, co-op, expert, MIS, operational)	IMPACT UPON THE BUSINESS	SIZE
Estimated life of the new system	IMPACT UPON THE BUSINESS	SIZE
Number of user departments to be affected by the new system	INITIAL INHERENT RISK	SIZE
Extent to which system builds upon existing systems	INITIAL INHERENT RISK	SIZE
Extent to which new system changes business practices	INITIAL INHERENT RISK	SIZE
Extent new system is part of other business changes	INITIAL INHERENT RISK	SIZE
Extent of planned integration of this system with others	INITIAL INHERENT RISK	SIZE
Does the development have user support?	INITIAL INHERENT RISK	SIZE
Vulnerability of business during implementation	INITIAL INHERENT RISK	SIZE
Need for system to conform to laws & external regulations	LEGAL RISK	SIZE
Overall size score from the control matrix of this activity	OVERALL [MINPLAN] SIZE SCORE	SIZE
Extent of problem of controlling access to the new system	ACCESS CONTROL	CONTROL
Number of input points to the system	ACCESS CONTROL	CONTROL
Degree of control reliance upon password control	ACCESS CONTROL	CONTROL
Likely difficulty in creating the required database	DATA CONTROL	CONTROL
Reliance upon time sharing processing	DEPENDENCE UPON THIRD PARTIES	CONTROL
Reliance upon proprietary software	DEPENDENCE UPON THIRD PARTIES	CONTROL
Extent to which software suppliers are on a learning curve	DEPENDENCE UPON THIRD PARTIES	CONTROL
Extent to which hardware suppliers are on a learning curve	DEPENDENCE UPON THIRD PARTIES	CONTROL
Extent of adequacy of time allowed for the system's design	DEVELOPMENT TIME CONSTRAINTS	CONTROL
Time criticality of the planned implementation date	DEVELOPMENT TIME CONSTRAINTS	CONTROL
Overall control score from the control matrix of this activity	OVERALL [MINPLAN] CONTROL SCORE	CONTROL
Likely quality of project management	PROJECT CONTROL RISK	CONTROL
Risk associated with implementation method	PROJECT CONTROL RISK	CONTROL
Use of modern project management techniques	PROJECT CONTROL RISK	CONTROL
Allowance for post project audit	PROJECT CONTROL RISK	CONTROL
Extent project management suppliers are on a learning curve	PROJECT CONTROL RISK	CONTROL

Table 2.1 continued

CONSIDERATIONS APPLICABLE TO:	Universes of IT Activities ("Auditable IT Units")	
CONSIDERATION DESCRIPTION	FACTOR DESCRIPTION	BRACKET
Proportion of project management by contractors	PROJECT CONTROL RISK	CONTROL
Degree of top management involvement	QUALITY OF DIRECTION	CONTROL
Quality of documentation of existing systems	QUALITY OF DP CONTROL	CONTROL
Quality of internal control in existing, old system	QUALITY OF INTERNAL CONTROL	CONTROL
Adequacy of likely steering committee arrangements	QUALITY OF MANAGEMENT	CONTROL
Likely competence of user staff to use the system	QUALITY OF USER STAFF	CONTROL
User departments' staff turnover	QUALITY OF USER STAFF	CONTROL
Past experience of IS with the IT software technology	QUALITY & EXPERIENCE OF TECHNICAL STAFF	CONTROL
Past experience of IS with the IT hardware technology	QUALITY & EXPERIENCE OF TECHNICAL STAFF	CONTROL
Past experience of IS designing in this business area	QUALITY & EXPERIENCE OF TECHNICAL STAFF	CONTROL
Extent to which new system is "state of the art"	QUALITY & EXPERIENCE OF TECHNICAL STAFF	CONTROL
Proportion of analysis and programming by contractors	QUALITY & EXPERIENCE OF TECHNICAL STAFF	CONTROL
Past experience of IS developing systems of this size	QUALITY & EXPERIENCE OF TECHNICAL STAFF	CONTROL
IS staff turnover	QUALITY & EXPERIENCE OF TECHNICAL STAFF	CONTROL
Time criticality of regular processing cycle	RELATIVE REQUIREMENT FOR CONTROL	CONTROL
Requirement for confidentiality	RELATIVE REQUIREMENT FOR CONTROL	CONTROL
Risk of industrial espionage	RELATIVE REQUIREMENT FOR CONTROL	CONTROL
Extent to which new system needs new operating software	TECHNICAL CONTROL RISK	CONTROL
Extent new system needs commissioning of new hardware	TECHNICAL CONTROL RISK	CONTROL
Use of modern systems development tools (e.g. CASE)	TECHNICAL CONTROL RISK	CONTROL
Likely effectiveness of programme desk checking	TECHNICAL CONTROL RISK	CONTROL
DP method (in-house mainframe, PC, facilities mgt, bureau, t-s)	TECHNICAL CONTROL RISK	CONTROL
Reliability of chosen proprietary software, if any	TECHNICAL CONTROL RISK	CONTROL
Reliability of chosen hardware	TECHNICAL CONTROL RISK	CONTROL
Likely adequacy of planned system test	TECHNICAL CONTROL RISK	CONTROL
Availability of IT competence in this area	TECHNICAL CONTROL RISK	CONTROL
Extent to which temporary clerical staff will be required	USER CONTROL	CONTROL
Extent to which users will be able to monitor output	USER CONTROL	CONTROL
Likely quality of user manual at implementation date	USER CONTROL	CONTROL
Extent to which users will be able to monitor processing	USER CONTROL	CONTROL
Extent to which user resources are adequate to test	USER CONTROL	CONTROL
Extent to which user resources are adequate to advise	USER CONTROL	CONTROL
Degree of segregation of duties in user departments	USER CONTROL	CONTROL
Extent to which user resources are adequate to implement	USER CONTROL	CONTROL
Adequacy of likely user involvement in the project	USER CONTROL	CONTROL
Extent to which users will be able to monitor input	USER CONTROL	CONTROL
Extent to which users will be able to monitor files	USER CONTROL	CONTROL
Extent of potential vulnerability to abuse by in-house users	VULNERABILITY FROM STAFF	CONTROL
Extent to which outsiders interface directly with the system	VULNERABILITY TO ABUSE	CONTROL
Need for new audit software before implementation	AUDITABILITY	AUDIT

Table 2.1 continued

CONSIDERATIONS APPLICABLE TO:	Universes of IT Activities ("Auditable IT Units")	
CONSIDERATION DESCRIPTION	FACTOR DESCRIPTION	BRACKET
Need for embedded audit software	AUDITABILITY	AUDIT
Likely auditability of the new system	AUDITABILITY	AUDIT
Expressed concern of general management	BIAS OF MANAGEMENT FOR AUDIT ATTENTION	AUDIT
Extent of audit resources needed to make an impact	COST EFFECTIVENESS OF INTERNAL AUDIT	AUDIT
Likely welcome of internal audit by project team	LIKELY INTERNAL AUDIT EFFECTIVENESS	AUDIT
Inherent control risk in this type of system	OPPORTUNITY TO BENEFIT FROM AN INTERNAL AUDIT	AUDIT
Extent to which internal audit might make a contribution	OPPORTUNITY TO BENEFIT FROM AN INTERNAL AUDIT	AUDIT
Likely competence of internal audit	OPPORTUNITY TO BENEFIT FROM AN INTERNAL AUDIT	AUDIT
Extent to which control is a management variable	OPPORTUNITY TO BENEFIT FROM AN INTERNAL AUDIT	AUDIT
Extent of involvement of external audit	RELIANCE PLACED ON EXTERNAL REVIEW AGENCIES	AUDIT
Likely effectiveness of IS quality assurance review	RELIANCE PLACED ON OTHER INTERNAL REVIEW AGENCIES	AUDIT
Importance of this system to external audit	REQUIREMENT FOR PRE-AUDIT BY INTERNAL AUDIT	AUDIT
Importance of this system to external review agencies	REQUIREMENT FOR PRE-AUDIT BY INTERNAL AUDIT	AUDIT
Importance of system to the statutory compliance function	REQUIREMENT FOR PRE-AUDIT BY INTERNAL AUDIT	AUDIT
Impact of new system upon the annual accounts	REQUIREMENT FOR PRE-AUDIT BY INTERNAL AUDIT	AUDIT

Table 2.2   IT environment audit universe: selected factors with considerations

BRACKET	FACTOR DESCRIPTION	CONSIDERATION DESCRIPTION
SIZE	BUSINESS PARTNER SENSITIVITY	Degree of potential supplier sensitivity to system failure
SIZE	BUSINESS PARTNER SENSITIVITY	Degree of potential customer sensitivity to system failure
SIZE	CATEGORY OF RISK	Nature of risk if system fails (e.g. lost info., cash, profit)
SIZE	NUMBER OF USER DEPARTMENTS IMPACTED UPON BY THIS ACTIVITY	Number of user departments to be affected by the new system
SIZE	OVERALL [MINPLAN] SIZE SCORE	Overall size score from the control matrix of this activity
CONTROL	ACCESS CONTROL VULNERABILITY	Extent of problem of controlling access to the new system
CONTROL	ACCESS CONTROL VULNERABILITY	Degree of control reliance upon password control
CONTROL	ACCESS CONTROL VULNERABILITY	Number of input points to the system
CONTROL	DATA CONTROL	Likely difficulty in creating the required database
CONTROL	DEPENDENCE UPON THIRD PARTIES	Extent to which software suppliers are on a learning curve
CONTROL	DEPENDENCE UPON THIRD PARTIES	Reliance upon proprietary software
CONTROL	DEPENDENCE UPON THIRD PARTIES	Extent to which hardware suppliers are on a learning curve
CONTROL	DEVELOPMENT TIME CONSTRAINTS	Extent of adequacy of time allowed for the system's design
CONTROL	OVERALL [MINPLAN] CONTROL SCORE	Overall control score from the control matrix of this activity
CONTROL	QUALITY OF DIRECTION AND MANAGEMENT	Adequacy of likely steering committee arrangements
CONTROL	QUALITY OF DIRECTION AND MANAGEMENT	Degree of top management involvement
CONTROL	QUALITY & EXPERIENCE OF TECHNICAL STAFF	Past experience of IS with the IT software technology
CONTROL	QUALITY & EXPERIENCE OF TECHNICAL STAFF	Past experience of IS developing systems of this size
CONTROL	QUALITY & EXPERIENCE OF TECHNICAL STAFF	Past experience of IS designing in this business area
CONTROL	QUALITY & EXPERIENCE OF TECHNICAL STAFF	Proportion of analysis and programming by contractors
CONTROL	QUALITY & EXPERIENCE OF TECHNICAL STAFF	Past experience of IS with the IT hardware technology
CONTROL	QUALITY & EXPERIENCE OF TECHNICAL STAFF	Extent to which new system is "state of the art"
CONTROL	QUALITY & EXPERIENCE OF TECHNICAL STAFF	IS staff turnover
CONTROL	RELATIVE REQUIREMENT FOR CONTROL	Requirement for confidentiality
CONTROL	RELATIVE REQUIREMENT FOR CONTROL	Risk of industrial espionage
CONTROL	TECHNICAL CONTROL RISK	Extent to which new system needs new operating software
CONTROL	TECHNICAL CONTROL RISK	Reliability of chosen hardware
CONTROL	TECHNICAL CONTROL RISK	Availability of IT competence in this area
CONTROL	TECHNICAL CONTROL RISK	Reliability of chosen proprietary software, if any
CONTROL	TECHNICAL CONTROL RISK	Extent new system needs commissioning of new hardware
CONTROL	VULNERABILITY FROM OUTSIDER ABUSE	Extent to which outsiders interface directly with the system
CONTROL	VULNERABILITY FROM STAFF	Extent of potential vulnerability to abuse by in-house users
AUDIT	AUDITABILITY	Need for embedded audit software
AUDIT	AUDITABILITY	Likely auditability of the new system
AUDIT	BIAS OF MANAGEMENT FOR AUDIT ATTENTION	Expressed concern of general management
AUDIT	COST EFFECTIVENESS OF INTERNAL AUDIT OF THIS ACTIVITY	Extent to which internal audit might make a contribution
AUDIT	COST EFFECTIVENESS OF INTERNAL AUDIT OF THIS ACTIVITY	Extent of audit resources needed to make an impact

Table 2.2　continued

BRACKET	FACTOR DESCRIPTION	CONSIDERATION DESCRIPTION
AUDIT	COST EFFECTIVENESS OF INTERNAL AUDIT OF THIS ACTIVITY	Likely competence of internal audit
AUDIT	COST EFFECTIVENESS OF INTERNAL AUDIT OF THIS ACTIVITY	Inherent control risk in this type of system
AUDIT	RELIANCE PLACED ON OTHER INTERNAL REVIEW AGENCIES	Likely effectiveness of IS quality assurance review

Table 2.3　IT environment audit universe: size matrix

WEIGHTING MATRIX (4 FACTORS, A to D)		A	B	C	D	
Chosen SIZE factors						
BUSINESS PARTNER SENSITIVITY	A	1	3	1	5	10
CATEGORY OF RISK	B	0.33	1	0.5	3	4.8
NUMBER OF USER DEPARTMENTS IMPACTED UPON BY THIS ACTIVITY	C	1	2	1	5	9
OVERALL [MINPLAN] SIZE SCORE	D	0.2	0.33	0.2	1	1.7
Weights		1	2	1	6	
Factor weighting (X / Y, rounded)		1	2	1	6	
		(A	+B	+C	+D	
Sum of columns		2.53	6.33	2.7	14	
Sum of columns divided by adjusted sum of rows		0.25	1.31	0.3	8.08	
Square root of above row figures (X)		0.5	1.14	0.55	2.84	
Minimum value in above row (Y)		0.5	0.5	0.5	0.5	

Table 2.4 IT environment audit universe: control matrix

WEIGHTING MATRIX (11 FACTORS, A to K)

Chosen CONTROL factors		A	B	C	D	E	F	G	H	I	J	K	
ACCESS CONTROL VULNERABILITY	A	1	0.6	1	1	5	2	1.5	1.5	1	1	1.8	17.4
DATA CONTROL	B	1.67	1	1	0.3	5	3	2	1	1	0.5	1	17.5
DEPENDENCE UPON THIRD PARTIES	C	1	1	1	0.7	5	2	1.5	1	0.8	0.5	0.6	15.1
DEVELOPMENT TIME CONSTRAINTS	D	1	3.33	1.43	1	5	3	2	1	1	1	2	21.8
OVERALL [MINPLAN] CONTROL SCORE	E	0.2	0.2	0.2	0.2	1	0.4	0.25	0.6	0.2	0.3	0.3	3.9
QUALITY OF DIRECTION AND MANAGEMENT	F	0.5	0.33	0.5	0.33	2.5	1	0.5	0.7	0.5	0.5	0.5	7.9
QUALITY & EXPERIENCE OF TECHNICAL STAFF	G	0.67	0.5	0.67	0.5	4	2	1	2	1	1.5	1	14.8
RELATIVE REQUIREMENT FOR CONTROL	H	0.67	1	1	1	1.67	1.43	0.5	1	0.7	1	1	11
TECHNICAL CONTROL RISK	I	1	1	1.25	1	5	2	1	1.43	1	1	1	16.7
VULNERABILITY FROM OUTSIDER ABUSE	J	1	2	2	1	3.33	2	0.67	1	1	1	2	17
VULNERABILITY FROM STAFF	K	0.56	1	1.67	0.5	3.33	2	1	1	1	0.5	1	13.6
Weights		1	1	1	1	6	3	2	2	1	1	2	
Factor weighting (X / Y, rounded)		(A	+B	+C	+D	+E	+F	+G	+H	+I	+J	+K	
Sum of columns		9.26	12	11.7	7.53	40.8	20.8	11.9	12.2	9.2	8.8	12.2	
Sum of columns divided by adjusted sum of rows		0.53	0.69	0.78	0.35	10.6	2.65	0.8	1.12	0.55	0.52	0.9	
Square root of above row figures (X)		0.73	0.83	0.88	0.59	3.26	1.63	0.9	1.06	0.74	0.72	0.95	
Minimum value in above row (Y)		0.59	0.59	0.59	0.59	0.59	0.59	0.59	0.59	0.59	0.59	0.59	

Table 2.5   IT environment audit universe: audit matrix

WEIGHTING MATRIX (4 FACTORS, A to D)						

Chosen AUDIT factors						
		A	B	C	D	
		-----------	-----------	-----------	-----------	
AUDITABILITY	A	1	2	1	2	6
BIAS OF MANAGEMENT FOR AUDIT ATTENTION	B	0.5	1	2	1	4.5
COST EFFECTIVENESS OF INTERNAL AUDIT OF THIS ACTIVITY	C	1	0.5	1	0.5	3
RELIANCE PLACED ON OTHER INTERNAL REVIEW AGENCIES	D	0.5	1	2	1	4.5
		-----------	-----------	-----------	-----------	
Weights		1	1	2	1	
		-----------	-----------	-----------	-----------	
Factor weighting (X / Y, rounded)		1	1	2	1	
		(A	+B	+C	+D	
		-----------	-----------	-----------	-----------	
Sum of columns		3	4.5	6	4.5	
Sum of columns divided by adjusted sum of rows		0.5	1	2	1	
Square root of above row figures (X)		0.71	1	1.41	1	
Minimum value in above row (Y)		0.71	0.71	0.71	0.71	

Table 2.6   IT environment audit universe: audit risk formula

	SIZE:				CONTROL:												AUDIT:			
	1	2	1	6	1	1	1	1	6	3	2	2	1	1	2		1	1	2	1
20	(A	+B	+C	+D)	(A	+B	+C	+D	+E	+F	+G	+H	+I	+J	+K)		(A	+B	+C	+D)
		n1									n2								n3		

At least one factor must be scored within each of the three sets of brackets.

Each factor scored is scored on a scale 1 through 5 (see Table 2.8)

The score given to a factor is weighted by the weight shown above the factor letter.

Within a set of brackets the weighted factor scores are summed.

The sum of the contents of the SIZE brackets only is multiplied by 20.

The sum of each of the brackets is divided by n1, n2 or n3 respectively.

n1 is the sum of the weights of the SIZE factors scored.

n2 is 5 x the sum of the weights of the CONTROL factors scored.

n3 is 5 x the sum of the weights of the AUDIT factors scored.

The maximum possible score for an auditable unit using this formula is 100.

Table 2.7   IT environment audit universe: factors in formula

SIZE FACTORS -

A   BUSINESS PARTNER SENSITIVITY

B   CATEGORY OF RISK

C   NUMBER OF USER DEPARTMENTS IMPACTED UPON BY THIS ACTIVITY

D   OVERALL [MINPLAN] SIZE SCORE

CONTROL FACTORS -

A   ACCESS CONTROL VULNERABILITY

B   DATA CONTROL

C   DEPENDENCE UPON THIRD PARTIES

D   DEVELOPMENT TIME CONSTRAINTS

E   OVERALL [MINPLAN] CONTROL SCORE

F   QUALITY OF DIRECTION AND MANAGEMENT

G   QUALITY & EXPERIENCE OF TECHNICAL STAFF

H   RELATIVE REQUIREMENT FOR CONTROL

I   TECHNICAL CONTROL RISK

J   VULNERABILITY FROM OUTSIDER ABUSE

K   VULNERABILITY FROM STAFF

AUDIT FACTORS -

A   AUDITABILITY

B   BIAS OF MANAGEMENT FOR AUDIT ATTENTION

C   COST EFFECTIVENESS OF INTERNAL AUDIT OF THIS ACTIVITY

D   RELIANCE PLACED ON OTHER INTERNAL REVIEW AGENCIES

Table 2.8   IT environment audit universe: scoring system

SIZE FACTORS

A   BUSINESS PARTNER SENSITIVITY

[Largest size]

5=   Would probably have disastrous impact upon both customer and supplier base
4=   Would probably have disastrous impact upon either customer or supplier base
3=   Impact would probably be highly material upon customer and/or supplier base
2=   Impact would probably be significant upon customer and/or supplier base
1=   Would probably have negligible impact upon customer and supplier relationships

[Smallest size]

B   CATEGORY OF RISK

[Largest size]

5=   Potential loss of large quantities of valuable information
4=   Large potential loss of cash or other asset, or equivalent increase in liability
3=   Significant potential political impact and/or loss of reputation
2=   Loss of profit
1=   Accounting error with or without balance sheet and profit and loss account impact

[Smallest size]

C   NUMBER OF USER DEPARTMENTS IMPACTED UPON BY THIS ACTIVITY

[Largest size]

5=   Over 20
4=   16 - 20
3=   11 - 16
2=   6 - 10
1=   0 - 5

[Smallest size]

D   OVERALL [MINPLAN] SIZE SCORE

[Largest size]

5=
4=
3=   (This score to be computed from the control matrix for this activity)
2=
1=

[Smallest size]

Table 2.8   continued

CONTROL FACTORS

A   ACCESS CONTROL VULNERABILITY

[Largest control risk]

5=
4=   Score on a range "1" to "5" where "5" represents a very large number of terminal-
       based access points often remotely located, in an environment over which
3=   (a) physical access is/will be difficult to control, and (b) much dependence
       is/will be placed upon password control.
2=
1=

[Smallest control risk]

B   DATA CONTROL

[Largest control risk]

5=   The creation and maintenance of the required database presents major difficulties
4=   The creation and maintenance of the required database presents some significant
       challenges
3=   There are only minor challenges associated with the development and maintenance
       of the required database
2=   [not used]
1=   There is no significant database requirement associated with this activity

[Smallest control risk]

C   DEPENDENCE UPON THIRD PARTIES

[Largest control risk]

5=   Almost total reliance upon both software and hardware suppliers who are relatively
       inexperienced in both the technology and this application of it
4=   Extensive use of outside hardware and/or software developers
3=   Most of the software development is by in-house personnel
2=   Some reliance is being placed upon third parties
1=   No reliance is being placed upon third parties

[Smallest control risk]

D   DEVELOPMENT TIME CONSTRAINTS

[Largest control risk]

5=   Seriously inadequate time has been budgeted for implementation of this project, and
       other business developments depend upon timely completion of this activity
4=   Seriously inadequate time has been budgeted for implementation of this project, but
       no other business developments depend upon timely completion of this activity
3=   The time schedule and availability of resources is tight
2=   Deferment of implementation would raise only minor problems
1=   There are no time constraints

[Smallest control risk]

Table 2.8   continued

E   OVERALL [MINPLAN] CONTROL SCORE
[Largest control risk]
5= 4= 3=   (This score to be computed from the control matrix for this activity) 2= 1=
[Smallest control risk]
------- --
F   QUALITY OF DIRECTION AND MANAGEMENT
[Largest control risk]

5=
4=   Score on a scale "1" to "5" where "1" indicates top quality management involvement
        throughout, evidenced by (a) the grades of management involved, (b) the functions
3=   which the management represent, and (c) the existence of an effective steering
        committee for this activity
2=
1=

[Smallest control risk]
------- --
G   QUALITY & EXPERIENCE OF TECHNICAL STAFF
[Largest control risk]

5=
4=   Score on a scale "1" to "5" according to the past experience of in-house technical
        staff with (a) the relevant hardware technology, (b) the relevant software technology,
3=   (c) the development of projects of this size, and (d) work within this area of the
        business
2=
1=

[Smallest control risk]
------- --
H   RELATIVE REQUIREMENT FOR CONFIDENTIALITY
[Largest control risk]
5=   Very special needs to secure confidentiality 4=   [not used] 3=   Some needs to secure confidentiality 2=   [not used] 1=   No special needs to secure confidentiality
[Smallest control risk]

Table 2.8 continued

I   TECHNICAL CONTROL RISK

[Largest control risk]

5=   ALL major elements of hardware, software, design methodologies and support
       services are complex and completely unproven in practice
4=   SOME major elements of hardware, software, design methodologies and support
       services are complex and completely unproven in practice
3=   There are novelties in the approach but they are not of major risk
2=   The development utilises no new methods but in-house experience is low
1=   The development utilises no novel features

[Smallest control risk]

J   VULNERABILITY FROM OUTSIDER ABUSE

[Largest control risk]

5=   The activity is highly vulnerable to potentially acutely damaging unauthorised
       logical (ie. "system use") as well as physical (ie. "breaking and entering") access
4=   The activity interfaces operationally with customers and suppliers in contexts which
       are hard to control
3=   The activity interfaces operationally with customers and suppliers but without undue
       risk
2=   There is a small risk of unintended outsider egress
1=   There is no intended opportunity for outsiders to interface with the system

[Smallest control risk]

K   VULNERABILITY FROM STAFF

[Largest control risk]

5=   The activity is highly vulnerable to potentially acutely damaging unauthorised
       activity by employees
4=   The activity interfaces operationally with many users in contexts which are hard
       to control
3=   The activity interfaces operationally with many users but without undue risk
2=   There is a small risk of unintended insider manipulation
1=   There is no intended opportunity for insiders to interface with the system

[Smallest control risk]

Table 2.8 continued

AUDIT FACTORS

A   AUDITABILITY

[Maximum justification for allocation of internal audit resource]

5=   Maximum audit involvement essential to create/maintain the activities auditability
4=   Some special audit involvement is justified so as to create/maintain auditability
3=   There is no special justification for audit involvement in order to create/maintain
      auditability
2=   Audit involvement can be scaled down to some extent as auditability is automated
1=   Audit involvement can be scaled down very significantly as auditability is automated

[Minimum justification for allocation of internal audit resource]

B   BIAS OF MANAGEMENT FOR AUDIT ATTENTION

[Maximum justification for allocation of internal audit resource]

5=   The audit committee of the board is expressing acute concern
4=   The audit committee of the board is expressing some concern
3=   Top management is expressing acute concern
2=   There is some concern being expressed by management
1=   No special concern has been expressed to the internal audit function

[Minimum justification for allocation of internal audit resource]

C   COST EFFECTIVENESS OF INTERNAL AUDIT OF THIS ACTIVITY

[Maximum justification for allocation of internal audit resource]

5=   Internal audit is likely to achieve excellent results quickly
4=   Internal audit is likely to achieve good results quite quickly
3=   Internal audit is likely to achieve good results without undue investment of audit
      resources
2=   Internal audit may achieve satisfactory results without undue investment of audit
      resources
1=   Internal audit is unlikely to achieve useful results even following the investment
      of excessive amounts of audit resources

[Minimum justification for allocation of internal audit resource]

D   RELIANCE PLACED ON OTHER INTERNAL REVIEW AGENCIES

[Maximum justification for allocation of internal audit resource]

5=
4=   Score on a range "1" to "5" where "1" indicates that the scope of internal
       audit reviews comprehensively cover ALL material aspects; and complete
3=   reliance may be placed upon this work.
       A further factor to be considered is the adequacy of the reporting lines of these
2=   other reviews.
1=

[Minimum justification for allocation of internal audit resource]

Table 2.9   IT environment audit universe: audit risk index

Chapter Ref.	Auditable Unit (i.e. Audit)	Audit Group	Principal Audit Location for Fieldwork	Date of Last Audit	Date of Planned Audit
ch 4	IT Strategic Planning	IT Audit Group			
ch 5	IT Organisation	IT Audit Group			
ch 6	Contingency Planning	IT Audit Group			
ch 7	Databases	IT Audit Group			
ch 8	Electronic Data Interchange	IT Audit Group			
ch 9	System Development	IT Audit Group			
ch 10	Facilities Management and Bureaux	IT Audit Group			
ch 11	Personal Computers and Workstations	IT Audit Group			
ch 12	Local Area Networks	IT Audit Group			
ch 13	Electronic Office	IT Audit Group			
ch 14	Expert Systems	IT Audit Group			
ch 15	IT Sites	IT Audit Group			
ch 16	IT Accounting	IT Audit Group			
ch 17	System Access Control	IT Audit Group			
ch 18	Back-up and Media	IT Audit Group			
ch 19	Processing Operations	IT Audit Group			
ch 20	Systems/Operating Software	IT Audit Group			
ch 21	Software Maintenance	IT Audit Group			
ch 22	Software Package Selection	IT Audit Group			
ch 23	User Support	IT Audit Group			
ch 24	BACS	IT Audit Group			
ch 25	Viruses	IT Audit Group			
ch 26	Spreadsheet Design	IT Audit Group			
ch 27	Data Protection (Data Protection Act)	IT Audit Group			

Audit Code Number	Audit Units Needed	Audit Risk Score	Size Score	Control Score	Audit Score	Size: 1 (A	2 +B	1 +C	6 +D)	Control: 1 (A	1 +B	1 +C	1 +D	6 +E	3 +F	2 +G	2 +H	1 +I	1 +J	2 +K)	Audit: 1 (A	1 +B	2 +C	1 +D)
IT001	24	23.5	2.9	0.7	0.6	2	2	5	3	1	1	1	3	5	4	3	5	4	1	1	3	1	3	5
IT002	28	27.8	3.8	0.6	0.6	1	4	5	4	2	1	1	2	5	4	3	3	1	1	1	3	1	3	5
IT003	27	26.6	3.7	0.6	0.6	4	5	5	3	1	1	2	3	5	2	3	3	1	1	3	3	1	3	5
IT004	43	42.7	3.3	0.8	0.8	2	5	3	3	3	5	5	1	5	5	2	5	1	5	3	5	4	3	5
IT005	31	31.1	3.0	0.6	0.8	3	4	1	3	3	3	4	1	5	1	2	5	2	4	2	4	5	3	5
IT006	22	22.1	2.8	0.7	0.6	2	3	2	3	1	3	3	1	5	2	3	3	2	3	4	3	1	3	5
IT007	19	19.1	2.5	0.6	0.6	1	2	2	3	1	1	5	1	5	4	1	3	3	2	2	3	1	3	5
IT008	24	24.4	2.7	0.7	0.6	2	1	5	3	4	3	2	1	5	3	3	3	3	2	4	4	1	3	5
IT009	20	19.7	2.1	0.7	0.6	2	2	3	2	4	4	2	3	5	3	3	3	3	2	4	4	1	3	5
IT010	15	14.9	2.0	0.6	0.6	1	3	1	2	2	1	2	2	5	2	3	3	5	1	2	3	1	3	5
IT011	15	15.4	1.8	0.7	0.6	1	2	1	2	1	3	5	1	5	3	5	3	5	1	2	3	1	3	5
IT012	26	25.9	3.6	0.6	0.6	3	2	5	4	1	1	3	2	5	3	2	3	1	2	2	3	1	3	5
IT013	20	19.8	3.1	0.5	0.6	1	1	4	4	1	2	1	1	5	3	3	1	1	1	1	3	1	3	5
IT014	31	31.5	3.2	0.8	0.6	2	5	2	3	5	2	4	3	5	3	2	5	4	5	5	3	1	3	5
IT015	24	24.1	3.4	0.6	0.6	2	5	4	3	1	1	2	2	5	2	2	3	4	2	2	3	1	3	5
IT016	26	25.9	3.6	0.6	0.6	1	3	5	4	2	1	2	1	5	3	2	3	3	1	2	3	1	3	5
IT017	15	14.9	2.5	0.7	0.4	1	1	4	3	1	1	5	1	5	3	4	3	3	3	2	3	1	1	5
IT018	18	17.9	2.2	0.7	0.6	1	2	5	2	2	2	3	3	5	3	3	3	1	3	3	3	1	3	5
IT019	12	12.4	1.6	0.6	0.6	3	2	3	1	1	1	1	2	5	3	4	3	3	3	2	3	1	3	5
IT020	15	15.0	2.3	0.5	0.6	2	2	5	2	1	1	1	1	5	3	3	1	1	1	2	3	1	3	5
IT021	28	27.9	2.6	0.7	0.8	3	5	1	2	2	1	4	1	5	2	5	5	2	4	2	4	4	3	5
IT022	43	43.5	3.4	0.7	0.9	1	5	5	3	4	1	4	1	5	3	4	1	1	5	4	3	5	5	5
IT023	14	13.7	1.7	0.6	0.6	1	1	2	2	1	1	4	1	5	3	4	3	1	1	2	4	1	3	5
IT024	15	15.1	2.1	0.6	0.6	2	3	1	2	1	2	1	1	5	2	3	5	1	1	2	3	1	3	5

Table 2.10a   IT environment audit universe: audit needs assessment

AUDIT NEEDS ASSESSMENT

Seq. No.	Audit Title	Audit Group	Audit Code Number	Audit Risk Score
1	IT Strategic Planning	IT Audit Group	IT001	23.5
2	IT Organisation	IT Audit Group	IT002	27.8
3	Contingency Planning	IT Audit Group	IT003	26.6
4	Databases	IT Audit Group	IT004	42.7
5	Electronic Data Interchange	IT Audit Group	IT005	31.1
6	System Development	IT Audit Group	IT006	22.1
7	Facilities Management and Bureaux	IT Audit Group	IT007	19.1
8	Personal Computers and Workstations	IT Audit Group	IT008	24.4
9	Local Area Networks	IT Audit Group	IT009	19.7
10	Electronic Office	IT Audit Group	IT010	14.9
11	Expert Systems	IT Audit Group	IT011	15.4
12	IT Sites	IT Audit Group	IT012	25.9
13	IT Accounting	IT Audit Group	IT013	19.8
14	System Access Control	IT Audit Group	IT014	31.5
15	Back-up and Media	IT Audit Group	IT015	24.1
16	Processing Operations	IT Audit Group	IT016	25.9
17	Systems/Operating Software	IT Audit Group	IT017	14.9
18	Software Maintenance	IT Audit Group	IT018	17.9
19	Software Package Selection	IT Audit Group	IT019	12.4
20	User Support	IT Audit Group	IT020	15.0
21	BACS	IT Audit Group	IT021	27.9
22	Viruses	IT Audit Group	IT022	43.5
23	Spreadsheet Design	IT Audit Group	IT023	13.7
24	Data Protection (Data Protection Act)	IT Audit Group	IT024	15.1

Maximum Actual Cycle Interval (months)	Minimum Audit Duration (days)	Needed Auditor Days Over Actual Audit Cycle				Needed Auditor Days: Annual Equivalent of Audit Cycle Days				Auditor Mix Needed(%)		
		Mgr	Snr	Asst	Tot	Mgr	Snr	Asst	Tot	Mgr	Snr	Asst
12	10	4.7	10.0	10.0	24.7	4.7	10.0	10.0	24.7	20.0	40.0	40.0
12	20	5.6	20.0	20.0	45.6	5.6	20.0	20.0	45.6	20.0	40.0	40.0
12	10	5.3	10.7	10.7	26.6	5.3	10.7	10.7	26.6	20.0	40.0	40.0
12	10	8.5	17.1	17.1	42.7	8.5	17.1	17.1	42.7	20.0	40.0	40.0
12	10	6.2	12.4	12.4	31.1	6.2	12.4	12.4	31.1	20.0	40.0	40.0
12	10	4.4	10.0	10.0	24.4	4.4	10.0	10.0	24.4	20.0	40.0	40.0
12	10	3.8	10.0	10.0	23.8	3.8	10.0	10.0	23.8	20.0	40.0	40.0
12	10	4.9	10.0	10.0	24.9	4.9	10.0	10.0	24.9	20.0	40.0	40.0
12	10	3.9	10.0	10.0	23.9	3.9	10.0	10.0	23.9	20.0	40.0	40.0
12	10	3.0	10.0	10.0	23.0	3.0	10.0	10.0	23.0	20.0	40.0	40.0
12	10	3.1	10.0	10.0	23.1	3.1	10.0	10.0	23.1	20.0	40.0	40.0
12	10	5.2	10.4	10.4	25.9	5.2	10.4	10.4	25.9	20.0	40.0	40.0
12	10	4.0	10.0	10.0	24.0	4.0	10.0	10.0	24.0	20.0	40.0	40.0
12	10	12.6	12.6	10.0	35.2	12.6	12.6	10.0	35.2	40.0	40.0	20.0
12	10	4.8	10.0	10.0	24.8	4.8	10.0	10.0	24.8	20.0	40.0	40.0
12	10	5.2	10.4	10.4	25.9	5.2	10.4	10.4	25.9	20.0	40.0	40.0
12	10	3.0	10.0	10.0	23.0	3.0	10.0	10.0	23.0	20.0	40.0	40.0
12	10	3.6	10.0	10.0	23.6	3.6	10.0	10.0	23.6	20.0	40.0	40.0
12	10	2.5	10.0	10.0	22.5	2.5	10.0	10.0	22.5	20.0	40.0	40.0
12	10	3.0	10.0	10.0	23.0	3.0	10.0	10.0	23.0	20.0	40.0	40.0
6	10	5.6	10.0	10.0	25.6	11.1	20.0	20.0	51.1	40.0	30.0	30.0
12	10	8.7	17.4	17.4	43.5	8.7	17.4	17.4	43.5	20.0	40.0	40.0
24	10	5.5	10.9	10.9	27.4	2.7	5.5	5.5	13.7	20.0	40.0	40.0
6	10	1.5	10.0	10.0	21.5	3.0	20.0	20.0	43.0	20.0	40.0	40.0

Table 2.10b   IT environment audit universe: auditors needed assessment

AUDITORS NEEDED ASSESSMENT

TOTAL AUDIT RISK SCORE:		555
AUDITOR DAYS PER YEAR	Manager	122.84
	Senior	546.37
	Assistant	543.79
	TOTAL	1213.00
DURATION IN MONTHS OF STANDARD AUDIT CYCLE		12
AUDIT UNITS (days/cycle) PER POINT OF AUDIT RISK SCORE:		1.00
AUDITOR ESTABLISHMENT NEEDED	Director	1.00
	Manager	1.36
	Senior	3.04
	Assistant	3.02
	TOTAL	8.42
ANNUAL PRODUCTIVE DAYS BY AUDITOR LEVEL	Manager	200
	Senior	200
	Assistant	200
% PRODUCTIVE TIME AVAILABLE FOR AUDITS	Manager	45
	Senior	90
	Assistant	90
% STANDARD AUDIT MIX BY STAFF CATEGORY	Manager	20
	Senior	40
	Assistant	40
MINIMUM AUDIT DURATION (DAYS)		10

Table 2.11 IT - based applications audit universe: selected factors with considerations

BRACKET	FACTOR DESCRIPTION	CONSIDERATION DESCRIPTION
SIZE	AMOUNT OF TURNOVER AT RISK	Amount of business turnover subject to this new system
SIZE	BUSINESS PARTNER SENSITIVITY	Degree of potential supplier sensitivity to system failure
SIZE	BUSINESS PARTNER SENSITIVITY	Degree of potential customer sensitivity to system failure
SIZE	CATEGORY OF RISK	Nature of risk if system fails (e.g. lost info., cash, profit)
SIZE	LIKELY RECOVERY COST	Likely recovery cost
SIZE	LEGAL RISK	Need for system to conform to laws & external regulations
SIZE	OVERALL [MINPLAN] SIZE SCORE	Overall size score from the control matrix of this activity
CONTROL	OVERALL [MINPLAN] CONTROL SCORE	Overall control score from the control matrix of the activity
CONTROL	QUALITY OF APPLICATION DOCUMENTATION	Quality of documentation of existing systems
CONTROL	QUALITY OF USER STAFF	User departments' staff turnover
CONTROL	RELATIVE REQUIREMENT FOR CONTROL	Time criticality of regular processing cycle
CONTROL	RELATIVE REQUIREMENT FOR CONTROL	Requirement for confidentiality
CONTROL	RELATIVE REQUIREMENT FOR CONTROL	Risk of industrial espionage
CONTROL	USER CONTROL	Extent that users will be able to monitor processing
CONTROL	USER CONTROL	Extent that users will be able to monitor input
CONTROL	USER CONTROL	Extent that users will be able to monitor files
CONTROL	USER CONTROL	Extent that users will be able to monitor output
CONTROL	USER CONTROL	Degree of segregation of duties in user departments
CONTROL	VULNERABILITY TO OUTSIDER ABUSE	Extent that outsiders interface directly with the system
AUDIT	BIAS OF MANAGEMENT FOR AUDIT ATTENTION	Expressed concern of general management
AUDIT	OPPORTUNITY TO BENEFIT FROM AN INTERNAL AUDIT	Extent that internal audit might make a contribution
AUDIT	RELIANCE PLACED ON EXTERNAL REVIEW AGENCIES	Extent of involvement of external audit
AUDIT	RELIANCE PLACED ON OTHER INTERNAL REVIEW AGENCIES	Likely effectiveness of IS quality assurance review
AUDIT	IMPORTANCE OF THIS APPLICATION TO EXTERNAL REVIEW AGENCIES	Importance of this system to external review agencies

Table 2.12   IT - based applications audit universe: audit risk formula

	SIZE:						CONTROL:						AUDIT:				
	2	3	4	1	1	8	4	1	1	2	2	1	2	1	3	1	1
20	(A	+B	+C	+D	+E	+F)	(A	+B	+C	+D	+E	+F)	(A	+B	+C	+D	+E)

$$\overline{\qquad n1 \qquad} \qquad \overline{\qquad n2 \qquad} \qquad \overline{\qquad n3 \qquad}$$

At least one factor must be scored within each of the three sets of brackets.
Each factor scored is scored on a scale 1 through 5.
The score given to a factor is weighted by the weight shown above the factor letter.
Within a set of brackets the weighted factor scores are summed.
The sum of the contents of the SIZE brackets only is multiplied by 20.
The sum of each of the brackets is divided by n1, n2 or n3 respectively.
n1 is the sum of the weights of the SIZE factors scored.
n2 is 5 x the sum of the weights of the CONTROL factors scored.
n3 is 5 x the sum of the weights of the AUDIT factors scored.

The maximum possible score for an auditable unit using this formula is 100.

Table 2.13   IT - based applications audit universe: factors in formula

SIZE FACTORS -

A AMOUNT OF TURNOVER AT RISK

B BUSINESS PARTNER SENSITIVITY

C CATEGORY OF RISK

D LEGAL RISK

E LIKELY RECOVERY COST

F OVERALL [MINPLAN] SIZE SCORE

CONTROL FACTORS -

A OVERALL [MINPLAN] CONTROL SCORE

B QUALITY OF APPLICATION DOCUMENTATION

C QUALITY OF USER STAFF

D RELATIVE REQUIREMENT FOR CONTROL

E USER CONTROL

F VULNERABILITY TO OUTSIDER ABUSE

AUDIT FACTORS -

A BIAS OF MANAGEMENT FOR AUDIT ATTENTION

B IMPORTANCE OF THIS APPLICATION TO EXTERNAL REVIEW AGENCIES

C OPPORTUNITY TO BENEFIT FROM AN INTERNAL AUDIT

D RELIANCE PLACED ON EXTERNAL REVIEW AGENCIES

E RELIANCE PLACED ON OTHER INTERNAL REVIEW AGENCIES

Table 2.14   IT systems/applications under development audit universe: selected factors with considerations

BRACKET	FACTOR DESCRIPTION	CONSIDERATION DESCRIPTION
------	----------------------------	--------------------------------
SIZE	AMOUNT OF TURNOVER AT RISK	Amount of business turnover subject to this new system
SIZE	CATEGORY OF RISK	Nature of risk if system fails (e.g. lost info., cash, profit)
SIZE	COST OF SYSTEM	Estimated cost of the new system development
SIZE	IMPACT UPON THE BUSINESS	Risk of violating legal requirements
SIZE	IMPACT UPON THE BUSINESS	System nature (strategic, co-op, expert, MIS, operational)
SIZE	IMPACT UPON THE BUSINESS	Risk of violating data protection legislation
SIZE	IMPACT UPON THE BUSINESS	Degree of 'political' sensitivity
SIZE	IMPACT UPON THE BUSINESS	Likely impact of the new system upon the total business
SIZE	IMPACT UPON THE BUSINESS	Estimated life of the new system
SIZE	INITIAL INHERENT RISK	Number of user departments to be affected by the new system
SIZE	INITIAL INHERENT RISK	Vulnerability of business during implementation
SIZE	INITIAL INHERENT RISK	Extent to which new system changes business practices
SIZE	INITIAL INHERENT RISK	Extent of planned integration of this system with others
SIZE	INITIAL INHERENT RISK	Extent new system is part of other business changes
SIZE	INITIAL INHERENT RISK	Extent to which system builds upon existing systems
--------------	--	--
CONTROL	ACCESS CONTROL	Degree of control reliance upon password control
CONTROL	ACCESS CONTROL	Extent of problem of controlling access to the new system
CONTROL	ACCESS CONTROL	Number of input points to the system
CONTROL	DATA CONTROL	Likely difficulty in creating the required database
CONTROL	DEPENDENCE UPON THIRD PARTIES	Extent to which software suppliers are on a learning curve
CONTROL	DEPENDENCE UPON THIRD PARTIES	Extent to which hardware suppliers are on a learning curve
CONTROL	DEVELOPMENT TIME CONSTRAINTS	Extent of adequacy of time allowed for the system's design
CONTROL	DEVELOPMENT TIME CONSTRAINTS	Time criticality of the planned implementation date
CONTROL	PROJECT CONTROL RISK	Risk associated with implementation method
CONTROL	PROJECT CONTROL RISK	Likely quality of project management
CONTROL	PROJECT CONTROL RISK	Extent to which project management suppliers are on a learning curve
CONTROL	QUALITY OF DIRECTION	Degree of top management involvement
CONTROL	QUALITY OF USER STAFF	Likely competence of user staff to use the system
CONTROL	QUALITY & EXPERIENCE OF TECHNICAL STAFF	Past experience of IS developing systems of this size
CONTROL	QUALITY & EXPERIENCE OF TECHNICAL STAFF	Proportion of analysis and programming by contractors
CONTROL	QUALITY & EXPERIENCE OF TECHNICAL STAFF	Past experience of IS with the IT software technology
CONTROL	QUALITY & EXPERIENCE OF TECHNICAL STAFF	Extent to which new system is "state of the art"
CONTROL	QUALITY & EXPERIENCE OF TECHNICAL STAFF	Past experience of IS designing in this business area
CONTROL	QUALITY & EXPERIENCE OF TECHNICAL STAFF	Past experience of IS with the IT hardware technology
CONTROL	TECHNICAL CONTROL RISK	Likely adequacy of planned system test
CONTROL	TECHNICAL CONTROL RISK	Use of modern systems development tools (e.g. CASE)
CONTROL	TECHNICAL CONTROL RISK	Reliability of chosen hardware

Table 2.14   continued

BRACKET	FACTOR DESCRIPTION	CONSIDERATION DESCRIPTION
-------	-------------------------	-------------------------------
CONTROL	TECHNICAL CONTROL RISK	Extent to which new system needs new operating software
CONTROL	TECHNICAL CONTROL RISK	Availability of IT competence in this area
CONTROL	TECHNICAL CONTROL RISK	Extent new system needs commissioning of new hardware
CONTROL	USER CONTROL	Extent to which users will be able to monitor files
CONTROL	USER CONTROL	Extent to which users will be able to monitor processing
CONTROL	USER CONTROL	Extent to which user resources are adequate to test
CONTROL	USER CONTROL	Extent to which user resources are adequate to advise
CONTROL	USER CONTROL	Extent to which users will be able to monitor output
CONTROL	USER CONTROL	Adequacy of likely user involvement in the project
AUDIT	AUDITABILITY	Likely auditability of the new system
AUDIT	AUDITABILITY	Need for embedded audit software
AUDIT	AUDITABILITY	Need for new audit software before implementation
AUDIT	COST EFFECTIVENESS OF INTERNAL AUDIT	Extent of audit resources needed to make an impact
AUDIT	OPPORTUNITY TO BENEFIT FROM AN INTERNAL AUDIT	Likely competence of internal audit
AUDIT	REQUIREMENT FOR PRE-AUDIT BY INTERNAL AUDIT	Impact of new system upon the annual accounts
AUDIT	REQUIREMENT FOR PRE-AUDIT BY INTERNAL AUDIT	Importance of this system to external review agencies
AUDIT	REQUIREMENT FOR PRE-AUDIT BY INTERNAL AUDIT	Importance of system to the statutory compliance function
AUDIT	REQUIREMENT FOR PRE-AUDIT BY INTERNAL AUDIT	Importance of this system to external audit

Table 2.15   IT systems/applications under development audit universe: audit risk formula

```
     SIZE:                    CONTROL:                          AUDIT:
     1   2   1   2   2     2   1   1   2   1   3   2   2   2   2     3   1   2   3
    (A  +B  +C  +D  +E )  (A  +B  +C  +D  +E  +F  +G  +H  +I  +J )  (A  +B  +C  +D )
    ─────────────────────────────────────────────────────────────────────────────
              n1                              n2                           n3
```

At least one factor must be scored within each of the three sets of brackets.
Each factor scored is scored on a scale 1 through 5.
The score given to a factor is weighted by the weight shown above the factor letter.
Within a set of brackets the weighted factor scores are summed.
The sum of the contents of the SIZE brackets only is multiplied by 20.
The sum of each of the brackets is divided by n1, n2 or n3 respectively.
n1 is the sum of the weights of the SIZE factors scored.
n2 is 5 x the sum of the weights of the CONTROL factors scored.
n3 is 5 x the sum of the weights of the AUDIT factors scored.

The maximum possible score for an auditable unit using this formula is 100.

**Table 2.16   IT systems/applications under development audit universe:
factors in formula**

	SIZE FACTORS -
A	AMOUNT OF TURNOVER AT RISK
B	CATEGORY OF RISK
C	COST OF SYSTEM
D	IMPACT UPON THE BUSINESS
E	INITIAL INHERENT RISK
	--
	CONTROL FACTORS -
A	ACCESS CONTROL
B	DATA CONTROL
C	DEPENDENCE UPON THIRD PARTIES
D	DEVELOPMENT TIME CONSTRAINTS
E	PROJECT CONTROL RISK
F	QUALITY OF DIRECTION
G	QUALITY OF USER STAFF
H	QUALITY & EXPERIENCE OF TECHNICAL STAFF
I	TECHNICAL CONTROL RISK
J	USER CONTROL
	--
	AUDIT FACTORS -
A	AUDITABILITY
B	COST EFFECTIVENESS OF INTERNAL AUDIT
C	OPPORTUNITY TO BENEFIT FROM AN INTERNAL AUDIT
D	REQUIREMENT FOR PRE-AUDIT BY INTERNAL AUDIT

3

USING CONTROL MATRICES TO HIGHLIGHT RISKS

Scope

In Chapter 2 we examined the development of audit risk formulae to assist in determining the appropriate amount of audit resource to be allocated to each IT auditable unit, that is to each potential audit. That would be the technique we would recommend to be used when drawing up a future programme of audits to be conducted.

*In this chapter we explain a matrix technique to be used as an aid **within** any audit in order to identify the principal risk areas within the activity which is subject to audit so as to enable the audit resources being expended on that auditable unit to be applied to best effect. Perhaps the easiest way to understand the purpose of this matrix technique is to consider that it replaces the internal control questionnaire (ICQ) or internal control evaluation questionnaire (ICEQ): it is designed before the audit fieldwork commences and completed early in the fieldwork so as to provide a means of assessing the control problems and determining the further audit work to be done and the points to be made to management in the audit report.*

*Each chapter in Parts II and III of this book explores the control and audit implications of a key IT activity which might be the subject of an audit, and included at the end of each of those chapters are one or two control matrices which follow the approach explained in this chapter. In working through this chapter readers may wish to refer to some of those control matrices. For each chapter in Part II of the book, which deals with activities having a strong strategic purpose, we have included two control matrices – one oriented **positively** in that it addresses management's **objectives**, and the other oriented **negatively** in that it addresses **exposures**. We explain the distinctions between these two styles of matrix later in this chapter. Due to limitations of space within this book we have restricted ourselves to one matrix for each chapter in Part III – oriented* *negatively towards exposures – with the exception of Chapter 16 on IT Accounting where we have included both types of control matrix.*

Audit resources are being challenged. This is partly because the scope of auditing has broadened and partly because the complexity and scale of businesses has increased. It also has to do with the accelerating pace of change in modern businesses. It may also be because audit resources have been scaled down – even though in many cases there are now regulatory requirements for internal audit where there were none before. Whether or not this means that auditing is less effective today depends in part upon whether audit professionalism has improved so as to rise to these challenges. Certainly audit functions need effective techniques to identify high risk areas in order to be able to focus their scarce resources where the potential to benefit from audit is greatest, and in order to be able to quickly draw to management's attention where improvements are most needed. In times when audit functions have to be highly selective in what they review, it is also helpful to have documented justification for their assessment of risk which determined the focus of their work.

INTERNAL CONTROL QUESTIONNAIRES

Within an audit auditors have traditionally used the internal control questionnaire to point up the areas of control weakness. In essence the ICQ was a list of 'key' questions – the answers to which could be interpreted by the auditor to indicate whether there were control weaknesses. So the questions were answered early in the audit fieldwork and the remainder of the audit time would be spent probing the identified areas of weakness and working up recommendations for improving control to put before management.

The ICQ was a vague and voluminous tool. The technique of the ICQ generally did not do effectively any of the following which the control matrix technique explained in this chapter has been designed to achieve:

- the ICQ did not specifically relate particular controls to particular objectives or exposures

- the ICQ did not show that individual controls have a different potential degree of effectiveness

- the ICQ forced Yes/No answers about compliance with controls when in reality partial compliance is more common, and partial compliance is better than no compliance at all

- the ICQ did not combine the potential for a control to be effective with the extent to which it was being complied with in order to give a measure of the control's actual effectiveness in a particular instance

- the ICQ did not highlight the existence and effect of compensating controls (where one working control compensates for the failure of another) or redundant controls (where control procedures fulfil no purpose even though they may be complied with religiously)

- the ICQ did not allow for some objectives being inherently more important than others (or some exposures being inherently more potentially damaging than others)

- the completed ICQ gave no summary of its implications. Interpretation by the auditor of the significance of control weaknesses was difficult. It was a poor tool to use from which to draft the audit report.

USING SPREADSHEET SOFTWARE TO DESIGN CONTROL MATRICES

Spreadsheets provide an excellent opportunity to design control matrices so as to explore the relationships between *exposures* and *controls* in more precise and useful ways than ICQs permitted, although the first uses of control matrices predated the development of spreadsheet software.[1]

THE VIRUSES EXAMPLE TO ILLUSTRATE THE MATRIX TECHNIQUE

The rest of this chapter provides an explanation of the control matrix technique using, for clarity of the illustration, a very small example of a matrix with only five *exposures* and five *controls*. The audit topic selected for this illustration is viruses. In practice the control matrix for viruses would probably be significantly larger – with more *exposures* and more *controls*: Chapter 25 gives a more realistic example of a control matrix for the audit of viruses with fifteen *exposures* and twenty-two *controls*, and in other chapters of this book there are examples with as many as twenty *exposures* and forty *controls*. The size of the matrix is determined by the size of the system being analysed and by the level of detail to which the auditor wishes to take the subject. In general too much detail is counter-productive as it tends to conceal the major issues.

The orientation of the viruses example in this chapter is *negative* in that it

---

[1] e.g. *vide,* W. C. Mair, D. M. Wood and K. W. Davis: *Computer Control & Audit,* [Institute of Internal Auditors Inc., 1972]

deals with *exposures* and *controls*. The technique described works just as well *positively* with management's *objectives* across the top axis and the *measures* which should be in place to improve management's opportunities to achieve their objectives being shown as the vertical axis. The topic of viruses lends itself to being dealt with in terms of exposures as management really have no objectives with regard to viruses other than to avoid them.

EXPOSURES AND CONTROLS

Table 3.1 shows just five illustrative exposures and controls. The exposures and controls may not necessarily strike the reader as fitting his or her perception of managing the virus threat within their enterprise – each user of this technique should tailor the matrix to their needs. Similarly, other entries in the matrix may not necessarily be appropriate to a particular enterprise.

Exposures are unwanted outcomes which management should endeavour to avoid. Controls are the procedures which should be in place to reduce or eliminate the risk of the exposures. It is apparent from Table 3.1 that there are points of intersection between each exposure and each control which we shall use numerically to measure the effectiveness of each control.

Allowing for differing degrees of importance of *Exposures*

While this example has identified five potential exposures, some may be more important than others and it would be preferable that the amount of audit attention given to an exposure varied according to its importance. Before this can be achieved it is necessary to measure each exposure's importance. The degree of importance of an exposure is a function of its *inherent risk* to the enterprise adjusted by the extent to which it is under control (*control risk*). This parallels the approach we took to audit needs assessment in Chapter 2. We discuss control risk later.

The way this technique allows for *inherent risk* is illustrated in Tables 3.2 and 3.3. Towards the top of Table 3.2 two dimensions of *inherent risk* are catered for. First, what is called a *Scale* or *Type* score. To provide this score for each exposure, Table 3.3 is used as if it were a ladder. Keeping the nature of the exposure in mind the ladder is climbed from the bottom rung and the rung number is selected which applies to the highest category of risk that in all likelihood this exposure represents; it is that number which appears in the *Scale* or *Type* row of the matrix in Table 3.2. Once again, the reader may not necessarily concur with all of the judgements which have been made in designing this control matrix – to some extent they are dependent upon an assumed business environment which may differ from the reader's.

The second dimension of inherent risk is its *Size* ranking (Table 3.2). This is a simple three-point scale where the chosen value indicates the auditor's judgement of the likely size of the unwanted outcome which was selected in the *Scale* row for a particular exposure. So the *Scale* score needs to be selected before the *Size* ranking can be determined.

Several different categories on the ladder given in Table 3.3 may be applicable to a particular exposure. In general the one which represents the highest rung on the scale should be selected and recorded on the matrix. To be more precise, the scale and size scores should be considered to be linked and an applicable pair which together represents the highest number (when the chosen *Scale* and *Size* are multiplied together) should be chosen. Thus, for instance, if an exposure could be either the fourth or fifth rungs of the ladder and of large or medium probable size respectively, then the *Scale* score selected should be '4' as four multiplied by the relevant *Size* score of '3' results in a higher value than the alternative ('5' multiplied by '2' for medium size).

Calculating initial *Risk*

Now that we have determined the two dimensions of inherent risk we can calculate the initial overall risk score for each of the exposures. This has been done towards the top of Table 3.4 where a score of '4' indicates the most important category of risk and a score of '1' would mean that the risk was insignificantly low. The formula used to produce this risk score is given later in this chapter. For the moment this risk score disregards control as no assumptions have yet been made as to whether or not the controls are effective or being complied with. So the risk score on Table 3.4 is based on inherent risk only.

Measuring *Control*

Table 3.5 starts to develop the procedure for measuring *control*. There are three measures of control where each control intersects with each exposure.

Best – The extent to which the control has the potential to reduce or entirely eliminate the exposure – assuming it were always being followed by management and staff exactly as intended. A score of '5' would mean that this control would entirely eliminate the exposure if it were being followed by management and staff all the time exactly as intended. A score of '0' means it would have no effect.

Test – The extent to which this control is being complied with. A score of '5' means 100 per cent compliance. A score of 2 corresponds to 40% compliance. A score of '0' means no compliance.

Both – A combination of the *Best* [B] and the *Test* [T] scores using the formula:

$$[B-(5-T) = \textit{Both score}]$$

Table 3.6 gives illustrative *Best* control scores for the extent to which each control has the potential to reduce each exposure. The calculated risk scores remain unchanged from Table 3.4 since Table 3.6 makes no assumptions that there is any compliance with any of these controls.

Compliance testing

Finally, Table 3.7 gives sample compliance scores. It is only these compliance scores which have to be entered during the fieldwork of the audit. The control matrix designed before the outset of the audit fieldwork would have the data shown in Table 3.6. If the spreadsheet is designed efficiently the compliance *Test* score need be entered once only and the spreadsheet will spread the score across the line and immediately calculate the *Both* scores. This has been done in Table 3.7. To arrive at the *Test* scores the auditors will probably continue with their established methods of compliance testing, although this technique requires them to assess their results on a numeric scale ('0' through to '5') for each test. It is often preferable to use subjective judgement rather than scientific techniques to arrive at the *Test* scores as this frees up more time for what follows in the audit after completion of the control matrix, which is often more beneficial to management.

Risk scores which take account of *Control*

The *Risk* scores at the top of each column have been modified in Table 3.7 since each is now calculated on all the data in the column and some reliance can be placed on certain controls which are now known to be complied with to some extent. The formula to compute each *Risk* score makes use of the *Type*, *Size* and all of the *Both* scores as follows where B is the sum of the cubes of the *Both* scores in the column:

$Type \times Size \times [125 - B] = Risk$ of '4' if greater than 1,500

$= Risk$ of '3' if between 751 and 1,500

$= Risk$ of '2' if between 1 and 750

$= Risk$ of '1' if less than or equal to 0

Users of this technique may wish to develop their own formula for producing the *Risk* score from the data in the column. Alternatively, if they feel this formula is too lax or excessively demanding, users may interpret the significance of the resultant *Risk* scores differently. A key feature of this formula is that by making use of cubes of the *Both* scores it places as much reliance upon two *Both* scores of '4' as on one *Both* score of '5'.

Making use of the results of a control matrix

The *Risk* scores represent the main output of this matrix technique. It is intended that a *Risk* score of '4' indicates a critically important exposure due to its inherent nature and the relative absence of effective control over it. Having completed the control matrix early in the audit fieldwork, the auditors will divide the rest of their audit time so that they focus first upon exposures with *Risk* scores of '4' and proportionately less so on those with lower scores. There is no need to spend any further time on exposures with *Risk* scores of '1' as these exposures are either inherently marginal or they have been eliminated by excellent controls which are functioning as intended. The auditors' focus is likely to be partly upon further testing to determine whether the exposures have actually been exploited leading to real errors or losses. Auditors often call this type of testing *substantive* or *weakness* testing. Some internal auditors would argue that probing control weaknesses in this way may not be an appropriate part of their remit although different considerations would apply for external auditors. Another part of the auditors' focus on the high risk exposures is likely to be (a) to devote time to work up recommendations to put to management which, if implemented, would have the effect of reducing the exposures, and (b) to persuade management to agree to and implement those recommendations. The matrix will be useful to illustrate to management the potential impact of these changes upon the levels of risk in the system.

The bottom of Table 3.7 gives overall inherent risk and control risk scores for viruses within the sample enterprise. These can be useful in audit contexts which require the auditors to give overall ratings for each audit. They can also be useful for future audit needs assessment purposes as explained in Chapter 2.

Objectives-oriented matrices

Although our example has been *Exposures* oriented, we should not lose sight that the technique is as effective if the matrix shows *Objectives* across the horizontal axis and *Measures* as the vertical axis. We use the expression *Measures* rather than *Controls* for positively-oriented matrices, as many would consider that management do not achieve their objectives merely by adhering to controls. The positive orientation can make the audit process much more acceptable to management. Management's mission is not just to avoid exposures: they are primarily in business to achieve objectives.

SUBJECTIVITY v. OBJECTIVITY

Once again, we must acknowledge that this matrix tool does not remove auditor subjectivity. The titles of the columns and rows are a matter of judgement as are the *Scale, Size* and *Best* scores. But it is valuable that the auditors are being required to record their judgement in numeric form as it forces the auditors to both make and record their judgements. The judgements which are behind a control matrix can be the combined, informed judgement of senior auditors and management. The matrix tool can then make use of their experienced judgement when it is applied by more junior, less experienced auditors. In this sense it is an expert system. Over time a matrix can be improved in the light of experience. It is a valuable and concise part of audit 'documentation'. It is of course an example of automating the audit by making use of the computer.

Table 3.1   Exposures and controls

A - Exporting viruses to customers and suppliers
B - Damaging computer-controlled production processes
C - Causing damage to software
D - Corrupting computer-based data
E - Upsetting office procedures

VIRUSES (Abbreviated example)	EXPOSURES				
	A	B	C	D	E
CONTROLS					
1 Up-to-date anti-virus scanning software is installed and used on all computers.	?	?	?	?	?
-	-	-	-	-	-
2 All incoming diskettes, other media and portable computers are scanned on entry.	?	?	?	?	?
-	-	-	-	-	-
3 Pirated and games software are not allowed to be used on company computers.	?	?	?	?	?
-	-	-	-	-	-
4 Back-up copies of software and data are taken regularly and kept securely.	?	?	?	?	?
-	-	-	-	-	-
5 All staff are effectively trained and procedures are applied universally.	?	?	?	?	?
-	-	-	-	-	-

Table 3.2   Allowing for inherent risk of exposures

A - Exporting viruses to customers and suppliers
B - Damaging computer-controlled production processes
C - Causing damage to software
D - Corrupting computer-based data
E - Upsetting office procedures

	VIRUSES (Abbreviated example)			EXPOSURES				
				A	B	C	D	E
				=	=	=	=	=
	Scale - see Table 3.3 (6 is most serious)	Type		6	3	5	4	1
	Size (3 is maximum)	Size		3	3	2	3	3
		-	-	-	-	-	-	-
	CONTROLS							
1	Up-to-date anti-virus scanning software is installed and used on all computers.			?	?	?	?	?
-				-	-	-	-	-
2	All incoming diskettes, other media and portable computers are scanned on entry.			?	?	?	?	?
-				-	-	-	-	-
3	Pirated and games software are not allowed to be used on company computers.			?	?	?	?	?
-				-	-	-	-	-
4	Back-up copies of software and data are taken regularly and kept securely.			?	?	?	?	?
-				-	-	-	-	-
5	All staff are effectively trained and procedures are applied universally.			?	?	?	?	?
-				-	-	-	-	-

Table 3.3   Category scale for assessing the nature of the inherent risk

(START CLIMBING THIS LADDER FROM THE BOTTOM)	
Point of Scale	
6	Failure to achieve business objectives, and/or loss of credibility
5	Systems failure
4	Loss of control of the corporate database
3	Damaging delay
2	Unnecessary financial costs
1	Delay of no commercial significance

Table 3.4 Calculated risk scores

A - Exporting viruses to customers and suppliers
B - Damaging computer-controlled production processes
C - Causing damage to software
D - Corrupting computer-based data
E - Upsetting office procedures

	VIRUSES (Abbreviated example)			EXPOSURES				
				A	B	C	D	E
	Calculated Risk Score:	Risk		4	3	3	3	2
				-	-	-	-	-
	Scale - see Table 3.3 (6 is most serious)	Type		6	3	5	4	1
	Size (3 is maximum)	Size		3	3	2	3	3
		-	-	-	-	-	-	-
	CONTROLS							
1	Up-to-date anti-virus scanning software is installed and used on all computers.			?	?	?	?	?
-				-	-	-	-	-
2	All incoming diskettes, other media and portable computers are scanned on entry.			?	?	?	?	?
-				-	-	-	-	-
3	Pirated and games software are not allowed to be used on company computers.			?	?	?	?	?
-				-	-	-	-	-
4	Back-up copies of software and data are taken regularly and kept securely.			?	?	?	?	?
-				-	-	-	-	-
5	All staff are effectively trained and procedures are applied universally.			?	?	?	?	?
-				-	-	-	-	-

Table 3.5   Control - potential, compliance and actual

A - Exporting viruses to customers and suppliers
B - Damaging computer-controlled production processes
C - Causing damage to software
D - Corrupting computer-based data
E - Upsetting office procedures

VIRUSES (Abbreviated example)		EXPOSURES				
		A	B	C	D	E
		=	=	=	=	=
Calculated Risk Score	Risk	4	3	3	3	2
		-	-	-	-	-
Scale - see Table 3.3 (6 is most serious)	Type	6	3	5	4	1
Size (3 is maximum)	Size	3	3	2	3	3
-	-	-	-	-	-	-
CONTROLS						
	Best					
1 Up-to-date anti-virus scanning software	Test	?				
is installed and used on all computers.	Both					
-	-	-	-	-	-	-
	Best					
2 All incoming diskettes, other media and	Test	?				
portable computers are scanned on entry.	Both					
-	-	-	-	-	-	-
	Best					
3 Pirated and games software are not allowed	Test	?				
to be used on company computers.	Both					
-	-	-	-	-	-	-
	Best					
4 Back-up copies of software and data are	Test	?				
taken regularly and kept securely.	Both					
-	-	-	-	-	-	-
	Best					
5 All staff are effectively trained and	Test	?				
procedures are applied universally.	Both					
-	-	-	-	-	-	-

Table 3.6 Example control potential scores

A - Exporting viruses to customers and suppliers
B - Damaging computer-controlled production processes
C - Causing damage to software
D - Corrupting computer-based data
E - Upsetting office procedures

VIRUSES (Abbreviated example)			A	B	C	D	E
Calculated Risk Score	Risk		4	3	3	3	2
Scale - see Table 3.3 (6 is most serious)	Type		6	3	5	4	1
Size (3 is maximum)	Size		3	3	2	3	3
CONTROLS							
1 Up-to-date anti-virus scanning software	Best		2	4	3	2	3
is installed and used on all computers.	Test	?	?	?	?	?	?
	Both						
2 All incoming diskettes, other media and	Best		4	4	4	4	4
portable computers are scanned on entry.	Test	?	?	?	?	?	?
	Both						
3 Pirated and games software are not allowed	Best		1	2	2	2	2
to be used on company computers.	Test	?	?	?	?	?	?
	Both						
4 Back-up copies of software and data are	Best			1	3	3	4
taken regularly and kept securely.	Test	?		?	?	?	?
	Both						
5 All staff are effectively trained and	Best		1	2	2	2	2
procedures are applied universally.	Test	?	?	?	?	?	?
	Both						

Table 3.7   Control matrix after inserting compliance scores

A - Exporting viruses to customers and suppliers
B - Damaging computer-controlled production processes
C - Causing damage to software
D - Corrupting computer-based data
E - Upsetting office procedures

VIRUSES (Abbreviated example)		EXPOSURES				
		A	B	C	D	E
		=	=	=	=	=
Calculated Risk Score:	Risk	4	2	3	3	2
	-	-	-	-	-	-
Scale - see Table 3.3 (6 is most serious)	Type	6	3	5	4	1
Size (3 is maximum)	Size	3	3	2	3	3
	-	-	-	-	-	-
CONTROLS						
	Best		2	4	3	2	3
1 Up-to-date anti-virus scanning software	Test	4	4	4	4	4	4
is installed and used on all computers.	Both		1	3	2	1	2
-	-	-	-	-	-	-
	Best		4	4	4	4	4
2 All incoming diskettes, other media and	Test	4	4	4	4	4	4
portable computers are scanned on entry.	Both		3	3	3	3	3
-	-	-	-	-	-	-
	Best		1	2	2	2	2
3 Pirated and games software are not allowed	Test	3	3	3	3	3	3
to be used on company computers.	Both						
-	-	-	-	-	-	-
	Best			1	3	3	4
4 Back-up copies of software and data are	Test	2		2	2	2	2
taken regularly and kept securely.	Both						1
-	-	-	-	-	-	-
	Best		1	2	2	2	2
5 All staff are effectively trained and	Test						
procedures are applied universally.	Both						
-	-	-	-	-	-	-
MIDPLAN Inherent Risk (Size)						
Score [5 is worst risk; 1 best]	3					
MIDPLAN Overall Control						
Score [5 is worst risk; 1 best]	3					

Part II

THE STRATEGIC DIRECTION

4

IT STRATEGIC PLANNING

Scope

This chapter broadly covers the approach to undertaking an IT Strategic Planning exercise from the selection of the appropriate methods, scoping the exercise, establishing the framework, initiating the process and gaining the commitment of affected parties, gathering the data and conducting the required interviews, to confirming the accuracy of data and assumptions, and circulating the results.

Information Technology Strategic Planning is not primarily about Information Technology, but the business activities that are supported by the use of IT. The essence of IT Strategic Planning is to ensure that IT delivers effective solutions to business problems, provides and maximises competitive advantages for the organisation, accurately targets the corporate critical success factors, and enables the organisation to achieve its business objectives.

In order to be relevant and effective the process needs to be directly linked to the objectives and goals of the corporate strategic planning process so as to ensure that the eventual recommendations are fully justified on business grounds. By the adoption of this form of motivation the process can avoid the pitfall whereby the current trends in information technology drive and determine the business direction rather than support and facilitate business achievements. The resultant IT plan should aim to address a realistic time period where the main components and constraints can be accurately projected or interpreted, for example three to five years.

In fulfilling the key business requirements, the strategic plan should not only clarify the role of existing and additional application systems, but evaluate the need for a whole range of IT related practices and recommend, when applicable, the relevant changes, for example:

- determine the approach to maintaining or extending the life of existing business application systems
- identify the need for new systems to increase competitive edge, increase efficiency, etc.

- maximise the cost-effective use of IT resources

- provide increased efficiency, etc. through the use of accurate and reliable management information

- determine the future hardware platform(s) and communications strategies

- introduce structured methods for system development, package selection, etc.

- develop and apply standards in all areas of IT operation in order to enhance quality factors

- provide tools and techniques to support IT and users alike

- determine the optimum organisation and staffing structures

- consider the appropriateness of using Facility Management contractors.

In the course of the process it is easy to over concentrate upon the key application systems which either already exist or need to be actively considered. However, the whole IT environment needs to be considered so that the quality and effectiveness of all IT related services and functions can be appraised. There is no point in registering the requirement for an enhanced business application if the existing resources are incapable of developing and accurately maintaining such a system.

There are a number of recognised IT Strategic Planning methodologies, most of which are based on established management and organisational theories. Broadly speaking, the overall structure of the process can be summarised as follows:

- determine the current business structure and use of IT

- determine, via an assessment of the business objectives and plans, the future IT requirements and specifically target those activities where IT systems and practices can add value

- produce a phased and justified plan, defined in IT terms, to achieve the migration from the current to the required future state.

The process should be driven from the top of an organisation, and it is crucial to obtain and maintain senior management commitment if the appropriate key functional goals are to be fully identified and achieved. Major exercises of this nature can be unsettling to staff unless the objectives are clearly communicated, perhaps by a series of informal meetings where the concepts can be explained, the potential benefits defined, and the exercise placed in the appropriate context.

It is essential that senior management should clearly establish the scope and bounds of the Strategic Planning exercise by defining those business areas to be included, the time period to be considered by the plan and the project structure, etc. Such scoping will, of course, be partly dependent upon the relevant organisational structure and prevailing financial constraints. Full details of the project scope will need to be circulated and clearly communicated to all project team members.

A project team should be formed which adequately represents all the interested or affected parties within the organisation and there should be a balance established between representatives from the user and IT communities. Management should further demonstrate their commitment to the exercise by ensuring that all the requisite resources are made available to the project team. If necessary, team members should receive suitable training in the use and application of the selected planning methodology.

The planning project should be subject to overall project management and work within predefined timescales. Key deliverables should be identified and their production monitored in relation to the established target dates. Inevitably the planning project will require the accurate recording and analysis of considerable amounts of data about the organisation, its business activities, the current and projected use of Information Technology, etc. Care should be taken to ensure that there is a suitable framework in place to accurately capture, record and manipulate all the relevant data.

Software packages exist which aid the recording, interpretation and analysis of the relevant planning data. Their use can also aid the future maintenance and updating of the plan. Irrespective of the method of data recording used, it should be ensured that the level of details held will prove sufficient to support the project without unnecessarily over-burdening the project team resources.

Rather than 're-invent the wheel' the organisation can opt to utilise a recognised and structured planning methodology and/or obtain guidance from external consultants. Setting aside the possible requirement to import the relevant planning and interpretive skills, the use of external consultants can introduce an enhanced degree of objectivity into the process and provide a balance to any existing long-held viewpoints which may obscure the identification of a more appropriate project direction.

Although the planning methods may vary in their precise application, there are a number of common and necessary elements, as follows:

- identification and analysis of current business areas and their related plans

- identification and classification of corporate objectives, goals, and targets (possibly as the output of a general business strategic planning exercise)

- establishing the relationship of the above factors to existing computer based systems and classifying and risk assessing such systems

- classify the business areas in terms of their present (and future) earnings capability, competitive strategy (low cost versus differentiation)

- examine business activities/actions and highlight those which add-value, have high levels of associated information and/or incur high levels of cost. Such activities can then be considered as targets for support by use of IT

- analysis of corporate data (modelling the existing structure and determining the necessary future form to support affected business operations)

- identification of activities or operations where some advantage could be gained by the use of IT

- identify those business areas/activities where the use of IT could improve the competitive advantage, beneficially affect the organisation's position in relation to suppliers, rivals and/or customers

- identify those areas of present IT practice which fall short of delivering reliable and good quality services

- distil out the actions required and report upon same.

The majority of the above data can be obtained by means of interviews with key user and IT managers. Accordingly there is always the danger that individual managers will present a biased or unbalanced view of their requirements, etc. In order to ensure that the impressions carried into the planning process are balanced, accurate and suitably representative, it will be necessary to qualify key findings by obtaining independent confirmation or qualification of the relevant details.

Key statistics and accounting data used in the project need to be gathered from, and reconciled to, reliable sources. Additionally, it is likely that some of the data used in the exercise will be of a sensitive or commercially confidential nature, and it will be necessary to ensure that such data is adequately protected from leakage or misuse.

It is usual for established methods of business classification and management theory to be applied to the business activities under review; such methods can provide the necessary logical synergy between driving business considerations and the most relevant application of IT techniques to achieve the desired improvements in either efficiency, cost-effectiveness, or competitive advantage.

The planning process should ideally also include data modelling which can underpin the future development of systems. Corporate information is a valuable resource, and whereas key data is generally stable, the processes which use it are variable over time. It is therefore important to build data into the systems structure and use it to drive future development and maximise the flow of common data through integrated systems, avoiding duplications and redundancy. This data-oriented approach has a further significance in relation to the application and use of Database technologies, which are further explored in Chapter 7.

Initial findings and recommendations should be converted into pragmatic action plans, feasibility studies, etc. and circulated for discussion, revision and ratification. In organisations with formal project review and authorisation structures it may also be necessary to further appraise the output of the strategic planning project for viability, etc. The discrete project suggestions generated as a consequence of the plan will then be subject to any formal methods of project control that are in place.

Senior management should fully review and ratify the contents of the plan and satisfy themselves that it comprehensively complies with the initial project scope. Board approval of the plan (or elements therein) may also have to be sought.

The final plan should ideally include the following elements:

- Management Report

- Set of prioritised IT Projects (including amendments to existing applications)

- Action Specifications and Statements (covering hardware, software, communications, organisational changes, standards and methods, tools and techniques, etc.)

- Data Strategy

- Requirement for Feasibility Studies

- Technical Evaluations (i.e. hardware and platform considerations).

If the IT Plan contains suggestions for new projects or the introduction of revised practices, these may have to be separately appraised for viability and cost/benefit justification purposes.

Once accepted, the progress of the individual plan recommendations will require to be monitored, perhaps by a management IT Steering Committee. Subsequent amendments to the direction and substance of the plan contents will have to be fully justified and ratified by senior management.

Obviously the cost of producing an effective, comprehensive and realistic IT Strategic Plan can be considerable and require significant amounts of managers' time to complete, However, if the scope and execution of the planning exercise were correctly handled it could remain relevant for some time and it should not be necessary to repeat the full exercise in the short term. The plan should be revisited and reworked in the event of any significant business, environmental or technological changes. Any significant changes to corporate direction (i.e. a major acquisition or company merger) should be related to the IT Plan and the impacts fully assessed and evaluated.

Control matrix examples

Given that IT Strategic Planning, as a process, has the potential for directly affecting the success of an organisation, and therefore will require the application of strong management direction, we have provided both Objective- and Exposure-oriented matrix examples as Tables 4.1 and 4.2 respectively. Full details of the relevant *Scales* used in the examples (i.e. numbers 2 & 4) are provided in Appendix 5.

The example values attributed to these matrices aim to reflect significant levels of impact in organisations which are relatively heavily committed to the use of IT and where the process of Strategic Planning would potentially affect the achievement of a variety of critical corporate objectives. The *Best* scores used aim to reflect a generally optimistic view of the effectiveness of both the measures and controls in place. Both the examples include a strong emphasis on establishing the appropriate environment, commitment and resources for the planning exercise so as to enhance its prospects of success.

You will note that the example *Measures* and *Controls* provided are predominantly the same; this is due, in part, to the nature of strategic planning and its' intrinsic structural linkages with business objectives and corporate direction. It follows, therefore, that the management controls in place would strongly resemble the driving business objectives and measures.

It should be stressed that the example values and data used in the matrices throughout this book do not aim to fully represent any one specific business environment. A variety of values are applied to the examples with a view to reflecting a range of underlying situations such as one would encounter in the real business world. Therefore it is highly probable that readers would wish to edit the contents of these examples so as to more accurately match the relevant scenarios in their own organisations. The application of the supporting methodology using a spreadsheet readily permits the evolution of each matrix and the revision of the applicable key measures and controls.

Table 4.1   Strategic Planning - Objectives

Overall Inherent Risk (Size) Score [5 is worst risk; 1 is best] = 2.54

A Maximise competitive advantage by use of IT
B Ensure IT planning is linked to corporate objectives
C Ensure the commitment and involvement of key managers
D Accurately determine/communicate scope of planning exercise
E Utilise a proven & acceptable methodology and support tools

F Provide adequate resources and expertise to achieve project
G Provide means to record, analyse and report on required data
H Ensure the accuracy & reliability of data, assumptions, etc.
I Ensure circulation and discussion of recommendations, etc.
J Generate pragmatic action plans, feasibility studies, etc.
K Monitor progress and implementation of recommendations
L Periodically revisit, update and revise the plan
M Protect commercially sensitive planning data from leakage

I T Strategic Planning		OBJECTIVES												
		A	B	C	D	E	F	G	H	I	J	K	L	M
		=	=	=	=	=	=	=	=	=	=	=	=	=
Calculated Risk Score:	Risk	3	3	3	3	2	3	3	3	3	3	2	2	2
		-	-	-	-	-	-	-	-	-	-	-	-	-
Scale 2 (6 is most serious)	Type	6	6	5	4	6	5	4	5	5	5	6	5	6
Size (3 is maximum)	Size	2	2	2	2	1	2	2	2	2	2	1	1	1
MEASURES	-	-	-	-	-	-	-	-	-	-	-	-	-	-
1 Chosen method involves detailed examination of activities and identifies beneficial uses of IT	Best		5											
	Test	?	?											
	Both													
-	-	-	-	-	-	-	-	-	-	-	-	-	-	-
2 Planning Project is linked to established corporate targets, etc. as per five year plan	Best		4	5										
	Test	?	?	?										
	Both													
-	-	-	-	-	-	-	-	-	-	-	-	-	-	-
3 Planning Project is sponsored by the Chief Executive and ratified by the Board	Best				4									
	Test	?			?									
	Both													
-	-	-	-	-	-	-	-	-	-	-	-	-	-	-
4 Briefing meetings held and documents circulated detailing the objectives of exercise	Best				4	4								
	Test	?			?	?								
	Both													
-	-	-	-	-	-	-	-	-	-	-	-	-	-	-
5 Managers made aware of the need for their active involvement as a means of shaping the future	Best				4									
	Test	?			?									
	Both													
-	-	-	-	-	-	-	-	-	-	-	-	-	-	-
6 Initial scoping exercise was conducted with the assistance of external consultants	Best				5									
	Test	?			?									
	Both													
-	-	-	-	-	-	-	-	-	-	-	-	-	-	-
7 Project team and key managers signed-off the Scope Proposal	Best				4	4								
	Test	?			?	?								
	Both													
-	-	-	-	-	-	-	-	-	-	-	-	-	-	-

Table 4.1   continued

			A	B	C	D	E	F	G	H	I	J	K	L	M
8	Chosen to use method X from ABC consultants. Previous users contacted for comments, etc.	Best					5								
		Test	?				?								
		Both													
-		-	-	-	-	-	-	-	-	-	-	-	-	-	-
9	Supporting software tool obtained and training undertaken	Best						3	5						
		Test	?					?	?						
		Both													
-		-	-	-	-	-	-	-	-	-	-	-	-	-	-
10	Project team formed from affected users and ITstaff	Best						4							
		Test	?					?							
		Both													
-		-	-	-	-	-	-	-	-	-	-	-	-	-	-
11	External consultants appointed as advisors and quality control	Best						4							
		Test	?					?							
		Both													
-		-	-	-	-	-	-	-	-	-	-	-	-	-	-
12	Project team members attended two day methodology training course	Best						4							
		Test	?					?							
		Both													
-		-	-	-	-	-	-	-	-	-	-	-	-	-	-
13	Key business assumptions were obtained from corporate plan - all tested by project group	Best								4					
		Test	?							?					
		Both													
-		-	-	-	-	-	-	-	-	-	-	-	-	-	-
14	Underlying assumptions were documented and agreed with the Board	Best								5					
		Test	?							?					
		Both													
-		-	-	-	-	-	-	-	-	-	-	-	-	-	-
15	All data examined by project sub-group to verify accuracy and relevance	Best								4					
		Test	?							?					
		Both													
-		-	-	-	-	-	-	-	-	-	-	-	-	-	-
16	Data held on system is subsequently reviewed for accuracy	Best								5					
		Test	?							?					
		Both													
-		-	-	-	-	-	-	-	-	-	-	-	-	-	-
17	Preliminary findings circulated - meetings held and agreement obtained	Best									4				
		Test	?								?				
		Both													
-		-	-	-	-	-	-	-	-	-	-	-	-	-	-
18	Action Plans produced and signed-off by relevant users and IT representatives	Best										5			
		Test	?									?			
		Both													
-		-	-	-	-	-	-	-	-	-	-	-	-	-	-
19	Feasibility sub-projects were scoped and initiated	Best										4			
		Test	?									?			
		Both													
-		-	-	-	-	-	-	-	-	-	-	-	-	-	-

Table 4.1   continued

			A	B	C	D	E	F	G	H	I	J	K	L	M
	Timetables established for	Best											5		
20	implementing changes, etc. -	Test	?										?		
	monitored and managed	Both													
-		-	-	-	-	-	-	-	-	-	-	-	-	-	-
	Plan reviewed every six months	Best												3	
21	and monitored accordingly	Test	?											?	
		Both													
-		-	-	-	-	-	-	-	-	-	-	-	-	-	-
	System access and report	Best													5
22	circulation is restricted -	Test	?												?
	password control on software	Both													
-		-	-	-	-	-	-	-	-	-	-	-	-	-	-

A Maximise competitive advantage by use of IT

B Ensure IT planning is linked to corporate objectives

C Ensure the commitment and involvement of key managers

D Accurately determine/communicate scope of planning exercise

E Utilise a proven & acceptable methodology and support tools

F Provide adequate resources and expertise to achieve project

G Provide means to record, analyse and report on required data

H Ensure the accuracy & reliability of data, assumptions, etc.

I Ensure circulation and discussion of recommendations, etc.

J Generate pragmatic action plans, feasibility studies, etc.

K Monitor progress and implementation of recommendations

L Periodically revisit, update and revise the plan

M Protect commercially sensitive planning data from leakage

Table 4.2   Strategic Planning - Exposures
Overall Inherent Risk (Size) Score [5 is worst risk; 1 is best] = 2.50

A Failure to identify where IT offers competitive advantages
B Plans fail to relate to established corporate objectives
C Lack of management commitment/involvement
   - objectives fail
D Inadequate/inappropriate scoping of exercise - incomplete
E Absence of reliable and proven planning method - error,cost
F Inadequate project resources - delay, error, failure, etc.
G Absence of required expertise - error, delay, cost, failure
H Inadequate/inflexible means of recording plan data - errors

I Inaccurate/unreliable data and/or assumptions - error, delay
J Failure to provide planning timescale, deadlines - over-run
K Inadequate discussion/agreement of recommendations
   - dispute
L Failure to provide relevant and pragmatic action plans
M Failure to conduct feasibility studies - cost, error, failure
N Failure to monitor progress on actions - lost opportunities
O Failure to maintain up-to-date plan - lost opportunities
P Inadequate security over commercially sensitive data - leaks

IT Strategic Planning		EXPOSURES															
		A	B	C	D	E	F	G	H	I	J	K	L	M	N	O	P
Calculated Risk Score	Risk	2	3	3	3	3	3	3	3	3	2	2	3	3	3	2	3
Scale 4 (6 is most serious)	Type	6	6	6	4	5	5	5	4	6	3	6	6	4	6	6	4
Size (3 is maximum)	Size	1	2	2	2	2	2	2	2	2	1	2	2	2	2	1	2
CONTROLS																	
1 Chosen method involves detailed examination of activities and identifies beneficial uses of IT	Best		5	4													
	Test	?	?	?													
	Both																
2 Planning Project is linked to established corporate targets, etc. as per five year plan	Best			5													
	Test	?		?													
	Both																
3 Planning Project is sponsored by the Chief Executive and ratified by the Board	Best			5													
	Test	?		?													
	Both																
4 Briefing meetings held and documents circulated detailing the objectives of exercise	Best			4													
	Test	?		?													
	Both																
5 Managers made aware of the need for their active involvement as a means of shaping the future	Best			4													
	Test	?		?													
	Both																
6 Initial scoping exercise was conducted with the assistance of external consultants	Best			4													
	Test	?		?													
	Both																
7 Project team and key managers signed-off the Scope Proposal	Best			4	5												
	Test	?		?	?												
	Both																

Table 4.2   continued

			A	B	C	D	E	F	G	H	I	J	K	L	M	N	O	P
8	Chosen to use method X from ABC consultants. Previous users contacted for comments, etc.	Best					5											
		Test	?				?											
		Both																
-		-	-	-	-	-	-	-	-	-	-	-	-	-	-	-	-	-
9	Supporting software tool obtained and training undertaken	Best								5								
		Test	?							?								
		Both													.			
-		-	-	-	-	-	-	-	-	-	-	-	-	-	-	-	-	-
10	Project team formed from affected users and IT staff	Best						4										
		Test	?					?										
		Both																
-		-	-	-	-	-	-	-	-	-	-	-	-	-	-	-	-	-
11	External consultants appointed as advisors and quality control	Best						4	5									
		Test	?					?	?									
		Both																
-		-	-	-	-	-	-	-	-	-	-	-	-	-	-	-	-	-
12	Project team members have attended two day methodology training course	Best						3	3									
		Test	?					?	?									
		Both																
-		-	-	-	-	-	-	-	-	-	-	-	-	-	-	-	-	-
13	Key business assumptions were obtained from corporate plan - all tested by project group	Best									4							
		Test	?								?							
		Both																
-		-	-	-	-	-	-	-	-	-	-	-	-	-	-	-	-	-
14	Underlying assumptions were documented and agreed with the Board	Best									5							
		Test	?								?							
		Both																
-		-	-	-	-	-	-	-	-	-	-	-	-	-	-	-	-	-
15	All data examined by project sub-group to verify accuracy and relevance	Best									4							
		Test	?								?							
		Both																
-		-	-	-	-	-	-	-	-	-	-	-	-	-	-	-	-	-
16	Data held on system is subsequently reviewed for accuracy, etc.	Best									4							
		Test	?								?							
		Both																
-		-	-	-	-	-	-	-	-	-	-	-	-	-	-	-	-	-
17	Project is managed using the prevailing method - deadlines established and monitored	Best										5						
		Test	?									?						
		Both																
-		-	-	-	-	-	-	-	-	-	-	-	-	-	-	-	-	-
18	Preliminary findings circulated - meetings held and agreement obtained	Best											4					
		Test	?										?					
		Both																
-		-	-	-	-	-	-	-	-	-	-	-	-	-	-	-	-	-
19	Action Plans produced and signed-off by relevant users and IT representatives	Best											4					
		Test	?										?					
		Both																
-		-	-	-	-	-	-	-	-	-	-	-	-	-	-	-	-	-

Table 4.2   continued

			A	B	C	D	E	F	G	H	I	J	K	L	M	N	O	P
20	Feasibility sub-projects were scoped and initiated	Best													4			
		Test	?												?			
		Both																
-		-	-	-	-	-	-	-	-	-	-	-	-	-	-	-	-	-
21	Timetables established for implementing changes, etc.- monitored and managed	Best														5		
		Test	?													?		
		Both																
-		-	-	-	-	-	-	-	-	-	-	-	-	-	-	-	-	-
22	Plan reviewed every six months and monitored accordingly	Best															4	
		Test	?														?	
		Both																
-		-	-	-	-	-	-	-	-	-	-	-	-	-	-	-	-	-
23	System access and report circulation is restricted - password control on software	Best																5
		Test	?															?
		Both																
-		-	-	-	-	-	-	-	-	-	-	-	-	-	-	-	-	-

A Failure to identify where IT offers competitive advantages
B Plans fail to relate to established corporate objectives
C Lack of management commitment/involvement
   - objectives fail
D Inadequate/inappropriate scoping of exercise - incomplete
E Absence of reliable and proven planning method - error,cost
F Inadequate project resources - delay, error, failure, etc.
G Absence of required expertise - error, delay, cost, failure
H Inadequate/inflexible means of recording plan data - errors

I Inaccurate/unreliable data and/or assumptions - error, delay
J Failure to provide planning timescale, deadlines - over-run
K Inadequate discussion/agreement of recommendations
   - dispute
L Failure to provide relevant and pragmatic action plans
M Failure to conduct feasibility studies - cost, error, failure
N Failure to monitor progress on actions - lost opportunities
O Failure to maintain up-to-date plan - lost opportunities
P Inadequate security over commercially sensitive data - leaks

5

IT ORGANISATION

Scope

This chapter addresses the organisational, administrative and management activities governing the IT facilities, incorporating the following aspects:

- *the establishment of Terms of Reference for the IT function*

- *determination of optimum organisational structure and staffing (allowing for adequate segregation of key duties)*

- *provision of adequate resources to meet prevailing obligations*

- *ensuring that staff are suitably skilled to meet their responsibilities*

- *determination of constructive procedures, policies and standards*

- *providing direct linkages with the IT Planning process*

- *determining optimum service levels and establishing related agreements with business management*

- *monitoring performance relative to prevailing requirements*

- *provision of effective corporate communications and thereby supporting the maintenance of staff motivation and awareness.*

Specific IT Accounting aspects are addressed separately in Chapter 16.

Many of the elements either featured or mentioned in this chapter are also explored in greater detail in subsequent chapters, however this apparent duplication is intentional. The elements are addressed here in the context of being relevant to the adequacy of the overall management framework and approach at a strategic level, whereas the specific subject chapters expand upon the detailed tactical requirements of such elements.

The Information Technology requirements of an organisation can be addressed in a variety of ways, for example:

- by a separate division or free-standing functional area

- as a central service provided as either a part or sub-division of a prime function, i.e. accounting

- devolved across the operational functions or divisions

- as a service provided and managed by a Facilities Management company on behalf of the organisation

- handled by a bureau or time sharing service

- as part of a shared service with another organisation.

The majority of this chapter's contents are relative to some form of internal and discrete IT responsibility and organisation, albeit that the underlying principles can be easily adapted so as to apply in most other situations. See Chapter 10 for further exploration of Facilities Management and Bureaux operations.

The controlling organisation should ideally consider the establishment of an operating brief or Terms of Reference for the IT function, denoting areas of specific responsibility (such as data security) and the range of services that are required. This document will also set the scene for determining the appropriate and optimum organisational structure in light of the required tasks and main objectives. Additionally the Terms of Reference can act as a cornerstone of any relevant Service Level agreements.

The adopted organisational structure should provide for adequate segregation of key duties and thereby protect the integrity of the data processing aspects of the operation thus ensuring the quality and reliability of business data. More importantly, it should provide logical groupings of staff with the requisite skills to effectively address their responsibilities and the needs or objectives of the company. The structure should also enable the development of effective internal and external channels of communication.

The provision of adequate resources (including staff) to meet the IT division obligations is of paramount importance. As an initial step it is ideal to establish, for the whole organisation, an IT Strategic Plan built upon the needs, aspirations and objectives of the major business areas (this process is fully explored in Chapter 4 – IT Strategic Planning). Having established the direction of the business and the related IT requirements, it is further necessary to identify the impact of the obligations upon staffing levels, skill requirements, new facilities, etc. and to provide a planned and cost-effective approach to fulfilling the defined objectives. Having defined such a plan and obtained senior group management ratification of same, the necessary policies, procedures, procurement, etc. can be established.

It is unlikely that the wider business, trading and technical environments will remain conveniently static: accordingly the structure and administration of the

IT function will benefit from periodic review so that it remains relevant and effective in accordance with both evolutionary and enforced changes.

Many of the day-to-day personnel requirements, such as recruitment, administration, etc., will more likely be handled, for the whole organisation, by a discrete Human Resources function. Any specific IT related requirements should be accurately determined and advised to this function. Job descriptions should ideally be universally in place and define the duties and responsibilities for each particular role. Where an organisation is heavily dependent upon IT facilities and the related skills of relatively few employees, the application of succession planning techniques can provide mechanisms to ensure that the level of ongoing support is progressively addressed and that future eventualities have been considered.

Given that the IT environment demands high skill levels in relatively precise areas of activity, it is necessary to ensure that the IT function has the appropriate mix and levels of skills to enable the continuing maintenance of operations and services. Training needs should be accurately identified, targeted and addressed, perhaps as a part of regular staff appraisals.

The fidelity bonding of IT employees may be necessary in those situations where exposure to commercially sensitive data or the potential for fraud or misuse of corporate facilities is in question. Additional screening processes may be necessary for staff selected for positions of trust. In any event, appropriate levels of indemnity insurance cover will need to be in place to protect the company against the impact of staff malpractice or failure of duty.

The procedures required for any particular function or department should combine the general rules affecting the organisation as a whole (i.e. Health & Safety, Security, etc.) with those specific to the IT environment or role being performed (i.e. the proper use of equipment, the logical security requirements, etc.). Any legal requirements should also be addressed by such procedures.

Specific operating procedures, defined policies or standards should be established for governing such elements as

- departmental and individual responsibilities

- staff policies (including training, disciplinary procedures, etc.)

- safety and security

- Data Protection Act implications

- operations and workflow

- programming standards

- system development standards

- documentation standards

- Machine Room best practice

- access control and logical security policy

- contingency planning in the event of a disaster

- software change control

- service levels and user support facilities

- authorisations

- accounting policy.

The existence of such detailed procedures and policies should aim to positively contribute to the quality, security and integrity of the various activities handled by the IT organisation and be capable of monitoring for either compliance or infringement.

The definition and day-to-day application of procedures and standards can be viewed by employees as unnecessary barriers to the achievement of fundamental goals. These attitudes can therefore result in such mechanisms being partially or ineffectively applied if there is an absence of monitoring and control mechanisms. The setting of procedures, standards, etc. should ideally avoid undue bureaucracy and their definition can benefit from appropriate degrees of input from the affected parties. The underlying concepts (i.e. increased quality and reliability) can be 'sold' to staff as part of involving them in the formulation process.

All policies can benefit from regular or ongoing review in order to ensure their continued relevance and effectiveness, as there is little point in wasting valuable resources slavishly following pointless or outdated routines where the true cost of control significantly outweighs the potential exposures.

The setting of required IT function service levels will obviously be intrinsically related to the operational needs of the business activities, but may also have to include the determination of critical periods, allowance for essential maintenance and back-up activities, the timetable for data up-date, etc. Mechanisms should be in place to monitor the provision of service and enable the prompt detection of potential points of failure in achieving the acceptable levels. Facilities should be available to enable the prompt rectification of problems and the restoration of full services.

Most of the constituent factors mentioned in this chapter will require the existence of comprehensive records, logs, etc. in order to enable the correct application, monitoring, assessment and control of same.

Amongst the major contributory factors to the effectiveness of staff are their levels of awareness of both corporate and IT related matters, whether they feel that they can actively contribute to the achievement of established targets, and the degrees of motivation and trust instilled by management. Whether or not the workforce are sufficiently aware and motivated is, in major part, related to either the management style or the effectiveness of formal methods of internal communications throughout the company. The dissemination of pertinent company information can be achieved in a number of ways, for example by regular newsletters, departmental meetings or management briefings. Irrespective of the selected method the aim should be to inform staff to the required degree and engender an atmosphere of involvement and trust.

Control matrix examples

The establishment of an effective and sound IT organisational structure can have a direct impact upon the success or otherwise of the overall business. Additionally, it can be so designed to develop, incorporate and apply a range of operational policies, standards and procedures which can all contribute to a culture of control designed to minimise a range of risks and exposures. For these prime reasons we have provided (in Tables 5.1 and 5.2) two example matrices for IT Organisation; one each for *Objectives* and *Exposures*. Full details of the relevant *Scales* used in these examples (i.e. numbers 2 and 4) are provided in Appendix 5.

The establishment of the structural and administrative framework is a fundamental process and the example data values represent a high level of relevance. It will be noted that selected *Measures* and *Controls* affect more than one *Objective* or *Exposure*, occasionally with varying degrees of effectiveness. The supplied *Best* score values reflect a range of middle to high levels of expectation in terms of anticipated effectiveness of measures and controls.

Table 5.1   Organisation - Objectives

Overall Inherent Risk (Size) Score [5 is worst risk; 1 is best] = 3.44

A Define the operational framework & responsibilities for IT
B Ensure corporate objectives are translated into IT plans
C Establish IT Service Level agreements to support objectives
D Determine required IT resources & staff to meet objectives
E Establish relevant & effective IT organisational structure
F Provide segregation of key duties to protect integrity
G Ensure skill profile & levels adequately match requirements
H Provide adequate & targeted staff training to meet needs
I Minimise exposure to staff fraud and/or misconduct

J Provide definitions of Dept. & individual responsibilities
K Provide documented procedures for all IT Dept. Functions
L Establish & apply adequate standards and policies
M Ensure accuracy, security & integrity of user systems/data
N Ensure continuity of operations in the event of failure, etc
O Provide means of recording & monitoring performance level
P Ensure that legal requirements are adequately addressed
Q Provide effective channels for internal communication
R Ensure that IT action plans remain relevant

I T Organisation		OBJECTIVES																	
		A	B	C	D	E	F	G	H	I	J	K	L	M	N	O	P	Q	R
Calculated Risk Score:	Risk	4	4	4	3	3	3	3	3	3	3	3	3	4	4	3	2	3	4
Scale 2 (6 is most serious)	Type	5	6	6	6	3	4	6	3	4	4	5	5	6	6	6	3	3	6
Size (3 is maximum)	Size	3	3	3	2	3	3	2	3	2	2	2	2	3	3	2	2	3	3
MEASURES																			
1 Terms of Reference provided for IT Division - agreed at Board level	Best		5																
	Test	?	?																
	Both																		
2 IT Strategic Planning exercise undertaken - based upon the corporate business objectives	Best		4																
	Test	?	?																
	Both																		
3 IT Action Plans generated by Strategic Plan - define resource skill & procedural requirements	Best		5		4			3											
	Test	?	?		?			?											
	Both																		
4 Operational criteria & service level requirements assessed and agreed with users	Best			5															
	Test	?		?															
	Both																		
5 Manpower planning undertaken for IT division + annual review of remuneration package	Best				5														
	Test	?			?														
	Both																		
6 Organisation structure reflects logical grouping of activities & lines of communication, etc.	Best					4													
	Test	?				?													
	Both																		
7 Key duties (i.e. processing, programming, data control, etc.) are adequately segregated	Best						5		4										
	Test	?					?		?										
	Both																		

Table 5.1   continued

			A	B	C	D	E	F	G	H	I	J	K	L	M	N	O	P	Q	R
8	Assessment of existing staff skills undertaken as basis for planning and training needs	Best							4	3										
		Test	?						?	?										
		Both																		
-		-	-	-	-	-	-	-	-	-	-	-	-	-	-	-	-	-	-	-
9	Training plan developed which reflects environmental changes and requirement targets	Best								4										
		Test	?							?										
		Both																		
-		-	-	-	-	-	-	-	-	-	-	-	-	-	-	-	-	-	-	-
10	All staff in positions of trust or commercial sensitivity are fidelity bonded	Best									4									
		Test	?								?									
		Both																		
-		-	-	-	-	-	-	-	-	-	-	-	-	-	-	-	-	-	-	-
11	Each department had documented terms of reference	Best										4								
		Test	?									?								
		Both																		
-		-	-	-	-	-	-	-	-	-	-	-	-	-	-	-	-	-	-	-
12	Job descriptions in place which define responsibilities, authority, etc.	Best										4								
		Test	?									?								
		Both																		
-		-	-	-	-	-	-	-	-	-	-	-	-	-	-	-	-	-	-	-
13	Operations Department procedures established and monitored	Best											4		2	3				
		Test	?										?		?	?				
		Both																		
-		-	-	-	-	-	-	-	-	-	-	-	-	-	-	-	-	-	-	-
14	System Development methodology and standards implemented	Best											4	4	3					
		Test	?										?	?	?					
		Both																		
-		-	-	-	-	-	-	-	-	-	-	-	-	-	-	-	-	-	-	-
15	Data Control procedures have been established	Best											4		4					
		Test	?										?		?					
		Both																		
-		-	-	-	-	-	-	-	-	-	-	-	-	-	-	-	-	-	-	-
16	Programming standards defined and in place	Best											4	4						
		Test	?										?	?						
		Both																		
-		-	-	-	-	-	-	-	-	-	-	-	-	-	-	-	-	-	-	-
17	Safety standards defined and implemented	Best											3							
		Test	?										?							
		Both																		
-		-	-	-	-	-	-	-	-	-	-	-	-	-	-	-	-	-	-	-
18	Access Control and logical security policy in place	Best											4	4						
		Test	?										?	?						
		Both																		
-		-	-	-	-	-	-	-	-	-	-	-	-	-	-	-	-	-	-	-
19	Documentation requirement standards established	Best											4	4	4					
		Test	?										?	?	?					
		Both																		
-		-	-	-	-	-	-	-	-	-	-	-	-	-	-	-	-	-	-	-

Table 5.1   continued

No	Item		A	B	C	D	E	F	G	H	I	J	K	L	M	N	O	P	Q	R
20	Data back-up and media handling procedure/policy in place and monitored	Best												4	4	4				
		Test	?											?	?	?				
		Both																		
-		-	-	-	-	-	-	-	-	-	-	-	-	-	-	-	-	-	-	-
21	Disaster & Contingency Plan formulated and tested at least annually	Best														5				
		Test	?													?				
		Both																		
-		-	-	-	-	-	-	-	-	-	-	-	-	-	-	-	-	-	-	-
22	All policies, procedures and standards subject to annual review and update	Best										3	4	4		4				
		Test	?									?	?	?		?				
		Both																		
-		-	-	-	-	-	-	-	-	-	-	-	-	-	-	-	-	-	-	-
23	Various performance records and logs maintained and subject to ongoing monitoring	Best															5			
		Test	?														?			
		Both																		
-		-	-	-	-	-	-	-	-	-	-	-	-	-	-	-	-	-	-	-
24	Performance problems are reacted to and reported upon	Best															4			
		Test	?														?			
		Both																		
-		-	-	-	-	-	-	-	-	-	-	-	-	-	-	-	-	-	-	-
25	Health & Safety, Data Protection Act, etc. issues are addressed by relevant managers	Best																4		
		Test	?															?		
		Both																		
-		-	-	-	-	-	-	-	-	-	-	-	-	-	-	-	-	-	-	-
26	Dept. level meetings held monthly to circulate corporate & IT objectives, performance, etc.	Best																	4	
		Test	?																?	
		Both																		
-		-	-	-	-	-	-	-	-	-	-	-	-	-	-	-	-	-	-	-
27	Quarterly company magazine produced - reinforces current direction, etc.	Best																	3	
		Test	?																?	
		Both																		
-		-	-	-	-	-	-	-	-	-	-	-	-	-	-	-	-	-	-	-
28	IT Division plans are reviewed annually in association with the corporate business plans	Best																		5
		Test	?																	?
		Both																		
-		-	-	-	-	-	-	-	-	-	-	-	-	-	-	-	-	-	-	-

A Define the operational framework & responsibilities for IT
B Ensure corporate objectives are translated into IT plans
C Establish IT Service Level agreements to support objectives
D Determine required IT resources & staff to meet objectives
E Establish relevant & effective IT organisational structure
F Provide segregation of key duties to protect integrity
G Ensure skill profile & levels adequately match requirements
H Provide adequate & targeted staff training to meet needs
I Minimise exposure to staff fraud and/or misconduct

J Provide definitions of Dept. & individual responsibilities
K Provide documented procedures for all IT Dept. Functions
L Establish & apply adequate standards and policies
M Ensure accuracy, security & integrity of user systems/data
N Ensure continuity of operations in the event of failure, etc
O Provide means of recording & monitoring performance level
P Ensure that legal requirements are adequately addressed
Q Provide effective channels for internal communication
R Ensure that IT action plans remain relevant

Table 5.2   Organisation - Exposures

Overall Inherent Risk (Size) Score [5 is worst risk; 1 is best] = 3.85

A Inadequate definition of IT function & responsibilities
B Failure to achieve group objectives due to lack of IT plan
C Inadequate/inappropriate IT service provision to business
D Inadequate IT resources to provide required service level
E Inadequate and/or inappropriately skilled IT staff
F Inappropriate IT organisation structure to support business
G Fraud and abuse due to inadequate segregation of key duties
H Inadequate or poorly targeted staff training - delay, error
I Appointment of unsuitable staff to positions of trust
J Failure to define & assign areas of responsibility - delay

K Absence of adequate operational procedures - error, cost
L Insecure or inadequate computer operation processes - delay
M Failure to develop/maintain good quality, reliable systems
N System failures due to poor programing standards - costs
O Insecure systems/operations - failure to support business
P Inaccurate, unreliable user data - error, disruption, costs
Q Inability to recover processing after failures or disaster
R Loss of data/facilities - disruption to business, losses
S Failure to monitor performance levels - disrupt business
T Failure to maintain awareness of business/IT requirements

	IT Organisation	EXPOSURES	A	B	C	D	E	F	G	H	I	J	K	L	M	N	O	P	Q	R	S	T
	Calculated Risk Score:	Risk	4	4	4	4	4	3	3	3	3	2	3	3	4	4	4	4	4	4	3	4
	Scale 4 (6 is most serious)	Type	6	6	6	6	5	5	4	4	4	6	5	6	5	5	6	6	6	6	6	6
	Size (3 is maximum)	Size	3	3	3	3	3	2	2	2	2	1	2	2	3	3	3	3	3	3	2	3
	CONTROLS																						
1	Terms of reference provided for IT Division - agreed at Board level	Best		5																		
		Test	?	?																		
		Both																				
2	IT Strategic Planning exercise undertaken - based upon the corporate business objectives	Best		5	4																	
		Test	?	?	?																	
		Both																				
3	IT Action Plans generated by Strategic Plan - define resource skill & procedural requirements	Best		4	4	4																
		Test	?	?	?	?																
		Both																				
4	Operational criteria & service level requirements assessed and agreed with users	Best		4	4	3																
		Test	?	?	?	?																
		Both																				
5	Manpower planning undertaken for IT division + annual review of remuneration package	Best		3		3	4															
		Test	?	?		?	?															
		Both																				
6	Hardware requirements plan has been developed	Best		4	3	4																
		Test	?	?	?	?																
		Both																				
7	Organisation structure reflects logical grouping of activities & lines of communication, etc.	Best						5														
		Test	?					?														
		Both																				

Table 5.2   continued

#	Description		A	B	C	D	E	F	G	H	I	J	K	L	M	N	O	P	Q	R	S	T
8	Key duties (i.e. processing, programming, data control, etc.) are adequately segregated	Best							5													
		Test	?						?													
		Both																				
-		-	-	-	-	-	-	-	-	-	-	-	-	-	-	-	-	-	-	-	-	-
9	Assessment of existing staff skills undertaken as basis for planning and training needs	Best					4			4												
		Test	?				?			?												
		Both																				
-		-	-	-	-	-	-	-	-	-	-	-	-	-	-	-	-	-	-	-	-	-
10	Training plan developed which reflects environmental changes and requirement targets	Best								4												
		Test	?							?												
		Both																				
-		-	-	-	-	-	-	-	-	-	-	-	-	-	-	-	-	-	-	-	-	-
11	All staff in positions of trust or commercial sensitivity are fidelity bonded	Best									5											
		Test	?								?											
		Both																				
-		-	-	-	-	-	-	-	-	-	-	-	-	-	-	-	-	-	-	-	-	-
12	Each department has documented terms of reference	Best										4										
		Test	?									?										
		Both																				
-		-	-	-	-	-	-	-	-	-	-	-	-	-	-	-	-	-	-	-	-	-
13	Job descriptions in place which define responsibilities, authority, etc.	Best										4										
		Test	?									?										
		Both																				
-		-	-	-	-	-	-	-	-	-	-	-	-	-	-	-	-	-	-	-	-	-
14	Operations Department procedures established and monitored	Best										4	4	5								
		Test	?									?	?	?								
		Both																				
-		-	-	-	-	-	-	-	-	-	-	-	-	-	-	-	-	-	-	-	-	-
15	System Development methodology and standards implemented	Best													5							
		Test	?												?							
		Both																				
-		-	-	-	-	-	-	-	-	-	-	-	-	-	-	-	-	-	-	-	-	-
16	Data Control procedures have been established	Best												4								
		Test	?											?								
		Both																				
-		-	-	-	-	-	-	-	-	-	-	-	-	-	-	-	-	-	-	-	-	-
17	Programming standards defined and in place	Best													4	5						
		Test	?												?	?						
		Both																				
-		-	-	-	-	-	-	-	-	-	-	-	-	-	-	-	-	-	-	-	-	-
18	Access control and logical security policy in place	Best												4	3			4	4			
		Test	?											?	?			?	?			
		Both																				
-		-	-	-	-	-	-	-	-	-	-	-	-	-	-	-	-	-	-	-	-	-
19	Documentation requirement standards established	Best											4	4	4	3	3		4			
		Test	?										?	?	?	?	?		?			
		Both																				
-		-	-	-	-	-	-	-	-	-	-	-	-	-	-	-	-	-	-	-	-	-

Table 5.2   continued

			A	B	C	D	E	F	G	H	I	J	K	L	M	N	O	P	Q	R	S	T
20	Data back-up and media handling procedure/policy in place and monitored	Best															3	4	4	4		
		Test	?														?	?	?	?		
		Both																				
-			-	-	-	-	-	-	-	-	-	-	-	-	-	-	-	-	-	-	-	-
21	Disaster & Contingency Plan formulated and tested at least annually	Best																	5	4		
		Test	?																?	?		
		Both																				
-			-	-	-	-	-	-	-	-	-	-	-	-	-	-	-	-	-	-	-	-
22	Data validation processes are incorporated into all key systems	Best																4				
		Test	?															?				
		Both																				
-			-	-	-	-	-	-	-	-	-	-	-	-	-	-	-	-	-	-	-	-
23	Data exception reporting facilities established	Best																4				
		Test	?															?				
		Both																				
-			-	-	-	-	-	-	-	-	-	-	-	-	-	-	-	-	-	-	-	-
24	Copies of all programs are stored off-site in secure facility	Best																		4		
		Test	?																	?		
		Both																				
-			-	-	-	-	-	-	-	-	-	-	-	-	-	-	-	-	-	-	-	-
25	Various performance records and logs maintained and subject to ongoing monitoring	Best																			5	
		Test	?																		?	
		Both																				
-			-	-	-	-	-	-	-	-	-	-	-	-	-	-	-	-	-	-	-	-
26	Performance problems are reacted to and reported upon	Best																			4	
		Test	?																		?	
		Both																				
-			-	-	-	-	-	-	-	-	-	-	-	-	-	-	-	-	-	-	-	-
27	I T Division plans are reviewed annually in association with the corporate business plans	Best																				5
		Test	?																			?
		Both																				
-			-	-	-	-	-	-	-	-	-	-	-	-	-	-	-	-	-	-	-	-
28	Dept. level meetings held monthly to circulate corporate & IT objectives, performance,etc.	Best																				4
		Test	?																			?
		Both																				
-			-	-	-	-	-	-	-	-	-	-	-	-	-	-	-	-	-	-	-	-

A Inadequate definition of IT function & responsibilities
B Failure to achieve group objectives due to lack of IT plan
C Inadequate/inappropriate IT service provision to business
D Inadequate IT resources to provide required service level
E Inadequate and/or inappropriately skilled IT staff
F Inappropriate IT organisation structure to support business
G Fraud and abuse due to inadequate segregation of key duties
H Inadequate or poorly targeted staff training - delay, error
I Appointment of unsuitable staff to positions of trust
J Failure to define & assign areas of responsibility - delay

K Absence of adequate operational procedures - error, cost
L Insecure or inadequate computer operation processes - delay
M Failure to develop/maintain good quality, reliable systems
N System failures due to poor programing standards - costs
O Insecure systems/operations - failure to support business
P Inaccurate, unreliable user data - error, disruption, costs
Q Inability to recover processing after failures or disaster
R Loss of data/facilities - disruption to business, losses
S Failure to monitor performance levels - disrupt business
T Failure to maintain awareness of business/IT requirements

6

CONTINGENCY PLANNING

Scope

Contingency planning is a process which aims to counteract the effects of potential disasters affecting the IT capabilities of an organisation thereby ensuring that it can recommence IT operations as quickly as possible in support of business operations. The two principal considerations are the cost-effectiveness and timescale of applying the contingency plan measures. The plan should clearly define the actions and responsibilities applicable in a disaster scenario, but its development should not distract management from the separate provision of effective day-to-day measures, policies and standards which can contribute either to controlled operations or the prevention and containment of potential disaster situations.

Reference should also be made to Chapter 15 (IT Sites), Chapter 18 (Back-up and Media Handling) and Chapter 10 (Facilities Management).

This chapter covers the development of a suitable Contingency and Recovery plan, and the testing and ongoing maintenance of same.

Any number of IT consultants will be able to provide convincing (and alarming) evidence that if an organisation is heavily dependent upon IT resources, and is unfortunate enough to succumb to the effects of a major disaster affecting its computing centre, it will only be able to survive as a going concerning for 'n' days, weeks or months unless it has adequate contingency plans and arrangements in place. However, the impacts of such major events can be mitigated by the application of good practices in the form of sensible everyday procedures and controls.

There can be considerable internal debate about what constitutes a disaster, and the likelihood of any given event actually happening (e.g. the ubiquitous Jumbo jet landing, unintentionally, on your computing centre). Each organisation must review such odds according to their location (e.g. their proximity to Heathrow Airport or an oil refinery) and any other 'local' circumstances. However when considering the requirements of contingency planning, it is easier to assume that, for whatever reason, the computing facility has been destroyed and that you are faced with recreating sufficient facilities to enable the business to carry on trading; we will leave all the shades of grey for the real event, but it is generally wise to plan for the worst scenario.

Of course, the nature of computer facilities will vary considerably, and no one standard recovery plan will be able to cope with the precise and perhaps very complex arrangements that will undoubtedly apply from company to company. However, there are degrees of consistency in the approach to determining a suitable plan, and to ensuring that all realistic and applicable elements have been adequately addressed.

There must a clear view of what constitutes the minimum combination of required hardware configuration and applications so as to enable the relevant key business functions to continue their operations. A register of all existing equipment and software is of assistance in this respect and can further support the necessary insurance claims in the event of loss or damage. Additionally, such a register may also exist to support the fixed asset accounting entries.

It is essential that all business users are consulted during the development of an IT recovery plan so that the application systems and related facilities that are critical to their operations are correctly identified and prioritised.

Although a planned approach to recovery is essential (if for no other reason than to ensure that all the points on the checklist have been addressed), the type and quality of the day-to-day operating procedures and practices can play a crucial role in the ability to survive a disaster. For example, adequate data and systems back-up, the off-site storage of media and adequate systems and procedural documentation, can all positively contribute to the speed and effectiveness of recovery from disruption, etc. Furthermore, adequate attention to matters of general physical security, fire detection and control, etc. can also contribute to the avoidance of potential disasters. Matters of best practice in a number of operational areas will positively contribute to both the prevention of avoidable problems and the general ability to promptly recover.

In the event of a potential emergency, for example a suspected fire, there should be existing and separate generalised instructions covering the safe and controlled evacuation of the buildings. Although such measures are applied prior to the declaration of a disaster requiring the use of a contingency plan, their regular testing can improve their effectiveness and by so doing potentially avert the necessity to subsequently invoke the contingency plan.

All considerations about contingency planning have to be relative to the cost of providing the recovery facilities and identifying beforehand the critical and key processes without which the company would die commercially. A form of risk assessment can assist in this process and bring into focus a suitable approach to providing the most appropriate and cost-effective recovery facilities.

The terms Cold Start, Warm Start and Hot Start are generally applied to differentiate between the various basic approaches to re-establishing a computing capability, and the definitions of these terms given below may be of use. Please note that such facilities can be provided by (a) specialist organisations who levy an annual premium according to the requirements, (b) reciprocal arrangements with other companies with appropriate facilities, or (c) by the company itself.

- *Cold Start* Normally an empty facility, perhaps owned by the company and very basically equipped with power, etc. Although the ongoing costs/ premiums may be low, the timescale required to get the facility operational can be longer than the critical survival period for the business, and is also dependent upon all the relevant suppliers and contractors responding with appropriate speed and effectiveness.

- *Warm Start* Normally provided by a specialist bureau or other large scale user with spare processing capacity, etc. of a compatible type to that used by the company. Alternatively a portable or mobile facility can be used which can be sited at any convenient and secure location (for example the company car park).

- *Hot Start* The most expensive option, this is a completely equipped facility with a normally idle machine. Usually made available to a fixed number of subscribers to apportion the cost of provision.

The option that a company chooses will depend on a number of factors including the extent to which their business is dependent upon IT, the related cost-effectiveness of the premiums associated with each option, and the criticality of the timescale associated with recovery of prime facilities, etc.

In certain businesses, for example the financial sector, the organisation may have dual computing facilities on separate sites with the ability to switch either all or the priority processing to one or other in the event of a major failure. This is an expensive option beyond the financial resources of most organisations, although there are a number of other incidental benefits in normal operations, such as the ability to archive data automatically to the other site.

Given that the costs of providing effective contingency measures can be substantial, each organisation should identify and comprehensively review the degree of dependency they have upon IT operations and the related impact of an IT context disaster on their ability to continue trading, cash flow, market valuation, etc. When considering contingency planning initially, a project team should be formed, reflecting all the required fields of expertise, to consider all the aspects of the recovery process.

All contingency planning projects should be supported or sponsored by senior management to reflect the significance of the process. The plan must be comprehensively documented and define specific responsibilities. There should be clarity as to who declares a disaster situation and invokes use of the plan.

The following aspects should be addressed, when appropriate to an installation, in the contingency planning process:

- identify the relevant personnel and plan management structure

- provide a documented Contingency Plan, allocating specific responsibilities and defining the structure for reporting and meetings, etc.

- identify and document the minimum hardware configuration for all types of computers, peripherals

- record the systems software requirements

- include a prioritised list of required application systems

- document the communications requirements incorporating the cabling, hardware, external lines and service circuits

- schedule all the data required to initiate and maintain company applications and operations, taking into account the effectiveness of existing back-up processes in safeguarding the recovery processes

- the provision of sufficient and suitable buildings and premises to facilitate the recovery

- ensure that all the initial and critical actions are clearly identified and allocated to named individuals

- address all the physical security aspects

- promptly provide power, light, air conditioning and heating facilities

- ensure the availability of telephones, fax and any other business communication facilities

- maintain accurate records of key staff contacts including out of hours telephone numbers

- address the housing and accommodation of key staff

- consider transport requirements for equipment, staff and supplies to and between the affected company sites

- ensure the availability of system documentation (which should be securely stored off-site to provide further assurance)

- provide all the necessary operating and procedural instructions (including configuration details for operating systems, etc.)

- establish accounting and budgetary controls over the recovery exercise

- establish responsibilities for the procurement of goods and services within defined and permitted mandates

- provide adequate office equipment, furniture, consumables and stationery

- consider the need for catering facilities, especially for remotely located temporary sites

- allocate responsibility for handling public and media relations so as to present a uniform and positive corporate image in the best interests of the company

- consider issues of compliance with local planning regulations, legal requirements, health and safety issues, etc.

- provide for adequate communication channels within the project team, ensuring that the co-ordinator or senior manager is kept up-to-date with progress, problems, etc.

- establish contact and maintain liaison with insurers.

The following internal and external contacts will need to be established and fully briefed upon their role if a disaster should strike and how they will be contacted in the actual event.

Internal
Legal services (or company solicitor)
IT management
   – Hardware specialists
   – Software specialists
   – Communications specialists
   – Operations staff
   – Database administration
   – Data input
User management representatives
Building and Facilities staff
Transport Dept.
Administration
Accounting
Salvage staff.

It may be preferable to form staff into various teams during a disaster situation, each being responsible for a particular aspect of the recovery process; team leaders can then present a report of the team progress, etc. to the co-ordinating group or committee.

External

Insurers (including any consideration of liability for injury or loss of life in the disaster)

Stand-by facility contractors

Building Surveyors and contractors

Computer and other hardware vendors/suppliers

Software suppliers

Electricity supplier

Telecommunications equipment and lines suppliers

Suppliers of ancillary equipment (i.e. generators)

Bureaux and/or FM contractors

Water, gas and fuel providers

Suppliers of sundries and consumables (i.e. discs, tapes, listing paper, etc.)

Local planning authorities

Security service organisations

Police & Fire service (i.e. in respect of damaged premises, etc.).

In seeking assurances from external suppliers or contractors, it can be understandably difficult to pin them down to specific obligations for some theoretical event that may take place at an unknown time, and the best you can achieve may be a rather vague letter of commitment.

Once agreed at senior management level, and suitably documented, the plan should be kept up-to-date with the details of the necessary contacts. Once documented, sufficient copies of the plan should be circulated to team members; additional copies should be kept off-site to cover the possible destruction or loss of the originals. Version control should be applied to the plan and all amendments issued by the co-ordinating officer.

Testing the plan, either in part or entirely, does present some problems, for example the cost and disruption of business, the ability to create a realistic and practical test scenario, and being able to realistically test the effectiveness of the action of external suppliers. However, avoiding testing the plan in advance in a controlled way potentially results in extra unforeseen factors being encountered for the first time in the understandably frenzied atmosphere of a real disaster situation. Any organisation which has a high level of IT dependency should attempt to objectively test whether it can demonstrate the necessary state of readiness in the event of a disaster. This can be achieved in a fragmented way, by evaluating a discrete part (or parts) of the plan (i.e. testing the ability to rebuild the key applications and retrieve and load the relevant data). Whenever the plan is tested, the results should be reviewed for effectiveness, speed of actions, etc. and any necessary amendments and improvements agreed and incorporated. In any event, the plan should be subject to regular review to ensure the relevance of the contacts, systems configuration, and all other quantifiable factors.

The regular testing of general fire and emergency evacuation drills also has a relevance to the contingency environment; valuable lessons can be learnt by reviewing the performance of such drills, thereby enabling any identified deficiencies to be accordingly addressed.

Control matrix examples

There is an obvious corporate strategic importance in successfully addressing this subject and therefore two example matrices are provided covering management *Objectives* (Table 6.1) and potential *Exposures* (Table 6.2). The various elements described above will cater (to varying degrees) for the needs of both management objectives and the avoidance of potential risks. The exposures described in the Table 6.2 example are oriented towards the cause (e.g. failure to effectively handle public and media relations), enabling the reader to interpret the nature and extent of the likely effects of such shortcomings in their own context.

The *Scale* data used in the example matrices are related to Scale 2 for the *Objectives* contained in Table 6.1, and Scale 4 for the *Exposures* reflected in Table 6.2. Supporting details for these and other *Scales* are provided in Appendix 5.

A high level of IT dependence is assumed in the use of example *Type* and *Size* data, with a relatively optimistic view of the *Measures* and *Control* examples.

Table 6.1 Contingency Planning - Objectives

Overall Inherent Risk (Size) Score [5 is worst risk; 1 is best] = 3.00

A Ensure that the potential for disaster is minimised
B Plan to ensure critical IT operations are promptly resumed
C Ensure that following a disaster, impacts are minimised
D Assess & record the minimum IT configuration required
E Assess & select the best/cost-effective recovery solution
F Ensure all internal resources are identified and alerted
G Ensure all external resources are identified and alerted
H Provide capability to rebuild required applications & data

I Provide management, communications & resource structures
J Ensure that insurance considerations are addressed
K Ensure correct liaison with local authorities, police, fire
L Ensure that damaged & recovery sites are secure and safe
M Ensure systems, procedure & plan documents are valid/secure
N Ensure public/media relations are handled in best interests
O Ensure the plan is documented and tested for effectiveness
P Ensure the plan contents remain relevant and up-to-date

Contingency Planning		OBJECTIVES	A	B	C	D	E	F	G	H	I	J	K	L	M	N	O	P
Calculated Risk Score:		Risk	3	4	4	3	3	3	3	3	3	2	2	2	3	2	3	3
Scale 2 (6 is most serious)		Type	6	6	6	6	6	4	6	6	3	6	3	6	5	6	6	5
Size (3 is maximum)		Size	2	3	3	2	2	3	2	2	3	1	2	1	2	1	2	2
MEASURES																		
1	Existing physical security, fire detection/control measures are of an acceptable standard	Best		4														
		Test	?	?														
		Both																
2	Regular fire and evacuation drills are conducted, and assessed for effectiveness	Best		3														
		Test	?	?														
		Both																
3	Contingency Planning Project created an agreed Recovery Plan - defines responsibilities,etc.	Best			4	4	4											
		Test	?		?	?	?											
		Both																
4	Plan allows for Warm-Start facility to be operational for critical tasks within 8 days	Best			4	4	3											
		Test	?		?	?	?											
		Both																
5	Plan contains full details of the critical hardware & software configuration requirements	Best				4	5											
		Test	?			?	?											
		Both																
6	The Warm-Start option was chosen following extensive research & assessment of all options	Best					5											
		Test	?				?											
		Both																
7	All recovery options were subjected to cost/benefit analysis & lead-time review	Best					4											
		Test	?				?											
		Both																

Table 6.1 continued

#			A	B	C	D	E	F	G	H	I	J	K	L	M	N	O	P
8	Key internal and external contacts are documented in the Plan	Best						4	4									
		Test	?					?	?									
		Both																
-		-	-	-	-	-	-	-	-	-	-	-	-	-	-	-	-	-
9	All affected staff are made aware of their plan responsibilities	Best						4										
		Test	?					?										
		Both																
-		-	-	-	-	-	-	-	-	-	-	-	-	-	-	-	-	-
10	All external suppliers were contacted & assurances obtained in writing - updated annually	Best							5									
		Test	?						?									
		Both																
-		-	-	-	-	-	-	-	-	-	-	-	-	-	-	-	-	-
11	Current copies of application software & data are stored and identified in off-site store	Best								4								
		Test	?							?								
		Both																
-		-	-	-	-	-	-	-	-	-	-	-	-	-	-	-	-	-
12	Systems documentation copies are stored off-site as back-up	Best								4					4			
		Test	?							?					?			
		Both																
-		-	-	-	-	-	-	-	-	-	-	-	-	-	-	-	-	-
13	Regular tests are conducted to prove ability to reconstruct key applications	Best								4								
		Test	?							?								
		Both																
-		-	-	-	-	-	-	-	-	-	-	-	-	-	-	-	-	-
14	Plan defines the management structure of recovery situation & who should invoke the plan	Best								4								
		Test	?							?								
		Both																
-		-	-	-	-	-	-	-	-	-	-	-	-	-	-	-	-	-
15	Lines of communication are defined in the plan, together with meeting/report requirements	Best								4								
		Test	?							?								
		Both																
-		-	-	-	-	-	-	-	-	-	-	-	-	-	-	-	-	-
16	Internal staff resources formed into teams, each addressing a particular area of activity	Best								4								
		Test	?							?								
		Both																
-		-	-	-	-	-	-	-	-	-	-	-	-	-	-	-	-	-
17	Insurers are aware of plan - which calls for day one contact & recording of expenditure, etc.	Best										5						
		Test	?									?						
		Both																
-		-	-	-	-	-	-	-	-	-	-	-	-	-	-	-	-	-
18	Plan defines contact points for local authority, police & fire. Planning requirements confirmed	Best											4					
		Test	?										?					
		Both																
-		-	-	-	-	-	-	-	-	-	-	-	-	-	-	-	-	-

Table 6.1 continued

No.	Description	Type		A	B	C	D	E	F	G	H	I	J	K	L	M	N	O	P
19	Security Services company used to patrol/guard damaged and recovery sites	Best													4				
		Test	?												?				
		Both																	
-		-	-	-	-	-	-	-	-	-	-	-	-	-	-	-	-	-	-
20	Surveyor will inspect damaged site and recommend any repairs or making safe	Best													4				
		Test	?												?				
		Both																	
-		-	-	-	-	-	-	-	-	-	-	-	-	-	-	-	-	-	-
21	Operating instructions, user procedure documentation stored off-site. Identified as critical	Best														4			
		Test	?													?			
		Both																	
-		-	-	-	-	-	-	-	-	-	-	-	-	-	-	-	-	-	-
22	Copies of the Contingency Plan also stored off-site	Best														4			
		Test	?													?			
		Both																	
-		-	-	-	-	-	-	-	-	-	-	-	-	-	-	-	-	-	-
23	All press/media enquiries will be routed to Press Liaison Officer; briefed by management	Best															5		
		Test	?														?		
		Both																	
-		-	-	-	-	-	-	-	-	-	-	-	-	-	-	-	-	-	-
24	Plan allows for appropriate announcement/advertising of impact on trading operations	Best															4		
		Test	?														?		
		Both																	
-		-	-	-	-	-	-	-	-	-	-	-	-	-	-	-	-	-	-
25	Plan is fully documented and signed-off by senior management	Best																4	
		Test	?															?	
		Both																	
-		-	-	-	-	-	-	-	-	-	-	-	-	-	-	-	-	-	-
26	Plan is tested once per year (without prior internal notice) in a simulation exercise	Best																4	
		Test	?															?	
		Both																	
-		-	-	-	-	-	-	-	-	-	-	-	-	-	-	-	-	-	-
27	Test results/performance are reviewed and adjustments to plan are recommended	Best																3	3
		Test	?															?	?
		Both																	
-		-	-	-	-	-	-	-	-	-	-	-	-	-	-	-	-	-	-
28	Plan contents reviewed annually and relevant managers requested to confirm accuracy of contents	Best																	4
		Test	?																?
		Both																	
-		-	-	-	-	-	-	-	-	-	-	-	-	-	-	-	-	-	-
29	Master copy of the plan is maintained - updates circulated under version control	Best																	4
		Test	?																?
		Both																	
-		-	-	-	-	-	-	-	-	-	-	-	-	-	-	-	-	-	-

A Ensure that the potential for disaster is minimised
B Plan to ensure critical IT operations are promptly resumed
C Ensure that following a disaster, impacts are minimised
D Assess & record the minimum IT configuration required
E Assess & select the best/cost-effective recovery solution
F Ensure all internal resources are identified and alerted
G Ensure all external resources are identified and alerted
H Provide capability to rebuild required applications & data
I Provide management, communications & resource structures
J Ensure that insurance considerations are addressed
K Ensure correct liaison with local authorities, police, fire
L Ensure that damaged & recovery sites are secure and safe
M Ensure systems, procedure & plan documents are valid/secure
N Ensure public/media relations are handled in best interests
O Ensure the plan is documented and tested for effectiveness
P Ensure the plan contents remain relevant and up-to-date

Table 6.2   Contingency Planning - Exposures

Overall Inherent Risk (Size) Score [5 is worst risk; 1 is best] = 3.40

A Ineffective measures to prevent/detect potential disasters
B Absence of a planned approach to effective recovery of IT
C Failure to minimise/contain business impacts
D Failure to identify the minimum IT requirements to survive
E Failure to assess/select the appropriate recovery solution
F Inadequate/inappropriate internal planning representation
G Absence of management commitment to contingency planning
H Failure to identify and document all required resources
I Failure to allocate clear responsibilities/provide training
J Failure to involve external sources & obtain commitments

K Failure to provide effective plan management/communications
L Inability to rebuild applications and data for key systems
M Failure to involve / alert insurers at appropriate stage
N Inadequate liaison with local authority, police & fire
O Absence of up-to-date systems, procedural & plan documents
P Failure to effectively handle public/media relations
Q Failure to provide power, gas, water, telephones, etc.
R Failure to address security, staff welfare & safety issues
S Failure to ensure the plan is up to date and relevant
T Failure to adequately test the plan

Contingency Planning		EXPOSURES	A	B	C	D	E	F	G	H	I	J	K	L	M	N	O	P	Q	R	S	T
Calculated Risk Score:	Risk		3	4	4	4	4	3	2	4	4	3	3	4	3	2	3	2	3	3	3	2
Scale 4 (6 is most serious)	Type		5	6	6	6	6	4	6	5	5	6	6	6	3	3	3	6	3	3	3	6
Size (3 is maximum)	Size		2	3	3	3	3	3	1	3	3	2	2	3	3	2	3	1	3	3	3	1
CONTROLS																						
1 Existing physical security, fire detection/control measures are of an acceptable standard	Best			4		2																
	Test		?	?		?																
	Both																					
2 Regular fire and evacuation drills are conducted, and assessed for effectiveness	Best			4																		
	Test		?	?																		
	Both																					
3 Contingency Planning Project created an agreed Recovery Plan - defines responsibilities, etc.	Best			5	4	2	3															
	Test		?	?	?	?	?															
	Both																					
4 Plan allows for Warm-Start facility to be operational for critical tasks within 5 days	Best			4	4	4	4															
	Test		?	?	?	?	?															
	Both																					
5 Plan contains full details of the critical hardware & software configuration requirements	Best			3	3	5				3												
	Test		?	?	?	?				?												
	Both																					
6 The Warm-Start option was chosen following extensive research & assessment of all options	Best			3			5															
	Test		?	?			?															
	Both																					
7 All recovery options were subjected to cost/benefit analysis & lead-time review	Best						4															
	Test		?				?															
	Both																					

Table 6.2   continued

			A	B	C	D	E	F	G	H	I	J	K	L	M	N	O	P	Q	R	S	T
8	Membership of Project team reflected all appropriate functions and skills	Best						5														
		Test	?					?														
		Both																				
-		-	-	-	-	-	-	-	-	-	-	-	-	-	-	-	-	-	-	-	-	-
9	Key internal and external contacts are documented in the Plan	Best						4		3												
		Test	?					?		?												
		Both																				
-		-	-	-	-	-	-	-	-	-	-	-	-	-	-	-	-	-	-	-	-	-
10	Project sponsored by the IT Director	Best							5													
		Test	?						?													
		Both																				
-		-	-	-	-	-	-	-	-	-	-	-	-	-	-	-	-	-	-	-	-	-
11	All affected staff made aware of their plan responsibilities	Best							4													
		Test	?						?													
		Both																				
-		-	-	-	-	-	-	-	-	-	-	-	-	-	-	-	-	-	-	-	-	-
12	Internal staff resources formed into teams, each addressing a particular area of activity	Best							4	4												
		Test	?						?	?												
		Both																				
-		-	-	-	-	-	-	-	-	-	-	-	-	-	-	-	-	-	-	-	-	-
13	Staff briefing/training is conducted. Test runs of plan are also undertaken	Best							4													
		Test	?						?													
		Both																				
-		-	-	-	-	-	-	-	-	-	-	-	-	-	-	-	-	-	-	-	-	-
14	All external suppliers were contacted & assurances obtained in writing - updated annually	Best									5											
		Test	?								?											
		Both																				
-		-	-	-	-	-	-	-	-	-	-	-	-	-	-	-	-	-	-	-	-	-
15	Plan defines the management structure of recovery situation & who should invoke the plan	Best											5									
		Test	?										?									
		Both																				
-		-	-	-	-	-	-	-	-	-	-	-	-	-	-	-	-	-	-	-	-	-
16	Lines of communication are defined in the plan, together with meeting/report requirements	Best											4									
		Test	?										?									
		Both																				
-		-	-	-	-	-	-	-	-	-	-	-	-	-	-	-	-	-	-	-	-	-
17	Current copies of application software & data are stored and identified in off-site store	Best												4								
		Test	?											?								
		Both																				
-		-	-	-	-	-	-	-	-	-	-	-	-	-	-	-	-	-	-	-	-	-
18	Systems documentation copies are stored off-site as back-up	Best												4								
		Test	?											?								
		Both																				
-		-	-	-	-	-	-	-	-	-	-	-	-	-	-	-	-	-	-	-	-	-
19	Regular tests are conducted to prove ability to reconstruct key applications	Best												4								
		Test	?											?								
		Both																				
-		-	-	-	-	-	-	-	-	-	-	-	-	-	-	-	-	-	-	-	-	-

Table 6.2   continued

			A	B	C	D	E	F	G	H	I	J	K	L	M	N	O	P	Q	R	S	T
	Insurers are aware of plan -	Best													5							
20	which calls for day one contact	Test	?													?							
	& recording of expenditure, etc.	Both																					
-		-	-	-	-	-	-	-	-	-	-	-	-	-	-	-	-	-	-	-	-	-
	Plan defines contact points for	Best														5						
21	local authority, police & fire.	Test	?														?						
	Planning requirements confirmed	Both																					
-		-	-	-	-	-	-	-	-	-	-	-	-	-	-	-	-	-	-	-	-	-
	Operating instructions, user	Best															4					
22	procedure documentation stored	Test	?															?					
	off-site. Identified as critical	Both																					
-		-	-	-	-	-	-	-	-	-	-	-	-	-	-	-	-	-	-	-	-	-
	Copies of Contingency Plan	Best															4					
23	also stored off-site	Test	?															?					
		Both																					
-		-	-	-	-	-	-	-	-	-	-	-	-	-	-	-	-	-	-	-	-	-
	All press/media enquiries will	Best																5				
24	be routed to Press Liaison	Test	?																?				
	Officer; briefed by management	Both																					
-		-	-	-	-	-	-	-	-	-	-	-	-	-	-	-	-	-	-	-	-	-
	Plan allows for appropriate	Best																4				
25	announcement/advertising of	Test	?																?				
	impact on trading operations	Both																					
-		-	-	-	-	-	-	-	-	-	-	-	-	-	-	-	-	-	-	-	-	-
	Responsibility is allocated to	Best																	5			
26	arrange for utilities and	Test	?																	?			
	telephone services	Both																					
-		-	-	-	-	-	-	-	-	-	-	-	-	-	-	-	-	-	-	-	-	-
	Security Services company used	Best																		4		
27	to patrol/guard damaged and	Test	?																		?		
	recovery sites	Both																					
-		-	-	-	-	-	-	-	-	-	-	-	-	-	-	-	-	-	-	-	-	-
	Surveyor will inspect damaged	Best																		4		
28	site and recommend any repairs	Test	?																		?		
	or making safe	Both																					
-		-	-	-	-	-	-	-	-	-	-	-	-	-	-	-	-	-	-	-	-	-
	Plan is fully documented and	Best																		3		
29	signed-off by senior management	Test	?																		?		
		Both																					
-		-	-	-	-	-	-	-	-	-	-	-	-	-	-	-	-	-	-	-	-	-
	Plan contents reviewed annually	Best																		4		
30	and relevant managers requested	Test	?																		?		
	to confirm accuracy of contents	Both																					
-		-	-	-	-	-	-	-	-	-	-	-	-	-	-	-	-	-	-	-	-	-
	Master copy of the plan is	Best																		4		
31	maintained - updates circulated	Test	?																		?		
	under version control	Both																					
-		-	-	-	-	-	-	-	-	-	-	-	-	-	-	-	-	-	-	-	-	-

Table 6.2   continued

			A	B	C	D	E	F	G	H	I	J	K	L	M	N	O	P	Q	R	S	T
32	Plan is tested once per year (without prior internal notice) in a simulation exercise	Best																				4
		Test	?																			?
		Both																				
-		-	-	-	-	-	-	-	-	-	-	-	-	-	-	-	-	-	-	-	-	-
33	Test results/performance are reviewed and adjustments to plan are recommended	Best																			3	4
		Test	?																			?	?
		Both																				
-		-	-	-	-	-	-	-	-	-	-	-	-	-	-	-	-	-	-	-	-	-

A Ineffective measures to prevent/detect potential disasters
B Absence of a planned approach to effective recovery of IT
C Failure to minimise/contain business impacts
D Failure to identify the minimum IT requirements to survive
E Failure to assess/select the appropriate recovery solution
F Inadequate/inappropriate internal planning representation
G Absence of management commitment to contingency planning
H Failure to identify and document all required resources
I Failure to allocate clear responsibilities/provide training
J Failure to involve external sources & obtain commitments

K Failure to provide effective plan management/communications
L Inability to rebuild applications and data for key systems
M Failure to involve/alert insurers at appropriate stage
N Inadequate liaison with local authority, police & fire
O Absence of up-to-date systems, procedural & plan documents
P Failure to effectively handle public/media relations
Q Failure to provide power, gas, water, telephones, etc.
R Failure to address security, staff welfare & safety issues
S Failure to ensure the plan is up to date and relevant
T Failure to adequately test the plan

7

DATABASES

Scope

This chapter includes an exploration of some of the benefits of Database technologies, the initiation and set-up of Database facilities and subsequent ongoing use and maintenance of same.

The text includes references to Data Dictionaries, which can either be free-standing or integrated into the Database Management System (DBMS). The use of database techniques can be strongly associated with initiatives designed to attain competitive advantage and therefore it is suggested that reference to Chapter 4 (IT Strategic Planning) may be useful.

We do not fully describe the process of evaluating and selecting a DBMS. However, Software Package Selection is discussed in detail in Chapter 22.

In essence, a database is a collection of structured data kept separate from the applications that use it. In the context of this text, the term Database implies the control of data at a significant functional or corporate level. The use of Database technology should represent a controlled approach to the definition and use of essential corporate information. The contents of a database are normally defined within a Data Dictionary (DDS), and a Database Management System (DBMS) provides facilities to store, update and retrieve the relevant data.

The database approach is ideally suited to organisations which require a sharing of data throughout the business or where a number of separate applications need to access the same data on a consistent basis. The decision to adopt a database approach is more likely to be driven by strategic business considerations rather than purely technical ones as the effective application of the technique can offer considerable benefits in relation to efficient usage of data for either planning or operational purposes.

The use of a database can provide considerable flexibility for an organisation and assist the achievement of corporate objectives. However, the success of the process will be directly related to the quality, accuracy and integrity of the business data as managed by the DBMS. It is likely that the data will have an inestimable value to the company and therefore it should be adequately and effectively protected from unauthorised access, amendment, leakage, and destruction.

The use of a database approach has the following advantages:

- ensures the consistent definition and use of data

- provides a stable reflection of the organisation in data terms (this remains fairly constant, whereas the use of such data tends to vary over time in step with changing business needs, corporate direction or external influences)

- avoids duplicate data items being used by different systems with the attendant problems of misinterpretation or inability to compare

- allows for the efficient use of mass storage facilities and enables accurate storage capacity planning

- keeps data separate from the applications/programs, thus avoiding the need to extensively amend programs if and when data has to be restructured

- generally supports the concept of system and data ownership, allowing 'owners' to grant access rights to their data

- facilitates the control of access to data and the granting of permission to either read, write, or update

- permits data to be interrogated or enquired upon by the use of Query Languages (such as SQL)

- the DBMS can provide mechanisms to ensure the integrity of data and assist in the recovery of the database in the event of a failure or the corruption of the records.

It is worth noting that the indiscriminate use of Query Languages can make a heavy demand upon resources, thereby affecting the performance of production tasks. Accordingly their use should be controlled and sufficient training in their efficient use should be provided.

There are some potential disadvantages of using the database approach.

(a) Holding all the relevant corporate data within one large scale mechanism can represent additional risks, unless the DBMS offers strong access and integrity controls, and permits the controlled and accurate recovery from system problems or failures.

(b) There is considerable cost and effort in transferring from a conventional data storage scenario to a database, as it requires an accurate modelling of data and possibly amendments to existing applications so that they can access the database record formats.

(c)   Given that the concept supports access to unique data items by a number of application systems, there can be attendant problems in satisfactorily identifying a single data owner.

There are a range of facilities available in current database software which counteract some of these concerns, but in any event the knowledge and skills of Database Administration staff becomes crucial if the mechanisms are to be effective and the commercial interests of the company adequately protected.

A precursor to adopting the database approach is the undertaking of a comprehensive examination and modelling of all corporate data. This exercise will assist in the determination of the most appropriate data structure to serve the business. Business users should be actively involved in the modelling process which may form part of an associated IT Strategic Planning exercise.

As noted above, there is considerable cost in the moving over to database techniques and it is essential that all the impacts upon existing system functionality are accurately identified with a view to assessing the necessary amendments to applications. As with any other major IT project the conversion to database should be subject to ratification by senior management after examination of a full cost / benefit analysis and justification.

Selecting the appropriate database software for a specific scenario will need to be subject to careful consideration involving an appraisal of the available products and their suppliers. Contact and discussion with existing users can be invaluable as part of the assessment of product and service reliability. Chapter 22 describes the approach to be considered when evaluating software packages.

If adopted the database approach will undoubtedly require some organisational changes especially the establishment of a suitably trained establishment to handle the administration of the eventual database. It is usual to appoint a Database Administrator who acts as an essential link between the user and IT communities and independently ensures that the database retains its integrity. The Database Administrator should ensure that only necessary and authorised amendments are made to the Data Dictionary and DBMS and that the related application system amendments are accurately applied.

The initial set-up of the database structure will need to be verified and all the DBMS functions suitably tested before live use. Additionally the initial loading of data, perhaps from a range of source systems, will also need to be controlled and reconciled back to source controls to confirm that it is complete, accurate and authorised. Before live use, the back-up and recovery processes should be fully tested and the users suitably assured that the mechanisms are in place to provide adequate coverage in the event of a major corruption or disaster. The procedures to use in the event of a disaster need to be recorded in the Contingency Plan and responsibilities allocated to named individuals. Any subsequent amendments to the database structure should be reviewed for their impact and fully tested with both the feeder and output systems before being authorised for application to the live version of the DBMS.

The Database Administration staff should monitor the operation of DBMS and promptly react to any suggestion of problems reported about the integrity of data, etc.

Control matrix examples

Accurate data can be commercially critical to an organisation, and therefore two example matrices have been provided covering both *Objective* and *Exposure* orientations (Tables 7.1 and 7.2 respectively). The contents of both matrices cover the initial implementation of database techniques and the ongoing use of same. If your company has already implemented a database, the example *Objectives* and *Exposures* relative to the initial establishment of such facilities can be accordingly disregarded. The values of the example data represent a relatively high dependency upon database techniques and a fairly optimistic view of the effectiveness of the applied measures and controls.

The *Objective* example matrix (per Table 7.1) utilises *Scale* 6 which can be strongly associated with the achievement of objectives via the use of information. The *Exposures* example (Table 7.2) makes use of *Scale* 4. Full details of both these *Scales* is contained in Appendix 5.

Table 7.1   Databases - Objectives

Overall Inherent Risk (Size) Score [5 is worst risk; 1 is best] = 3.94

A Ensure accurate assessment & modelling of corporate data
B Ensure the accurate assessment of data storage requirements
C Ensure selection of suitably flexible, reliable, secure DBMS
D Establish & communicate concept of data & systems ownership
E Establish accurate and secure data access rights
F Assess/plan for impact of database upon existing systems
G Protect data from unauthorised access, amendment, etc.
H Ensure the accurate set-up of database structure
I Ensure all database facilities are tested prior to live use
J Ensure accuracy/completeness of data loaded onto database

K Provide relevant knowledge & skills to manage the database
L Ensure the integrity of the database at all times
M Ensure subsequent amendments to DBMS & DDS are authorised
N Ensure the operational availability of data
O Ensure the efficient use of Query Languages
P Ensure database can be recovered in the event of a failure
Q Provide adequate data back-up facilities
R Ensure that DBMS activity is logged and monitored

Databases	OBJECTIVES	A	B	C	D	E	F	G	H	I	J	K	L	M	N	O	P	Q	R
Calculated Risk Score	Risk	4	3	3	3	3	3	4	3	4	4	4	4	3	4	3	4	4	3
Scale 6 (6 is the most serious)	Type	6	3	6	5	6	3	6	6	6	6	5	6	5	6	3	6	6	4
Size (3 is maximum)	Size	3	3	2	2	2	3	3	2	3	3	3	3	2	3	3	3	3	3
MEASURES																			
1 Data modelling exercise was conducted as part of the Strategic Planning project	Best	5																	
	Test	?	?																
	Both																		
2 Corporate data model has been accepted and agreed by divisional management	Best		4		4														
	Test	?	?		?														
	Both																		
3 Capacity planning implications determined from data modelling & workload estimates	Best			5															
	Test	?		?															
	Both																		
4 Selection of DBMS subject to software evaluation and selection methodology	Best			5															
	Test	?		?															
	Both																		
5 Requirements specification for DBMS used to match with available products	Best				4														
	Test	?			?														
	Both																		
6 DBMS reliability and security factors reviewed as part of 5 above	Best				4														
	Test	?			?														
	Both																		
7 Revised approach to systems and data ownership presented at management briefing sessions	Best				4														
	Test	?			?														
	Both																		

Table 7.1 continued

#				A	B	C	D	E	F	G	H	I	J	K	L	M	N	O	P	Q	R
	Data modelling exercise	Best						4													
8	included allocation of initial	Test	?					?													
	data access types & rights	Both																			
-		---------	-	-	-	-	-	-	-	-	-	-	-	-	-	-	-	-	-	-	-
	Necessary amendments to existing	Best							4												
9	programs identified, justified	Test	?						?												
	and developed per plan	Both																			
-		---------	-	-	-	-	-	-	-	-	-	-	-	-	-	-	-	-	-	-	-
	Access rights effectively	Best								5											
10	controlled via definition in	Test	?							?											
	DDS/DBMS - agreed by owners	Both																			
-		---------	-	-	-	-	-	-	-	-	-	-	-	-	-	-	-	-	-	-	-
	Database structure entered and	Best									5										
11	verified independently by	Test	?								?										
	owners	Both																			
-		---------	-	-	-	-	-	-	-	-	-	-	-	-	-	-	-	-	-	-	-
	Full test project applied to	Best										4									
12	DBMS following the initial	Test	?								?										
	configuration. Amendments applied	Both																			
-		---------	-	-	-	-	-	-	-	-	-	-	-	-	-	-	-	-	-	-	-
	Data conversion process subject	Best										5									
13	to plan, including reconciliation	Test	?								?										
	of loaded data to source	Both																			
-		---------	-	-	-	-	-	-	-	-	-	-	-	-	-	-	-	-	-	-	-
	Experienced Database	Best												4							
14	Administrator employed, plus	Test	?										?								
	staff attended training course	Both																			
-		---------	-	-	-	-	-	-	-	-	-	-	-	-	-	-	-	-	-	-	-
	DBMS has built-in integrity	Best													5						
15	checking facilities, i.e. valid	Test	?											?							
	pointers, block sums, etc.	Both																			
-		---------	-	-	-	-	-	-	-	-	-	-	-	-	-	-	-	-	-	-	-
	DBMS provides warning of any	Best													4						
16	integrity problems and suggests	Test	?											?							
	corrective action(s)	Both																			
-		---------	-	-	-	-	-	-	-	-	-	-	-	-	-	-	-	-	-	-	-
	Administrator supervises any	Best													4						
17	necessary recovery processes,	Test	?											?							
	ensuring adequate fallback	Both																			
-		---------	-	-	-	-	-	-	-	-	-	-	-	-	-	-	-	-	-	-	-
	All subsequent database	Best														4					
18	amendments are authorised by	Test	?												?						
	owners. Applied by Administrator	Both																			
-		---------	-	-	-	-	-	-	-	-	-	-	-	-	-	-	-	-	-	-	-
	Revised data details are	Best														4					
19	reported to owners for	Test	?												?						
	verification, etc.	Both																			
-		---------	-	-	-	-	-	-	-	-	-	-	-	-	-	-	-	-	-	-	-

Table 7.1 continued

#			A	B	C	D	E	F	G	H	I	J	K	L	M	N	O	P	Q	R
	Service level agreements have	Best														4				
20	been established and documented	Test	?													?				
		Both																		
-		---------	-	-	-	-	-	-	-	-	-	-	-	-	-	-	-	-	-	-
	All database down-time, etc. is	Best													3					
21	recorded and fault analysis is	Test	?												?					
	reported	Both																		
-		---------	-	-	-	-	-	-	-	-	-	-	-	-	-	-	-	-	-	-
	Data back-up & running of the	Best													3					
22	integrity checks conducted	Test	?												?					
	overnight to minimise disruption	Both																		
-		---------	-	-	-	-	-	-	-	-	-	-	-	-	-	-	-	-	-	-
	User training provided for	Best														3				
23	Query Languages	Test	?													?				
		Both																		
-		---------	-	-	-	-	-	-	-	-	-	-	-	-	-	-	-	-	-	-
	Overnight batch processing of	Best														4				
24	extensive Query Language runs	Test	?													?				
	to prevent production disruption	Both																		
-		---------	-	-	-	-	-	-	-	-	-	-	-	-	-	-	-	-	-	-
	Query Language runs greater	Best														4				
25	than X minutes are switched to	Test	?													?				
	background to avoid degradation	Both																		
-		---------	-	-	-	-	-	-	-	-	-	-	-	-	-	-	-	-	-	-
	Approved users can download	Best														4				
26	sections of the database to PC	Test	?													?				
	for localised analysis, etc.	Both																		
-		---------	-	-	-	-	-	-	-	-	-	-	-	-	-	-	-	-	-	-
	DBMS includes effective tracking	Best															4			
27	of transactions, with before &	Test	?														?			
	after images to enable recovery	Both																		
-		---------	-	-	-	-	-	-	-	-	-	-	-	-	-	-	-	-	-	-
	Overnight data back-ups	Best																4	5	
28	available to aid recovery	Test	?															?	?	
		Both																		
-		---------	-	-	-	-	-	-	-	-	-	-	-	-	-	-	-	-	-	-
	Back-up is daily - data is	Best																4		
29	retained in secure off-site	Test	?															?		
	media store	Both																		
-		---------	-	-	-	-	-	-	-	-	-	-	-	-	-	-	-	-	-	-
	All accesses are authorised	Best																		4
30	and logged	Test	?																	?
		Both																		
-		---------	-	-	-	-	-	-	-	-	-	-	-	-	-	-	-	-	-	-
	Logs are interrogated for	Best																		4
31	exceptional entries for	Test	?																	?
	management purposes	Both																		
-		---------	-	-	-	-	-	-	-	-	-	-	-	-	-	-	-	-	-	-

Table 7.1   continued

			A	B	C	D	E	F	G	H	I	J	K	L	M	N	O	P	Q	R
	Diagnostic routines are	Best																		4
32	regularly applied for review	Test	?																	?
	and action	Both																		
-		---------	-	-	-	-	-	-	-	-	-	-	-	-	-	-	-	-	-	-

A Ensure accurate assessment & modelling of corporate data
B Ensure the accurate assessment of data storage requirements
C Ensure selection of suitably flexible, reliable, secure DBMS
D Establish & communicate concept of data & systems ownership
E Establish accurate and secure data access rights
F Assess/plan for impact of database upon existing systems
G Protect data from unauthorised access, amendment, etc.
H Ensure the accurate set-up of database structure
I Ensure all database facilities are tested prior to live use
J Ensure accuracy/completeness of data loaded onto database

K Provide relevant knowledge & skills to manage the database
L Ensure the integrity of the database at all times
M Ensure subsequent amendments to DBMS & DDS are
   authorised
N Ensure the operational availability of data
O Ensure the efficient use of Query Languages
P Ensure database can be recovered in the event of a failure
Q Provide adequate data back-up facilities
R Ensure that DBMS activity is logged and monitored

Table 7.2 Databases - Exposures

Overall Inherent Risk (Size) Score [5 is worst risk; 1 is best] = 3.15

A Inaccurate assessment of corporate data structure
B Failure to account for data storage implications - disruption
C Acquisition of unsuitable, unreliable or insecure DBMS
D No accountability due to absence of Data/Systems ownership
E Failure to effectively communicate database advantages
F Failure to establish accurate and secure data access rights
G Failure to identify impact of database on existing systems
H Failure to adequately modify existing systems for database
I Unauthorised access to and amendment of data - error, costs
J Incorrect set-up of database structure - error, cost, delay

K Inadequate testing of database prior to live use - disruption
L Loading of incorrect, inaccurate or incomplete data
M Absence of required knowledge and skills to manage database
N Integrity of database not assured and monitored - failure
O Application of unauthorised/inaccurate database amendments
P Data not available as and when required by the business
Q Inefficient use of Query Languages - production disrupted
R Inability to recover database following failure, etc.
S Inadequate data back-up - disruption, delay, costs
T DBMS activity not logged and monitored - inefficiency, etc.

Databases		EXPOSURES																			
		A	B	C	D	E	F	G	H	I	J	K	L	M	N	O	P	Q	R	S	T
Calculated Risk Score	Risk	4	3	4	3	2	4	3	3	3	3	4	3	3	4	3	4	2	3	3	3
Scale 4 (6 is most serious)	Type	6	3	6	4	3	5	4	3	4	6	5	4	4	5	4	6	3	5	5	4
Size (3 is maximum)	Size	3	3	3	2	2	3	2	3	3	2	3	3	3	3	2	3	2	2	2	2
CONTROLS																						
1 Data modelling exercise was conducted as part of the Strategic Planning project	Best		5																			
	Test	?	?																			
	Both																					
2 Corporate data model has been accepted and agreed by divisional management	Best		4			4																
	Test	?	?			?																
	Both																						
3 Capacity planning implications determined from data modelling & workload estimates	Best			5																			
	Test	?		?																			
	Both																						
4 Selection of DBMS subject to software evaluation and selection methodology	Best				5																		
	Test	?			?																		
	Both																						
5 Requirements specification for DBMS used to match with available products	Best				4																		
	Test	?			?																		
	Both																						
6 DBMS reliability and security factors reviewed as part of 5 above	Best				4																		
	Test	?			?																		
	Both																						
7 Revised approach to systems and data ownership presented at management briefing sessions	Best					4	4																
	Test	?				?	?																
	Both																						

Table 7.2 continued

			A	B	C	D	E	F	G	H	I	J	K	L	M	N	O	P	Q	R	S	T
8	Data modelling exercise included allocation of initial data access types & rights	Best						5														
		Test	?					?														
		Both																				
-		-	-	-	-	-	-	-	-	-	-	-	-	-	-	-	-	-	-	-	-	-
9	Necessary amendments to existing programs identified, justified and developed per plan	Best							4													
		Test	?						?													
		Both																				
-		-	-	-	-	-	-	-	-	-	-	-	-	-	-	-	-	-	-	-	-	-
10	All systems modified and tested with test version of the database before live use	Best							4													
		Test	?						?													
		Both																				
-		-	-	-	-	-	-	-	-	-	-	-	-	-	-	-	-	-	-	-	-	-
11	Access rights effectively controlled via definition in DDS/DBMS - agreed by owners	Best				3				5												
		Test	?			?				?												
		Both																				
-		-	-	-	-	-	-	-	-	-	-	-	-	-	-	-	-	-	-	-	-	-
12	Database structure entered and verified independently by owners	Best									5											
		Test	?								?											
		Both																				
-		-	-	-	-	-	-	-	-	-	-	-	-	-	-	-	-	-	-	-	-	-
13	Full test project applied to DBMS following the initial configuration. Amendments applied	Best										4										
		Test	?									?										
		Both																				
-		-	-	-	-	-	-	-	-	-	-	-	-	-	-	-	-	-	-	-	-	-
14	Data conversion process subject to plan, including reconciliation of loaded data to source	Best											5									
		Test	?										?									
		Both																				
-		-	-	-	-	-	-	-	-	-	-	-	-	-	-	-	-	-	-	-	-	-
15	Experienced Database Administrator employed, plus staff attended training course	Best													4							
		Test	?												?							
		Both																				
-		-	-	-	-	-	-	-	-	-	-	-	-	-	-	-	-	-	-	-	-	-
16	DBMS has built-in integrity checking facilities, i.e. valid pointers, block sums, etc.	Best													5							
		Test	?												?							
		Both																				
-		-	-	-	-	-	-	-	-	-	-	-	-	-	-	-	-	-	-	-	-	-
17	DBMS provides warning of any integrity problems and suggests corrective action(s)	Best													4							
		Test	?												?							
		Both																				
-		-	-	-	-	-	-	-	-	-	-	-	-	-	-	-	-	-	-	-	-	-
18	Administrator supervises any necessary recovery processes, ensuring adequate fallback	Best													4							
		Test	?												?							
		Both																				
-		-	-	-	-	-	-	-	-	-	-	-	-	-	-	-	-	-	-	-	-	-
19	All subsequent database amendments are authorised by owners. Applied by Administrator	Best														4						
		Test	?													?						
		Both																				
-		-	-	-	-	-	-	-	-	-	-	-	-	-	-	-	-	-	-	-	-	-

Table 7.2   continued

#	Statement		A	B	C	D	E	F	G	H	I	J	K	L	M	N	O	P	Q	R	S	T
	Revised data details are	Best															4					
20	reported to owners for	Test	?														?					
	verification, etc.	Both																				
-		-	-	-	-	-	-	-	-	-	-	-	-	-	-	-	-	-	-	-	-	-
	Service level agreements have	Best															4					
21	been established and documented.	Test	?														?					
	Performance is monitored	Both																				
-		-	-	-	-	-	-	-	-	-	-	-	-	-	-	-	-	-	-	-	-	-
	All database down-time, etc. is	Best															4					
22	recorded and fault analysis is	Test	?														?					
	reported	Both																				
-		-	-	-	-	-	-	-	-	-	-	-	-	-	-	-	-	-	-	-	-	-
	Data back-up & running of the	Best															4					
23	integrity checks conducted	Test	?														?					
	overnight to minimise disruption	Both																				
-		-	-	-	-	-	-	-	-	-	-	-	-	-	-	-	-	-	-	-	-	-
	User training provided for	Best															4					
24	Query Languages	Test	?														?					
		Both																				
-		-	-	-	-	-	-	-	-	-	-	-	-	-	-	-	-	-	-	-	-	-
	Overnight batch procesing of	Best															4					
25	extensive Query Language runs	Test	?														?					
	to prevent production disruption	Both																				
-		-	-	-	-	-	-	-	-	-	-	-	-	-	-	-	-	-	-	-	-	-
	Query Language runs greater	Best															4					
26	than X minutes are switched to	Test	?														?					
	background to avoid degradation	Both																				
-		-	-	-	-	-	-	-	-	-	-	-	-	-	-	-	-	-	-	-	-	-
	Approved users can download	Best															4					
27	sections of the database to PC	Test	?														?					
	for localised analysis, etc.	Both																				
-		-	-	-	-	-	-	-	-	-	-	-	-	-	-	-	-	-	-	-	-	-
	DBMS includes effective tracking	Best																	5			
28	of transactions, with before &	Test	?																?			
	after images to enable recovery	Both																				
-		-	-	-	-	-	-	-	-	-	-	-	-	-	-	-	-	-	-	-	-	-
	Overnight data back-ups	Best																	4	5		
29	available to aid recovery	Test	?																?	?		
		Both																				
-		-	-	-	-	-	-	-	-	-	-	-	-	-	-	-	-	-	-	-	-	-
	Back-up is daily - data is	Best																		4		
30	retained in secure off-site	Test	?																	?		
	media store	Both																				
-		-	-	-	-	-	-	-	-	-	-	-	-	-	-	-	-	-	-	-	-	-
	All accesses are authorised	Best																				5
31	and logged	Test	?																			?
		Both																				
-		-	-	-	-	-	-	-	-	-	-	-	-	-	-	-	-	-	-	-	-	-

Table 7.2   continued

			A	B	C	D	E	F	G	H	I	J	K	L	M	N	O	P	Q	R	S	T
	Logs are interrogated for	Best																					3
32	exceptional entries for	Test	?																				?
	management reporting purposes	Both																					
-		-	-	-	-	-	-	-	-	-	-	-	-	-	-	-	-	-	-	-	-	-	-
	Diagnostic routines are	Best																					4
33	regularly applied for review	Test	?																				?
	and action	Both																					
-		-	-	-	-	-	-	-	-	-	-	-	-	-	-	-	-	-	-	-	-	-	-

A Inaccurate assessment of corporate data structure

B Failure to account for data storage implications - disruption

C Acquisition of unsuitable, unreliable or insecure DBMS

D No accountability due to absence of Data/Systems
  ownership

E Failure to effectively communicate database advantages

F Failure to establish accurate and secure data access rights

G Failure to identify impact of database on existing systems

H Failure to adequately modify existing systems for database

I Unauthorised access to and amendment of data - error, costs

J Incorrect set-up of database structure - error, cost, delay

K Inadequate testing of database prior to live use - disruption

L Loading of incorrect, inaccurate or incomplete data

M Absence of required knowledge and skills to manage
  database

N Integrity of database not assured and monitored - failure

O Application of unauthorised/inaccurate database amendments

P Data not available as and when required by the business

Q Inefficient use of Query Languages - production disrupted

R Inability to recover database following failure, etc.

S Inadequate data back-up - disruption, delay, costs

T DBMS activity not logged and monitored - inefficiency, etc.

8

ELECTRONIC DATA INTERCHANGE

Scope

The use of Electronic Data Interchange is now increasingly common as a means of electronically transferring business and transaction data between trading partners. Indeed some organisations insist that their suppliers adopt the process as a condition of either establishing or maintaining a trading relationship. For the user it can represent an additional competitive edge and contribute to internal efficiency gains and cost savings.

This chapter covers the assessment of using EDI within an organisation, its benefits, a discussion of the key control issues and the implementation and operation of EDI facilities. Although EDI can encompass data exchange via magnetic media, the following text primarily relates to data transmission exchanges via either a VAN (Value-Added Network) or a VADS (Value-Added & Data Service).

The National Computing Centre (NCC) defines EDI as 'The transfer of structured data, by agreed message standards, from one computer system to another, by electronic means.' It is important to establish that the use of EDI is not primarily a technical issue, but the means to either generate new business opportunities or sustain and enhance existing trading relationships. However the technical factors do need to be assessed and addressed if the business benefits are to be fully realised and the reliability of the relative data assured.

In practice the transfer of data can be achieved by the use of electronic mailbox services, private communication networks or the exchange of magnetic media. Although the emphasis is usually placed upon the exchange of data between trading partners, the technique can also be applied to transfers within an organisation (i.e. between subsidiaries and the holding company).

Electronic Data Interchange VANs (Value-Added Networks) which support the transfer of relevant data have been established and operated by, among others, IBM, SD-Scicon, AT & T, and British Telecom. Please note that VANs are also referred to as VADS (Value Added & Data Services).

The requirement to implement EDI facilities may arise from an internal strategic initiative, but can also come from a dominant trading partner as a condition for continuing a business relationship. In any event, it is likely that an organisation will wish to seek suitable external advice before embarking on a significant involvement with EDI facilities.

A number of bodies have been established to support the adoption and development of the EDI process and provide the necessary data formats, transaction standards and communication protocols. It is not our intention to explore the various standards (for example EDIFACT or TRADACOMS) in any detail, but to simply emphasise that users should ensure that their application systems and EDI software are capable of conforming to the prevailing requirements of these established and recognised standards.

Some business sectors have developed their own EDI projects which provide a framework for their particular requirements, for example:

CEFIC for the Chemical industry
ODETTE for the Automotive industry
EDIFICE for the Computing and Electronic industries
UNICORN for the Ferry /Holiday industry
SWIFT for Banking
EDICON for the Construction industry.

The benefits and impacts of EDI will include the following, though not all of these may apply to your business sector or organisation. We have divided the factors into three groups, namely those which impact upon the strategic level business considerations, potential benefits in relation to operational considerations, and where they offer or generate further trading opportunities.

Strategic

(a) The operation of a faster and more accurate Trading Cycle, thus enhancing the trading image of the business.

(b) The introduction and/or use of Just-in-Time Manufacturing techniques which can minimise stock holdings, facilitate the flexible use of the workforce, etc.

(c) As a means to remain competitive in response to highly competitive market entrants.

(d) By adding value to the overall service offered to customers and the establishment of a more responsive business relationship.

(e) Generally improving relationships with suppliers/customers and maintaining their loyalty.

Operational

(a) The reduction of costs, in terms of manual processing (re-keying, verification, document reconciliation and filing), postage, paper, reduced stock holdings (in relation to released floor space, storage and insurance costs).
(b) The potential for improving cash flow as a consequence of more accurate invoicing and transaction matching, hopefully resulting in more timely payment settlements.
(c) A reduction in data errors as the re-keying of transaction data is avoided. Additionally there should be fewer delivery and other errors.
(d) An overall discernible improvement in the quality of service to customers.

Opportunities

(a) The ability to offer and maintain a competitive edge due to faster service turnround, extension of IT facilities made available to customers, and so on.
(b) Ability to counteract competitor encroachment or as an additional barrier to new entrants into the same market.

It will be necessary to undertake a full review of the business consequences of using EDI paying particular attention to the strategic and long term considerations. If the use of EDI is being forced upon an organisation by a dominant trading partner, the matter of joint funding of the exercise will have to be suitably explored. Full account will need to taken of the impact upon existing operational arrangements, and where necessary due regard taken of the future staffing and training requirements.

There are some risks (or negative factors) related to EDI; perhaps the most important of these relate to the current legal situation. The law can be said to lag behind the changes in the business arena brought about by new methods, and EDI has generated the need for new definitions of the legal status of the transmitted data. The EDI Association (EDIA) has developed legal guidelines on forms of contract, for example defining at what point the contract is formed, which has particular relevance when transactions are international. It is suggested that users establish, with their trading partners, an Interchange Agreement which clearly specifies the relevant conditions, legal interpretations, responsibilities, etc.

The legal standing of EDI transactions has not (to our knowledge) been challenged in the courts. Currently paper documents have to be retained for fixed periods and this requirement also applies to electronic data. The ability to enable access to such transactions in the future has to be considered (i.e. assuming that the technology that created the data is still available, at the appropriate time, to retrieve it!).

Some transactions currently require support with an actual document (such as the Bill of Lading which conveys the right of ownership). Legal guidance may have to be sought to provide the necessary assurances in specific trading operations.

H.M. Customs and Excise will have to be informed of the intended use of EDI, especially where there are VAT or international trading implications. The Customs and Excise will normally have to inspect an EDI installation and signify their approval of its ongoing use.

Some form of specific EDI software will be required to act as an interface between the source application system (i.e. Purchase Ordering) and the network link to the trading partner operated normally by a third party service provider. This software will handle the following aspects of the related processes.

Outgoing Data

- Data extraction from source application

- Data structuring and encoding in accord with relevant transaction and format standards

- Data transmission via the network.

Incoming Data

- Data received from trading partner via the network

- De-coding of received data

- Update of de-coded data on relevant application.

It is vital that the transaction data passed through the system is accurate, suitably authorised and authenticated as part of the transmission and receipt processes. Transactions should be reconciled between the EDI system and either the source or target applications in order to ensure completeness and integrity. VAN suppliers should confirm the data security arrangements for those processing aspects within their sphere of control, and users should be satisfied as to the effectiveness of such measures (i.e. the authentication of network traffic).

It is possible that some of the transaction data passing through the EDI routes may be of either a commercially sensitive or confidential nature (especially that moving between companies in the same group). Measures such as encryption may have to be employed to provide added security in these circumstances.

Ideally the software should provide some form of document/transaction archive facility to enable the trailing of transactions in the absence of paper-based transaction trails. Additionally it may be possible to use this archived data for interrogation and enquiry purposes. The selection of EDI software and communication services should include the production of a requirements specification for matching against the available products. The requirements for effectively and comprehensively evaluating package software are more fully explored in Chapter 22.

As with the introduction of all new business systems, a full testing program will need to be implemented before live usage, and the results accepted by both or all parties affected by the system. If, as is likely, the use of EDI has significant trading and operational implications for an organisation, documented plans should be established to cater for the contingency arrangements necessary in the event of a major failure, disruption or disaster scenario. (See Chapter 6 – Contingency Planning for more details).

Control matrix examples

In the appropriate circumstance, EDI can make a significant contribution to business success, therefore we have provided example matrices which address both the business Objective and risk Exposure views of its use. The Objective example is provided as Table 8.1 and the Exposure-oriented version is Table 8.2 and the contents are provided in the context of Scales 2 and 4 respectively.

The examples include middle to high range values for *Type* and *Size* scores thus reflecting a significant but not overly crucial dependence upon EDI techniques. (See Appendix 5 for full details of the relevant Scale narratives). This scenario suggests that there is considerable use of such facilities in some business areas but that it is not critical to the organisation as a whole.

Table 8.1   EDI - Objectives

Overall Inherent Risk (Size) Score [5 is worst risk; 1 is best] = 2.67

A Assess & monitor strategic & operational advantages of EDI
B Ensure that EDI interfaces with corporate & IT strategies
C Maintain satisfactory relationship with customers/suppliers
D Assess & monitor the trading, admin., and cost advantages
E Accurately assess and plan for business implications of EDI
F Address the legal issues & establish Interchange Agreements
G Create new business opportunities via the use of EDI
H Ensure the evaluation & selection of appropriate software
I Ensure operational impacts, staff training, etc. are addressed

J Ensure accuracy of data, etc. from feeder applications
K Ensure that EDI software and VAN are secure
L Ensure EDI systems are satisfactorily tested before use
M Ensure that adequate authentication is applied
N Ensure all transactions are reconciled to source/target
O Ensure commercially sensitive data remains confidential
P Ensure Customs & Excise approval of new system is obtained
Q Ensure that transactions are trailed and archived
R Provide contingency plans in case of systems failure, etc.

	Electronic Data Interchange	OBJECTIVES	A	B	C	D	E	F	G	H	I	J	K	L	M	N	O	P	Q	R
	Calculated Risk Score	Risk	4	4	4	3	3	3	2	3	3	3	3	3	3	3	2	2	2	3
	Scale 2 (6 is most serious)	Type	6	6	6	3	5	4	6	4	4	6	4	4	4	4	6	4	3	6
	Size (3 is maximum)	Size	3	3	3	3	2	2	1	2	2	2	2	2	2	2	1	1	2	2
	MEASURES																			
1	Feasibility Study implemented and report issued	Best		4			4													
		Test	?	?			?													
		Both																			
2	EDI used to reduce stocks, offer faster, more flexible service to customers, etc.	Best		4		2														
		Test	?	?		?														
		Both																			
3	All EDI initiatives are correlated to critical success factors per Strategic Plan	Best		5					3											
		Test	?	?					?											
		Both																			
4	Measurable targets established for EDI. Management monitoring in place	Best		3			4													
		Test	?	?			?													
		Both																			
5	Data accuracy improved and re-keying reduced	Best		3		3														
		Test	?	?		?														
		Both																			
6	Discussions held with customers and agreements reached for way forward	Best				4			3											
		Test	?			?			?											
		Both																			
7	Major supplier already extensively uses EDI	Best				3														
		Test	?			?														
		Both																			

Table 8.1   continued

				A	B	C	D	E	F	G	H	I	J	K	L	M	N	O	P	Q	R
8	Data processing, administration and distribution cost savings monitored against expectations	Best		3			4														
		Test	?	?			?															
		Both																				
-		-	-	-	-	-	-	-	-	-	-	-	-	-	-	-	-	-	-	-	-
9	Some operational re-organisation was necessary. New skills have been acquired	Best						4				4									
		Test	?					?				?										
		Both																				
-		-	-	-	-	-	-	-	-	-	-	-	-	-	-	-	-	-	-	-	-
10	Interchange Agreements negotiated with partners - expert legal advice was sought	Best							5												
		Test	?						?													
		Both																				
-		-	-	-	-	-	-	-	-	-	-	-	-	-	-	-	-	-	-	-	-
11	Adoption of relevant standards will enable planned European ventures to proceed	Best								3											
		Test	?							?												
		Both																				
-		-	-	-	-	-	-	-	-	-	-	-	-	-	-	-	-	-	-	-	-
12	Package evaluation methodology applied to selection of EDI communications & software	Best								4											
		Test	?							?												
		Both																				
-		-	-	-	-	-	-	-	-	-	-	-	-	-	-	-	-	-	-	-	-
13	Recognised standard communication protocol and proven system were selected	Best								4											
		Test	?							?												
		Both																				
-		-	-	-	-	-	-	-	-	-	-	-	-	-	-	-	-	-	-	-	-
14	Staff training provided and experienced manager recruited	Best										4									
		Test	?									?										
		Both																				
-		-	-	-	-	-	-	-	-	-	-	-	-	-	-	-	-	-	-	-	-
15	Data is validated upon input to feeding applications	Best											5								
		Test	?										?									
		Both																				
-		-	-	-	-	-	-	-	-	-	-	-	-	-	-	-	-	-	-	-	-
16	Incoming EDI data is checked by interface validation processes	Best										4									
		Test	?									?										
		Both																				
-		-	-	-	-	-	-	-	-	-	-	-	-	-	-	-	-	-	-	-	-
17	VAN operator's External Auditors provided written assurance of security measures	Best												4							
		Test	?											?								
		Both																				
-		-	-	-	-	-	-	-	-	-	-	-	-	-	-	-	-	-	-	-	-
18	Security features satisfactorily tested prior to live use of system	Best												4	5						
		Test	?											?	?							
		Both																				
-		-	-	-	-	-	-	-	-	-	-	-	-	-	-	-	-	-	-	-	-
19	All transmissions initiated via tamper-proof electronic signature/authorisation	Best												4		4					
		Test	?											?		?						
		Both																				
-		-	-	-	-	-	-	-	-	-	-	-	-	-	-	-	-	-	-	-	-

Table 8.1 continued

		A	B	C	D	E	F	G	H	I	J	K	L	M	N	O	P	Q	R
20 Full test plan applied during trial period - results were satisfactory (retained on file)	Best											4	5						
	Test	?										?	?						
	Both																		
-	-	-	-	-	-	-	-	-	-	-	-	-	-	-	-	-	-	-	-
21 System provides for key encryption of message data	Best											4				4			
	Test	?										?				?			
	Both																		
-	-	-	-	-	-	-	-	-	-	-	-	-	-	-	-	-	-	-	-
22 Keys to encryption system are changed regularly and kept secure	Best											3				3			
	Test	?										?				?			
	Both																		
-	-	-	-	-	-	-	-	-	-	-	-	-	-	-	-	-	-	-	-
23 Access to EDI software is controlled by user-id and password	Best												3						
	Test	?											?						
	Both																		
-	-	-	-	-	-	-	-	-	-	-	-	-	-	-	-	-	-	-	-
24 All message data is reconciled between EDI logs and relevant application source/target	Best														5				
	Test	?													?				
	Both																		
-	-	-	-	-	-	-	-	-	-	-	-	-	-	-	-	-	-	-	-
25 Archive database subject to access controls	Best															4			
	Test	?														?			
	Both																		
-	-	-	-	-	-	-	-	-	-	-	-	-	-	-	-	-	-	-	-
26 Archive data back-up to tape on weekly basis	Best															3		3	
	Test	?														?		?	
	Both																		
-	-	-	-	-	-	-	-	-	-	-	-	-	-	-	-	-	-	-	-
27 System was inspected by Customs & Excise prior to use - written approval obtained	Best																5		
	Test	?															?		
	Both																		
-	-	-	-	-	-	-	-	-	-	-	-	-	-	-	-	-	-	-	-
28 Common transaction reference used on source & EDI system - micro-film records available	Best																	4	
	Test	?																?	
	Both																		
-	-	-	-	-	-	-	-	-	-	-	-	-	-	-	-	-	-	-	-

A Assess & monitor strategic & operational advantages of EDI
B Ensure that EDI interfaces with corporate & IT strategies
C Maintain satisfactory relationship with customers/suppliers
D Assess & monitor the trading, admin., and cost advantages
E Accurately assess and plan for business implications of EDI
F Address the legal issues & establish Interchange Agreements
G Create new business opportunities via the use of EDI
H Ensure the evaluation & selection of appropriate software
I Ensure operational impacts, staff training, etc. are addressed

J Ensure accuracy of data, etc. from feeder applications
K Ensure that EDI software and VAN are secure
L Ensure EDI systems are satisfactorily tested before use
M Ensure that adequate authentication is applied
N Ensure all transactions are reconciled to source/target
O Ensure commercially sensitive data remains confidential
P Ensure Customs & Excise approval of new system is obtained
Q Ensure that transactions are trailed and archived
R Provide contingency plans in case of systems failure, etc.

Table 8.1   continued

			A	B	C	D	E	F	G	H	I	J	K	L	M	N	O	P	Q	R
	On-line interrogation of EDI	Best																	3	
29	archive is possible	Test	?																?	
		Both																		
-		-	-	-	-	-	-	-	-	-	-	-	-	-	-	-	-	-	-	-
	Stand-by equipment and	Best																		3
30	communications facilities are	Test	?																	?
	available per Contingency Plan	Both																		
-		-	-	-	-	-	-	-	-	-	-	-	-	-	-	-	-	-	-	-
	Transfer using magnetic media	Best																		4
31	is available if required	Test	?																	?
		Both																		
-		-	-	-	-	-	-	-	-	-	-	-	-	-	-	-	-	-	-	-

A Assess & monitor strategic & operational advantages of EDI
B Ensure that EDI interfaces with corporate & IT strategies
C Maintain satisfactory relationship with customers/suppliers
D Assess & monitor the trading, admin., and cost advantages
E Accurately assess and plan for business implications of EDI
F Address the legal issues & establish Interchange Agreements
G Create new business opportunities via the use of EDI
H Ensure the evaluation & selection of appropriate software
I   Ensure operational impacts, staff training, etc. are addressed

J Ensure accuracy of data, etc. from feeder applications
K Ensure that EDI software and VAN are secure
L Ensure EDI systems are satisfactorily tested before use
M Ensure that adequate authentication is applied
N Ensure all transactions are reconciled to source/target
O Ensure commercially sensitive data remains confidential
P Ensure Customs & Excise approval of new system is obtained
Q Ensure that transactions are trailed and archived
R Provide contingency plans in case of systems failure, etc.

Table 8.2   EDI - Exposures

Overall Inherent Risk (Size) Score [5 is worst risk; 1 is best] = 3.25

A Inadequate assessment of strategic/operational advantages
B Failure to integrate EDI initiatives with Strategic Plan
C Failure to get customer/supplier agreement to use of EDI
D Inadequate customer/supplier liaison during implementation
E Failure to monitor EDI performance/benefits - erode profit
F Failure to assess/address business implications of EDI
G Failure to research/agree upon legal status of transactions
H Failure to determine & agree relevant trading conditions
I Failure to use EDI to create new business opportunities
J Inadequate assessment of communications & software needs

K Failure to adequately plan the implementation - error, delay
L Failure to train staff and amend procedures accordingly
M Inaccurate data passed through system - costs, reputation
N EDI software and/or VAN insecure - leakage, fraud, error, cost
O Inadequate testing of communications/software - delay, costs
P Failure to authenticate messages - fraud, loss, error, costs
Q Failure to reconcile transactions to source/target systems
R Leakage of commercially sensitive data - impact on business
S Failure to obtain Customs & Excise approval of system
T Inadequate trailing, archiving and contingency arrangements

Electronic Data Interchange	EXPOSURES	A	B	C	D	E	F	G	H	I	J	K	L	M	N	O	P	Q	R	S	T
Calculated Risk Score	Risk	4	3	3	3	2	2	3	3	2	3	3	4	4	4	3	3	3	3	3	4
Scale 4 (6 is most serious)	Type	6	6	6	6	5	6	6	6	6	5	6	3	6	6	5	4	4	6	3	5
Size (3 is maximum)	Size	3	2	2	2	1	1	2	2	1	2	2	3	3	3	3	3	3	3	2	3
CONTROLS																					
1 Feasibility Study implemented	Best	4	3				2	2	2	3											
and report issued recommending	Test	?	?	?			?	?	?	?											
future approach - Board approved	Both																				
2 EDI used to reduce stocks,	Best		3				3														
offer faster more flexible	Test	?	?				?														
service to customers, etc.	Both																				
3 All EDI initiatives are	Best		5																		
correlated to critical success	Test	?	?																		
factors per Strategic Plan	Both																				
4 Measurable targets established	Best					4															
for EDI. Management monitoring	Test	?				?															
is in place	Both																				
5 Data accuracy improved and	Best						3														
re-keying reduced	Test	?					?														
	Both																				
6 Discussions held with customers	Best				4	4															
and agreements reached, defining	Test	?			?	?															
future business relationship	Both																				
7 Major supplier already	Best				4	4															
uses EDI. Company should adopt	Test	?			?	?															
EDI to maintain supply, etc.	Both																				

Table 8.2   continued

			A	B	C	D	E	F	G	H	I	J	K	L	M	N	O	P	Q	R	S	T
8	Data processing, administration and distribution cost savings monitored against expectations	Best					4															
		Test	?				?															
		Both																					
-		-	-	-	-	-	-	-	-	-	-	-	-	-	-	-	-	-	-	-	-	-
9	Some operational re-organisation was necessary. New skills have been acquired	Best					3							3								
		Test	?				?							?								
		Both																					
-		-	-	-	-	-	-	-	-	-	-	-	-	-	-	-	-	-	-	-	-	-
10	Interchange Agreements negotiated with partners - expert legal advice was sought	Best			4				4	4												
		Test	?		?				?	?												
		Both																					
-		-	-	-	-	-	-	-	-	-	-	-	-	-	-	-	-	-	-	-	-	-
11	Adoption of relevant standards will enable planned European ventures to proceed	Best		3	3						4											
		Test	?	?	?						?											
		Both																					
-		-	-	-	-	-	-	-	-	-	-	-	-	-	-	-	-	-	-	-	-	-
12	Package evaluation methodology applied to selection of EDI communications and software	Best										5										
		Test	?									?										
		Both																					
-		-	-	-	-	-	-	-	-	-	-	-	-	-	-	-	-	-	-	-	-	-
13	Recognised standard communication protocol and proven systems were selected	Best										5										
		Test	?									?										
		Both																					
-		-	-	-	-	-	-	-	-	-	-	-	-	-	-	-	-	-	-	-	-	-
14	Staff training provided and experienced manager recruited	Best											4	4								
		Test	?										?	?								
		Both																					
-		-	-	-	-	-	-	-	-	-	-	-	-	-	-	-	-	-	-	-	-	-
15	Data is validated upon input to feeding application	Best													4							
		Test	?												?							
		Both																					
-		-	-	-	-	-	-	-	-	-	-	-	-	-	-	-	-	-	-	-	-	-
16	Incoming EDI data is checked by interface validation processes	Best													4							
		Test	?												?							
		Both																					
-		-	-	-	-	-	-	-	-	-	-	-	-	-	-	-	-	-	-	-	-	-
17	VAN operator's External Auditors provided written assurance of security measures applied	Best													4							
		Test	?												?							
		Both																					
-		-	-	-	-	-	-	-	-	-	-	-	-	-	-	-	-	-	-	-	-	-
18	Security features satisfactorily tested prior to live use of system - results on file	Best													4	5						
		Test	?												?	?						
		Both																					
-		-	-	-	-	-	-	-	-	-	-	-	-	-	-	-	-	-	-	-	-	-
19	All transactions initiated via tamper-proof electronic signature/authorisation	Best															4					
		Test	?														?					
		Both																					
-		-	-	-	-	-	-	-	-	-	-	-	-	-	-	-	-	-	-	-	-	-

Table 8.2 continued

		A	B	C	D	E	F	G	H	I	J	K	L	M	N	O	P	Q	R	S	T
20 Full test plan applied during trial period - results were satisfactory (retained on file)	Best														4	5					
	Test	?													?	?					
	Both																				
-	-	-	-	-	-	-	-	-	-	-	-	-	-	-	-	-	-	-	-	-	-
21 System provides for key encryption of message data	Best														4						
	Test	?													?						
	Both																				
-	-	-	-	-	-	-	-	-	-	-	-	-	-	-	-	-	-	-	-	-	-
22 Keys to encryption system are changed regularly and kept secure	Best														4						
	Test	?													?						
	Both																				
-	-	-	-	-	-	-	-	-	-	-	-	-	-	-	-	-	-	-	-	-	-
23 Access to EDI software is controlled by user-id and password	Best														4						
	Test	?													?						
	Both																				
-	-	-	-	-	-	-	-	-	-	-	-	-	-	-	-	-	-	-	-	-	-
24 All message data is reconciled between EDI logs and relevant application source/target	Best																	5			
	Test	?																?			
	Both																				
-	-	-	-	-	-	-	-	-	-	-	-	-	-	-	-	-	-	-	-	-	-
25 Archive database subject to access controls	Best														4			4			
	Test	?													?			?			
	Both																				
-	-	-	-	-	-	-	-	-	-	-	-	-	-	-	-	-	-	-	-	-	-
26 Archive data back-up to tape on weekly basis - copy kept off-site	Best																				4
	Test	?																			?
	Both																				
-	-	-	-	-	-	-	-	-	-	-	-	-	-	-	-	-	-	-	-	-	-
27 System was inspected by Customs & Excise prior to use - written approval obtained	Best																			5	
	Test	?																		?	
	Both																				
-	-	-	-	-	-	-	-	-	-	-	-	-	-	-	-	-	-	-	-	-	-
28 Common transaction reference used on source & EDI systems - micro-film records available	Best																				4
	Test	?																			?
	Both																				
-	-	-	-	-	-	-	-	-	-	-	-	-	-	-	-	-	-	-	-	-	-

A Inadequate assessment of strategic/operational advantages
B Failure to integrate EDI initiatives with Strategic Plan
C Failure to get customer/supplier agreement to use of EDI
D Inadequate customer/supplier liaison during implementation
E Failure to monitor EDI performance/benefits - erode profit
F Failure to assess/address business implications of EDI
G Failure to research/agree upon legal status of transactions
H Failure to determine & agree relevant trading conditions
I Failure to use EDI to create new business opportunities
J Inadequate assessment of communications & software needs
K Failure to adequately plan the implementation - error, delay
L Failure to train staff and amend procedures accordingly
M Inaccurate data passed through system - costs, reputation
N EDI software and/or VAN insecure - leakage, fraud, error, cost
O Inadequate testing of communications/software - delay, costs
P Failure to authenticate messages - fraud, loss, error, costs
Q Failure to reconcile transactions to source/target systems
R Leakage of commercially sensitive data - impact on business
S Failure to obtain Customs & Excise approval of system
T Inadequate trailing, archiving and contingency arrangements

Table 8.2   continued

			A	B	C	D	E	F	G	H	I	J	K	L	M	N	O	P	Q	R	S	T
	On-line interrogation of EDI	Best																				4
29	archive is possible to provide	Test	?																			?
	staff with transaction details	Both																				
-		-	-	-	-	-	-	-	-	-	-	-	-	-	-	-	-	-	-	-	-	-	-
	Stand-by equipment and	Best																				4
30	communications facilities are	Test	?																			?
	available per Contingency Plan	Both																				
-		-	-	-	-	-	-	-	-	-	-	-	-	-	-	-	-	-	-	-	-	-	-
	Transfer using magnetic media	Best																				4
31	is available in the event of	Test	?																			?
	communications failure	Both																				
-		-	-	-	-	-	-	-	-	-	-	-	-	-	-	-	-	-	-	-	-	-	-

A Inadequate assessment of strategic/operational advantages

B Failure to integrate EDI initiatives with Strategic Plan

C Failure to get customer/supplier agreement to use of EDI

D Inadequate customer/supplier liaison during implementation

E Failure to monitor EDI performance/benefits - erode profit

F Failure to assess/address business implications of EDI

G Failure to research/agree upon legal status of transactions

H Failure to determine & agree relevant trading conditions

I Failure to use EDI to create new business opportunities

J Inadequate assessment of communications & software needs

K Failure to adequately plan the implementation - error, delay

L Failure to train staff and amend procedures accordingly

M Inaccurate data passed through system - costs, reputation

N EDI software and/or VAN insecure - leakage, fraud, error, cost

O Inadequate testing of communications/software - delay, costs

P Failure to authenticate messages - fraud, loss, error, costs

Q Failure to reconcile transactions to source/target systems

R Leakage of commercially sensitive data - impact on business

S Failure to obtain Customs & Excise approval of system

T Inadequate trailing, archiving and contingency arrangements

9

SYSTEM DEVELOPMENT

Scope

This chapter addresses the controlled and structured approach to developing application systems in-house as a means of ensuring that well-structured and controlled systems are developed in accord with the needs of the business activities. The contents include the establishment of a suitable development framework which should aim to ensure that systems are constructed in accord with the user's functional requirements and any prevailing standards and policies. The contents can be generally relevant to developments for a variety of hardware platforms.

The establishment of appropriate supporting policies and standards is featured in Chapter 5 (IT Organisation). The ongoing maintenance or amendment of operational application systems is specifically addressed by Chapter 21 (Software Maintenance).

The in-house development of business application systems can be an extremely costly process and the organisation will need to justify such developments on either business or cost/benefit grounds. Chapter 4 (IT Strategic Planning) explored the requirement for all development, software acquisition, etc. to support business objectives and the need to improve or maintain corporate competitive advantage. For the purpose of structuring this chapter, it has been assumed that the motivation and direction for developing systems has stemmed from the results of the Strategic Planning exercise, either in the form of a firm proposal or the need to more fully explore the feasibility of undertaking the related development project.

Despite the overriding requirement for all system proposals to be adequately supported by driving business objectives, the characteristics and proposed life of the relevant systems may vary. For example a relatively inexpensive PC-based solution may be necessary to support the short term requirements of a new business initiative which management consider to be experimental; in this case it would be unwise to embark upon a major and costly systems development until the activity has a proven and sustainable market. This approach could be termed 'throwaway solutions' where the level of development expenditure is consciously restricted and the initial system solution may be discarded for a more comprehensive development when the demands of the business activity justify such a change. This type of solution is now feasible given the relative price of personal computers and indeed networking equipment, especially when the hardware is capable of general redeployment elsewhere in the organisation when its original use has passed. Additionally, the use of an amalgam of package and bespoke systems may provide the appropriate business support facilities within necessarily modest budgetary constraints.

The current culture for 'right-sizing' the corporate hardware platforms also has a direct effect upon management's expectations with regard to system development, in that the creation of large and complex mainframe systems that take two or three years to develop may no longer appear either relevant or justifiable. This is especially true for companies involved in fast-moving markets which may demand frequent changes in emphasis in order to remain competitive. However, there will still be a need to develop large, mainframe-based systems of this type where there is a justifiable relationship between both the scale and strategic significance of a particular business operation.

Chapter 4 (IT Strategic Planning) makes reference to the use of corporate data modelling techniques as a means of providing the stable foundation for all system usage within an organisation. This process aims to derive the essential data elements that can be used throughout the company in order to support the business whilst avoiding duplication and potential distortion of common data. If this technique is applied, it can perform an essential role in systems developments especially in relation to the interconnection of discrete systems so as to provide consistency and accuracy across the areas of management responsibility served by localised systems.

The creation of reliable and controlled systems is primarily a function of establishing an appropriate and well-controlled development environment and culture. The facilities should encompass relevant and workable standards and policies, the proactive involvement of users and the application of an overall guiding framework or methodology which incorporates all the requisite resources and factors. All these elements can be suitably focused in order to contribute to the reliability, integrity and quality of in-house systems.

There are any number of Structured Development Methodologies available which direct the development process through a number of defined stages, each with its own deliverables, control points, etc. The precise operation and associated terminology of these methods will vary. However, some or all of the following development lifecycle elements will normally apply to most development projects.

- *Project Initiation* Perhaps resulting from a Strategic Planning exercise. Obtaining management sponsorship and establishing Terms of Reference.

- *Feasibility Study* Consideration of all elements (risk assessment, hardware platforms, interfacing with existing systems, operational impacts, cost/ benefit analysis and other financial considerations).

- *Basic Design* Determining the user's requirements and producing a system requirements specification. At this stage matters such as required performance and reaction times, operational control and back-up requirements are identified and/or clarified.

- *Detailed Design* Developing a systems specification as the basis for subsequent construction.

- *Programming & Testing* Producing the required programs and subjecting same to thorough testing. This stage also generates essential documentation enabling the future ongoing support of the system.

- *Systems Testing and User Acceptance* Exhaustive testing of the complete system and any interfaces, etc. Satisfying user's requirements and obtaining their acceptance of the completed system.

- *Implementation* This stage may well need addressing progressively at earlier stages in the project as it aims to ensure that all the necessary preparations have been made for the smooth and effective implementation of the system. The necessary considerations include the provision of training, adequate user documentation, accurate conversion of existing data, correct set-up of appropriate system standing data, necessary amendments to operational or clerical practices, etc.

It is not our intention to provide definitive lists of all the required documents, key elements, etc. but to provide an overview of the key issues and principal considerations. The precise nature of deliverables will also vary between methodologies and be further dependent upon the type of development environment in place (for example either a fully or partially functional CASE scenario).

Selecting the appropriate IT solution is often commercially critical in terms of required levels of system performance or the flexibility and ease of future expansion; therefore the process of evaluating the most suitable hardware and/or communications platforms should feature in the feasibility stage of the development process.

In larger organisations there may be a form of IT Steering Committee, which is responsible for objectively reviewing systems proposals in light of company objectives, cost-effectiveness, etc. and for authorising the progression of a project to the next stage (for example from initiation to feasibility). The committee will normally comprise a combination of key user management, IT management, and more neutral members such as non-executive directors.

Underpinning the development process there should be an established set of company policies and standards governing the relevant stages, such as programming standards, documentation requirements, and user representation in projects. Such structures, if realistic, can all add to the quality and resilience of systems, and appropriately set the development benchmarks for users and developers alike. A degree of automation of the development process may apply, perhaps in the form of a CASE environment; such tools can also be used to 're-engineer' existing systems to cater for either changed operational circumstances or the adoption of different hardware platforms.

It is also essential that some form of Project Management control be applied, defining the key stages, recording the resource requirements, dependencies and timescales, and plotting the actual progress attained against the established target milestones and timescales.

One of the most significant stages in the development process is the establishment of user requirements. This process has to be approached very openly, otherwise it is possible that the existing scenario is simply transferred, warts and all, into a new environment. It is important to consider the future direction of the related business activity and to cater for suitable flexibility in the system structure and design. If this stage of the process is either rushed or inadequately addressed, it is possible that some of the necessary functionality will be omitted; in such cases the incorporation of the additional functions or features at a later stage of the development can be disproportionately expensive and may require other aspects to be substantially re-engineered.

User representation in any project is vital if the resultant system is to meet the operational requirements. Although computer awareness and literacy are becoming more widespread, there can still be a considerable cultural gulf between users and systems providers. Additionally, development staff may have limited practical experience of business functions and therefore the overall project team may not share a common language for identifying and expressing key issues. In order that the related project will achieve a successful conclusion, it may be necessary to provide opportunities for all parties to assimilate the key elements and considerations.

However thorough the functional specification process, it is possible that further enhancements or facilities may be identified during the course of the development project. Such potential subsequent amendments will have to be fully assessed and justified before incorporation into the eventual systems design. Any specific impact upon project budgets and overall timescales will also need to be assessed and suitably approved before progressing with the necessary amendments.

Most development projects require the contribution of a wide range of skills, from the more obvious user knowledge and developer's programming abilities, through to awareness of specific hardware platforms, operating systems, and communications protocols. Therefore it is important that the required skills are made available to the project, and if necessary, to effectively address any specific training needs or involve staff with the requisite experience and knowledge. Each application is likely to have its own unique key factors or operational requirements (for example, the incorporation of data encryption facilities), which must be adequately identified and addressed in the development process if the resultant system is to make an effective and secure contribution to company activities. The appropriate formulation of the project group representation can aid this process from the earliest stage.

Adequate testing (of both the individual programs and the full system) is crucial, and should be planned well in advance and extensively documented. Sets of suitably representative test data should be prepared and the expected results of tests recorded for comparison with the actual test results. Testing documentation should be retained so that any future system amendments can be accordingly assessed. As user and development staff may change over a period of time, it is critical that systems are appropriately supported by adequate documentation, so that those who follow can quickly assimilate the structure and purpose of the relevant areas and apply prompt and accurate corrective action.

Mechanisms should be defined which protect the operational integrity of the system and enable the recovery from failure or disruption. (Also see Chapter 6 – Contingency Planning). Security concerns will require assessment so that the most appropriate and cost-effective measures can be incorporated into the design. Similarly, suitable transaction trailing and archive processes should be incorporated into the system's operational structure to provide ongoing protection of data.

In some situations, periods of parallel running alongside the existing system may be relevant, until such time as all parties are satisfied with the functionality and performance of the new system. This approach can be useful when the adoption of a new system is to be phased into live usage, as it provides fall-back facilities in the event of problems being encountered. Furthermore, it can offer the possibility of comparing the output generated by both systems as a means of ensuring accuracy of processing on the new system.

System implementation requirements will need to be fully identified and a plan may be drawn up, the contents of which should be accepted by all the affected parties. Aspects such as procedural documentation, user training, access control set-up, etc. will need to be appropriately addressed by such a plan. Following the implementation of the 'live' system, mechanisms should be in place to monitor actual performance and the achievement of actual benefits against the expected levels. Serious shortfalls will need to be investigated further and any subsequent amendments to the system duly identified.

Control matrix examples

Systems developments have obvious connections with the achievement of business objectives but can also present challenges to management in their ability to counter wasteful use of expensive resources; therefore example matrices for both the *Objective* and *Exposure* orientations have been provided as Tables 9.1 and 9.2 respectively. It will be noted that the *Measures* and *Controls* provided in the two examples are essentially the same, this is because the achievement of many corporate goals in this context will be dependent upon the establishment of a stable and controlled development environment enhanced by the presence of effective control mechanisms. However, as previously stated, the data in the following matrices is provided only for illustrative purposes with a view to suggesting some of the desirable mechanisms that may be deemed necessary.

For the purpose of the example data, a considerable degree of in-house development with a strategically significant impact has been assumed; additionally the adopted view of the effectiveness of the mechanisms in place is decidedly optimistic.

Appendix 5 includes details of all the standard *Scales* used with the example matrices throughout this book. The supplied examples provided for this subject utilise *Scales* 2 and 4 for *Objectives* and *Exposures* respectively.

Table 9.1 System Development - Objectives
Overall Inherent Risk (Size) Score [5 is worst risk; 1 is best] = 3.06

A Ensure developments comply with Strategic Plan objectives
B Provide a structured environment/method for quality systems
C Ensure projects are subject to effective feasibility review
D Establish adequate programming and other standards/ policies
E Ensure all projects are justified on business/cost grounds
F Ensure all development proposals are reviewed & authorised
G Ensure all developments incorporate adequate security, etc.
H Ensure user involvement and/or representation in projects
I Provide adequately trained & proficient development staff

J Establish an effective project management framework
K Ensure accurate determination of functional requirements
L Ensure system structures remain flexible for the future
M Ensure all developments are subject to effective testing
N Ensure all systems are supported by adequate documentation
O Ensure users test their systems and signify acceptance
P Ensure all implementation issues are identified & addressed
Q Monitor actual system performance & achievement of benefits

System Development	OBJECTIVES		A	B	C	D	E	F	G	H	I	J	K	L	M	N	O	P	Q
Calculated Risk Score	Risk		4	4	3	4	3	2	3	3	3	2	4	3	3	3	3	3	2
Scale 2 (6 is most serious)	Type		6	5	5	5	3	5	6	4	5	3	6	6	4	5	4	3	3
Size (3 is maximum)	Size		3	3	2	3	3	1	2	2	2	2	3	2	3	2	2	3	2
MEASURES																			
1 All project proposals are reviewed against the objectives & output of Strategic Plan	Best			5															
	Test	?		?															
	Both																			
2 IT Steering Committee examines all proposals and authorises relevant projects	Best			5				5											
	Test	?		?				?											
	Both																			
3 A recognised structured development methodology is in place, with defined deliverables	Best			5															
	Test	?		?															
	Both																			
4 Methodology facilitates adequate levels of documentation and project support	Best			4															
	Test	?		?															
	Both																			
5 Full feasibility study and cost/ benefit justification required as part of development method	Best				4		4												
	Test	?			?		?												
	Both																			
6 All options are considered at feasibility stage	Best				4														
	Test	?			?														
	Both																			
7 Programming, documentation and testing standards in place to support quality developments	Best					5		4											
	Test	?				?		?											
	Both																			

Table 9.1   continued

			A	B	C	D	E	F	G	H	I	J	K	L	M	N	O	P	Q
8	Company policies define security and control considerations - including recovery procedures	Best							4										
		Test	?						?										
		Both																	
-		-	-	-	-	-	-	-	-	-	-	-	-	-	-	-	-	-	-
9	Systems design & documentation must specifiy all control, security & trail features	Best							4										
		Test	?						?										
		Both																	
-		-	-	-	-	-	-	-	-	-	-	-	-	-	-	-	-	-	-
10	Users are held responsible for the quality of 'their' systems & development involvement	Best								4									
		Test	?							?									
		Both																	
-		-	-	-	-	-	-	-	-	-	-	-	-	-	-	-	-	-	-
11	Users are involved in defining functional and operational requirements for systems	Best								4			4						
		Test	?							?			?						
		Both																	
-		-	-	-	-	-	-	-	-	-	-	-	-	-	-	-	-	-	-
12	IT staff skill profiles are analysed - used as basis for determining training requirement	Best									4								
		Test	?								?								
		Both																	
-		-	-	-	-	-	-	-	-	-	-	-	-	-	-	-	-	-	-
13	Skill levels maintained to address current and future requirements	Best									4								
		Test	?								?								
		Both																	
-		-	-	-	-	-	-	-	-	-	-	-	-	-	-	-	-	-	-
14	Project management system used for all projects - defines milestones, dependencies, etc.	Best										5							
		Test	?									?							
		Both																	
-		-	-	-	-	-	-	-	-	-	-	-	-	-	-	-	-	-	-
15	Functional requirement specification determined by wide-ranging project team	Best											4						
		Test	?										?						
		Both																	
-		-	-	-	-	-	-	-	-	-	-	-	-	-	-	-	-	-	-
16	Requirements specification is signed-off by key user management	Best											4						
		Test	?										?						
		Both																	
-		-	-	-	-	-	-	-	-	-	-	-	-	-	-	-	-	-	-
17	All new developments are linked to corporate data model requirements	Best												4					
		Test	?											?					
		Both																	
-		-	-	-	-	-	-	-	-	-	-	-	-	-	-	-	-	-	-
18	Project feasibility addresses potential future needs, scale of operations, etc.	Best												4					
		Test	?											?					
		Both																	
-		-	-	-	-	-	-	-	-	-	-	-	-	-	-	-	-	-	-
19	Testing standards are defined in company policy	Best													4				
		Test	?												?				
		Both																	
-		-	-	-	-	-	-	-	-	-	-	-	-	-	-	-	-	-	-

Table 9.1 continued

				A	B	C	D	E	F	G	H	I	J	K	L	M	N	O	P	Q
	Users are involved in systems	Best														3		4		
20	testing and sign-off of results	Test	?													?		?		
		Both																		
-		-	-	-	-	-	-	-	-	-	-	-	-	-	-	-	-	-	-	-
	Documentation requirements are	Best															4			
21	defined in methodology and	Test	?														?			
	company standards	Both																		
-		-	-	-	-	-	-	-	-	-	-	-	-	-	-	-	-	-	-	-
	Documentation should support	Best															4			
22	the current operation and any	Test	?														?			
	future amendments, etc.	Both																		
-		-	-	-	-	-	-	-	-	-	-	-	-	-	-	-	-	-	-	-
	All implementation issues (i.e.	Best																	4	
23	training, documents, etc.) are	Test	?																?	
	subject to a planning process	Both																		
-		-	-	-	-	-	-	-	-	-	-	-	-	-	-	-	-	-	-	-
	Post-implementation review is	Best																		4
24	conducted after X months -	Test	?																	?
	benefits assessed against target	Both																		
-		-	-	-	-	-	-	-	-	-	-	-	-	-	-	-	-	-	-	-

A Ensure developments comply with Strategic Plan objectives

B Provide a structured environment/method for quality systems

C Ensure projects are subject to effective feasibility review

D Establish adequate programming and other standards/policies

E Ensure all projects are justified on business/cost grounds

F Ensure all development proposals are reviewed & authorised

G Ensure all developments incorporate adequate security, etc.

H Ensure user involvement and/or representation in projects

I Provide adequately trained & proficient development staff

J Establish an effective project management framework

K Ensure accurate determination of functional requirements

L Ensure system structures remain flexible for the future

M Ensure all developments are subject to effective testing

N Ensure all systems are supported by adequate documentation

O Ensure users test their systems and signify acceptance

P Ensure all implementation issues are identified & addressed

Q Monitor actual system performance & achievement of benefits

Table 9.2   System Development - Exposures

Overall Inherent Risk (Size) Score [5 is worst risk; 1 is best] = 3.20

A Failure to connect developments to strategic objectives
B Inadequate systems due to lack of structured approach
C Inconsistent & variable development approach - poor quality
D Failure to justify development on business or cost grounds
E Inadequate feasibility review of all appropriate options
F Absence of high-level review and approval of proposals
G Inadequate programming and other standards/policies - error
H Failure to address security, control & trailing issues
I Failure to involve users in projects - poor functionality
J Inadequate representation of required skills in project
K Absence of required development skills in IT Dept. - delay
L Failure to efficiently manage/monitor development projects
M Inadequate determination of functional requirements - delay
N Inflexible system design - failure to adapt for future use
O Inadequate documentation - unable to support system/changes
P Failure to apply adequate testing - error, delay, disruption
Q Failure to obtain user acceptance of system - delay, dispute
R Inadequate identification of, or planning for, implementation
S Absence of sufficient user training or documentation - error
T Failure to monitor for achievement of benefits/performance

#	System Development		A	B	C	D	E	F	G	H	I	J	K	L	M	N	O	P	Q	R	S	T
	Calculated Risk Score	Risk	3	4	3	3	3	3	4	3	3	3	3	3	4	4	3	4	3	3	3	2
	Scale 4 (6 is most serious)	Type	6	5	5	6	6	6	5	4	6	4	3	6	6	5	3	5	6	3	4	2
	Size (3 is maximum)	Size	2	3	2	2	2	2	3	3	2	2	3	2	3	3	3	3	2	3	3	3
	CONTROLS																					
1	All project proposals are reviewed against the objectives & output of Strategic Plan	Best		5																		
		Test	?	?																		
		Both																				
2	IT Steering Committee examines all proposals and authorises relevant projects	Best		4				5														
		Test	?	?				?														
		Both																				
3	A recognised structured development methodology is in place, with defined deliverables	Best		5	5																	
		Test	?	?	?																	
		Both																				
4	Methodology facilitates adequate levels of documentation and project support	Best		3	3																	
		Test	?	?	?																	
		Both																				
5	Full feasibility study and cost/benefit justification required as a part of development method	Best				5	4															
		Test	?			?	?															
		Both																				
6	All options are considered at feasibility stage	Best				4	5															
		Test	?			?	?															
		Both																				
7	Programming, documentation and testing standards in place to support quality developments	Best							5													
		Test	?						?													
		Both																				

Table 9.2   continued

			A	B	C	D	E	F	G	H	I	J	K	L	M	N	O	P	Q	R	S	T
8	Company policies define security and control considerations - including recovery procedures	Best								4												
		Test	?							?												
		Both																				
-		-	-	-	-	-	-	-	-	-	-	-	-	-	-	-	-	-	-	-	-	-
9	Systems design & documentation must specifiy all control, security & trail features	Best								4												
		Test	?							?												
		Both																				
-		-	-	-	-	-	-	-	-	-	-	-	-	-	-	-	-	-	-	-	-	-
10	Users are held responsible for the quality of 'their' systems & development involvement	Best									5			4								
		Test	?								?			?								
		Both																				
-		-	-	-	-	-	-	-	-	-	-	-	-	-	-	-	-	-	-	-	-	-
11	Users are involved in defining functional and operational requirements for systems	Best									5			4								
		Test	?								?			?								
		Both																				
-		-	-	-	-	-	-	-	-	-	-	-	-	-	-	-	-	-	-	-	-	-
12	Project skill requirements are identified at outset, and a suitable/balanced team is formed	Best										4										
		Test	?									?										
		Both																				
-		-	-	-	-	-	-	-	-	-	-	-	-	-	-	-	-	-	-	-	-	-
13	IT staff skill profiles are analysed - used as basis for determining training requirements	Best											4									
		Test	?										?									
		Both																				
-		-	-	-	-	-	-	-	-	-	-	-	-	-	-	-	-	-	-	-	-	-
14	Skill levels maintained to address current and future requirements	Best											4									
		Test	?										?									
		Both																				
-		-	-	-	-	-	-	-	-	-	-	-	-	-	-	-	-	-	-	-	-	-
15	Project management system used for all projects - defines milestones, dependencies, etc.	Best												5								
		Test	?											?								
		Both																				
-		-	-	-	-	-	-	-	-	-	-	-	-	-	-	-	-	-	-	-	-	-
16	Experienced Project Managers are in place to support progress and maintain quality factors	Best												4								
		Test	?											?								
		Both																				
-		-	-	-	-	-	-	-	-	-	-	-	-	-	-	-	-	-	-	-	-	-
17	Functional requirement specification determined by wide-ranging project team	Best												5								
		Test	?											?								
		Both																				
-		-	-	-	-	-	-	-	-	-	-	-	-	-	-	-	-	-	-	-	-	-
18	Requirements specification is signed-off by key user management	Best												4	3							
		Test	?											?	?							
		Both																				
-		-	-	-	-	-	-	-	-	-	-	-	-	-	-	-	-	-	-	-	-	-
19	All new developments are linked to corporate data model requirements	Best													4							
		Test	?												?							
		Both																				
-		-	-	-	-	-	-	-	-	-	-	-	-	-	-	-	-	-	-	-	-	-

Table 9.2   continued

			A	B	C	D	E	F	G	H	I	J	K	L	M	N	O	P	Q	R	S	T
	Project feasibility addresses	Best														4						
20	potential future needs, scale of	Test	?														?						
	operations, etc.	Both																					
-		-	-	-	-	-	-	-	-	-	-	-	-	-	-	-	-	-	-	-	-	-	-
	Documentation requirements are	Best															4					
21	defined in methodology and	Test	?															?					
	company standards	Both																					
-		-	-	-	-	-	-	-	-	-	-	-	-	-	-	-	-	-	-	-	-	-	-
	Documentation should support	Best															4					
22	the current operation and any	Test	?															?					
	future amendments, etc.	Both																					
-		-	-	-	-	-	-	-	-	-	-	-	-	-	-	-	-	-	-	-	-	-	-
	Testing standards are defined	Best															5					
23	in company policy	Test	?															?					
		Both																					
-		-	-	-	-	-	-	-	-	-	-	-	-	-	-	-	-	-	-	-	-	-	-
	Users are involved in systems	Best															4	4				
24	testing and sign-off of results	Test	?															?	?				
		Both																					
-		-	-	-	-	-	-	-	-	-	-	-	-	-	-	-	-	-	-	-	-	-	-
	All implementation issues (i.e.	Best																		4	3	
25	training, documents, etc.) are	Test	?																	?	?	
	subject to a planning process	Both																					
-		-	-	-	-	-	-	-	-	-	-	-	-	-	-	-	-	-	-	-	-	-	-
	User training needs are	Best																			4	
26	identified at an early stage	Test	?																		?	
	and planned for	Both																					
-		-	-	-	-	-	-	-	-	-	-	-	-	-	-	-	-	-	-	-	-	-	-
	User documentation is addressed	Best																			4	
27	as a methodology deliverable -	Test	?																		?	
	must conform to company standard	Both																					
-		-	-	-	-	-	-	-	-	-	-	-	-	-	-	-	-	-	-	-	-	-	-
	Post-implementation review is	Best																				4
28	conducted after X months -	Test	?																			?
	benefits assessed against target	Both																					
-		-	-	-	-	-	-	-	-	-	-	-	-	-	-	-	-	-	-	-	-	-	-

A Failure to connect developments to strategic objectives
B Inadequate systems due to lack of structured approach
C Inconsistent & variable development approach - poor quality
D Failure to justify development on business or cost grounds
E Inadequate feasibility review of all appropriate options
F Absence of high-level review and approval of proposals
G Inadequate programming and other standards/policies - error
H Failure to address security, control & trailing issues
I Failure to involve users in projects - poor functionality
J Inadequate representation of required skills in project

K Absence of required development skills in IT Dept. - delay
L Failure to efficiently manage/monitor development projects
M Inadequate determination of functional requirements - delay
N Inflexible system design - failure to adapt for future use
O Inadequate documentation - unable to support system/ changes
P Failure to apply adequate testing - error, delay, disruption
Q Failure to obtain user acceptance of system - delay, dispute
R Inadequate identification of, or planning for, implementation
S Absence of sufficient user training or documentation - error
T Failure to monitor for achievement of benefits/performance

10

FACILITIES MANAGEMENT AND BUREAUX

Scope

This chapter includes the appraisal and selection of either FM or Bureaux services, the confirmation that such facilities will be secure, to required standards and levels of service, ensuring that the necessary protection is reflected in agreements/contracts, and the ongoing monitoring of service provision and costs. Before addressing the issues for these subjects, it is useful to establish some definitions.

- *Facilities Management (FM) This is where an external company takes over the responsibility for part or all of an organisation's computing services. This can include not only operating the existing systems, but also developing new applications. The actual hardware may remain at the client organisation's site or the processing may be transferred to the FM company facilities. The prime advantages are that the relevant costs are fixed and known for the organisation, and it no longer has to be directly concerned with changes in technology and recruiting suitably skilled staff. The ownership of the existing hardware may either transfer to the FM company or remain with the organisation.*

  A further possibility is that the organisation will pass over the current and future operation of all existing systems to the FM company, and concentrate its own resources on the development of necessary new applications.

- *Bureaux This is where a third party provides processing facilities, usually of a specific nature, for example payroll preparation. Such a service can also include the creation of software to meet the specific needs of a client.*

The use of IT facilities has changed rapidly over recent years, partly due to changes in technology and the performance capabilities of new equipment, but also as a consequence of focused management attention on methods of reducing the costs of providing and maintaining IT services at their former level, due mainly to recessionary effects. It can be true that maintaining in-house IT facilities with all the necessary ancillary skills can be expensive, especially as the skill requirements are constantly on the move with related changes in technology. Part of this process of change has been the rush towards 'downsizing', although the alternative and related term 'rightsizing' is perhaps more apt. Where such initiatives require substantial reinvestment in hardware and associated skills, management may reasonably question the necessity to carry all the burdens in house, when there are third parties with the required infrastructure, facilities and knowledge to assume the task, albeit at a price. Setting aside these potential advantages, management must also be aware of the risks associated with such a move and obtain suitable assurance that the third party is fully capable of providing a secure, reliable and stable service.

Before opting for the use of either Facilities Management or Bureaux services, an organisation should undertake an evaluation, which should include the following assessments.

(a)   A comprehensive review and cost/benefit analysis of their current IT arrangements for subsequent comparisons. The prime aim being to either reduce or contain IT-related costs.

(b)   A determination of requirements (i.e. service types, required service levels, data security considerations, and general control environment factors).

(c)   A full review of available third party services, including service/cost comparisons, ensuring that all the feasible options are appraised including retaining the status quo.

(d)   Structured research into the use of such services by existing users, obtaining their views and comments on supplier effectiveness, etc.

(e)   A detailed feasibility study of the shortlisted suppliers and matching with the previously defined requirements.

It is possible that the decision to review and/or adopt the use of FM or Bureaux services had resulted from a Strategic Planning exercise, in which case some of the necessary analysis of current position, options for the future, etc. may already have been addressed. In this context, opting to use such services can free the resources of an organisation to focus their attention upon other more pressing or strategically significant business activities. As stated previously, there may be financial and other practical benefits for the organisation by contracting out its IT activities, but these are only likely to be fully achieved if the supplier can provide the appropriate quality of service and this needs to be thoroughly checked out beforehand.

The success of either the FM or Bureaux option is primarily dependent upon the flexibility and realism of the conditions reflected in the contract established between the affected parties. Contracts and arrangements for Facilities

Management should include a clear and unambiguous definition of each party's duties, responsibilities, rights and liabilities. These definitions should incorporate the required level of service provision, including that for any special periods such as the accounting year-end or peak trading periods. Where responsibility lies for data handling and control will need to be established and the development and the necessary application of professional and effective standards and methods can obviously contribute to the quality of service and systems.

Management should ensure that contracts and arrangements for Bureaux define the performance and levels of service required. Additionally a mechanism for monitoring actual performance against the targets should also be established and effectively monitored. Specifications will need to be supplied for each application provided by the Bureaux, including user staff responsibilities and the extent of data validation and other checks that are applied; these specifications should be examined by the users and the adequacy of such measures appraised, agreed and amended when necessary. The ownership of programs used to process users' data should be clearly established, especially where the software has been specifically developed for the user. The user may wish to hold a copy of the program in these circumstances as an additional form of security.

A statement as to the methods employed by the Bureaux to protect the integrity and confidentiality of users' data (in various forms) should be provided and the contents agreed as realistic and acceptable. User data must be isolated from all other users' data handled by the same bureau. The contracts or agreements should include a clear description of the basis for calculating the costs applied to the provision of services and their ongoing review and amendment, with special attention being paid to the flexibility permitted to the bureaux in respect of increasing such charges.

Assuming that a considerable portion of processing affecting the business may be handled by external suppliers, care needs to be taken in the determination of liability arrangements in the event of loss or disruption of service, especially where this could adversely affect the ability of the user company to continue trading operations.

Full details of the methods employed by the bureaux to control work and the contents of files, etc. should be obtained and reviewed for apparent effectiveness. The provision of an adequate audit trail will also need to be confirmed. If new programs have been developed for the user, arrangements should allow for the comprehensive testing to the satisfaction of users prior to live use, indeed there is a strong case for the active involvement of users in contributing to the test program.

Service providers should be obligated to advise users of any amendments applied to the programs used on their behalf, and they will ideally need to seek prior agreement to any significant changes.

Users must review the details of the contingency arrangements established in the event of disruption of facilities, and be satisfied as to their effectiveness in the protection of their business interests.

A requirement common to both FM and Bureaux is a form of arrangement to allow the user's auditors either access to the FM/bureaux operation for review purposes, or (more likely) the ability to seek assurance from the bureaux auditors. Additionally, in the case of FM, auditors (and indeed other interested parties) should ideally have interrogation access to the data held so that it can be confirmed as both complete and accurate. Again, in both cases, user staff involved in entering data into the relevant bureaux systems should have adequate supporting documentation and be sufficiently trained in respect of the system requirements.

The flow of work to and from bureaux should be recorded and checked upon return to ensure correct and complete processing. It will be necessary to promptly identify errors or omissions and ensure that action is promptly taken to suitably correct them.

In the case of transferring significant operations to FM, a planned approach is essential in order to ensure, for example, the use of accurate initial data and the loading of the correct versions of application programs. During this process specific responsibilities will need to be established and accordingly allocated.

The charges for Bureaux services and the costs for FM should be monitored against expectations and any significant variations examined. Please note that the creation of appropriate accounting facilities for the IT environment are examined in Chapter 16.

Control matrix examples

Example matrices reflecting both the *Objective* (Table 10.1) and *Exposure* (Table 10.2) orientation are provided, as this subject has both very distinct strategic business implications and can potentially represent notable risks if not suitably controlled. The *Scale* data used for these examples is drawn from *Scale* 2 (Objectives) and *Scale* 4 (Exposures); the supporting narrative for these and all other *Scales* in contained in Appendix 5.

The examples are designed to represent an organisation which relies substantially upon either FM or Bureaux services and the value data reflects a relevant level of dependency. Please note that the anticipated effectiveness of selected controls (i.e. control numbers 5, 9, 10. and 12) recorded on the *Exposure* example intentionally suggests a pessimistic view.

Some of the *Objectives* and *Exposures* are common to both types of service (i.e. the requirement for securely handling company data). However, the examples incorporate coverage of both service scenarios, therefore if your organisation only utilises one or the other, the data will require editing accordingly to remove the explicit references to the non-applicable service.

Table 10.1 Facilities Management - Objectives
Overall Inherent Risk (Size) Score [5 is worst risk; 1 is best] = 3.16

A Ensure accurate assessment of current & future requirements
B Ensure that IT related costs are reduced / contained
C Ensure the comprehensive research of options for change
D Ensure that selected IT 3rd party is reputable & reliable
E Ensure 3rd party option will provide necessary flexibility
F Ensure that required service levels will be achieved
G Establish effective & protective contracts/agreements
H Ensure allocation of responsibilities, rights & liabilities
I Ensure adequate security is exercised over company data
J Ensure that company data is accurate and reliable
K Establish the ownership of programs and applications
L Ensure disruption/loss of service is effectively addressed
M Ensure company auditors can assess adequacy of operation
N Ensure that any new systems or amendments are agreed/ tested
O Ensure that transaction trailing is adequate
P Ensure costs & performance are monitored against targets
Q Ensure that 3rd party applies effective standards & methods
R Ensure migration to 3rd party is adequately planned, etc.
S Ensure that user staff are supported to achieve objectives

Facilities Management	OBJECTIVES		A	B	C	D	E	F	G	H	I	J	K	L	M	N	O	P	Q	R	S
Calculated Risk Score	Risk		4	3	3	3	3	4	3	3	3	4	2	4	2	3	2	3	3	2	3
Scale 2 (6 is most serious)	Type		6	6	5	6	6	6	6	4	6	6	3	6	3	4	3	5	4	3	3
Size (3 is maximum)	Size		3	2	2	2	2	3	2	3	2	3	2	3	2	2	2	2	3	2	3
MEASURES																					
1 Output of Strategic Planning exercise provided basis for future IT requirements	Best		5				4														
	Test		?	?			?														
	Both																				
2 Current & proposed alternatives are subject to cost/benefit analysis and comparison	Best		4	4	4																
	Test		?	?	?	?															
	Both																				
3 Formal evaluation & feasibility methods were used to assess 3rd party options	Best			4	5	3	4												3		
	Test		?		?	?	?	?											?		
	Both																				
4 Quality, service & operational criteria established for assessment of relevant suppliers	Best					4	3	4													
	Test		?			?	?	?													
	Both																				
5 Current users contacted and subject to standard interview, re. performance, quality, etc.	Best					3	3														
	Test		?			?	?														
	Both																				
6 Contract defines required minimum service levels and critical operational timetables	Best							5	4												
	Test		?					?	?												
	Both																				
7 Service level performance is subject to ongoing monitoring and feedback	Best							4										4			
	Test		?					?										?			
	Both																				

Table 10.1 continued

			A	B	C	D	E	F	G	H	I	J	K	L	M	N	O	P	Q	R	S
8	Comprehensive contract has been established; defines rights, responsibilities and liabilities	Best							5	5											
		Test	?						?	?											
		Both																			
-		-	-	-	-	-	-	-	-	-	-	-	-	-	-	-	-	-	-	-	-
9	All liability in the event of disruption or loss of service > X hours, lies with suppliers	Best							4												
		Test	?						?												
		Both																			
-		-	-	-	-	-	-	-	-	-	-	-	-	-	-	-	-	-	-	-	-
10	Data preparation, input, reporting & reconciliation procedures defined	Best							4	3											
		Test	?						?	?											
		Both																			
-		-	-	-	-	-	-	-	-	-	-	-	-	-	-	-	-	-	-	-	-
11	Company auditor undertook review of 3rd party controls prior to relationship	Best								4	4										
		Test	?							?	?										
		Both																			
-		-	-	-	-	-	-	-	-	-	-	-	-	-	-	-	-	-	-	-	-
12	Pilot exercise undertaken to assess live conditions - results were satisfactory	Best								4	4										
		Test	?							?	?										
		Both																			
-		-	-	-	-	-	-	-	-	-	-	-	-	-	-	-	-	-	-	-	-
13	Processed data is reconciled	Best							3		4										
		Test	?						?		?										
		Both																			
-		-	-	-	-	-	-	-	-	-	-	-	-	-	-	-	-	-	-	-	-
14	Programs developed for the company remain the property of the company - per contract	Best											5								
		Test	?										?								
		Both																			
-		-	-	-	-	-	-	-	-	-	-	-	-	-	-	-	-	-	-	-	-
15	Contingency plan is in place (reviewed prior to contract) and tested for effectiveness	Best												5							
		Test	?											?							
		Both																			
-		-	-	-	-	-	-	-	-	-	-	-	-	-	-	-	-	-	-	-	-
16	Contract specifies conditions of access for company auditors to obtain assurance re controls	Best													5						
		Test	?												?						
		Both																			
-		-	-	-	-	-	-	-	-	-	-	-	-	-	-	-	-	-	-	-	-
17	All amendments to existing programs are specified, developed, tested & signed-off	Best														4		3			
		Test	?													?		?			
		Both																			
-		-	-	-	-	-	-	-	-	-	-	-	-	-	-	-	-	-	-	-	-
18	New programs are developed using an effective development methodology and framework	Best														4		3			
		Test	?													?		?			
		Both																			
-		-	-	-	-	-	-	-	-	-	-	-	-	-	-	-	-	-	-	-	-
19	Full audit trail is available	Best															4				
		Test	?														?				
		Both																			
-		-	-	-	-	-	-	-	-	-	-	-	-	-	-	-	-	-	-	-	-

Table 10.1   continued

#			A	B	C	D	E	F	G	H	I	J	K	L	M	N	O	P	Q	R	S
	All relative costs are	Best																4			
20	monitored against budget and	Test	?															?			
	variances are investigated	Both																			
-		-	-	-	-	-	-	-	-	-	-	-	-	-	-	-	-	-	-	-	-
	Satisfactory operating	Best																	5		
21	procedures are in place - site	Test	?																?		
	is accredited with BS5750	Both																			
-		-	-	-	-	-	-	-	-	-	-	-	-	-	-	-	-	-	-	-	-
	Initial transfer process was	Best																		4	
22	subject to agreed implementation	Test	?																	?	
	plan - with milestones/targets	Both																			
-		-	-	-	-	-	-	-	-	-	-	-	-	-	-	-	-	-	-	-	-
	Training and new documentation	Best																			4
23	provided as per contract	Test	?																		?
		Both																			
-		-	-	-	-	-	-	-	-	-	-	-	-	-	-	-	-	-	-	-	-

A Ensure accurate assessment of current & future requirements
B Ensure that IT related costs are reduced / contained
C Ensure the comprehensive research of options for change
D Ensure that selected IT 3rd party is reputable & reliable
E Ensure 3rd party option will provide necessary flexibility
F Ensure that required service levels will be achieved
G Establish effective & protective contracts/agreements
H Ensure allocation of responsibilities, rights & liabilities
I Ensure adequate security is exercised over company data
J Ensure that company data is accurate and reliable

K Establish the ownership of programs and applications
L Ensure disruption/loss of service is effectively addressed
M Ensure company auditors can assess adequacy of operation
N Ensure that any new systems or amendments are agreed/ tested
O Ensure that transaction trailing is adequate
P Ensure costs & performance are monitored against targets
Q Ensure that 3rd party applies effective standards & methods
R Ensure migration to 3rd party is adequately planned, etc.
S Ensure that user staff are supported to achieve objectives

Table 10.2 Facilities Management - Exposures

Overall Inherent Risk (Size) Score [5 is worst risk; 1 is best] = 3.11

A Inadequate identification of future IT requirements
B Failure to reduce/contain IT related costs - erode profit
C Inadequate research and review of options for change
D Failure to achieve objectives due to unreliable 3rd party
E Failure of 3rd party to provide required future flexibility
F Business disruption, due to failure to achieve service level
G Absence of adequate contractual arrangements - dispute,etc
H Failure to allocate responsibilities, rights & liabilities
I Unauthorised access to, or loss of, company data - error
J Inaccurate company data - affects planning/decision making

K Disruption due to disputed ownership of programs, etc.
L Disruption, loss, etc. due to inadequate contingency planning
M Failure to obtain assurance on 3rd party controls
N Unauthorised or incorrect amendments to existing systems
O Absence of user involvement in new system developments
P Inadequate transaction trails - delay, error, etc.
Q Failure to monitor costs and performance - loss, delay, etc.
R Disruption of migration to 3rd party due to poor planning
S User staff inadequately supported - errors, disruption, etc.

Facilities Management	EXPOSURES	A	B	C	D	E	F	G	H	I	J	K	L	M	N	O	P	Q	R	S
Calculated Risk Score	Risk	4	2	2	4	2	4	2	3	3	3	2	4	3	3	4	2	2	3	3
Scale 4 (6 is most serious)	Type	6	6	6	6	6	6	6	5	4	6	6	6	4	5	6	3	6	5	4
Size (3 is maximum)	Size	3	1	1	3	1	3	1	2	3	2	1	3	3	2	3	2	1	2	2
CONTROLS	-																			
1 Output of Strategic Planning exercise provided basis for future IT requirements	Best		5		2											2				
	Test	?	?		?											?				
	Both																			
2 Current & proposed alternatives were subject to cost/benefit analysis and comparison	Best			5	3															
	Test	?		?	?															
	Both																			
3 Formal evaluation & feasibility methods were used to assess 3rd party options	Best			3	4	3	4	2												
	Test	?		?	?	?	?	?												
	Both																			
4 Quality, service & operational criteria established for assessment of relevant suppliers	Best				2	4	4	3												
	Test	?			?	?	?	?												
	Both																			
5 Current users contacted and subject to standard interview, re performance, quality, etc.	Best				3	3	2													
	Test	?			?	?	?													
	Both																			
6 Contract defines required minimum service levels and critical operational timetables	Best					3		4	2											
	Test	?				?		?	?											
	Both																			
7 Service level performance is subject to ongoing monitoring and feedback	Best						4											4		
	Test	?					?											?		
	Both																			

Table 10.2   continued

			A	B	C	D	E	F	G	H	I	J	K	L	M	N	O	P	Q	R	S
8	Comprehensive contract has been established; defines rights, responsibilities and liabilities	Best							5												
		Test	?						?												
		Both																			
-		-	-	-	-	-	-	-	-	-	-	-	-	-	-	-	-	-	-	-	-
9	All liability in the event of disruption or loss of service > X hours, lies with suppliers	Best							3	3											
		Test	?						?	?											
		Both																			
-		-	-	-	-	-	-	-	-	-	-	-	-	-	-	-	-	-	-	-	-
10	Data preparation, input, reporting & reconciliation procedures defined & applied	Best							2	3											
		Test	?						?	?											
		Both																			
-		-	-	-	-	-	-	-	-	-	-	-	-	-	-	-	-	-	-	-	-
11	Company auditors undertook review of 3rd party controls prior to relationship	Best				3				3	4	4		3	3	2		3			
		Test	?			?				?	?	?		?	?	?		?			
		Both																			
-		-	-	-	-	-	-	-	-	-	-	-	-	-	-	-	-	-	-	-	-
12	Pilot exercise undertaken to assess live conditions - results were satisfactory	Best				4				2	2	3									
		Test	?			?				?	?	?									
		Both																			
-		-	-	-	-	-	-	-	-	-	-	-	-	-	-	-	-	-	-	-	-
13	Processed data is reconciled	Best									5										
		Test	?								?										
		Both																			
-		-	-	-	-	-	-	-	-	-	-	-	-	-	-	-	-	-	-	-	-
14	Programs developed for the company remain the property of the company - per contract	Best											5								
		Test	?										?								
		Both																			
-		-	-	-	-	-	-	-	-	-	-	-	-	-	-	-	-	-	-	-	-
15	Contingency plan is in place (reviewed prior to contract) and tested for effectiveness	Best											5								
		Test	?										?								
		Both																			
-		-	-	-	-	-	-	-	-	-	-	-	-	-	-	-	-	-	-	-	-
16	Contract specifies conditions of access for company auditors to obtain assurance re controls	Best												5							
		Test	?											?							
		Both																			
-		-	-	-	-	-	-	-	-	-	-	-	-	-	-	-	-	-	-	-	-
17	All amendments to existing programs are specified, developed, tested & signed-off	Best													5						
		Test	?												?						
		Both																			
-		-	-	-	-	-	-	-	-	-	-	-	-	-	-	-	-	-	-	-	-
18	New programs are developed using an effective development methodology and framework	Best															5				
		Test	?														?				
		Both																			
-		-	-	-	-	-	-	-	-	-	-	-	-	-	-	-	-	-	-	-	-
19	Full audit trail is available	Best															4				
		Test	?														?				
		Both																			
-		-	-	-	-	-	-	-	-	-	-	-	-	-	-	-	-	-	-	-	-

Table 10.2   continued

			A	B	C	D	E	F	G	H	I	J	K	L	M	N	O	P	Q	R	S
	All relative costs are	Best																	5		
20	monitored against budget, and	Test	?																?		
	variances are fully investigated	Both																			
-		-	-	-	-	-	-	-	-	-	-	-	-	-	-	-	-	-	-	-	-
	Satisfactory operating	Best													4						
21	procedures are in place - site	Test	?												?						
	is accredited with BS5750	Both																			
-		-	-	-	-	-	-	-	-	-	-	-	-	-	-	-	-	-	-	-	-
	Initial transfer process was	Best																		5	
22	subject to agreed implementation	Test	?																	?	
	plan - with milestones/targets	Both																			
-		-	-	-	-	-	-	-	-	-	-	-	-	-	-	-	-	-	-	-	-
	Training and new documentation	Best																			4
23	provided as per contract	Test	?																		?
		Both																			
-		-	-	-	-	-	-	-	-	-	-	-	-	-	-	-	-	-	-	-	-

A Inadequate identification of future IT requirements
B Failure to reduce/contain IT related costs - erode profit
C Inadequate research and review of options for change
D Failure to achieve objectives due to unreliable 3rd party
E Failure of 3rd party to provide required future flexibility
F Business disruption, due to failure to achieve service level
G Absence of adequate contractural arrangements - dispute,etc
H Failure to allocate responsibilities, rights & liabilities
I Unauthorised access to, or loss of, company data - error
J Inaccurate company data - affects planning/decision making

K Disruption due to disputed ownership of programs, etc.
L Disruption, loss, etc. due to inadequate contingency planning
M Failure to obtain assurance on 3rd party controls
N Unauthorised or incorrect amendments to existing systems
O Absence of user involvement in new system developments
P Inadequate transaction trails - delay, error, etc.
Q Failure to monitor costs and performance - loss, delay, etc.
R Disruption of migration to 3rd party due to poor planning
S User staff inadequately supported - errors, disruption, etc.

11

PERSONAL COMPUTERS AND WORKSTATIONS

Scope

This chapter covers the key issues relating to the acquisition and use of Personal Computers, including ensuring the reliability of hardware, the protection of data and software, maintenance, upgrading, security, back-up, and staff training.

The contents are intended to encompass the use of Personal Computers as either free-standing units or terminals/workstations connected to either networks or mainframe systems. In this context the term 'Personal Computer' used throughout the following text implies all available options. Additionally the terms Personal Computer and Microcomputer are intended to be fully inter-changeable.

There are natural linkages with subjects explored in other chapters (e.g. System Access Control, Data Protection Act, Viruses, Software Package Selection, etc.), and, where applicable, any apparent overlap in coverage is intentional. The in-house development of PC software is not addressed here, but Chapter 9 covers all aspects of system development.

There has been a boom in end-user orientated computing with a related proliferation of both hardware and software aimed at handling a vast range of business tasks. Business has seized the opportunities offered by Personal Computers (and related devices) partly as a means of escape from the costly and restrictive constraints of traditional centralised mainframe installations and facilities. Many companies utilise personal computers to support rapid change, support new initiatives, enable the manipulation and analysis of corporate data, facilitate inter-department communications, contribute to staff productivity and motivate staff to become involved in the use of IT in their everyday activities.

However, although apparently reducing user dependence upon the IT specialists, adopting the widespread use of personal computers does present some risks, because along with the newly found freedom comes the related absence of the traditional disciplines and controlling technical restrictions which supported the secure and structured use of systems and data in either traditional batch processing or mainframe environments. There is the prime danger that allowing too free an approach to end-user computing can result in putting the key issues of business data security, integrity, reliability and confidentiality at risk, with the inevitable consequences for the business. Viewed in this context the relatively low value of the machine can belie the true commercial worth of the data it contains.

As well as their role in business, personal computers have a wide general leisure appeal and can, by their very nature, attract a lively interest, which can be of dual concern when the machines in question are essential to the operation of a business and can be easily subject to inquisitive exploration or tampering. In addition, personal computers are portable and desirable objects, therefore security measures should prevent their removal from the office without a suitable form of written authority.

It is necessary, therefore, to apply sensible restrictions and other controls over the use of personal computers, if the operation of the business is to be adequately protected. The degree to which such restrictions are applied will, among other factors, be relative to the potential risks associated with misuse. However, the level of control applied should be in balance with, and not adversely counteract, all the benefits of immediacy which personal computers can generically provide.

In assessing the requirements for personal computers or software, a prime consideration to bear in mind is the relevance of use of such facilities to the successful achievement of the business objectives. There is always the danger that PC hardware (and software) will be acquired for the wrong reasons in a fast-changing market, or that keeping on the leading edge of technology becomes more important than achieving corporate goals. Undoubtedly personal computers can be a tool in the achievement of corporate strategic objectives, but only if their acquisition and use is intermeshed with the defined business aims of the organisation and suitably justified on both financial and functional grounds.

Noted below are the key issues and measures relative to the effective and secure use of personal computers and related software. Some of the points noted are explored more fully in other chapters in this book (such as Media Handling and Back-up, Systems Access Control, Data Protection Act, Software Package Selection, Viruses, etc.).

ASSESSING REQUIREMENTS

Given the proliferation of hardware and software products available, and the ever-changing technical specifications, it is essential that requirements are initially accurately assessed. There are a number of established industry standards relative to both hardware and software and these should be selected in preference to obscure or unproven product ranges. Where existing facilities are being enhanced or extended, it should be confirmed that any additional equipment is technically compatible with that currently in use and that interconnection is both feasible and proven. It is important that early in the specification process a direct relationship is established between the policy and functional requirements of any IT Strategy and the identification of the equipment deemed suitable to achieve the underlying objectives.

All the costs and benefits associated with any changes should be identified and approved in accord with prevailing financial policies, especially where new business initiatives are involved which may have been subject to capital investment limits.

All factors relevant to technical and functional requirements will need to be identified, documented and agreed with all involved parties. A form of requirements specification is particularly useful when subsequently approaching external suppliers. The projected future needs will require consideration in this process and confirmation obtained that likely levels of growth and development can be suitably accommodated. Equipment should be chosen that demonstrates a clear technical upgrade path with the potential for expansion in line with projected requirements.

Another key issue is the matter of machine performance which can normally be expressed in terms of processor speed, response times, and the ability to deal effectively with considerable levels of mathematical calculations. Linked to the question of performance is the provision of adequate amounts of main and hard disk memory, the restriction of which may cause the operation of applications to either significantly degrade or even fail in execution as available memory is exhausted. Due consideration should be applied to the realistic requirements for data storage especially if data is to be downloaded from a central system for local manipulation or if local data back-up is a crucial operational requirement.

The requirement of additional peripheral equipment (such as printers, tape streamers, scanners, etc.) should be identified on a proven needs basis. There may be special requirements such as the ability to display very high quality graphics for design purposes, scanning documents for input or provision of communication and electronic mail facilities. All such functional variations should be fully specified and confirmed with users as correct, prior to being subject to justification and approval procedures.

ACQUISITION (OF HARDWARE AND SOFTWARE)

It is preferable to establish a corporate purchasing policy in relation to computer equipment and software in order that compatibility with existing equipment can be assured and any future upgrade paths can be achieved. Such a policy may have been generated as part of an IT Strategic Planning exercise and may therefore be linked to the achievement of specific business goals and objectives. Although the policy may define a preferred equipment manufacturer it is more likely to identify the base technical specification, i.e. processor generation or type. In this latter context, it is preferable that only industry standard products with a clear upgrade path are acquired.

The personal computer market is currently very competitive on price and a comprehensive appraisal of the market may be necessary in order to identify a combination of value for money and favourable terms. Management should ensure, by the establishment of suitable financial controls, that all the relevant costs are suitably justified and approved within the agreed budget constraints.

The application of effective equipment and software selection procedures is necessary to ensure compatibility between the identified requirements and the selected products. Chapter 22 provides specific guidance on evaluation of software packages. The capabilities of available equipment should be appraised in relation to the identified requirements and minimum technical and operational criteria for software products. The reliability, stability and reputation of potential suppliers and their products should be examined. The opinions of current users can be sought and a view taken on whether the product is well established and proven in the market. Assurance should be sought (in writing) that the products conform to any prevailing legislation or recognised standards (i.e. for screen radiation emissions).

In order to fully conform to the requirements specification established and agreed with the users, it may be necessary to enhance or modify the basic product; the full costs and implications of such actions should be clearly identified, documented and sanctioned by management prior to entering into any arrangements with suppliers.

The operational demands placed upon hardware may be such that any disruption of availability will need to be promptly rectified, therefore it is necessary to determine the quality, speed and cost of service arrangements. The initial and ongoing costs associated with service should be clearly identified and taken into account during the cost justification of projects.

The correct and efficient use of hardware and software is partially dependent upon the quality of product documentation and ideally this should be examined and appraised before purchasing the product(s). Consider the cost and effort involved in having to create in-house documentation if the supplied version appears inadequate or deficient.

The quality of ongoing customer support is another important factor to be considered. For instance, are users able to telephone the supplier in the event of difficulty, and can they expect a prompt response to all their enquiries or problems? Existing users may be able to provide an indication of the quality of after-sales support. If a supplier promotes his accreditation under BS5750 or ISO9000, confirm that the standard specifically applies to all of his activities and is not, for example, restricted to a distribution subsidiary.

Consider the licence and copyright aspects of software and ensure that subsequent compliance with conditions can be accommodated by the organisation. Clearly establish with the supplier the basis and likely costs for future software upgrades and build same into the budgets for ongoing costs. Users should be responsible for assessing the impact of new technology and software on their requirements for staffing, training, and operations. Training in the use of new software may be provided, at a price, by the suppliers or developers. Alternatively the software may feature integrated tutorial modules.

INSTALLATION (AND CONFIGURATION)

It is desirable to ensure that implementations of new or upgraded hardware and software are adequately planned and take account of all the impacts (i.e. power supplies, cabling, configuration, supply of consumables, staff training, testing, etc.).

When new or additional equipment and software is received, an inventory record should be maintained so that the items can be subsequently controlled and tracked, especially in relation to fixed asset implications. These records can then be subsequently used as a basis for confirming the continued existence of hardware and software and also for identifying the location of items which may require collective upgrade, maintenance, etc. In specific relation to software, such records can be used to aid the confirmation that all copies of package applications present on personal computers are correctly supported by the number of licence copies officially held by the company as part of a process of confirming compliance with software licensing conditions.

In order to ensure that personal computers achieve optimum performance in relation to the applications being used and their base technical specification, it will be necessary to determine an appropriate default configuration. Therefore it is recommended that the installation and configuration of personal computers is only undertaken by experienced staff in accordance with these established standards. This process will involve the setting of various parameters in the AUTOEXEC and CONFIG files used by the operating system to determine the operational characteristics of the machines. Unfortunately, editing access to these files is openly permitted within the facilities of the available operating systems and therefore users can either unintentionally or deliberately amend the contents and thereby adversely affect machine performance. There are add-in devices and software products available which prevent or restrict such access and their use is suggested where performance and overall reliability are critical considerations.

Ensure that the appropriate environmental conditions are provided for the operation of the equipment and that the siting of equipment takes account of any security considerations (i.e. the processing of confidential data) avoiding free or casual access to such machines. Additionally, ensure that the equipment is protected from the effects of high levels of static electricity and that any health and safety aspects are addressed (i.e. screen radiation, earthing of equipment, routing of cables, etc.). Power supply conditioners or spike suppressors may be required if the power supply is prone to variation, etc.

Provide users with clear guidelines as to the correct use and care of all equipment including printers, tape streamers, and other peripherals. Points of contact should be provided in the event of equipment failure or software faults; this may be a central User Support function (see Chapter 23 for more information). Ensure that all the necessary hardware and software manuals are made available to users.

Before loading software onto user computers ensure that all source disks are checked for the presence of virus infection and advise users to check all diskettes for possible infection before use on their equipment. (Chapter 25 discusses a range of precautions designed to prevent virus infections).

Take back-up copies of all software for use in the event of failure, system damage, etc. These copies should be stored securely and preferably away from the user area; not only to provide greater resilience in the event of a localised problem or disaster but also to avoid the inappropriate use or illegal copying of the source disks. Ideally, software should only be loaded and upgraded by suitably authorised staff who also ensure that adequate records are maintained of all software in use throughout the organisation.

The installation of software can be structured by use of separate directories as this can also aid the segregation of duties if supported by access controls applied at a directory level. It is strongly recommended that you only use industry standard Operating Systems with clear upgrade paths and compatibility and further ensure that any subsequent upgrades will not interfere with the continued operation of existing software by applying appropriate central testing before general distribution to end-users.

In order to ensure the consistent use of software products throughout the company all affected users will need to be correctly identified when applying upgrades; this can be achieved if accurate records of software copies related to users are maintained. To further guarantee overall consistency of usage, software upgrades and fixes should only be loaded by authorised support staff in a standard manner. Restrictions, in the form of access control systems or lockable diskette drives, can be applied to users to prevent them from loading unauthorised software or applying their own amendments to existing software and configuration files. Unless essential for running applications, all program language software (i.e. BASIC, C, etc.) should be removed from personal computers so as to avoid inappropriate usage.

Users should be encouraged to report any apparent shortfalls in terms of machine or application performance, and facilities will need to be provided to effectively address any such problems.

RESPONSIBILITIES, PROCEDURES AND TRAINING

The provision of written procedures on PC use and definitions of user responsibilities for equipment, systems and data can engender an atmosphere of collective responsibility and systems ownership. Users can be made aware that their actions can directly affect and enhance the quality of corporate data and that any malpractice will be regarded as a disciplinary offence. Maintain a general awareness of procedural requirements and ensure that the induction of new staff includes a briefing on the current requirements.

Ownership of company data should be made clear and the undue or unauthorised copying or amendment should be discouraged and actively prevented. Ensure that user access to data is granted on an authorised 'need to know' basis in agreement with the data owners (see Chapter 17 for details of System Access Control). Provide guidance (and training where necessary and justified) on compliance with the requirements of the Data Protection Act and ensure that all personal data is subject to the application of the principles contained in the Act. Consider providing users with supporting documentation (i.e. application system manuals) and assess the need for supporting training. Additionally ensure that the equipment is used in accordance with the manufacturer's/supplier's instructions and that users are aware of how to correctly handle, use and store magnetic media in order to protect the recorded data.

Although it is presently fashionable to establish 'No Smoking' policies in company premises for health related reasons, it is in any case preferable that staff do not smoke, eat, or drink when using personal computers because the equipment and related media can be damaged as a consequence of such actions.

When initiating the use of new systems, provide sufficient training in the use of both package and bespoke software and generally provide adequate support for users and facilitate the development of best practices throughout the company.

Prevent the illegal copying of software by employees and thereby avoid contravention of the software licence conditions. Establish a clear policy which connects the pirating of software with the staff disciplinary code. Additionally it will be necessary to prevent the loading and use of unauthorised software by users (e.g. computer game programs) as their presence may affect the consistent operation of the official applications and affect the performance of the hardware by, for example, utilising conflicting portions of memory. The use of devices to lock diskette drives can help to prevent the loading of unofficial programs but their presence can also be a barrier to the necessary back-up of data and systems by users. Such diskette locks can also prevent the booting of the system from unauthorised versions of the operating system.

Although the extent of virus infections may have been overplayed in the media, it is wise to ensure that all disks used on personal computers are checked for virus infection prior to use or loading. (See Chapter 25 for details of the methods aimed at the prevention and containment of virus infections).

In order to preserve their ability to conduct business activities ensure that users are fully aware of the necessity to take regular back-up copies of data and systems to enable recovery in the event of a failure.

SECURITY

This section summarises matters relevant to both physical and logical security in respect of personal computers with the objective of protecting data and systems from abuse, disruption, damage and unauthorised disclosure.

Ensure that access to the building is controlled and that the movement of computer equipment out of the premises is subject to a check for the appropriate authorisation. Users should be made aware of their custodial responsibilities for the security of computer hardware which can be underscored by the provision and application of a written PC Security Policy (including the definition of any disciplinary actions in cases of neglect or malpractice). Preventing or hindering the theft of computer hardware and associated devices can be a matter of using devices which firmly affix the equipment to desks. All company fixed assets should be recorded in an inventory and suitably identified with a distinctive non-removable company label and reference number. The accuracy of such records should be regularly confirmed by physical checks of equipment in use and the accounting for all asset records.

Given the personal dimension of end-user computing and the related levels of user responsibility for safe custody of equipment, staff and management alike need to be proactive in the prevention of unauthorised access to personal computing facilities. This can, for example, be demonstrated by the sensible location of computers, especially where sensitive or confidential data or systems are concerned.

Users are the first line of defence for system security and therefore must be responsible for preventing casual use of their computer, by using keyboard locks or not leaving their machines unattended whilst the system is active or connected to the mainframe or network. Mechanisms are available which automatically de-activate computers or terminals after a fixed period of inactivity in order to prevent unauthorised or opportunist use.

Undertaking a risk assessment relative to the use of PC equipment in the organisation can generate the requirement (in the appropriate circumstances) for measures designed to minimise or contain the impact of certain problems, failures, etc. For example it may be relevant to consider either the use of UPS (Uninterruptible Power Supplies) in order to provide continuity of supply in case of failure of the main system, or the acquisition of back-up or alternative equipment in order to maintain the more crucial processing operations. The use of lockable processor cases can aid the prevention of tampering with the internal circuitry. It may be necessary to protect network and other communication cabling from either tampering or damage if there is a high dependence upon such facilities.

Beyond the physical security considerations there are the connected matters of access to data, systems and corporate computing facilities. Access control measures can be established which aim to prevent unauthorised access or malpractice and these are fully examined in Chapter 17. However users should specifically be made aware of their basic responsibilities with regard to the safeguarding of their passwords from discovery or misuse.

Resident anti-virus software that operates automatically upon power-up can provide assurance about the potential for damaging infections.

Unauthorised access to utilities, DOS commands or 'Tools' software can, to varying degrees, result in disruption of PC facilities. For example, files can be erased, disks can be re-formatted with the associated loss of all the previously held data and software, and systems can be unofficially re-configured with a potential impact upon performance.

Taking into account the likelihood of disaster striking the personal computer operations and the perceived effectiveness of existing controls and measures, insurance cover arrangements should be examined for both their adequacy and appropriateness.

PROTECTION OF DATA

Prime application data should ideally be assigned to 'owners' who then determine the necessary access rights granted to all users which can be allocated and administered by the use of access control systems. Staff should protect their user passwords or other access control 'tokens' from unauthorised use and thereby contribute to the integrity and accuracy of corporate data and systems. The unauthorised copying of data files should be taken into account when constructing a corporate data access framework. If employees change roles or leave the company the person responsible for access security matters must ensure that the relevant access rights are promptly amended or revoked. Data owners and user management can be held responsible for ensuring the accuracy of authorised user and access right records. Additional access and physical security measures may have to be applied to the use of, and access to, confidential or commercially sensitive data.

A suitable data policy can be established which ensures that data are regularly backed-up and securely stored in relation to the underlying significance to the business. Back-up media will need to be accurately labelled, identified, suitably stored and protected from accidental erasure or removal. In order to be effective it is necessary to prove that data files are capable of rebuilding using the available back-up copies and/or transaction trails. If the data is held on network file servers, ensure that adequate back-up procedures are established and applied. With a number of users, perhaps from different departments, the clear allocation of security and back-up duties can be overlooked, a fact that only becomes apparent when the system has been affected and there are insufficient back-up copies to facilitate a full recovery.

Ensure that an agreed Contingency Plan for all personal computing is established for use in the event of a disaster or major failure and undertake periodic testing and evaluation of the plan so that it remains comprehensive and effective in recovering the personal computer data necessary for continued operations. If data held centrally is accessed for interrogation and other purposes ensure that mechanisms are in place to prevent the unauthorised amendment or corruption of 'live' data.

If true database methods are employed ensure that database management software contains facilities to maintain and determine the integrity of constituent data.

Limiting access to personal computing utilities and software 'tools' can further protect locally held company data from either unintentional or deliberate corruption or loss.

PROTECTION OF SOFTWARE

Ensure that the software is used in accordance with the supplier's instructions and that all the relevant user manuals and internal usage procedures are available. Disable the floppy disk drive (perhaps by drive locking devices) to prevent the unauthorised loading or copying of software; additionally control the access to and use of the keys when it is necessary to legitimately utilise the drive.

Ensure that the User Support department or a nominated individual holds back-up copies of software and controls any re-loading of same in accordance with the licence conditions. When loading software updates ensure that only supplier approved and tested software upgrades (or fixes) are applied and that previous versions of software are retained and suitably labelled to prevent inadvertent use.

Ensure that all media are checked for virus infection prior to use. Restrict access to utilities, file editors, tools, DOS (or equivalent) commands, as a means of preventing either deliberate or accidental disruption.

Ensure that adequate provision is made in the documented Contingency Plan for use in the event of a disaster or failure to cover the requirements for reloading the appropriate and current versions of all personal computer software (including operating systems).

MAINTENANCE AND FAULTS

In order to prolong the life of equipment and ensure the correct functioning of same, ensure that routine cleaning and preventative maintenance are conducted in accordance with the manufacturer's or supplier's recommendations. Adequate maintenance and service cover should be established and the provision of service should be monitored so that the supplier's maintenance obligations are observed.

Ensure that requests for assistance, etc. are co-ordinated and initially checked by user support staff; this offers the opportunity for rectifying minor or straightforward problems in-house without recourse to external agents where additional costs may be incurred. Ensure that all faults are reported, logged and followed-up; additionally ensure that down time as a result of machine or software faults is minimised. Also ensure that only supplier approved components are fitted to avoid invalidating the terms of any warranty or service contracts.

Control matrix examples

An organisation may utilise personal computers with a view to achieving a specific corporate goal or in the pursuit of gaining competitive advantage over a rival. However, the use of personal computers does, in itself, present some very real risks. In light of these factors and the strategic significance offered by personal computers two example matrices are provided with *Objective* and *Exposures* orientations as Tables 11.1 and 11.2 respectively. The *Size* data used in both examples reflects a medium to high reliance upon the use of Personal Computers. *Scales* 2 and 4 are used for the *Objectives* and *Exposures* respectively, narratives supporting all the *Scales* utilised in this book are contained in Appendix 5.

The objective-related example (per Table 11.1) is naturally aligned towards the achievement of important business-related issues and whereas the exposure matrix also highlights the consequences of not attaining such strategic goals, it also addresses the considerable potential for disruption, cost, etc. which would accompany poor levels of control. There is an intentional duplication of some measures data recorded on the objective example with the controls noted on the exposure matrix.

Table 11.1 Personal Computers - Objectives

Overall Inherent Risk (Size) Score [5 is worst risk; 1 is best] = 3.21

A Ensure Personal Computing contributes to company objectives
B Ensure hard and software is compatible with Strategic Plan
C Ensure the integrity and security of corporate data
D Ensure the integrity and security of corporate systems
E Ensure hardware and software is reliable, upgradable, etc.
F Prevent the loss, theft and damage of PC hard and software
G Ensure adequate assessment of all PC related requirements
H Ensure staff are suitably trained to maximise performance
I Prevent unauthorised use of/access to computing facilities

J Ensure that hardware is correctly installed & configured
K Ensure upgrades are correctly applied by authorised staff
L Ensure compliance with the Data Protection Act (1984)
M Prevent the infection of systems with viruses
N Prevent tampering with hardware, software or configuration
O Provide adequate facilities to recover from failure, etc.
P Ensure that sensitive data remains confidential
Q Minimise disruption due to equipment failure
R Ensure the consistent use of PCs throughout the company
S Maximise systems integration throughout the company

Personal Computers		OBJECTIVES																		
		A	B	C	D	E	F	G	H	I	J	K	L	M	N	O	P	Q	R	S
		=	=	=	=	=	=	=	=	=	=	=	=	=	=	=	=	=	=	=
Calculated Risk Score	Risk	4	4	4	4	3	2	4	3	3	3	3	2	3	3	4	3	3	3	3
Scale 2 (6 is most serious)	Type	6	6	6	6	5	2	5	4	5	5	4	4	6	4	6	5	6	4	5
Size (3 is maximum)	Size	3	3	3	3	2	2	3	2	2	2	2	1	2	3	3	2	2	2	2
MEASURES																					
1 Acquisition and use of Personal Computers is related to Strategic Plan requirements	Best	4	4																	3	4
	Test	?	?	?																?	?
	Both																				
2 Each business area has a plan for use of PCs in achieving business goals & objectives	Best	4	3																		
	Test	?	?	?																	
	Both																				
3 Preferred hardware platforms & software environments are defined in documented policy	Best		4					2												4	4
	Test	?		?				?												?	?
	Both																				
4 Only industry standard equipment is purchased	Best		2	3	2		4		3										4	4	4
	Test	?	?	?	?		?		?										?	?	?
	Both																				
5 Suitability of hardware & software is assessed by using established evaluation process	Best		4	2			4		3												4
	Test	?		?	?		?		?												?
	Both																				
6 System access controls are applied using user-ID and password	Best			4	4		4			4			4			4					
	Test	?		?	?		?			?			?			?					
	Both																				
7 Data owners define access rights and access system reflects these requirements	Best		4	4						4											
	Test	?	?	?						?											
	Both																				

Table 11.1 continued

			A	B	C	D	E	F	G	H	I	J	K	L	M	N	O	P	Q	R	S
	Equipment has to be compatible	Best		3			4		3											4	4
8	with existing systems and	Test	?		?		?		?											?	?
	capable of upgrade	Both																			
-		-	-	-	-	-	-	-	-	-	-	-	-	-	-	-	-	-	-	-	-
	Data back-up policy is in place	Best			4												4			3	
9	- defines frequency, method of	Test	?		?												?			?	
	storage, labelling, etc.	Both																			
-		-	-	-	-	-	-	-	-	-	-	-	-	-	-	-	-	-	-	-	-
	Critical data back-ups are	Best			4												4				
10	stored off-site in the secure	Test	?		?												?				
	media library	Both																			
-		-	-	-	-	-	-	-	-	-	-	-	-	-	-	-	-	-	-	-	-
	Contingency plan and measures	Best			4	4											4				
11	are in place in the event of	Test	?		?	?											?				
	failure, etc.	Both																			
-		-	-	-	-	-	-	-	-	-	-	-	-	-	-	-	-	-	-	-	-
	Unauthorised copying of data &	Best			3		3				4			4							
12	software is prevented by control	Test	?		?		?				?			?							
	over accessing utilities	Both																			
-		-	-	-	-	-	-	-	-	-	-	-	-	-	-	-	-	-	-	-	-
	Loading of unauthorised systems	Best			4	4					4			4							
13	& data is prevented by locking	Test	?		?	?					?			?							
	the floppy disk drives	Both																			
-		-	-	-	-	-	-	-	-	-	-	-	-	-	-	-	-	-	-	-	-
	Only approved/tested software	Best			4	4							5								
14	updates are loaded by User	Test	?		?	?							?								
	Support staff	Both																			
-		-	-	-	-	-	-	-	-	-	-	-	-	-	-	-	-	-	-	-	-
	All media is checked for virus	Best			4	4									4						
15	infection before use/update,	Test	?		?	?									?						
	etc.	Both																			
-		-	-	-	-	-	-	-	-	-	-	-	-	-	-	-	-	-	-	-	-
	Suppliers are investigated as	Best					4														
16	to their financial stability,	Test	?				?														
	reputation, etc.	Both																			
-		-	-	-	-	-	-	-	-	-	-	-	-	-	-	-	-	-	-	-	-
	All requirements, including	Best					3		4												
17	performance criteria, are	Test	?				?		?												
	assessed & matched to products	Both																			
-		-	-	-	-	-	-	-	-	-	-	-	-	-	-	-	-	-	-	-	-
	Upgrade path and costs are	Best					3		4												
18	fully assessed	Test	?				?		?												
		Both																			
-		-	-	-	-	-	-	-	-	-	-	-	-	-	-	-	-	-	-	-	-
	All hard and software is	Best					4														
19	registered, and non-removable	Test	?				?														
	inventory labels are attached	Both																			
-		-	-	-	-	-	-	-	-	-	-	-	-	-	-	-	-	-	-	-	-

Table 11.1 continued

			A	B	C	D	E	F	G	H	I	J	K	L	M	N	O	P	Q	R	S
	All equipment leaving the site	Best						4													
20	has to be supported by written	Test	?					?													
	authorisation	Both																			
-		-	-	-	-	-	-	-	-	-	-	-	-	-	-	-	-	-	-	-	-
	Procedures and policy defines	Best			3	3		3		3										4	
21	users responsibilities re	Test	?		?	?		?		?										?	
	security, use of PC, back-up	Both																			
-		-	-	-	-	-	-	-	-	-	-	-	-	-	-	-	-	-	-	-	-
	General & specific training	Best								4											
22	needs are identified and	Test	?							?											
	addressed	Both																			
-		-	-	-	-	-	-	-	-	-	-	-	-	-	-	-	-	-	-	-	-
	Unattended/dormant machines	Best									4										
23	will automatically log-off or	Test	?								?										
	go into stand-by mode	Both																			
-		-	-	-	-	-	-	-	-	-	-	-	-	-	-	-	-	-	-	-	-
	Installation/configuration is	Best									4		4								
24	undertaken by experienced	Test	?								?		?								
	User Support staff	Both																			
-		-	-	-	-	-	-	-	-	-	-	-	-	-	-	-	-	-	-	-	-
	User Support periodically check	Best									4		4								
25	that the configuration, etc. is	Test	?								?		?								
	correct	Both																			
-		-	-	-	-	-	-	-	-	-	-	-	-	-	-	-	-	-	-	-	-
	User Support staff are available	Best								4											
26	to provide assistance. User	Test	?							?											
	Group has been formed	Both																			
-		-	-	-	-	-	-	-	-	-	-	-	-	-	-	-	-	-	-	-	-
	Data Protection guidelines	Best												4							
27	issued and data model has been	Test	?											?							
	examined by Compliance Officer	Both																			
-		-	-	-	-	-	-	-	-	-	-	-	-	-	-	-	-	-	-	-	-
	All machines have resident	Best													4						
28	virus checking software - run	Test	?												?						
	automatically at power-up	Both																			
-		-	-	-	-	-	-	-	-	-	-	-	-	-	-	-	-	-	-	-	-
	Processor cases are protected	Best													4						
29	by locks	Test	?												?						
		Both																			
-		-	-	-	-	-	-	-	-	-	-	-	-	-	-	-	-	-	-	-	-
	Critical corporate data is	Best															4				
30	only held on machines located in	Test	?														?				
	secure executive areas	Both																			
-		-	-	-	-	-	-	-	-	-	-	-	-	-	-	-	-	-	-	-	-
	Access to data (at 30 above)	Best															4				
31	is restricted to key staff only	Test	?														?				
		Both																			
-		-	-	-	-	-	-	-	-	-	-	-	-	-	-	-	-	-	-	-	-

Table 11.1 continued

			A	B	C	D	E	F	G	H	I	J	K	L	M	N	O	P	Q	R	S
	All faults are reported to the	Best																	3		
32	Help Desk, registered and	Test	?																?		
	reacted to	Both																			
-		-	-	-	-	-	-	-	-	-	-	-	-	-	-	-	-	-	-	-	-
	Supplier (on-site) maintenance	Best																	3		
33	agreements ensure same day	Test	?																?		
	service response	Both																			
-		-	-	-	-	-	-	-	-	-	-	-	-	-	-	-	-	-	-	-	-
	Down-time is recorded and	Best																	3		
34	alternative processing is	Test	?																?		
	arranged whenever possible	Both																			
-		-	-	-	-	-	-	-	-	-	-	-	-	-	-	-	-	-	-	-	-
	Basic configuration & operating	Best																		4	4
35	system environment is	Test	?																	?	?
	compatible throughout company	Both																			
-		-	-	-	-	-	-	-	-	-	-	-	-	-	-	-	-	-	-	-	-

A Ensure Personal Computing contributes to company objectives

B Ensure hard and software is compatible with Strategic Plan

C Ensure the integrity and security of corporate data

D Ensure the integrity and security of corporate systems

E Ensure hardware and software is reliable, upgradable, etc.

F Prevent the loss, theft and damage of PC hard and software

G Ensure adequate assessment of all PC related requirements

H Ensure staff are suitably trained to maximise performance

I Prevent unauthorised use of/access to computing facilities

J Ensure that hardware is correctly installed & configured

K Ensure upgrades are correctly applied by authorised staff

L Ensure compliance with the Data Protection Act (1984)

M Prevent the infection of systems with viruses

N Prevent tampering with hardware, software or configuration

O Provide adequate facilities to recover from failure, etc.

P Ensure that sensitive data remains confidential

Q Minimise disruption due to equipment failure

R Ensure the consistent use of PCs throughout the company

S Maximise systems integration throughout the company

Table 11.2   Personal Computers - Exposures

Overall Inherent Risk (Size) [5 is worst risk; 1 is best] = 3.10

A Failure to conform with Strategic Plan & company objectives
B Acquisition of incompatible or unreliable hardware
C Purchase and use of unproven or inappropriate software
D Loss or corruption of corporate data - disruption, etc.
E Leakage of confidential or sensitive data - business damaged
F Unauthorised access to systems/data - damage, fraud, etc.
G Dealing with unreliable/unstable supplier - lack of support
H Inadequate determination of requirements - failed objectives
I Loss, theft of/damage to hardware - costs, disruption, etc.
J Inadequate procedures and/or staff training - error, etc.

K Inadequate user support - error, misuse, inconsistent use
L Unauthorised access/use of system configuration/utilities
M Inadequate installation & configuration of hardware - error
N Failure to plan implementation & address all implications
O Incorrect / unauthorised loading of software upgrades
P Unauthorised copying of software/data - breach of licence
Q Infection of system with viruses - delay, disruption, etc.
R Tampering with hardware - failure, disruption, costs, delay
S Inability to recover from failure, disaster, etc.
T Failure to promptly deal with faults/problems - disruption

Personal Computers		EXPOSURES																			
		A	B	C	D	E	F	G	H	I	J	K	L	M	N	O	P	Q	R	S	T
Calculated Risk Score	Risk	4	3	3	4	3	3	3	3	2	3	3	3	3	3	2	3	3	3	4	3
Scale 4 (6 is most serious)	Type	6	5	5	6	4	4	5	6	2	4	4	5	5	3	5	4	4	4	6	5
Size (3 is maximum)	Size	3	2	2	3	3	3	2	2	3	3	2	2	2	3	1	2	3	3	3	2
CONTROLS	-																				
1 Acquisition and use of Personal Computers is related to Strategic Plan requirements	Best		5	3																	
	Test	?	?	?																	
	Both																				
2 Each business area has a plan for use of PCs in achieving business goals & objectives	Best		4																		
	Test	?	?																		
	Both																				
3 Preferred hardware platforms & software environments are defined in documented policy	Best			4																	
	Test	?		?																	
	Both																				
4 Only industry standard equipment is purchased	Best			4																	
	Test	?		?																	
	Both																				
5 Suitability of hardware & software is assessed by using established evaluation process	Best			3	3																
	Test	?		?	?																
	Both																				
6 Only established and proven software packages are obtained	Best				4																
	Test	?			?																
	Both																				
7 Equipment has to be compatible with existing systems and capable of upgrade	Best		3	4																	
	Test	?	?	?																	
	Both																				

Table 11.2   continued

			A	B	C	D	E	F	G	H	I	J	K	L	M	N	O	P	Q	R	S	T
8	System access controls are applied using user-ID and password	Best				4	4	4														
		Test	?			?	?	?														
		Both																				
-		-	-	-	-	-	-	-	-	-	-	-	-	-	-	-	-	-	-	-	-	-
9	Data owners define access rights and access system reflects these requirements	Best				4	4	4														
		Test	?			?	?	?														
		Both																				
-		-	-	-	-	-	-	-	-	-	-	-	-	-	-	-	-	-	-	-	-	-
10	Data back-up policy is in place - defines frequency, method of storage, labelling, etc.	Best				4															4	
		Test	?			?															?	
		Both																				
-		-	-	-	-	-	-	-	-	-	-	-	-	-	-	-	-	-	-	-	-	-
11	Critical data back-ups are stored off-site in the secure media library	Best				4															4	
		Test	?			?															?	
		Both																				
-		-	-	-	-	-	-	-	-	-	-	-	-	-	-	-	-	-	-	-	-	-
12	Contingency plan and measures are in place in the event of failure, etc.	Best				4															4	
		Test	?			?															?	
		Both																				
-		-	-	-	-	-	-	-	-	-	-	-	-	-	-	-	-	-	-	-	-	-
13	Unauthorised copying of data & software is prevented by control over accessing utilities	Best				3								4				4				
		Test	?			?								?				?				
		Both																				
-		-	-	-	-	-	-	-	-	-	-	-	-	-	-	-	-	-	-	-	-	-
14	Loading of unauthorised systems & data is prevented by locking the floppy disk drives	Best				3														4		
		Test	?			?														?		
		Both																				
-		-	-	-	-	-	-	-	-	-	-	-	-	-	-	-	-	-	-	-	-	-
15	Critical corporate data is only held on machines located in secure executive areas	Best					4															
		Test	?				?															
		Both																				
-		-	-	-	-	-	-	-	-	-	-	-	-	-	-	-	-	-	-	-	-	-
16	Access to data (15 above) is restricted to key staff only	Best					4															
		Test	?				?															
		Both																				
-		-	-	-	-	-	-	-	-	-	-	-	-	-	-	-	-	-	-	-	-	-
17	Unattended/dormant machines will automatically log-off or go into stand-by mode	Best						4														
		Test	?					?														
		Both																				
-		-	-	-	-	-	-	-	-	-	-	-	-	-	-	-	-	-	-	-	-	-
18	Suppliers are investigated as to their finanacial stability, reputation, etc.	Best							5													
		Test	?						?													
		Both																				
-		-	-	-	-	-	-	-	-	-	-	-	-	-	-	-	-	-	-	-	-	-
19	All requirements, including performance criteria, are assessed & matched to products	Best							4													
		Test	?						?													
		Both																				
-		-	-	-	-	-	-	-	-	-	-	-	-	-	-	-	-	-	-	-	-	-

Table 11.2   continued

			A	B	C	D	E	F	G	H	I	J	K	L	M	N	O	P	Q	R	S	T
	Upgrade path and costs are	Best								4												
20	fully assessed	Test	?							?												
		Both																				
-		-	-	-	-	-	-	-	-	-	-	-	-	-	-	-	-	-	-	-	-	-
	All hard and software is	Best								4												
21	registered, and non-removable	Test	?							?												
	inventory labels are attached	Both																				
-		-	-	-	-	-	-	-	-	-	-	-	-	-	-	-	-	-	-	-	-	-
	All equipment leaving the site	Best								4												
22	has to be supported by written	Test	?							?												
	authorisation	Both																				
-		-	-	-	-	-	-	-	-	-	-	-	-	-	-	-	-	-	-	-	-	-
	Procedures and policy defines	Best										4	3									
23	users responsibilities re	Test	?									?	?									
	security, use of PC, back-up	Both																				
-		-	-	-	-	-	-	-	-	-	-	-	-	-	-	-	-	-	-	-	-	-
	General & specific training	Best										4	3									
24	needs are identified and	Test	?									?	?									
	addressed	Both																				
-		-	-	-	-	-	-	-	-	-	-	-	-	-	-	-	-	-	-	-	-	-
	Data Protection guidelines	Best										2	2									
25	issued and data model has been	Test	?									?	?									
	examined by Compliance Officer	Both																				
-		-	-	-	-	-	-	-	-	-	-	-	-	-	-	-	-	-	-	-	-	-
	Processor cases are protected	Best								3										4		
26	by locks	Test	?							?										?		
		Both																				
-		-	-	-	-	-	-	-	-	-	-	-	-	-	-	-	-	-	-	-	-	-
	User Support staff are available	Best											4									
27	to provide assistance. User	Test	?										?									
	Group has been formed	Both																				
-		-	-	-	-	-	-	-	-	-	-	-	-	-	-	-	-	-	-	-	-	-
	Configuration file is protected	Best												4								
28	from casual access	Test	?											?								
		Both																				
-		-	-	-	-	-	-	-	-	-	-	-	-	-	-	-	-	-	-	-	-	-
	Potentially damaging utilities	Best												4								
29	are removed from hard disks	Test	?											?								
		Both																				
-		-	-	-	-	-	-	-	-	-	-	-	-	-	-	-	-	-	-	-	-	-
	Installation/configuration is	Best													4							
30	undertaken by experienced	Test	?												?							
	User Support staff	Both																				
-		-	-	-	-	-	-	-	-	-	-	-	-	-	-	-	-	-	-	-	-	-
	Environmental, safety and	Best													4							
31	security factors considered	Test	?												?							
	prior to installation	Both																				
-		-	-	-	-	-	-	-	-	-	-	-	-	-	-	-	-	-	-	-	-	-

Table 11.2   continued

#	Description	Type	A	B	C	D	E	F	G	H	I	J	K	L	M	N	O	P	Q	R	S	T
32	User Support periodically check that the configuration, etc. is correct	Best												4								
		Test	?											?								
		Both																				
-		-	-	-	-	-	-	-	-	-	-	-	-	-	-	-	-	-	-	-	-	-
33	Basic configuration & operating system environment is compatible throughout company	Best													4							
		Test	?												?							
		Both																				
-		-	-	-	-	-	-	-	-	-	-	-	-	-	-	-	-	-	-	-	-	-
34	Implementation impact is assessed and planned for	Best														5						
		Test	?													?						
		Both																				
-		-	-	-	-	-	-	-	-	-	-	-	-	-	-	-	-	-	-	-	-	-
35	Only approved/tested software updates are loaded by User Support staff	Best															4					
		Test	?														?					
		Both																				
-		-	-	-	-	-	-	-	-	-	-	-	-	-	-	-	-	-	-	-	-	-
36	Software disks are not left with users, but retained by User Support Dept.	Best																4				
		Test	?															?				
		Both																				
-		-	-	-	-	-	-	-	-	-	-	-	-	-	-	-	-	-	-	-	-	-
37	All media is checked for virus infection before use/update	Best																	4			
		Test	?																?			
		Both																				
-		-	-	-	-	-	-	-	-	-	-	-	-	-	-	-	-	-	-	-	-	-
38	All machines have resident virus checking software - Run automatically at power-up	Best																	4			
		Test	?																?			
		Both																				
-		-	-	-	-	-	-	-	-	-	-	-	-	-	-	-	-	-	-	-	-	-
39	All faults are reported to the Help Desk, registered and reacted to	Best																				4
		Test	?																			?
		Both																				
-		-	-	-	-	-	-	-	-	-	-	-	-	-	-	-	-	-	-	-	-	-
40	Supplier (on-site) maintenance agreements ensure same day service response	Best																				4
		Test	?																			?
		Both																				
-		-	-	-	-	-	-	-	-	-	-	-	-	-	-	-	-	-	-	-	-	-

A Failure to conform with Strategic Plan & company objectives
B Acquisition of incompatible or unreliable hardware
C Purchase and use of unproven or inappropriate software
D Loss or corruption of corporate data - disruption, etc.
E Leakage of confidential or sensitive data - business damaged
F Unauthorised access to systems/data - damage, fraud, etc.
G Dealing with unreliable/unstable supplier - lack of support
H Inadequate determination of requirements - failed objectives
I Loss, theft of/damage to hardware - costs,disruption, etc.
J Inadequate procedures and/or staff training - error, etc.

K Inadequate user support - error, misuse, inconsistent use
L Unauthorised access/use of system configuration/utilities
M Inadequate installation & configuration of hardware - error
N Failure to plan implementation & address all implications
O Incorrect/unauthorised loading of software upgrades
P Unauthorised copying of software/data - breach of licence
Q Infection of system with viruses - delay, disruption, etc.
R Tampering with hardware - failure, disruption, costs, delay
S Inability to recover from failure, disaster, etc.
T Failure to promptly deal with faults/problems - disruption

12

LOCAL AREA NETWORKS

Scope

This chapter covers the initial assessment of needs, the installation and ongoing secure operation of the network. Various types of network exist (e.g. LAN, WAN, VAN) each with a variety of possible topologies (Star, Bus and Ring). Although this text and the example matrices in Tables 12.1 and 12.2 concentrate upon Local Area Networks, the elements can be generally applied to other networking and communication situations.

The use of LANs can provide the platform to facilitate a number of business-related system solutions, for example Distributed Processing, the ability to let business information flow throughout the organisation, and the support of team-related activities such as sales. In this context the use of LAN structures and technology can directly contribute to the attainment of critical strategic or short-term business objectives.

LAN technologies have reached a point of stability and are well proven in practice. The process of establishing a LAN is now easily accomplished with virtually all the required components available off the shelf. There are a number of different standards with the limited potential for interconnection between them, however the remaining barriers to establishing relatively inexpensive LAN solutions are likely to be addressed as part of continuing product development. Local Area Networks operate around a File Server which hosts the necessary general and application software for use by those connected to the system, and also stores the user data for use in such applications. Typically, the terminals will contain their own processing ability and are now more likely to be personal computers with suitable LAN communication boards.

Local Area Networks normally operate over a restricted area either in isolation or in conjunction with other network systems. Gateways are devices which provide linkages between systems (i.e. from a LAN to a WAN). Bridges (combinations of hardware and software) enable the interconnection of networks (i.e. two LANs in separate parts of an office complex). A wide range of technical standards exist; some are based on international agreements, whereas others are unique to hardware vendors; due care needs to be exercised to ensure that interconnection is technically feasible and that an industry standard product is selected for use.

Unauthorised access to file servers, gateway PCs and the terminals used to back-up the system can be further prevented by locating such equipment in secure lockable areas; additionally the relevant keyboards can be disabled by locking when not in use.

Network systems and configurations vary considerably, and the technical issues can be relatively complex. Although we will avoid delving too deeply into the technicalities, the intentionally broad nature of the *Objectives* and *Exposures* provided in the example matrices (Tables 12.1 and 12.2) can be related to most network and communication situations. It is possible that, in a large organisation, there will be a number of different generic network types in use.

Personal Computers are increasingly being used as terminals on networks, especially as they have additional capabilities and are an equivalent price to dedicated terminals. If the network offers onward connection to a mainframe system, the personal computers may have to emulate the more traditional 'dumb' terminal. Using personal computers as mainframe links also enables data to be downloaded and manipulated, etc. on the PC.

The Network Planning process is crucial, not only in determining the current requirements, but in ensuring that the system is capable of future expansion and enhancement in line with operational needs. It will be necessary to undertake a comprehensive assessment of functional and operational requirements which can be used subsequently to match to suitable available network products. Assurances will need to be sought from either the network system supplier or the software developer that all the required software will operate satisfactorily on the proposed network system. Particular attention may need to be paid to the relative performance of application software in a network environment, especially where response times are critical in business operational terms.

As is the case with Personal Computers, the use of Local Area Networks offers greater accessibility to information and systems, but requires the deliberate curbing of this openness in order to ensure that corporate data and systems are protected from unauthorised access, alteration and leakage. The degree of control applied will need to be pitched at a level appropriate to the commercial value, sensitivity and confidentiality of the data concerned.

Access control systems can be incorporated into the LAN environment and support the structuring of directories, files, etc. into logical groups associated with legitimate users. The use of some form of user identity and password system can then reinforce these logical divisions ensuring that only authorised users are allowed to gain access to their systems. Clear lines of responsibility will have to be established for administrating access controls on the behalf of users. The person nominated for this task should only act, in the set-up, amendment or deletion of permitted users, on the direct instruction of the relevant departmental or section managers. These managers should ensure that the details of the current permitted users on the access system are correct. Particular network systems are provided with usage monitoring systems and it is possible to log selected unusual events for subsequent management review. (See Chapter 17 for more detail on administering and controlling access systems). If data is especially confidential or commercially sensitive, the use of encryption will need to be considered.

Network systems are normally supplied with a high level user access facility, usually referred to as the Supervisor. This type of facility affords access to the higher functions of the system which could, in the wrong hands, present the opportunity for either disruption or delay. Such facilities will need to be suitably protected, perhaps with two levels of password access control. Additionally, the use of these access routes will have to be strictly limited to nominated employees who possess the requisite knowledge and skills.

It is important to provide clear procedural instructions to LAN users, especially in respect of responsibilities for backing-up the system. A straightforward solution is to periodically dump the contents of the server to a tape streamer cartridge, but a more selective back-up approach may be more workable as it enables each user to secure the appropriate portions of their own data. Users will need to be made aware of the necessity to undertake back-ups at intervals which most logically match their operating needs. They should also be provided with guidance on the media storage considerations. The overall objective should be the protection of valuable data and the setting of back-up processes which enable either the individual departments or the company as a whole to continue operating their business systems in the event of a disaster or localised problems. (Also refer to Chapter 18 for other Back-up and Media Handling considerations).

It is probable that the availability of network systems will be critical to those business areas actively using the facilities, therefore it will be necessary to provide effective channels of communication whenever the system fails, and the means to generally ensure that the agreed levels of service availability are maintained. Maintenance and repairs will need to be promptly and efficiently carried out. (Chapter 23 contains greater detail of the requirements of a User Support service).

Given that the technical issues are relatively complex, it is necessary to ensure that adequately experienced technical and support staff are available so as to avoid the costly disruption caused by network faults and failures. The loading of approved software amendments and the changing of systems configuration should only be applied by such qualified staff in accord with either the prevailing company policy or the official updates issued by the appropriate suppliers.

Control matrix examples

As the application of LAN technologies has the potential to support strategic business initiatives, the matrices provided include both an *Objective* (Table 12.1) and *Exposure* (Table 12.2) oriented example. Both examples reflect a low to mid-range dependency upon LAN-based systems for illustrative purposes. The *Objective* example uses *Scale* 2 and the *Exposure* matrix utilises *Scale* 4; these are both described in Appendix 5.

Table 12.1   Local Area Networks - Objectives

Overall Inherent Risk (Size) Score [5 is worst risk; 1 is best] = 2.47

A Ensure full assessment of Network/Communication requirement
B Ensure LAN installations and implementations are planned
C Ensure installation is capable of future expansion
D Ensure availability/reliability of network services
E Ensure that repairs and necessary maintenance are effective
F Prevent unauthorised access to network facilities
G Prevent unauthorised access to, or leakage of, user data

H Protect the integrity of network system software
I Provide secure locations for file servers, gateway PC, etc.
J Ensure controlled use of Supervisor & high-level facilities
K Provide monitoring facilities & detection of unusual events
L Provide experienced staff for network management
M Provide adequate user support
N Ensure external access to the network is limited/controlled
O Provide adequate & effective contingency and recovery plans

Local Area Networks		OBJECTIVES														
		A	B	C	D	E	F	G	H	I	J	K	L	M	N	O
		=	=	=	=	=	=	=	=	=	=	=	=	=	=	=
Calculated Risk Score	Risk	3	2	2	3	3	3	3	3	2	3	2	2	3	3	3
Scale 2 (6 is most serious)	Type	5	3	5	6	5	5	5	5	4	5	4	3	3	4	6
Size (3 is maximum)	Size	2	2	1	2	2	2	2	2	2	1	2	2	2	2	2
MEASURES																
1 Assessment of current and future requirements was undertaken as part of Strategic Planning	Best		5		4											
	Test	?	?		?											
	Both															
2 Network Controller co-ordinates installations, including cabling, configuration, tests, etc.	Best			4												
	Test	?		?												
	Both															
3 Most installations/major changes are carried out over weekends to minimise disruption, etc.	Best			2												
	Test	?		?												
	Both															
4 Industry standard hardware and software is used	Best			4	4											
	Test	?		?	?											
	Both															
5 Faults are reported to Help Desk with same-day response or escalation as appropriate	Best				5	5										
	Test	?			?	?										
	Both															
6 System availability and performance is monitored and managed	Best				3											
	Test	?			?											
	Both															
7 User-id and password system in place, including minimum length and enforced password changes	Best						4	4	4							
	Test	?					?	?	?							
	Both															

Table 12.1 continued

			A	B	C	D	E	F	G	H	I	J	K	L	M	N	O
8	Automatic log-off of PC if left unattended/dormant for more than ten minutes	Best						4	4								
		Test	?					?	?								
		Both															
-		-	-	-	-	-	-	-	-	-	-	-	-	-	-	-	-
9	User access is further restricted to relevant user applications and data	Best						4	4								
		Test	?					?	?								
		Both															
-		-	-	-	-	-	-	-	-	-	-	-	-	-	-	-	-
10	Access system is maintained by the Network Support Manager	Best						3	3	3							
		Test	?					?	?	?							
		Both															
-		-	-	-	-	-	-	-	-	-	-	-	-	-	-	-	-
11	Network software is only accessible via 'Supervisor' high-level user-ID & password	Best								5							
		Test	?							?							
		Both															
-		-	-	-	-	-	-	-	-	-	-	-	-	-	-	-	-
12	Only approved & tested network software updates are applied by the network support staff	Best								4							
		Test	?							?							
		Both															
-		-	-	-	-	-	-	-	-	-	-	-	-	-	-	-	-
13	File servers, gateway PCs & PCs used for overnight back-up are located in lockable areas	Best									4						
		Test	?								?						
		Both															
-		-	-	-	-	-	-	-	-	-	-	-	-	-	-	-	-
14	File Server keyboards are disabled by locks	Best									4						
		Test	?								?						
		Both															
-		-	-	-	-	-	-	-	-	-	-	-	-	-	-	-	-
15	'Supervisor' high-level user access is subject to enhanced access control	Best									4	5					
		Test	?								?	?					
		Both															
-		-	-	-	-	-	-	-	-	-	-	-	-	-	-	-	-
16	All events are logged, and pre-defined 'unusual' events are reported to Network Controller	Best											5				
		Test	?										?				
		Both															
-		-	-	-	-	-	-	-	-	-	-	-	-	-	-	-	-
17	System prevents users from logging-on to more than one terminal at the same time	Best						3	3				3				
		Test	?					?	?				?				
		Both															
-		-	-	-	-	-	-	-	-	-	-	-	-	-	-	-	-
18	Suitably experienced staff are provided in the Network Support Group	Best												4	4		
		Test	?											?	?		
		Both															
-		-	-	-	-	-	-	-	-	-	-	-	-	-	-	-	-
19	User manual and quick reference guides are available	Best													4		
		Test	?												?		
		Both															
-		-	-	-	-	-	-	-	-	-	-	-	-	-	-	-	-

Table 12.1 continued

			A	B	C	D	E	F	G	H	I	J	K	L	M	N	O
	Dial-up services are restricted	Best														5	
20	with additional authentication	Test	?													?	
	processes	Both															
-		-	-	-	-	-	-	-	-	-	-	-	-	-	-	-	-
	Network operations are included	Best															4
21	in the agreed Disaster and	Test	?														?
	Contingency Plan	Both															
-		-	-	-	-	-	-	-	-	-	-	-	-	-	-	-	-
	Alternative message routing is	Best															4
22	built into the central network	Test	?														?
		Both															
-		-	-	-	-	-	-	-	-	-	-	-	-	-	-	-	-
	Critical applications can resort	Best															4
23	to using off-line processing or	Test	?														?
	magnetic media transfer of data	Both															
-		-	-	-	-	-	-	-	-	-	-	-	-	-	-	-	-
	Data is backed-up on a daily	Best															4
24	basis. Complete system dump once	Test	?														?
	a week.	Both															
-		-	-	-	-	-	-	-	-	-	-	-	-	-	-	-	-

A Ensure full assessment of Network/Communication requirement

B Ensure LAN installations and implementations are planned

C Ensure installation is capable of future expansion

D Ensure availability/reliability of network services

E Ensure that repairs and necessary maintenance are effective

F Prevent unauthorised access to network facilities

G Prevent unauthorised access to, or leakage of, user data

H Protect the integrity of network system software

I Provide secure locations for file servers, gateway PC, etc.

J Ensure controlled use of Supervisor & high-level facilities

K Provide monitoring facilities & detection of unusual events

L Provide experienced staff for network management

M Provide adequate user support

N Ensure external access to the network is limited/controlled

O Provide adequate & effective contingency and recovery plans

Table 12.2 Local Area Networks - Exposures
Overall Inherent Risk (Size) Score [5 is worst risk; 1 is best = 2.26

A Inadequate assessment of network requirements - disruption
B Disruption, etc. due to poorly planned network installations
C Failure to adequately test network before live use - delay
D Failure to ensure future expansion capabilities - delay, etc.
E Disruption, etc. due to unreliable hardware and software
F Failure to achieve required service availability levels
G Failure to promptly & effectively resolve faults - delay, etc.
H Inadequate maintenance - disruption, loss of business, costs
I Unauthorised access to network - error, fraud, loss, etc.
J Unauthorised access to, or use of, data - error, leakage, etc

K Unauthorised access to, or amendment of, network software
L Unrestricted access to file servers, gateway PCs, etc.
M Access to 'Supervisor' facilities & utilities - disruption
N Failure to monitor & detect unusual events, etc. - error, etc
O Inadequate in-house experience of networks - delay, costs
P Failure to manage networks, handle changes, etc. - delay, etc
Q Inadequate user support - error, delay, disruption, etc.
R Uncontrolled external access to network facilities
S Inadequate contingency & recovery plans - business failure

Local Area Networks		EXPOSURES																		
		—	—	—	—	—	—	—	—	—	—	—	—	—	—	—	—	—	—	—
		A	B	C	D	E	F	G	H	I	J	K	L	M	N	O	P	Q	R	S
		=	=	=	=	=	=	=	=	=	=	=	=	=	=	=	=	=	=	=
Calculated Risk Score	Risk	2	2	3	2	3	2	2	2	3	3	3	3	3	3	2	2	2	3	3
		-	-	-	-	-	-	-	-	-	-	-	-	-	-	-	-	-	-	-
Scale 4 (6 is most serious)	Type	6	3	5	6	5	5	5	3	4	4	5	5	4	4	3	5	3	4	6
Size (3 is maximum)	Size	1	2	2	1	2	1	1	2	2	2	2	2	2	2	2	1	2	2	2
CONTROLS	-	-	-	-	-	-	-	-	-	-	-	-	-	-	-	-	-	-	-	-
Assessment of current and future	Best		5			5														
1 requirements was undertaken as	Test	?	?			?														
part of Strategic Planning	Both																			
-	-	-	-	-	-	-	-	-	-	-	-	-	-	-	-	-	-	-	-	-
Network Controller co-ordinates	Best			4																
2 installations, including cabling,	Test	?		?																
configuration, tests, etc.	Both																			
-	-	-	-	-	-	-	-	-	-	-	-	-	-	-	-	-	-	-	-	-
Network is subject to full	Best			5																
3 testing by Network Support	Test	?		?																
before live use	Both																			
-	-	-	-	-	-	-	-	-	-	-	-	-	-	-	-	-	-	-	-	-
Most installations/major changes	Best			3																
4 are carried out over weekends	Test	?		?																
to minimise disruption, etc.	Both																			
-	-	-	-	-	-	-	-	-	-	-	-	-	-	-	-	-	-	-	-	-
Industry standard hardware and	Best					4	3													
5 software is used	Test	?				?	?													
	Both																			
-	-	-	-	-	-	-	-	-	-	-	-	-	-	-	-	-	-	-	-	-
Faults are reported to Help Desk	Best					4	4													
6 with same-day response or	Test	?				?	?													
escalation as appropriate	Both																			
-	-	-	-	-	-	-	-	-	-	-	-	-	-	-	-	-	-	-	-	-
System availability and	Best					3	2													
7 performance is monitored and	Test	?				?	?													
managed	Both																			
-	-	-	-	-	-	-	-	-	-	-	-	-	-	-	-	-	-	-	-	-

Table 12.2   continued

			A	B	C	D	E	F	G	H	I	J	K	L	M	N	O	P	Q	R	S
8	Maintenance contract established with hardware supplier	Best								4											
		Test	?							?											
		Both																			
-		-	-	-	-	-	-	-	-	-	-	-	-	-	-	-	-	-	-	-	-
9	User-id and password system in place, including minimum length and enforced password changes	Best									4	4	4								
		Test	?								?	?	?								
		Both																			
-		-	-	-	-	-	-	-	-	-	-	-	-	-	-	-	-	-	-	-	-
10	Automatic log-off of PC if left unattended/dormant for more than ten minutes	Best									3	3									
		Test	?								?	?									
		Both																			
-		-	-	-	-	-	-	-	-	-	-	-	-	-	-	-	-	-	-	-	-
11	User access is further restricted to relevant user applications and data	Best										4									
		Test	?									?									
		Both																			
-		-	-	-	-	-	-	-	-	-	-	-	-	-	-	-	-	-	-	-	-
12	Access system is maintained by the Network Support Manager	Best									3	3	3								
		Test	?								?	?	?								
		Both																			
-		-	-	-	-	-	-	-	-	-	-	-	-	-	-	-	-	-	-	-	-
13	Network software is only accessible via 'Supervisor' high-level user-ID & password	Best											5								
		Test	?										?								
		Both																			
-		-	-	-	-	-	-	-	-	-	-	-	-	-	-	-	-	-	-	-	-
14	Only approved & tested network software updates are applied by the network support staff	Best											4								
		Test	?										?								
		Both																			
-		-	-	-	-	-	-	-	-	-	-	-	-	-	-	-	-	-	-	-	-
15	File servers, gateway PCs & PCs used for overnight back-up are located in lockable areas	Best												5							
		Test	?											?							
		Both																			
-		-	-	-	-	-	-	-	-	-	-	-	-	-	-	-	-	-	-	-	-
16	File Server keyboards are disabled by locks	Best												4							
		Test	?											?							
		Both																			
-		-	-	-	-	-	-	-	-	-	-	-	-	-	-	-	-	-	-	-	-
17	'Supervisor' high-level user access is subject to enhanced access control	Best											4		5						
		Test	?										?		?						
		Both																			
-		-	-	-	-	-	-	-	-	-	-	-	-	-	-	-	-	-	-	-	-
18	All events are logged, and pre-defined 'unusual' events are reported to Network Controller	Best														3					
		Test	?													?					
		Both																			
-		-	-	-	-	-	-	-	-	-	-	-	-	-	-	-	-	-	-	-	-
19	System prevents users from logging-on to more than one terminal at the same time	Best									3	3									
		Test	?								?	?									
		Both																			
-		-	-	-	-	-	-	-	-	-	-	-	-	-	-	-	-	-	-	-	-

Table 12.2 continued

			A	B	C	D	E	F	G	H	I	J	K	L	M	N	O	P	Q	R	S
20	Suitably experienced staff are provided in the Network Support Group	Best															4		4		
		Test	?														?		?		
		Both																			
-	-	-	-	-	-	-	-	-	-	-	-	-	-	-	-	-	-	-	-	-	-
21	User manual and quick reference guides are available	Best																	4		
		Test	?																?		
		Both																			
-	-	-	-	-	-	-	-	-	-	-	-	-	-	-	-	-	-	-	-	-	-
22	Day-to-day network management is handled by network support team per agreed procedures	Best																5			
		Test	?															?			
		Both																			
-	-	-	-	-	-	-	-	-	-	-	-	-	-	-	-	-	-	-	-	-	-
23	Dial-up services are restricted with additional authentication processes	Best																		4	
		Test	?																	?	
		Both																			
-	-	-	-	-	-	-	-	-	-	-	-	-	-	-	-	-	-	-	-	-	-
24	Network operations are included in the agreed Disaster and Contingency Plan	Best																			4
		Test	?																		?
		Both																			
-	-	-	-	-	-	-	-	-	-	-	-	-	-	-	-	-	-	-	-	-	-
25	Alternative message routing is built into the central network	Best																			4
		Test	?																		?
		Both																			
-	-	-	-	-	-	-	-	-	-	-	-	-	-	-	-	-	-	-	-	-	-
26	Critical applications can resort to using off-line processing or magnetic media transfer of data	Best																			3
		Test	?																		?
		Both																			
-	-	-	-	-	-	-	-	-	-	-	-	-	-	-	-	-	-	-	-	-	-
27	Data is backed-up on a daily basis. Complete system dump once a week.	Best																			4
		Test	?																		?
		Both																			
-	-	-	-	-	-	-	-	-	-	-	-	-	-	-	-	-	-	-	-	-	-

A Inadequate assessment of network requirements - disruption

B Disruption, etc. due to poorly planned network installations

C Failure to adequately test network before live use - delay

D Failure to ensure future expansion capabilities - delay, etc.

E Disruption, etc. due to unreliable hardware and software

F Failure to achieve required service availability levels

G Failure to promptly & effectively resolve faults - delay, etc.

H Inadequate maintenance - disruption, loss of business,costs

I Unauthorised access to network - error, fraud, loss, etc.

J Unauthorised access to, or use of, data - error, leakage, etc

K Unauthorised access to, or amendment of, network software

L Unrestricted access to file servers, gateway PCs, etc.

M Access to 'Supervisor' facilities & utilities - disruption

N Failure to monitor & detect unusual events, etc. - error, etc

O Inadequate in-house experience of networks - delay, costs

P Failure to manage networks, handle changes, etc. - delay, etc

Q Inadequate user support - error, delay, disruption, etc.

R Uncontrolled external access to network facilities

S Inadequate contingency & recovery plans - business failure

13

ELECTRONIC OFFICE

Scope

The provision of an integrated series of general office applications can aid staff in the efficient preparation of information in accordance with company-wide requirements which, in turn, facilitates the communication of that information throughout the company.

The term 'Electronic Office' used in this section relates to the provision of software and the supporting environment to cover any combination of the following functions:

- *word processing*

- *spreadsheets*

- *database system*

- *electronic mail*

- *accounting packages*

- *PC to mainframe links (i.e. for interrogation purposes)*

- *facsimile and/or Telex*

- *inter-department/function communications*

- *Desk Top Publishing (DTP)*

- *time planning/management or organiser systems*

- *project management systems*

- *data extraction and analysis systems*

- *decision support systems*

- *graphical or presentation systems*

- *design support tools.*

It is not our intention to examine in detail either the functionality or the issues for each of the above noted areas, but to consider the broader issues applicable to the introduction of the encompassing framework.

This chapter examines the determination of required facilities, the identification of suitable software, implementing selected facilities, provision of adequate staff training, ensuring controlled use of facilities, and monitoring the benefits.

The files are deliberately biased towards the applications supporting the concept of the electronic office, and although reference is made to broader issues, such as Personal Computer security and good practices, the detailed implications of these related matters are more specifically addressed in other chapters (i.e. Chapter 11 – Personal Computers and Workstations, Chapter 12 – Local Area Networks, Chapter 17 – System Access Control, Chapter 22 – Software Package Selection, and Chapter 27 – Data Protection Act).

Information is the lifeblood of most companies, and this needs to be current, accurate and capable of analysis and circulation. Staff at all levels of the organisation will require the means to create, edit, interpret, manipulate, and distribute the information relevant to their sphere of operation. Some of this data will be commercially sensitive or confidential and therefore suitable security measures will need to be established to protect it.

The electronic office concept aims to support the whole information process and provide other general facilities to aid day-to-day efficiency in the support of office and business activity-related tasks. Some aspects of this approach can be free-standing, while for others it is essential that there is the ability to freely transfer data between users in different areas and between application systems. In the case of data transfer between users, some form of communication facilities is required, for example Electronic Mail or other network-based file transfer systems.

The introduction of the electronic office concept can be related to a wider strategic move, in that it can provide for the prompt flow of data throughout the organisation in support of a specific business operation, but the main benefits will be related to improved staff efficiency, although this can also be a factor in the general achievement of business objectives. In environments where the quality of service is a key factor the provision of these facilities may provide direct support for the achievement of prompt turnround and response requirements.

There is a proliferation of general office software (for example spreadsheets and word processors) which now facilitate the movement of data between such applications, so that financial analysis data from the spreadsheet can be incorporated into a board report prepared using the word processor. If the company utilises industry standard products the transfer and movement of business data can be simply achieved. However, this open approach does raise questions about the security measures required to prevent data falling into the wrong hands and the means of ensuring that data retains its integrity and accuracy.

An initial step in acquiring and introducing an integrated environment would be to accurately and realistically assess the functional requirements of those products identified as necessary for the particular corporate situation. There could be a combination of general facilities (such as electronic mail) and more specialised applications (such as computer aided design). The normal rules of project justification should be applied to all these elements and their acquisition should fulfil a proven need. There has to be more to this process than merely providing the latest software toys and projecting an up-to-date image to the world at large.

If the company has a preferred hardware platform policy, the introduction of an electronic office approach will have to be reviewed in relation to that policy and take into account the specific requirements of each software package (i.e. in terms of memory requirements, minimum processor type, etc.)

The assessment of software packages is specifically addressed in Chapter 22, but it will normally be necessary to undertake a full evaluation of software facilities against the identified functional requirements. The issue of inter-connectivity of individual applications will have to be addressed if this type of functionality is both required and justified. Allowance should also have been made in the requirements specification for predicted future workloads, and particular attention should be paid to assessing the ability of software to cope with the identified demands. As part of the assessment of software packages, the reliability of the supplier will have to be taken into account together with the suitability of the defined upgrade path of the application(s). Costings for the acquisition of the software will need to incorporate the future upgrade and ongoing product support costs.

Staff or officers responsible for data security matters should be consulted and their advice sought on providing suitable and workable structures to retain control over data and system access, etc. The misuse of such facilities can be minimised by the application of such access controls and the general encouragement of good practices. Having researched and justified the project, the chosen applications should feature on the official company approved software list, which may be the subject of a preferred product policy against which all procurement will be subsequently matched. The establishment of such a policy can prevent the acquisition of unsuitable software which is incapable of successfully interfacing with the products already in place. Additionally, the policy can also act as the foundation for ensuring that no other products are held on company hardware, which simplifies the task of verifying the software present on computers. It is essential to assess the level of existing internal expertise in relation to the chosen product base, in order to ensure that the necessary training is provided in good time to enable the successful implementation of the integrated environment. The quality of application documentation should have been assessed as part of the initial product review process, but this may have to be augmented by the provision and application of localised procedures designed to enhance either the security of operations or the ease of usage. Points of reference will need to established so that new and existing users can obtain suitable support and guidance; some form of user support function may be relevant in larger organisations (See Chapter 23). It may be necessary to ensure that all the relevant applications are configured in a standard way as a means of ensuring the consistent use of the systems throughout the organisation.

Management will have to ensure that there are mechanisms and practices in place which encourage and support the considered use of these facilities and the maintenance of accurate and secure source data. The speed at which new forms of data can be created and presented may be outweighed by the fact that the data is inaccurate and therefore quite useless.

In order to protect ongoing operations, procedures defining data back-up and media-handling processes should be introduced (see Chapter 18). Following the implementation of this type of facility, it can be useful to canvass the opinion of users as a means of gauging such factors as the level of use of the systems, any particular common problems which may need to be addressed, the quality of support available, etc. There is a case, in larger installations, for the creation of a User Group which, through the medium of informal meetings, can discuss and hopefully resolve common problems; such groups can also provide a platform for the organisation to introduce concepts of good practice for application throughout the company.

Control matrix examples

If general efficiency and the easy manipulation of data are significant elements in the support of both general and specific business tasks, this process can have a notable impact upon the achievement of business objectives. For this reason we have supplied two example matrices, one each for *Objectives* and *Exposures* (See Tables 13.1 and 13.2). The *Objective* example makes use of *Scale* 6 as this can more readily reflect the relevance of information in the achievement of corporate objectives. *Scale* 4 is used in support of the *Exposure* example matrix (Table 13.2). Full details of the narratives for all *Scales* are contained in Appendix 5. The example values for *Type* and *Size* data are set between low and middle range levels.

Table 13.1   Electronic Office - Objectives

Overall Inherent Risk (Size) Score [5 is worst risk; 1 is best] = 2.20

A Improve efficiency & consistency of office/support tasks
B Enable the transfer & movement of data throughout company
C Ensure accurate assessment/justification of requirements
D Assess and monitor the benefits to be derived
E Fully evaluate quality & reliability of software/suppliers
F Match the functionality to the identified requirements
G Establish a policy for the purchasing of approved products
H Ensure software relates to the preferred hardware platform

I Adequately plan the implementation of software
J Provide relevant levels of training & in-house expertise
K Ensure compliance with software licence conditions
L Provide adequate procedural, technical & documentary
    support
M Ensure adequacy of product support and upgrade policy
N Ensure that software is consistently configured and used
O Prevent the abuse of software

	Electronic Office		OBJECTIVES														
			A	B	C	D	E	F	G	H	I	J	K	L	M	N	O
			=	=	=	=	=	=	=	=	=	=	=	=	=	=	=
	Calculated Risk Score	Risk	3	3	3	2	3	3	3	3	2	3	2	3	2	3	3
	Scale 6 (6 is most serious)	Type	5	5	5	3	4	5	4	4	5	4	3	4	5	4	4
	Size (3 is maximum)	Size	2	2	2	2	2	2	2	2	1	2	1	2	1	2	2
	MEASURES	-	-	-	-	-	-	-	-	-	-	-	-	-	-	-	-
	Review undertaken of present	Best		4		3											
1	arrangements and necessary	Test	?	?		?											
	changes recommended	Both															
-		-	-	-	-	-	-	-	-	-	-	-	-	-	-	-	-
	Identified the core functional	Best		4	4	3											
2	requirements to meet current	Test	?	?	?	?											
	and mid-term objectives	Both															
-		-	-	-	-	-	-	-	-	-	-	-	-	-	-	-	-
	Plan in place to achieve common	Best		4	5					5							
3	hardware and software usage at	Test	?	?	?					?							
	principal sites	Both															
-		-	-	-	-	-	-	-	-	-	-	-	-	-	-	-	-
	Cost/benefit justification	Best				4	3										
4	report produced for overall	Test	?			?	?										
	project - Agreed by Board	Both															
-		-	-	-	-	-	-	-	-	-	-	-	-	-	-	-	-
	Performance and cost monitoring	Best				3											
5	in place as part of MIS -	Test	?			?											
	Project costs monitored	Both															
-		-	-	-	-	-	-	-	-	-	-	-	-	-	-	-	-
	Prevailing Package Selection	Best					4	5	2						3		
6	Methodology applied to all	Test	?				?	?	?						?		
	software purchases	Both															
-		-	-	-	-	-	-	-	-	-	-	-	-	-	-	-	-
	Existing users contacted and	Best					4								4		
7	opinions obtained re quality	Test	?				?								?		
	of service, support, etc.	Both															
-		-	-	-	-	-	-	-	-	-	-	-	-	-	-	-	-

Table 13.1 continued

#	Description	Type	A	B	C	D	E	F	G	H	I	J	K	L	M	N	O
8	All purchasing is related to an established register of approved products	Best							5								
		Test	?						?								
		Both															
-		-	-	-	-	-	-	-	-	-	-	-	-	-	-	-	-
9	Strategic Plan defines the preferred hardware platform	Best							4								
		Test	?						?								
		Both															
-		-	-	-	-	-	-	-	-	-	-	-	-	-	-	-	-
10	Roll-out of software is planned and undertaken by the User Support team	Best								5				3		4	3
		Test	?							?				?		?	?
		Both															
-		-	-	-	-	-	-	-	-	-	-	-	-	-	-	-	-
11	In-house training is provided for key users	Best										4					
		Test	?									?					
		Both															
-		-	-	-	-	-	-	-	-	-	-	-	-	-	-	-	-
12	User Support staff attend relative supplier training sessions	Best										4	4				
		Test	?									?	?				
		Both															
-		-	-	-	-	-	-	-	-	-	-	-	-	-	-	-	-
13	Multi-user/multi-site licences obtained for all software	Best										3					
		Test	?									?					
		Both															
-		-	-	-	-	-	-	-	-	-	-	-	-	-	-	-	-
14	Register is maintained of software copies/versions for each personal computer (per ID)	Best										3					
		Test	?									?					
		Both															
-		-	-	-	-	-	-	-	-	-	-	-	-	-	-	-	-
15	Register at 14 above is verified periodically by User Support	Best										4				3	4
		Test	?									?				?	?
		Both															
-		-	-	-	-	-	-	-	-	-	-	-	-	-	-	-	-
16	User manuals are obtained and distributed	Best											4				
		Test	?										?				
		Both															
-		-	-	-	-	-	-	-	-	-	-	-	-	-	-	-	-
17	Help Desk/User Support provide telephone enquiry service to users	Best											4				
		Test	?										?				
		Both															
-		-	-	-	-	-	-	-	-	-	-	-	-	-	-	-	-

Table 13.1   continued

			A	B	C	D	E	F	G	H	I	J	K	L	M	N	O
18	Software upgrades obtained and applied by User Support	Best													4		
		Test	?												?		
		Both															
-		-	-	-	-	-	-	-	-	-	-	-	-	-	-	-	-
19	Original software diskettes are held by User Support	Best															4
		Test	?														?
		Both															
-		-	-	-	-	-	-	-	-	-	-	-	-	-	-	-	-

A Improve efficiency & consistency of office/support tasks
B Enable the transfer & movement of data throughout company
C Ensure accurate assessment/justification of requirements
D Assess and monitor the benefits to be derived
E Fully evaluate quality & reliability of software/suppliers
F Match the functionality to the identified requirements
G Establish a policy for the purchasing of approved products
H Ensure software relates to the preferred hardware platform

I Adequately plan the implementation of software
J Provide relevant levels of training & in-house expertise
K Ensure compliance with software licence conditions
L Provide adequate procedural, technical & documentary
   support
M Ensure adequacy of product support and upgrade policy
N Ensure that software is consistently configured and used
O Prevent the abuse of software

Table 13.2 Electronic Office - Exposures

Overall Inherent Risk (Size) Score [5 is worst risk; 1 is best] = 2.06

A Failure to achieve inter-site compatibility & data movement
B Inaccurate assessment of software requirements - cost, error
C Inaccurate assessment of costs & other impacts - delay, etc.
D Failure to accurately assess true benefits of requirements
E Purchase of unsuitable, poor quality software - delay, cost
F Failure to confirm acceptability or reliability of supplier
G Failure to match functionality to requirements - delay, cost
H Absence of approved product policy - inadequate or costly s/w

I Failure to ensure compatibility with preferred hardware
J Incorrect loading/configuration of software - error, etc.
K Uncontrolled roll-out/installation of software - misuse
L Inadequate training provision - error, time wastage, costs
M Absence of in-house expertise - delay, cost, error, etc.
N Failure to comply with software licence - support withdrawn
O Absence of manuals, procedures - delay, error, time wastage
P Product poorly supported or upgrades not applied
Q Software illegally copied by users - licence invalidation

#	Electronic Office	EXPOSURES		A	B	C	D	E	F	G	H	I	J	K	L	M	N	O	P	Q
			=	=	=	=	=	=	=	=	=	=	=	=	=	=	=	=	=	=
	Calculated Risk Score	Risk		2	3	2	2	3	3	3	3	2	2	2	2	2	2	2	3	2
	Scale 4 (6 is most serious)	Type		6	6	2	3	6	5	5	4	3	3	3	3	3	2	3	4	1
	Size (3 is maximum)	Size		1	2	2	2	2	2	2	2	2	2	2	2	2	1	2	2	1
	CONTROLS																			
1	Review undertaken of present arrangements and necessary changes recommended	Best		4	4															
		Test	?	?	?															
		Both																		
2	Identified the core functional requirements to meet current and mid-term objectives	Best		4	4			2												
		Test	?	?	?			?												
		Both																		
3	Plan in place to achieve common hardware and software usage at principal sites	Best		4	4							4								
		Test	?	?								?								
		Both																		
4	Cost/benefit justification report produced for overall project - Agreed by Board	Best					4	4												
		Test	?				?	?												
		Both																		
5	Performance and cost monitoring in place as part of MIS - Project costs monitored	Best					3													
		Test	?				?													
		Both																		
6	Prevailing Package Selection Methodology applied to all software purchases	Best		3	3	3	3	5	4	4		3								
		Test	?	?	?	?	?	?	?	?		?								
		Both																		
7	Existing users contacted and opinions obtained re quality of service, support, etc.	Best						4											3	
		Test	?					?											?	
		Both																		

Table 13.2 continued

			A	B	C	D	E	F	G	H	I	J	K	L	M	N	O	P	Q
8	All purchasing is related to an established register of approved products	Best								5									
		Test	?							?									
		Both																	
-		-	-	-	-	-	-	-	-	-	-	-	-	-	-	-	-	-	-
9	Strategic Plan defines the preferred hardware platform	Best								5									
		Test	?							?									
		Both																	
-		-	-	-	-	-	-	-	-	-	-	-	-	-	-	-	-	-	-
10	Roll-out of software is planned and undertaken by the User Support team	Best										5	5						
		Test	?									?	?						
		Both																	
-		-	-	-	-	-	-	-	-	-	-	-	-	-	-	-	-	-	-
11	In-house training is provided for key users	Best													4				
		Test	?												?				
		Both																	
-		-	-	-	-	-	-	-	-	-	-	-	-	-	-	-	-	-	-
12	User Support staff attend relative supplier training sessions	Best													4				
		Test	?												?				
		Both																	
-		-	-	-	-	-	-	-	-	-	-	-	-	-	-	-	-	-	-
13	Multi-user/multi-site software licences obtained for all software	Best													3				
		Test	?												?				
		Both																	
-		-	-	-	-	-	-	-	-	-	-	-	-	-	-	-	-	-	-
14	Register is maintained of software copies/versions for each personal computer (per ID)	Best													3				
		Test	?												?				
		Both																	
-		-	-	-	-	-	-	-	-	-	-	-	-	-	-	-	-	-	-
15	Register at 14 above is verified periodically by User Support	Best										3			4				
		Test	?									?			?				
		Both																	
-		-	-	-	-	-	-	-	-	-	-	-	-	-	-	-	-	-	-
16	User manuals are obtained and distributed	Best															5		
		Test	?														?		
		Both																	
-		-	-	-	-	-	-	-	-	-	-	-	-	-	-	-	-	-	-
17	Help Desk/User Support provide telephone enquiry service to users	Best															4		
		Test	?														?		
		Both																	
-		-	-	-	-	-	-	-	-	-	-	-	-	-	-	-	-	-	-
18	Software upgrades obtained and applied by User Support	Best															4		
		Test	?														?		
		Both																	
-		-	-	-	-	-	-	-	-	-	-	-	-	-	-	-	-	-	-
19	Original software diskettes are held by User Support	Best																	4
		Test	?																?
		Both																	
-		-	-	-	-	-	-	-	-	-	-	-	-	-	-	-	-	-	-

Table 13.2   continued

A Failure to achieve inter-site compatibility & data movement
B Inaccurate assessment of software requirements - cost, error
C Inaccurate assessment of costs & other impacts - delay, etc.
D Failure to accurately assess true benefits of requirements
E Purchase of unsuitable, poor quality software - delay, cost
F Failure to confirm acceptability or reliability of supplier
G Failure to match functionality to requirements - delay, cost
H Absence of approved product policy - inadequate or costly s/w

I Failure to ensure compatibility with preferred hardware
J Incorrect loading/configuration of software - error, etc.
K Uncontrolled roll-out/installation of software - misuse
L Inadequate training provision - error, time wastage, costs
M Absence of in-house expertise - delay, cost, error, etc.
N Failure to comply with software licence - support withdrawn
O Absence of manuals, procedures - delay, error, time wastage
P Product poorly supported or upgrades not applied
Q Software illegally copied by users - licence invalidation

14

EXPERT SYSTEMS

Scope

This chapter incorporates a review of the benefits of using Expert Systems, the selection of the relevant shell software, the gathering of accurate knowledge data, the construction of the system, testing, implementation, and appraisal of benefits achieved.

Expert Systems can be described as mechanisms capable of making judgements on subjects normally handled by specialists. They are normally made up of two main components.

- A Knowledge Base;

- A Set of Rules (or Heuristics), applied to the knowledge base and used to reach conclusions.

The eventual user normally has to either supply some key factors (such as location of pain and other symptoms for a medical diagnostic system), or follow a menu structure, or respond to questions until he/she reaches the precise situation or applicable condition. The relevant information or conclusion can then be supplied in the appropriate form.

Expert Systems are a type of Knowledge-Based System, and have been developed to provide general support for a variety of professional and specialist functions, such as:

- medical systems

- investment management

- insurance underwriting

- scientific

- Data Protection Act compliance.

Their use can be theoretically applied to any complex technical or specialist area. In organisations dependent to any significant degree upon some form of specialist or precise knowledge, the use of expert systems to supplant the use of skilled staff can have a strategic bearing. There could be a resultant reduction in the staffing of specialist areas or transversely a dispersion of expert knowledge to a wider range of users. This latter situation could, for example, have a direct effect upon the ability to cope with customer enquiries or the provision of a better quality service without the costly reliance upon knowledgeable staff who attract high salaries.

Although suppliers of knowledge-based and expert systems will normally provide a full design and development consultancy service, some systems are provided as a 'shell' which enables users to gather, record and structure their own relevant data, and develop the associated rules. The choice of the method most appropriate for a given organisation will be partially dependent upon the nature of the target expertise, the degree of familiarity required of the expert system shell, and whether the company is willing to travel the necessary learning curve. The construction of an effective and serviceable expert system may, in itself, generate the need to employ specialist help in the form of consultants. Among the benefits claimed for such systems are:

- reducing costs of consulting or employing relevant qualified persons

- spreading the relevant specialist knowledge throughout an organisation

- reducing delays in accessing the relevant information

- providing consistency of interpretation throughout the organisation.

The nature of an organisation will drive the appropriate usage of this type of system. For example, an insurance company which decides to construct a system covering case risk assessment may be able to make savings in centralised operations by reducing the number of suitably experienced staff or by redeploying them elsewhere. Alternatively, an organisation with relatively general knowledge requirements may have little justifiable need for such system support. In any event, a comprehensive cost/benefit analysis and feasibility study should be undertaken as part of the project justification process.

Particular care should be taken in handling the introduction of such systems, as staff will undoubtedly feel threatened by the implications, and may react by strongly resisting the process. It may be subsequently necessary to actively involve these same employees as part of the fact gathering processes, and the approach adopted should be carefully considered so as not to alienate them. Ensure that the intended use of the system is clearly and tactfully communicated to affected employees so as to avoid any undue resentment or resistance.

It is important that the knowledge rules are complete and adequately cater for all the possible through routes. The rules identified should be subject to comprehensive review to further ensure that they are correctly related and complete. Having constructed the expert system, it should be subjected to exhaustive testing against the requirements of a comprehensive testing plan; any problems or necessary changes identified during the testing should be agreed by the users and thence incorporated into the design. If the system is either commercially sensitive or critical to the operation of the company, appropriate security and access control facilities will have to be provided. If the system is going to be in general use, operational guidance may have to be provided for the eventual users.

The expert system product selected will need to allow for the application of any subsequent amendments of the structure necessary in light of changes in the market, external forces, changes in legislation, etc.

Control matrix examples

Having regard for the potential strategic implications for using Expert Systems, we have provided both *Objective* and *Exposure* related example matrices for this subject (Tables 14.1 & 14.2 below).

It is more likely that this type of system will be targeted on a limited number of functions within an organisation; however, the significance to the organisation of the selected function will vary between companies. The example *Type* and *Size* data reflects a relatively important area of corporate activity with potentially medium level benefit impacts. *Scales* 2 and 3 are used for the *Objective* and *Exposure* examples respectively and are fully described in Appendix 5. *Scale* 3 was specifically chosen in this instance as it provides a view of the relevance of key knowledge or information with respect to real impacts such as political sensitivity, reputation and loss of such information.

Table 14.1 Expert Systems - Objectives

Overall Inherent Risk (Size) Score [5 is worst risk; 1 is best] = 2.23

A Ensure potential for using Expert Systems is fully assessed
B Undertake comprehensive cost/benefit and feasibility study
C Evaluate all available options and select most appropriate
D Ensure that the 'Knowledge & Rules' components are accurate
E Aim to provide consistent, accessible & reliable data
F Ensure intentions are clearly and tactfully communicated
G Ensure the adequate testing of systems before live use

H Consider & plan for the smooth implementation of the system
I Ensure system is capable of subsequent maintenance & update
J Monitor the actual benefits achieved against expectations
K Provide the necessary skills to operate & maintain systems
L Ensure the ongoing availability of systems is safeguarded
M Provide effective security measures over critical data

Expert Systems		OBJECTIVES												
		A	B	C	D	E	F	G	H	I	J	K	L	M
		=	=	=	=	=	=	=	=	=	=	=	=	=
Calculated Risk Score	Risk	3	3	2	3	3	2	3	3	2	2	2	3	3
Scale 2 (6 is most serious)	Type	5	4	3	5	5	3	5	4	4	2	4	5	5
Size (3 is maximum)	Size	2	2	2	2	2	2	2	2	1	2	1	2	2
MEASURES	-	-	-	-	-	-	-	-	-	-	-	-	-	-
1 Relevant areas of expertise were identified as part of initial feasibility study	Best		5	4										
	Test	?	?	?										
	Both													
2 Expenditure on 'expert' support was compared to development costs for expert system	Best		4											
	Test	?	?											
	Both													
3 Development Project was costed & satisfactory return on capital was calculated	Best		4											
	Test	?	?											
	Both													
4 Feasibility exercise explored merits, disadvantages, etc. of all internal & external options	Best			4										
	Test	?		?										
	Both													
5 Internal & external 'Experts' were used to determine the necessary data and logic	Best				4	4								
	Test	?			?	?								
	Both													
6 End-users were consulted and operational factors were fully considered	Best				3	3	3		2					
	Test	?			?	?	?		?					
	Both													
7 Staff meetings & consultations were held and the necessary commitment was obtained	Best						4							
	Test	?					?							
	Both													

Table 14.1   continued

			A	B	C	D	E	F	G	H	I	J	K	L	M
8	50% of relevant staff reduction will be achieved by redeployment	Best						2		3					
		Test	?					?		?					
		Both													
-		-	-	-	-	-	-	-	-	-	-	-	-	-	-
9	System was subject to comprehensive testing - results documented	Best								5					
		Test	?							?					
		Both													
-		-	-	-	-	-	-	-	-	-	-	-	-	-	-
10	System amendments identified and change control applied to software modifications	Best				4	4								
		Test	?			?	?								
		Both													
-		-	-	-	-	-	-	-	-	-	-	-	-	-	-
11	Implementation plan produced	Best									4				
		Test	?								?				
		Both													
-		-	-	-	-	-	-	-	-	-	-	-	-	-	-
12	Staff training programme is in place	Best								3			4		
		Test	?							?			?		
		Both													
-		-	-	-	-	-	-	-	-	-	-	-	-	-	-
13	System output was compared to range of decisions made by experts during pilot phase	Best				4	4		4	4					
		Test	?			?	?		?	?					
		Both													
-		-	-	-	-	-	-	-	-	-	-	-	-	-	-
14	Selected method allows for the update of data and logic if circumstances change	Best									5				
		Test	?								?				
		Both													
-		-	-	-	-	-	-	-	-	-	-	-	-	-	-
15	Operational costs to be monitored against estimates and projected savings	Best										4			
		Test	?									?			
		Both													
-		-	-	-	-	-	-	-	-	-	-	-	-	-	-
16	Pilot program implemented and monitored for 6 months before full staff reductions applied	Best										4			
		Test	?									?			
		Both													
-		-	-	-	-	-	-	-	-	-	-	-	-	-	-
17	IT Department have relevant maintenance and technical skills - plus full documentation	Best										4			
		Test	?									?			
		Both													
-		-	-	-	-	-	-	-	-	-	-	-	-	-	-
18	Software and data backed-up on daily basis and stored off-site	Best												5	
		Test	?											?	
		Both													
-		-	-	-	-	-	-	-	-	-	-	-	-	-	-
19	System covered by Contingency Plan	Best												4	
		Test	?											?	
		Both													
-		-	-	-	-	-	-	-	-	-	-	-	-	-	-

Table 14.1   continued

			A	B	C	D	E	F	G	H	I	J	K	L	M
	System access restricted on a	Best													4
20	'Need to Know' basis	Test	?												?
		Both													
-		-	-	-	-	-	-	-	-	-	-	-	-	-	-
	Access controlled by use of	Best													5
21	user-id and password	Test	?												?
		Both													
-		-	-	-	-	-	-	-	-	-	-	-	-	-	-

A Ensure potential for using Expert Systems is fully assessed
B Undertake comprehensive cost/benefit and feasibility study
C Evaluate all available options and select most appropriate
D Ensure that the 'Knowledge & Rules' components are accurate
E Aim to provide consistent, accessible & reliable data
F Ensure intentions are clearly and tactfully communicated
G Ensure the adequate testing of systems before live use
H Consider & plan for the smooth implementation of the system
I Ensure system is capable of subsequent maintenance & update
J Monitor the actual benefits achieved against expectations
K Provide the necessary skills to operate & maintain systems
L Ensure the ongoing availability of systems is safeguarded
M Provide effective security measures over critical data

Table 14.2 Expert Systems - Exposures

Overall Inherent Risk (Size) Score [5 is worst risk; 1 is best] = 2.47

A Inappropriate use of Expert Systems - cost, operation impact
B Failure to undertake effective feasibility study - disruption
C Failure to undertake effective cost/benefit analysis - cost
D Inadequate assessment of development options - costs, delay
E Unstable/unsuitable software supplier or consultants - cost
F Failure to accurately determine 'Knowledge & Rules'
G Failure to effectively communicate intentions to staff

H Failure to adequately test systems - errors, image, costs
I Failure to plan implementation - disruption, delay, etc.
J Inability to maintain or update system - business impact
K Failure to monitor and react to benefits achieved - cost
L Absence of skills necessary to operate systems - disruption
M Inability to recover system in the event of a disaster
N Inadequate security measures - improper use, error, costs
O Loss of commercially sensitive data - image, business impact

	Expert Systems		EXPOSURES													
			—	—	—	—	—	—	—	—	—	—	—	—	—	—	—
			A	B	C	D	E	F	G	H	I	J	K	L	M	N	O
			=	=	=	=	=	=	=	=	=	=	=	=	=	=	=
	Calculated Risk Score	Risk	3	2	2	2	3	3	3	3	2	2	2	3	3	3	3
			-	-	-	-	-	-	-	-	-	-	-	-	-	-	-
	Scale 3 (6 is most serious)	Type	5	3	3	3	6	6	4	6	5	6	3	4	6	6	6
	Size (3 is maximum)	Size	2	2	2	2	2	2	2	2	1	1	2	2	2	2	2
	CONTROLS	-	-	-	-	-	-	-	-	-	-	-	-	-	-	-	-	-
	Relevant areas of expertise	Best		4	5												
1	were identified as a part of	Test	?	?	?												
	initial feasibility study	Both															
-		-	-	-	-	-	-	-	-	-	-	-	-	-	-	-	-
	Expenditure on 'expert' support	Best			4												
2	was compared to development	Test	?		?												
	costs for expert system	Both															
-		-	-	-	-	-	-	-	-	-	-	-	-	-	-	-	-
	Development project was costed	Best			4												
3	& satisfactory return on capital	Test	?		?												
	was calculated	Both															
-		-	-	-	-	-	-	-	-	-	-	-	-	-	-	-
	Feasibility exercise explored	Best			3	4	4										
4	merits, disadvantages, etc. of	Test	?		?	?	?										
	all internal & external options	Both															
-		-	-	-	-	-	-	-	-	-	-	-	-	-	-	-
	Products and suppliers were	Best					5										
5	appraised per Software	Test	?				?										
	Evaluation standards	Both															
-		-	-	-	-	-	-	-	-	-	-	-	-	-	-	-
	Internal & external 'Experts'	Best						5									
6	were used to determine the	Test	?					?									
	necessary data and logic	Both															
-		-	-	-	-	-	-	-	-	-	-	-	-	-	-	-
	End-users were consulted and	Best						2	3		2						
7	operational factors were fully	Test	?					?	?		?						
	considered	Both															
-		-	-	-	-	-	-	-	-	-	-	-	-	-	-	-

Table 14.2 continued

			A	B	C	D	E	F	G	H	I	J	K	L	M	N	O
8	Staff meetings & consultations were held and the necessary commitment was obtained	Best							4								
		Test	?						?								
		Both															
-		-	-	-	-	-	-	-	-	-	-	-	-	-	-	-	-
9	50% of relevant staff reduction will be achieved by redeployment	Best							2								
		Test	?						?								
		Both															
-		-	-	-	-	-	-	-	-	-	-	-	-	-	-	-	-
10	System was subject to comprehensive testing - results documented	Best								5							
		Test	?							?							
		Both															
-		-	-	-	-	-	-	-	-	-	-	-	-	-	-	-	-
11	System amendments identified and change control applied to software modifications	Best						3		3							
		Test	?					?		?							
		Both															
-		-	-	-	-	-	-	-	-	-	-	-	-	-	-	-	-
12	Implememtation plan produced	Best									5						
		Test	?								?						
		Both															
-		-	-	-	-	-	-	-	-	-	-	-	-	-	-	-	-
13	Staff training programme is in place	Best								3	2		3				
		Test	?							?	?		?				
		Both															
-		-	-	-	-	-	-	-	-	-	-	-	-	-	-	-	-
14	System output was compared to range of decisions made by experts during pilot phase	Best						4		4	3						
		Test	?					?		?	?						
		Both															
-		-	-	-	-	-	-	-	-	-	-	-	-	-	-	-	-
15	Selected method allows for the update of data and logic if circumstances change	Best										4					
		Test	?									?					
		Both															
-		-	-	-	-	-	-	-	-	-	-	-	-	-	-	-	-
16	Operational costs to be monitored against estimates and projected savings	Best											5				
		Test	?										?				
		Both															
-		-	-	-	-	-	-	-	-	-	-	-	-	-	-	-	-
17	Pilot program implemented and monitored for 6 months before full staff reductions applied	Best											4				
		Test	?										?				
		Both															
-		-	-	-	-	-	-	-	-	-	-	-	-	-	-	-	-
18	IT Department have relevant maintenance and technical skills - plus full documentation	Best											5				
		Test	?										?				
		Both															
-		-	-	-	-	-	-	-	-	-	-	-	-	-	-	-	-
19	Software and data backed-up on daily basis and stored off-site	Best													4		
		Test	?												?		
		Both															
-		-	-	-	-	-	-	-	-	-	-	-	-	-	-	-	-

Table 14.2 continued

			A	B	C	D	E	F	G	H	I	J	K	L	M	N	O
	System is covered by the	Best												4			
20	Contingency Plan	Test	?											?			
		Both															
-	-	-	-	-	-	-	-	-	-	-	-	-	-	-	-	-	-
	System access is restricted on	Best														4	4
21	a 'Need to Know' basis	Test	?													?	?
		Both															
-	-	-	-	-	-	-	-	-	-	-	-	-	-	-	-	-	-
	Access is controlled by the	Best														5	5
22	use of user-ID and password	Test	?													?	?
		Both															
-	-	-	-	-	-	-	-	-	-	-	-	-	-	-	-	-	-

A Inappropriate use of Expert Systems - cost, operation impact

B Failure to undertake effective feasibility study - disruption

C Failure to undertake effective cost/benefit analysis - cost

D Inadequate assessment of development options - costs, delay

E Unstable/unsuitable software supplier or consultants - cost

F Failure to accurately determine 'Knowledge & Rules'

G Failure to effectively communicate intentions to staff

H Failure to adequately test systems - errors, image, costs

I Failure to plan implementation - disruption, delay, etc.

J Inability to maintain or update system - business impact

K Failure to monitor and react to benefits achieved - cost

L Absence of skills necessary to operate systems - disruption

M Inability to recover system in the event of a disaster

N Inadequate security measures - improper use, error, costs

O Loss of commercially sensitive data - image, business impact

Part III

THE OPERATIONAL FRAMEWORK

15

IT SITES

Scope

This chapter covers the following subject areas relative to information technology sites:

- *Risk assessment of potential exposures*

- *Building and Physical security*

- *Physical damage and fire protection*

- *Provision and maintenance of appropriate environmental conditions for IT operations*

- *Procedures, instructions and drills*

- *Protection of and protection from personnel*

- *Insurance.*

The chapter contents are more naturally related to a traditional mainframe installation, but some of the factors (i.e. Security and Insurance) will generally apply in other computing location scenarios. Additionally, it has been assumed that the target computing installation already exists, although the chapter can be used in the context of assessing the acceptability of either new or potential IT sites. Most of the constituent subjects have strong connections with the process of Contingency Planning against the impacts of a major failure or disaster; Chapter 6 considers in greater detail the requirements for effective contingency planning. Please also note that logical access control matters, which are briefly mentioned here, are specifically addressed in Chapter 17.

Risk assessment of potential exposures

Where a computing facility is vital for business operations, a number of factors will need to be assessed in order to ensure that any associated risks are adequately contained or countered. It is usual for management (and auditors) to undertake an overall risk-assessment exercise which identifies and evaluates the broad range of risks and exposures associated with the particular installation, and to further ensure that the prevailing or planned measures are adequate to counter or neutralise the identified risks. The prime objective of such an exercise is to ensure that all the critical business operations can be effectively maintained costwise without undue disruption.

The assessment of the risks relevant to the IT site should incorporate matters relating to building and physical security, physical damage and fire protection, provision and maintenance of appropriate environmental conditions for IT operations, protection of and protection from personnel, and all related insurance cover issues. The following sections provide guidance on the aspects that should be considered within each of these main subject areas. The principal requirements should be formally documented, and where appropriate form the basis of established company procedures and regulations which are capable of being objectively monitored for effectiveness. Furthermore, having explored the potential risks, appropriate mechanisms can be incorporated into a formal contingency plan designed to counter the adverse effects of a major disaster befalling the installation. In assessing any risks one should always bear in mind the associated levels of probability, which can be borne out by, among other things, existing statistics and, in some instances, the application of common sense. It is comparatively easy to get carried away with the investigation of potential risks and to fail to take into account the likelihood of such situations occurring. However, for the sake of sanity it is recommended that practitioners should assume that, no matter how the event occurred, all the prime features of the computer installation can be disrupted and/or destroyed.

Building and Physical Security

Consider the location of the relevant building(s), for example are the perimeters either protected or patrolled and are there any potential hazards (i.e. main roads or airports) located nearby which will need to be addressed by specific security or other measures?

Access to critical computer facilities should, as a matter of course, be restricted and controlled. Physical security measures should be in place and all points of entry protected, for example by locks, card-key entry systems or security personnel. Visitors should be recorded upon arrival and departure; additionally they should be escorted during their time in the facility. Delivery drivers, cleaners and maintenance engineers should have restricted access only, be supervised and suitably identified, for example by distinctive lapel badges. Staff identity cards or passes should always be shown upon entry to the building and suitably inspected by security or reception staff. Despite the existence of staff pass systems, it is quite easy for the scrutiny of these to become lax and ineffective. The organisation should openly encourage all staff to challenge individuals they encounter on the premises and whom they do not personally recognise and ask for some proof of their identity.

Having gained access to the building, consideration should be given to only allowing staff (and of course visitors) access and movement to selected operational areas on a 'need to know' basis; this is especially true of the main computer room where access should be strictly limited to operations personnel only. If the building has a system of card-key access control in place there should be a clear policy on which building zones are accessible to which grades of staff. Responsibility for producing the cards and ensuring that zone restrictions are suitably programmed onto the cards will need to be explicitly allocated.

Specific arrangements should be defined for out of hours and/or weekend working. Most card-key access systems allow for the control in relation to permitted working hours or periods and can thereby prevent access during unusual or unexpected periods without the positive intervention of security personnel. However, whereas such access systems should prevent the unauthorised access to facilities by unauthorised persons, they should also be sensibly applied so as to aim to minimise the disruption caused by preventing authorised staff from access areas where they are normally permitted.

Selected items of valuable office equipment are portable and may naturally attract the attention of dishonest members of society. All equipment leaving the building should be inspected by security or reception staff, to confirm that the removal is suitably authorised. A positive culture of security awareness can be nurtured by management by clear actions and example.

Consideration should be given to the provision of intruder alarm systems and CCTV surveillance equipment. However, if the latter is installed it is only effective if the images are subject to ongoing monitoring. Additionally all alarm and surveillance equipment should be regularly inspected and maintained to ensure optimum operation. The effectiveness of alarm systems is further related to their nature and the type of location occupied by the IT installation. For example it is unlikely that passers-by would be around in the late evening to react to external alarm bells if the installation was located on an out-of-town industrial estate. In such a situation, some form of direct linkage of the alarm signal to the nearest police control centre or the presence of security patrols might prove to be more appropriate and effective.

With the unfortunate realities of terrorism and attacks launched against corporate targets, any organisation should have adequate precautions in place to counteract the relevant threats. For example, are suspicious or unattended parcels promptly and safely reacted to? There should be security procedures in place which define the necessary actions in the event of bomb threats, disturbances or other forms of unusual event. These requirements should take due account of staff safety concerns.

Physical damage and fire protection

Water, power and fuel supplies should be routed in such a way as to avoid impact upon and damage to IT facilities in the event of leakage, short-circuit, etc. The design or structure of the building should support the containment of fire, for example by means of self-closing fire doors, sealed cable conduits and fire-proof barriers. Adequate fire prevention measures should be established, documented and widely circulated to all staff. For example the accumulation of combustible materials in corridors should be avoided and smoking should not be permitted in the computer room.

Regular fire and emergency drills should be conducted and reviewed for their effectiveness. Responsibilities in the event of a fire or other emergency should be clearly established and reinforced by the regular drills and exercises. Computer room staff especially should be aware of their specific responsibilities with regard to controlled system closedown and evacuation. Additional safety considerations will need to be applied to any areas protected by inert gas-flooding systems.

Staff should be aware of the fire escape routes and the appropriate manner in which the building should be safely evacuated, having regard for their personal safety and the protection of company equipment and facilities. Visitors should be advised of the relevant evacuation route(s) and accounted for during emergencies or drills by reference to the visitor records maintained by reception or security staff.

Adequate and operative fire detection systems should be installed and subject to regular testing and maintenance. If there are direct communication links to the fire and police services, are they protected from tampering and tested at reasonable intervals?

Fire containment systems (i.e. sprinklers, extinguishers, acceptable gas-smothering facilities, etc.) should be appropriate, adequate and operative. The air conditioning plant should automatically switch off in the event of fire so as to avoid the spread of smoke, fumes and heat throughout the building. Due consideration needs to be given to the impact and effect of damage caused by the fire-fighting process. The fire services are usually only too happy to provide guidance and advice on the most effective methods to prevent, detect or contain the outbreak of fire.

Specific fireproof facilities should be considered for the on-site storage of media containing current data and systems as a further means of protecting the ability to continue critical processing.

Environmental conditions

Although some current computer technology is quite tolerant of environmental conditions such as temperature and humidity, most mainframe equipment still requires the provision of very specific conditions in which to operate. Adequate temperature and humidity control systems should be provided in accordance with the equipment manufacturer's recommendations.

Air conditioning plant of the required capacity should be available and have the ability and capacity to cope with comparatively abnormal conditions. Back-up or secondary systems should be in place to counteract the failure or malfunction of the prime systems. Monitoring of the overall environmental conditions can be performed by automated systems employing remote sensors; such systems can provide warning of unsuitable conditions which may give rise to equipment damage or failure. In the event of a notable failure, the required actions need to be promptly and accurately communicated to the relevant operators. If such an approach is utilised, there should also be adequate monitoring of the sensing devices for potential problems and regular inspection and maintenance to ensure that the monitoring equipment is correctly calibrated and operational.

External power sources can fail or be disrupted, thus causing interruption to the IT service provided to users, customers, etc. The provision of a local uninterruptible power supply (UPS) should provide sufficient power to enable the continuance of critical operations for a limited period, or alternatively allow the operations staff to perform a controlled power-down of the central systems. (Please note that it is also possible to provide UPS systems for local network systems and free-standing personal computers).

All environmental systems should be subject to regular and effective preventative maintenance. All malfunctions should be promptly reported and arrangements put in place to cater for emergency repairs to such equipment. The provision of suitable environmental systems should be taken into account when considering contingency planning in the event of a disaster. Any planned installation of additional equipment in the computer room must be assessed for the related impact (if any) upon the environmental systems.

Protection of and protection from personnel

All prevailing health and safety requirements relevant to the installation should be addressed and also be the subject of company procedures or guidelines, including the provision of suitable staff training when this is appropriate and necessary. Unambiguous procedures should be established which define the individual's responsibilities in relation to security matters, fire drills, safety, acceptable operational practices, etc. In defining and circulating staff procedures and standards, the specific requirements of contract and/or temporary staff will also need to be addressed. New employees should be subject to general assessment procedures designed to reveal any significant background factors. Staff being considered for positions requiring high degrees of personal trust or integrity can be subject to fidelity bonding.

Key duties must be subject to adequate segregation so as to avoid any potential for fraud, malpractice or abuse of systems or facilities. Organisational structures that avoid the concentration of key or critical knowledge/responsibility with one individual are to be encouraged so as to prevent undue over-dependence on a limited number of staff. Access to premises, computing facilities and information should be granted only on a proven needs basis and in agreement with the appropriate system or data custodians. In particular, production facilities should be protected from access by programmers and others outwith the operations department. Access to the main computer room should be restricted to operations staff only. The use of programmed card-keys can assist in reinforcing physical access restrictions to sensitive areas.

Clauses can be included in the contracts of employment for programmers and others involved in the creation of systems which clearly establish that the ownership of the intellectual property rights relative to application software is always granted to the organisation and that any breach of this right will be subject to disciplinary action being taken against the employee(s) involved. Any staff who have access to, or dealings with, corporate data should be the subject of procedural conditions affecting matters of commercial confidentiality, especially in relation to disclosure, use for personal gain, etc.

There is also a need to establish a realistic policy on system and data access rights which supports the role of data owners and the terms under which access is granted to all other staff. The security and data integrity aspects aside, facilities should be in place which effectively restrict access to both company systems and data. The ability to report attempted access violations can be incorporated into such an access control system, thereby enabling monitoring and appropriate reaction by management. When an employee leaves the company or is dismissed, all of his/her system access rights and privileges need to be promptly withdrawn.

Insurance

Mechanisms need to be established which ensure the provision of adequate and appropriate insurance cover for the following elements:

- material damage (e.g. to hardware, buildings)
- consequences of the damage (e.g. disruption of business, loss of data, etc.)

- risks to and from personnel or third parties (e.g. injury liability, negligence of staff, fraud, etc.).

Additionally, it is necessary to ensure that the terms of the prevailing cover suitably match the type of installation, business dependencies and likelihood of risks, etc. In assessing the risks associated with the installation, account must be taken of the reasonable actions and precautions that can be taken by management in order to reduce either the relevant risk or the related insurance costs.

Control matrix example

This subject has a more natural affinity with risk and accordingly the example provided in Table 15 is *Exposure* oriented. The example aims to reflect a major mainframe site scenario where the continued operation is critical to the company business, therefore the relevant data indicates a high level of dependency. The tone of the example is established by the use of *Scale* 4 which is described in Appendix 5.

A number of the example *Exposures* can represent a top-level or collective perspective of a noted risk (i.e. 'Disruption and losses due to disaster, emergency or fire') where it is implied that a range of specific constituent sub-risks could or may be included in the exposure. In practice these sub-elements of the summary exposure (i.e. fire, bomb attack, employee sabotage, etc.) can either be evaluated in terms of a number of controls recorded on the same matrix or as a consolidated view brought forward, as one overall control, from another more detailed, separate and supporting matrix. As can be appreciated, there are space limitations in the text fields of the matrix which describe the exposures (i.e. fields A to S in Table 15) and it is impossible to list all the probable effects in every case. Therefore it has been necessary, in some instances, to record the cause of the exposure rather than the effect. For example, the potential effects of exposure J ('Staff unaware of their security/safety responsibilities') could include loss of or damage to company property, liability for death or injury, legal costs, etc. For the most part the determination and recognition of these elements is a straightforward matter.

Table 15   IT Sites - Exposures

Overall Inherent Risk (Size) Score [5 is worst risk; 1 is best] = 3.53

A Ineffective measures due to inaccurate assessment of risks
B Disruption & losses due to disaster, emergency or fire
C Confusion, delay, etc. due to absence of adequate procedures
D Inadequate IT operation environmental systems - disruption
E Failure to maintain key environmental systems - down-time
F Interruption of IT facility power supply - down-time, etc.
G Unauthorised access to site, buildings and computer room
H Uncontrolled access afforded to vistors, cleaners, deliveries
I Failure to effectively deal with disturbances, bomb-threats
J Staff unaware of their security/safety responsibilities

K Removal of company equipment & property from premises
L Failure of security & alarm systems - processing disruption
M Inadequate fire/damage precautions - loss, injury, disruption
N Inadequate fire detection facilities - loss, injury, etc.
O Inadequate fire containment/control facilities - loss, etc.
P Damage from water leakage - cost, disruption, etc.
Q Inadequate protection of staff & visitors - injury, liability
R Damage & disruption caused by staff malpractice/
   misconduct
S Inadequate or inappropriate insurance cover - loss, delay

I T Sites		EXPOSURES	A	B	C	D	E	F	G	H	I	J	K	L	M	N	O	P	Q	R	S
Calculated Risk Score	Risk		4	4	3	3	3	3	4	3	3	2	3	3	4	4	4	3	3	3	4
Scale 4 (6 is most serious)	Type		6	6	5	5	5	5	6	5	6	3	2	5	6	6	6	5	5	5	6
Size (3 is maximum)	Size		3	3	2	2	2	2	3	2	2	3	2	2	2	3	3	3	2	2	3
CONTROLS																					
1 Risk and impact assessment for IT operations undertaken - used to determine actions & insurance	Best			5																	
	Test		?	?																	
	Both																				
2 Assessment reviewed annually to ensure account is taken of relevant changes, etc.	Best			4																	
	Test		?	?																	
	Both																				
3 Disaster & Recovery Contingency Plan established, responsibility allocated and actions defined	Best			4																	
	Test		?		?																
	Both																				
4 Contingency Plan is tested, at least, annually	Best			4																	
	Test		?		?																
	Both																				
5 Procedures established for dealing with fires, bomb threats, etc. - regular drills undertaken	Best			4	5						5										
	Test		?		?	?					?										
	Both																				
6 Custom built IT centre commissioned - includes relevant temperature & humidity systems	Best					4															
	Test		?			?															
	Both																				
7 Environment system (i.e. Air Conditioning) are monitored for correct operation and faults	Best					4	3														
	Test		?			?	?														
	Both																				

Table 15   continued

			A	B	C	D	E	F	G	H	I	J	K	L	M	N	O	P	Q	R	S
8	Back-up/secondary environment systems installed; automatically initiated upon prime failure	Best					4														
		Test	?				?														
		Both																			
-		-	-	-	-	-	-	-	-	-	-	-	-	-	-	-	-	-	-	-	-
9	Un-interruptible power supplies in place. Provides 2 hours of reserve power for closedown, etc.	Best					3	5													
		Test	?				?	?													
		Both																			
-		-	-	-	-	-	-	-	-	-	-	-	-	-	-	-	-	-	-	-	-
10	Programmes of preventive maintenance applied to all hardware & environment systems	Best					4														
		Test	?				?														
		Both																			
-		-	-	-	-	-	-	-	-	-	-	-	-	-	-	-	-	-	-	-	-
11	Main site protected by perimeter fencing with security gate-house to control site access	Best							4												
		Test	?						?												
		Both																			
-		-	-	-	-	-	-	-	-	-	-	-	-	-	-	-	-	-	-	-	-
12	Main building entrance manned with security personnel who check staff ID's & visitors	Best							4												
		Test	?						?												
		Both																			
-		-	-	-	-	-	-	-	-	-	-	-	-	-	-	-	-	-	-	-	-
13	Access beyond reception is controlled by key-card system - allocated on 'needs' basis	Best							4												
		Test	?						?												
		Both																			
-		-	-	-	-	-	-	-	-	-	-	-	-	-	-	-	-	-	-	-	-
14	All visitors registered and escorted whilst in building	Best							3	4											
		Test	?						?	?											
		Both																			
-		-	-	-	-	-	-	-	-	-	-	-	-	-	-	-	-	-	-	-	-
15	Other entrances kept locked or access is controlled by use of restricted key-cards	Best							3												
		Test	?						?												
		Both																			
-		-	-	-	-	-	-	-	-	-	-	-	-	-	-	-	-	-	-	-	-
16	Intruder alarm systems installed and regularly tested/serviced	Best							4												
		Test	?						?												
		Both																			
-		-	-	-	-	-	-	-	-	-	-	-	-	-	-	-	-	-	-	-	-
17	Main computer room observed by CCTV and recording systems	Best							4												
		Test	?						?												
		Both																			
-		-	-	-	-	-	-	-	-	-	-	-	-	-	-	-	-	-	-	-	-
18	Premises are patrolled after normal working hours	Best							3												
		Test	?						?												
		Both																			
-		-	-	-	-	-	-	-	-	-	-	-	-	-	-	-	-	-	-	-	-
19	Key-cards programmed with permitted zones and time period restrictions per job type	Best							4												
		Test	?						?												
		Both																			
-		-	-	-	-	-	-	-	-	-	-	-	-	-	-	-	-	-	-	-	-

Table 15   continued

			A	B	C	D	E	F	G	H	I	J	K	L	M	N	O	P	Q	R	S
20	Delivery staff are not permitted unattended access to the main building	Best								4												
		Test	?							?												
		Both																				
-		-	-	-	-	-	-	-	-	-	-	-	-	-	-	-	-	-	-	-	-	-
21	Security procedure manual is in place - Contracts of employment specify employee responsibility	Best										5										
		Test	?									?										
		Both																				
-		-	-	-	-	-	-	-	-	-	-	-	-	-	-	-	-	-	-	-	-	-
22	Goods moving in/out of site are inspected for relevant authority	Best											4									
		Test	?										?									
		Both																				
-		-	-	-	-	-	-	-	-	-	-	-	-	-	-	-	-	-	-	-	-	-
23	Building systems monitored 24 hours and any faults/failures are reported for same day repair	Best											4									
		Test	?										?									
		Both																				
-		-	-	-	-	-	-	-	-	-	-	-	-	-	-	-	-	-	-	-	-	-
24	Building design caters for damage limitation (i.e. routing of water pipes, etc.).	Best												4		4						
		Test	?											?		?						
		Both																				
-		-	-	-	-	-	-	-	-	-	-	-	-	-	-	-	-	-	-	-	-	-
25	Smoking is not permitted anywhere on the site	Best												4								
		Test	?											?								
		Both																				
-		-	-	-	-	-	-	-	-	-	-	-	-	-	-	-	-	-	-	-	-	-
26	Fire Wardens are responsible for ensuring that combustible waste removed, fire doors closed, etc.	Best												3								
		Test	?											?								
		Both																				
-		-	-	-	-	-	-	-	-	-	-	-	-	-	-	-	-	-	-	-	-	-
27	Fire detection & alarm systems installed & linked to fire station - tested & serviced	Best											4		4							
		Test	?										?		?							
		Both																				
-		-	-	-	-	-	-	-	-	-	-	-	-	-	-	-	-	-	-	-	-	-
28	Building evacuation drills are regularly undertaken & reviewed for effectiveness	Best														4		4				
		Test	?													?		?				
		Both																				
-		-	-	-	-	-	-	-	-	-	-	-	-	-	-	-	-	-	-	-	-	-
29	Automatic shut-off of air conditioning and power-down of computer in event of fire	Best														3						
		Test	?													?						
		Both																				
-		-	-	-	-	-	-	-	-	-	-	-	-	-	-	-	-	-	-	-	-	-
30	Main computer room protected by ozone friendly gas-smothering system - triggered when empty	Best															5					
		Test	?														?					
		Both																				
-		-	-	-	-	-	-	-	-	-	-	-	-	-	-	-	-	-	-	-	-	-
31	Adequate extinguishers (number and type) are located on advice from Fire Service	Best															3					
		Test	?														?					
		Both																				
-		-	-	-	-	-	-	-	-	-	-	-	-	-	-	-	-	-	-	-	-	-

Table 15   continued

			A	B	C	D	E	F	G	H	I	J	K	L	M	N	O	P	Q	R	S
32	All Health & Safety requirements are provided, and assessed by Health & Safety Officer	Best																	4		
		Test	?																?		
		Both																			
-		-	-	-	-	-	-	-	-	-	-	-	-	-	-	-	-	-	-	-	-
33	New employees are vetted and fidelity bonded before engagement	Best																	3		
		Test	?																?		
		Both																			
-		-	-	-	-	-	-	-	-	-	-	-	-	-	-	-	-	-	-	-	-
34	System access control policy in place to limit potential for damaging systems & facilities	Best																	4		
		Test	?																?		
		Both																			
-		-	-	-	-	-	-	-	-	-	-	-	-	-	-	-	-	-	-	-	-
35	Key I T duties are segregated	Best																	4		
		Test	?																?		
		Both																			
-		-	-	-	-	-	-	-	-	-	-	-	-	-	-	-	-	-	-	-	-
36	Activity logs are maintained and monitored for attempted security violations	Best																	3		
		Test	?																?		
		Both																			
-		-	-	-	-	-	-	-	-	-	-	-	-	-	-	-	-	-	-	-	-
37	Legal Dept. undertake annual review of insurance cover based upon risk assessment	Best																			5
		Test	?																		?
		Both																			
-		-	-	-	-	-	-	-	-	-	-	-	-	-	-	-	-	-	-	-	-

A Ineffective measures due to inaccurate assessment of risks
B Disruption & losses due to disaster, emergency or fire
C Confusion, delay, etc. due to absence of adequate procedures
D Inadequate IT operation environmental systems - disruption
E Failure to maintain key environmental systems - down-time
F Interruption of IT facility power supply - down-time, etc.
G Unauthorised access to site, buildings and computer room
H Uncontrolled access afforded to vistors, cleaners, deliveries
I Failure to effectively deal with disturbances, bomb-threats
J Staff unaware of their security/safety responsibilities

K Removal of company equipment & property from premises
L Failure of security & alarm systems - processing disruption
M Inadequate fire/damage precautions - loss, injury, disruption
N Inadequate fire detection facilities - loss, injury, etc.
O Inadequate fire containment/control facilities - loss, etc.
P Damage from water leakage - cost, disruption, etc.
Q Inadequate protection of staff & visitors - injury, liability
R Damage & disruption caused by staff malpractice/ misconduct
S Inadequate or inappropriate insurance cover - loss, delay

16

IT ACCOUNTING

Scope

This chapter addresses the establishment of a general accounting framework encompassing all specific aspects of information technology. The contents are constructed in the wider context of a separate IT division and are intended to include the ability to charge end users in respect of resources used. However it is acknowledged that not every organisation chooses to charge back operating and other IT costs.

Obviously, the nature of computing facilities operated by an organisation, and the methods chosen to account for such activities, will vary considerably. Therefore, it is unlikely that the scenario provided will directly apply in every respect, and it is presented as a very broad template against which individual readers can map their own situations more precisely. General accounting functions such as Accounts Payable, Payroll, etc. are not addressed in detail as the contents concentrate upon the IT-specific accounting aspects.

The type of accounting information required in relation to computing and other IT activities will, of course, very much depend on the organisation, its general accounting policies, the significance of IT activities, proportion of in-house systems development, etc. We do not intend to counterbalance the arguments for any particular accounting strategy, but steer a broad course by discussing a range of issues and suggested general mechanisms. For the most part, the accounting requirements applied to an information technology division or operation will need to follow standard good practice and generally accepted methods. However, there are some discrete elements which may require additional or special consideration (e.g. calculating meaningful charges for facility usage, maintaining accurate project level cost records, etc.).

It has been broadly assumed that IT policy is driven by a business related IT Strategic Plan, and that there are adequate mechanisms to ensure that projects are subject to feasibility study and cost/benefit appraisal. We have divided the general IT accounting considerations into the following areas, each of which is addressed in detail in the following sub-sections:

- general considerations
- Cost Centres
- Fixed Assets
- budgets
- Project Costing
- authorities
- charging out
- monitoring benefits.

General considerations

It is, of course, essential to ensure that the accounts and applied policies all comply with the prevailing fiscal and taxation legislation and recognised accounting standards. Senior management will need to define an appropriate accounting policy structure, and obtain agreement to same from affected management. The appropriate degrees of accounting detail (for cost type, etc.) should be determined, agreed and documented.

Care should be taken in selecting and implementing a comprehensive, accurate and timely accounting facility giving due regard to the security of accounting data and ensuring that the accounting system is protected from unauthorised access, and that transactions are suitably authorised. Generally ensure that accurate accounting information is provided and processed within the established timescales.

In order to further ensure the quality of accounting data confirm that control accounts and key banking accounts are regularly reconciled and that this is evidenced. Ensure that accounts received from suppliers are scrutinised, agreed-to orders approved, and paid in accordance with the agreed trading terms but having regard for the cashflow considerations for the company.

Establish a suitable accounting authority structure and determine a meaningful and agreed method for charging for services (see sections below). Also ensure that management information generated or derived from the accounts system is accurate and reliable.

Cost centres

IT organisational structures will vary, but the following example represents a logical sub-division of main activities for cost identification purposes.

- management & administration

- hardware & software (including purchase, lease, rental, maintenance, etc.)
- operations (including data preparation, production control, operators, technical support, help desk, Bureaux charges, etc.)
- systems (in-house development and maintenance)
- network & communications (lines, usage costs and relevant hardware).

It should be possible to derive all manner of cost details for the following types of activities:

- running production facilities (by system)
- providing third party services
- developing new systems (by project)
- maintaining/modifying existing systems, etc.

Fixed assets

It is preferable that the company has an agreed assets policy and this should include the regulations applicable to the IT division. This policy should incorporate the agreed depreciation approach for all types of capital equipment. All hardware and other capitalised items for the IT function should be recorded on an Assets Register or Inventory system. Ensure that all equipment (especially personal computers and other removable items) is suitably labelled and identified. It is possible that IT equipment could be located on a number of remote sites, perhaps even in branches and retail outlets, therefore the inventory system should be capable of recording the physical location of the item(s). The existence of assets should be periodically verified as part of the substantiation of asset values reflected in the corporate accounts.

Disposals of fixed assets will need to be suitably authorised in line with established authority limits and regulations. Evidence of the action taken in respect of asset disposals will need to be retained as part of the trial supporting the relevant accounting entries.

Budgets

The budgeting system should reflect the appropriate level of detail and ensure that only agreed and ratified versions of the budgets are held. The department or functional level budgets should be agreed with the responsible managers and any subsequent amendments will need to be agreed and ratified by the Board. The budgeting system should be protected from unauthorised access. Accurate and timely budget versus actual reports should be circulated and mechanisms established so that significant variations can be fully investigated and reported upon.

Project costing

Ensure that projects (development and capital investment) are cost justified and suitably approved. Organisations may choose to establish a financial limit above which all projects are subject to formal appraisal and approval processes. However, if this approach is adopted, mechanisms can be placed to detect the fragmentation of larger projects into smaller units that are individually valued below the justification financial limit. One solution is to route all project proposals via a Steering Committee where individual projects of a similar nature can be identified. Tight budgetary control can also be effective in ensuring that overall costs are contained in line with established objectives.

Establish comprehensive costing records for all approved projects (i.e. system developments) and ensure relevant entries are accurate, authorised and within the budgetary constraints. Provide regular and accurate project cost progress reports to management and project teams and ensure that any potential overspends are promptly detected, investigated and reported upon to senior management. Establish the key stages for each project (i.e. feasibility, design, construction, implementation, etc.) and provide structured accounts to support each stage.

Authorities

It may be relevant to establish an appropriate authority structure in respect of the following:

- purchases
- authority to pay creditors
- project charging
- budget amendments.

In order to be further effective authorities can be linked to the organisational structure; the aims should be to provide realistic and effective tiered mandate levels. It is imperative to structure the authority procedures so as to avoid possible conflicts of interest, and to ensure that there is adequate segregation of duties and prevent fraudulent payments being made.

Charging out

Charging for the use of mainframe computing facilities is a matter for management policy. Operating systems normally include facilities for accumulating various usage data and the means of applying a unit charge to calculate costs. Alternatively such usage accounting mechanisms can be provided as an add-on facility. However there are a number of possible bases for the calculation of usage charges and a combination of these may be applicable in specific situations, including, for example:

- dividing the total cost of providing a service and applying this pro-rata based upon a measure or division of time usage

- operator or data preparation hours worked at an agreed rate

- number of operator key depressions

- number of records or lines produced

- less allowances for errors/necessary corrections

- hourly charge for computer runs (can either be measured by the computer or manually)

- based on machine resource usage (i.e. central processor minutes, file inputs and outputs, lines printed, etc.)

- identifying charges based upon access by approved users (with unique identification) and related to 'Account Users'.

The selection of the most appropriate method will be dependent upon the nature of processing, stability of volumes, the level of overheads apparent, etc. in a particular situation. Whatever method or basis is selected, the terms and details should be clearly defined, circulated to affected parties and generally acknowledged as fair. Charging for services on a usage basis can raise user awareness and instil a degree of responsibility in their use of facilities.

Monitoring benefits

It is usual for new IT-related projects to be subject to formal cost/benefit analysis as part of the initial feasibility study. Therefore, it is logical and good practice to ensure that the anticipated benefits are actually subsequently realised. Projects and systems should be subject to a post-implementation review which should, among other things, accurately identify the actual costs and benefits against expectations. A mechanism should therefore exist which enables the identification and accumulation of the appropriate accounting data.

Control matrix examples

The subject of IT Accounting may have a strategic significance in relation to the success of a company or group, especially in overtly competitive markets. Additionally, it is likely that the establishment of a well-controlled business environment will be dependent upon the existence of sound accounting mechanisms and controls. For these reasons, two example matrices have been provided, one each for *Objectives* and *Exposures* (per Tables 16.1 and 16.2).

Given that investment in and expenditure upon computing and related activities can represent substantial proportions of total outgoings, the example *Type* and *Size* data reflects high levels of relativity. *Scales* 1 and 3 are used respectively for the *Objective* and *Exposure* example matrices; *Scale* 1 establishes the scene with regard to the importance of accounting information as a tool in both the assessment and achievement of corporate objectives. *Scale* 3 is used to symbolise the basic distortion and corruption of accounting information in support of the noted *Exposures*. Appendix 5 contains the supporting narratives for all the *Scales* used in the examples provided throughout this book.

Table 16.1 IT Accounting - Objectives
Overall Inherent Risk (Size) Score [5 is worst risk; 1 is best] = 3.73

A Agree, establish and apply IT Accounting Policies
B Ensure accounts & information are accurate, complete, timely
C Ensure accounts comply with prevailing legislation/standard
D Establish an effective authority & approval procedure
E Ensure accounts reflect the organsiation/operational needs
F Ensure cost & expenditure data is sufficiently detailed
G Ensure that assets are suitably recorded and protected
H Establish an accurate & timely budget & reporting system

I Ensure adequate particiption in, and agreement of budgets
J Ensure significant budget variances are detected/actioned
K Ensure that budget amendments are authorised
L Ensure development project costs are monitored ex. budget
M Ensure that development projects are cost justified
N Determine an accurate, fair & appropriate charging basis
O Monitor & assess actual project benefits versus expectation

I T Accounting			OBJECTIVES														
			A	B	C	D	E	F	G	H	I	J	K	L	M	N	O
			=	=	=	=	=	=	=	=	=	=	=	=	=	=	=
	Calculated Risk Score	Risk	4	4	3	3	3	4	4	3	3	3	4	4	4	4	3
	Scale 1 (6 is most serious)	Type	6	6	6	3	6	5	5	4	4	4	5	5	5	6	4
	Size (3 is maximum)	Size	3	3	2	3	2	3	3	3	3	3	3	3	3	3	3
	MEASURES	-															
1	Various accounting policies discussed with affected managers and ratified by Board	Best		5														
		Test	?	?														
		Both																
2	Accounting procedures developed and based upon agreed policies	Best		4	4	3												
		Test	?	?	?	?												
		Both																
3	Reliable and proven Accounting system installed	Best			4													
		Test	?		?													
		Both																
4	Access to accounting system is controlled by use of passwords	Best			4													
		Test	?		?													
		Both																
5	Accounting timetable established and managed by Senior Accountant	Best			4													
		Test	?		?													
		Both																
6	Accounting data input is subject to approval and completeness checks	Best			4													
		Test	?		?													
		Both																
7	Accounts procedures & methods are reviewed by Group Chief Accountant for compliance, etc.	Best				5												
		Test	?			?												
		Both																

Table 16.1   continued

			A	B	C	D	E	F	G	H	I	J	K	L	M	N	O
8	Mandated staff & levels have been established for invoice, charging approval, etc.	Best				4											
		Test	?			?											
		Both															
-		-	-	-	-	-	-	-	-	-	-	-	-	-	-	-	-
9	Cost centres established for each major functional area per organisation chart	Best						5									
		Test	?					?									
		Both															
-		-	-	-	-	-	-	-	-	-	-	-	-	-	-	-	-
10	Chart of Accounts agreed by functional management and group accounting staff	Best							5								
		Test	?						?								
		Both															
-		-	-	-	-	-	-	-	-	-	-	-	-	-	-	-	-
11	Fixed Assets register in place - each entry is identified with unique reference number	Best							4								
		Test	?						?								
		Both															
-		-	-	-	-	-	-	-	-	-	-	-	-	-	-	-	-
12	All asset items are marked with non-removable company label with ref. number - checked annually	Best							4								
		Test	?						?								
		Both															
-		-	-	-	-	-	-	-	-	-	-	-	-	-	-	-	-
13	Depreciation policy in place - reflected in fixed asset register and calculations	Best							3								
		Test	?						?								
		Both															
-		-	-	-	-	-	-	-	-	-	-	-	-	-	-	-	-
14	Movement of all assets is subject to written authority	Best							3								
		Test	?						?								
		Both															
-		-	-	-	-	-	-	-	-	-	-	-	-	-	-	-	-
15	All asset disposals authorised in writing by IT Director - terms etc. are also documented	Best							4								
		Test	?						?								
		Both															
-		-	-	-	-	-	-	-	-	-	-	-	-	-	-	-	-
16	Budgeting procedure established & ratified by senior management	Best								4							
		Test	?							?							
		Both															
-		-	-	-	-	-	-	-	-	-	-	-	-	-	-	-	-
17	Budgets set and agreed in accord with IT business plan and approved by Board	Best								4	4						
		Test	?							?	?						
		Both															
-		-	-	-	-	-	-	-	-	-	-	-	-	-	-	-	-
18	Budgets versus Actual reports produced & circulated monthly for management attention	Best										4					
		Test	?									?					
		Both															
-		-	-	-	-	-	-	-	-	-	-	-	-	-	-	-	-
19	Significant variances are subject of Board reporting	Best										4					
		Test	?									?					
		Both															
-		-	-	-	-	-	-	-	-	-	-	-	-	-	-	-	-

Table 16.1   continued

			A	B	C	D	E	F	G	H	I	J	K	L	M	N	O
20	All budget amendment proposals have to be ratified by the Board	Best											5				
		Test	?										?				
		Both															
-	-	-	-	-	-	-	-	-	-	-	-	-	-	-	-	-	-
21	All projects (development and others) are subject to cost / benefit & feasibility analysis	Best													4		
		Test	?												?		
		Both															
-	-	-	-	-	-	-	-	-	-	-	-	-	-	-	-	-	-
22	Cost justification is applied to all projects - Steering Committee authorises projects	Best													4		
		Test	?												?		
		Both															
-	-	-	-	-	-	-	-	-	-	-	-	-	-	-	-	-	-
23	Monthly project costs versus budget reports are produced for management sign-off	Best												5			
		Test	?											?			
		Both															
-	-	-	-	-	-	-	-	-	-	-	-	-	-	-	-	-	-
24	Appropriate charging basis was agreed with main users - subject to annual review	Best														4	
		Test	?													?	
		Both															
-	-	-	-	-	-	-	-	-	-	-	-	-	-	-	-	-	-
25	Actual costs, etc. monitored for 12 months following project implementation	Best															4
		Test	?														?
		Both															
-	-	-	-	-	-	-	-	-	-	-	-	-	-	-	-	-	-

A Agree, establish and apply IT Accounting Policies
B Ensure accounts & information are accurate, complete, timely
C Ensure accounts comply with prevailing legislation/standard
D Establish an effective authority & approval procedure
E Ensure accounts reflect the organsiation/operational needs
F Ensure cost & expenditure data is sufficiently detailed
G Ensure that assets are suitably recorded and protected
H Establish an accurate & timely budget & reporting system
I Ensure adequate particiption in, and agreement of budgets
J Ensure significant budget variances are detected/actioned
K Ensure that budget amendments are authorised
L Ensure development project costs are monitored ex. budget
M Ensure that development projects are cost justified
N Determine an accurate, fair & appropriate charging basis
O Monitor & assess actual project benefits versus expectation

Table 16.2 IT Accounting - Exposures

Overall Inherent Risk (Size) Score [5 is worst risk; 1 is best] = 3.75

A Inaccurate accounts due to absence of policies/procedures
B Distortion of accounts due to unauthorised access to system
C Inaccurate, incomplete or delayed accounts - decision error
D Failure to comply with prevailing legislation or standards
E Absence of effective authority & approval - fraud, loss, etc
F Not all main function costs sufficiently identified
G Failure to identify or control assets - loss, cost, etc.
H Unauthorised disposal of Fixed Assets - loss, fraud, etc.

I Failure to establish & monitor budgets - erode profits,etc.
J Inadequate management involvement in agreeing budgets
K Unauthorised amendment of budgets - distortion, erode profit
L Failure to detect or remedy significant budget variances
M Absence of accurate project costing system - excess costs
N Failure to accurately cost-justify projects - erode profit
O Failure to accurately monitor/assess project benefits
P Absence of accurate/credible facilities charging process

I T Accounting		EXPOSURES	A	B	C	D	E	F	G	H	I	J	K	L	M	N	O	P
Calculated Risk Score	Risk		4	3	4	3	4	4	4	2	4	2	4	4	4	4	4	3
Scale 3 (6 is most serious)	Type		6	5	6	4	5	6	5	2	5	3	5	5	5	5	5	3
Size (3 is maximum)	Size		3	2	3	3	3	3	3	3	3	2	3	3	3	3	3	3
CONTROLS																		
1 Various accounting policies discussed with affected managers and ratified by Board	Best			5														
	Test		?	?														
	Both																	
2 Accounting procedures developed and based upon agreed policies	Best			4		4												
	Test		?	?		?												
	Both																	
3 Access to accounting system is controlled by use of passwords - changed regularly	Best				5	4												
	Test		?		?	?												
	Both																	
4 Reliable and proven Accounting system installed	Best					3												
	Test		?			?												
	Both																	
5 Accounting timetable established and managed by Senior Accountant	Best					3												
	Test		?			?												
	Both																	
6 Accounting data input is subject to approval and completeness checks	Best					4												
	Test		?			?												
	Both																	
7 Accounts procedures & methods are reviewed by Group Chief Accountant for compliance, etc.	Best					5												
	Test		?			?												
	Both																	

Table 16.2 continued

#			A	B	C	D	E	F	G	H	I	J	K	L	M	N	O	P
8	Mandated staff & levels have	Best					4											
	been established for invoice,	Test	?				?											
	charging approval, etc.	Both																
-		-	-	-	-	-	-	-	-	-	-	-	-	-	-	-	-	-
9	Cost centres established for	Best						4										
	each major functional area per	Test	?					?										
	organisation chart	Both																
-		-	-	-	-	-	-	-	-	-	-	-	-	-	-	-	-	-
10	Chart of Accounts agreed by	Best						4										
	functional management and group	Test	?					?										
	accounting staff per policies	Both																
-		-	-	-	-	-	-	-	-	-	-	-	-	-	-	-	-	-
11	Fixed Assets register in place -	Best							4									
	each entry is identified with	Test	?						?									
	unique reference number	Both																
-		-	-	-	-	-	-	-	-	-	-	-	-	-	-	-	-	-
12	All asset items are marked with	Best							4									
	non-removable company label with	Test	?						?									
	ref. number - checked annually	Both																
-		-	-	-	-	-	-	-	-	-	-	-	-	-	-	-	-	-
13	Depreciation policy in place -	Best							4									
	reflected in fixed asset	Test	?						?									
	register and calculations	Both																
-		-	-	-	-	-	-	-	-	-	-	-	-	-	-	-	-	-
14	Movement of all assets is	Best							3									
	subject to written authority	Test	?						?									
		Both																
-		-	-	-	-	-	-	-	-	-	-	-	-	-	-	-	-	-
15	All asset disposals authorised	Best							4	4								
	in writing by IT Director -	Test	?						?	?								
	terms, etc. are also documented	Both																
-		-	-	-	-	-	-	-	-	-	-	-	-	-	-	-	-	-
16	Budgeting procedure established	Best									4							
	& ratified by senior management	Test	?								?							
		Both																
-		-	-	-	-	-	-	-	-	-	-	-	-	-	-	-	-	-
17	Budgets set and agreed in accordance	Best									4	4						
	with IT business plan and	Test	?								?	?						
	approved by Board	Both																
-		-	-	-	-	-	-	-	-	-	-	-	-	-	-	-	-	-
18	All budget amendment proposals	Best												5				
	have to be ratified by the	Test	?											?				
	Board	Both																
-		-	-	-	-	-	-	-	-	-	-	-	-	-	-	-	-	-
19	Budgets versus Actual reports	Best												4				
	produced & circulated monthly	Test	?											?				
	for management attention	Both																
-		-	-	-	-	-	-	-	-	-	-	-	-	-	-	-	-	-

Table 16.2   continued

			A	B	C	D	E	F	G	H	I	J	K	L	M	N	O	P
20	Significant variances are subject of Board reporting	Best												4				
		Test	?											?				
		Both																
-		-	-	-	-	-	-	-	-	-	-	-	-	-	-	-	-	-
21	Monthly project costs versus budget reports are produced for management sign-off	Best												5				
		Test	?											?				
		Both																
-		-	-	-	-	-	-	-	-	-	-	-	-	-	-	-	-	-
22	All projects (development and others) are subject to cost / benefit & feasibility analysis	Best													4			
		Test	?												?			
		Both																
-		-	-	-	-	-	-	-	-	-	-	-	-	-	-	-	-	-
23	Cost justification is applied to all projects - Steering Committee authorises projects	Best													4			
		Test	?												?			
		Both																
-		-	-	-	-	-	-	-	-	-	-	-	-	-	-	-	-	-
24	Actual costs, etc. monitored for 12 months following project implementation	Best														5		
		Test	?													?		
		Both																
-		-	-	-	-	-	-	-	-	-	-	-	-	-	-	-	-	-
25	Appropriate charging basis was agreed with main users - subject to annual review	Best																5
		Test	?															?
		Both																
-		-	-	-	-	-	-	-	-	-	-	-	-	-	-	-	-	-

A Inaccurate accounts due to absence of policies/procedures
B Distortion of accounts due to unauthorised access to system
C Inaccurate, incomplete or delayed accounts - decision error
D Failure to comply with prevailing legislation or standards
E Absence of effective authority & approval - fraud, loss, etc
F Not all main function costs sufficiently identified
G Failure to identify or control assets - loss, cost, etc.
H Unauthorised disposal of Fixed Assets - loss, fraud, etc.

I Failure to establish & monitor budgets - erode profits,etc.
J Inadequate management involvement in agreeing budgets
K Unauthorised amendment of budgets - distortion, erode profit
L Failure to detect or remedy significant budget variances
M Absence of accurate project costing system - excess costs
N Failure to accurately cost-justify projects - erode profit
O Failure to accurately monitor/assess project benefits
P Absence of accurate/credible facilities charging process

17

SYSTEM ACCESS CONTROL

Scope

This chapter concentrates upon the provision of logical access controls designed to prevent unauthorised access to systems and data. Although mention is made, in passing, to physical methods of security and control, these are explicitly explored in Chapter 15 – IT Sites. The contents aim to address all types of computer, but there is a deliberate bias towards mainframe and on-line systems due to the greater concentration of data and systems supported by these types of environment. However, the underlying concerns will be common to most situations; only the nature and scale of the relevant measures and controls are likely to differ.

The fundamental aims of system access control are to prevent the unauthorised use, modification, loss and corruption of systems and data, thereby avoiding disruption of business activities, and misuse of costly facilities.

Although the first line of defence is normally a physical one, we shall be concentrating upon logical methods of control. However, the siting of terminals in secure and lockable areas, or the fitting of locks to disable keyboards can, at least, initially discourage individuals from attempting abuse of computing facilities or causing malicious damage to systems and data. All security measures should be a balance between the relative value of the target for protection and the costs of providing that protection, and so partly for this reason we shall not be examining some of the more extreme (or esoteric) forms of controls which may be more suited to very high security applications (i.e. in government or military establishments). Additionally, although measures should obviously protect against inappropriate use by unauthorised persons, they should not unduly hinder the progress of appropriate activities undertaken by authorised staff, lest they be either circumvented or devalued by employees as unnecessary barriers to getting the job done.

A fundamental principle in establishing an effective access mechanism is that all systems and data should have a logical owner, and any rights of access, for whatever reason, should be sanctioned by that owner. Additionally it is also crucial that, in order to maintain the integrity and validity of data and systems, IT department staff should have no ability to directly affect user systems and data. Access to a system may provide a user (or indeed an unauthorised person) with a range of facilities, for example:

- ability to access various systems or interconnected machine environments

- ability to read or enquire upon data (which may fall outwith their realm of ownership, be of a confidential or commercially sensitive nature)

- ability to amend or update data

- ability to amend system standing data (e.g. VAT rate, loan interest rate)

- ability to delete or erase files

- ability to run programs

- ability to copy data

- ability to modify programs or configuration software, etc.

The access may relate to on-line systems, data entry processes, personal computers (perhaps acting as mainframe terminals), network systems, etc. All the possible variations of systems will generate different control and limitation needs in line with their basic technology, normal use, importance to the organisation, value of data, etc. Each scenario will be specific to the organisation concerned and should be subject to an objective review in order to identify the significant risks that require to be countered.

It can be seen that there is a requirement to tailor access controls and access rights (or permissions) to the particular situation. For example, a mainframe-driven on-line system may provide the potential for users to access a wide range of different services and applications; ideally each user should only be granted access to those systems he/she has a right to use. Furthermore, the type of access should also be taken into account (i.e. read only, amend, etc.). This detailed 'mapping' of access rights, as agreed by the owner of the system, is essential if the data and systems are to be adequately protected.

In order for the access control system to be able to allocate the appropriate access rights to an individual, there must be a method of uniquely identifying that individual, and positively confirming his/her identity when establishing contact with the target systems. These requirements are normally met by the use of a User Identity (or User-ID) linked to a password (or PIN – Personal Identification Number) which have to be entered correctly before access is permitted. The user-ID and password may grant access to a given range of facilities, or the user may require a different identity (and password) for each separate system.

In large installations, it is usual to allocate the responsibility for managing, updating and monitoring access rights to a specific individual (for example the Security Administrator); the tasks of this responsibility should ideally include:

- maintaining accurate records of all users and their access rights

- establishing the access rights for new users with the agreement and authority of the system/data owners

- ensuring that staff leavers are promptly deleted from the records and that their access permissions are revoked

- catering for changes in access rights with changed responsibility, etc.

- monitoring the system(s) for attempted access violations

- ensuring that initial passwords are securely issued

- ensuring that passwords are changed regularly to maintain the effectiveness of the access measures

- promoting good system security practice throughout the organisation, etc.

The activities of the Security Administrator will have to be monitored (i.e. by system owners), so that he/she is not able to set up bogus users, etc. Data/Systems owners should be able to check that the users established on the access system are reconciled to the current staff in the appropriate department(s).

There are a number of additional access-related considerations and these are noted below:

- avoid the use of obvious or simple passwords (i.e. car registration numbers, birthdays, names of pets, etc.)

- users should be made aware of their responsibilities and protect their passwords from misuse (i.e. avoid being observed when entering a password)

- passwords should be a minimum length and contain numbers or other characters in order to reduce the chance of random discovery

- passwords should not consist of blanks or spaces

- passwords should *not* be written down or appear in clear form on input screens or system printouts

- Security Administrators should not have access to live user passwords

- passwords should be changed regularly and the re-use of previous codes must be avoided (this can be enforced by the access system)

- terminal systems should only allow a limited number of failed access attempts before locking out

- users may be restricted to the use of a particular terminal (identified by a hard-coded identification reference)

- access may only be granted within certain time periods

- users should not be able to log-on to more than one terminal at a time

- attempted violations should be promptly reported and investigated

- terminals left logged-on but unused or unattended should be automatically logged-off to avoid unauthorised or opportunist use

- all accesses should be recorded on the systems journals as to date, time, user-ID, terminal-ID, etc.

- directory structures can be used to support the allocation of files to specific user areas and thereby augment access arrangements (this approach can also be applied in a personal computer situation).

In organisations where a charge is made for the use of computer facilities, the user-id can be used to determine the relevant cost centre. Users may detect unauthorised system usage by an unexpected increase in the appropriate charges, and may require staff to keep a manual record of on-line sessions by recording the time connected which is normally provided by the system at the end of a session. This record can then be compared to either a report generated from the system journal or the usage information supplied in support of the accounting charge.

Beyond the needs of conventional users, there will be high-level users, usually in the technical operations area, who will be granted wide and potentially damaging access rights. These individuals are obviously placed in positions of great trust, and may have access to powerful utilities and operating system level facilities the misuse of which can have notable implications for the organisation. Such facilities should be further protected, perhaps by a further layer of access controls, prior authority to use the facilities, the automatic logging of such usage or the independent reporting of their use to management.

There should be separate program libraries for development and production (i.e. 'live') purposes, and access should be restricted in order to avoid the use of unauthorised programs for live systems, or to prevent unauthorised amendments being applied to production versions.

In situations where a very high level of security is required, the signals transmitted between the terminal and the host computer may be encrypted so as to avoid discovery of passwords by electronic eavesdropping.

Control matrix example

An *Exposure*-oriented example matrix is provided as Table 17 with *Scale* 4 being used to graduate the type of exposures; details of this and all other *Scales* can be found in Appendix 5. There is an intentional bias towards a mainframe environment scenario in the example data. This subject can have great significance in organisations with, for example, high dependency upon distributed systems or on-line data entry. The example data values reflect a medium to high relevance.

Table 17   System Access Control - Exposures

Overall Inherent Risk (Size) Score [5 is worst risk; 1 is best] = 3.00

A Unauthorised access to systems - error, disruption, delay
B Unauthorised access to/amendment of data - disruption, etc.
C Unauthorised use of computing facilities - costs, disruption
D Absence of access policy/procedures - haphazard approach
E Failure to establish system ownership & agree access rights
F Users not restricted in their access and actions - disruption
G Inadequate password standards - ineffective access controls
H Failure to detect attempted violations & security breaches

I Failure to maintain up-to-date & accurate access records
J Unauthorised use of 'logged-on' terminals left unattended
K Failure to maintain effectiveness of access measures
L Failure to adequately protect confidential data - leakage
M Insecure dispatch of initial password - interception & use
N Failure to account for and record system activity - misuse
O Failure to control access to 'high-level' facilities
P Unauthorised access to production program library

System Access Control	EXPOSURES	A	B	C	D	E	F	G	H	I	J	K	L	M	N	O	P
		=	=	=	=	=	=	=	=	=	=	=	=	=	=	=	=
Calculated Risk Score	Risk	4	4	3	3	3	4	3	3	3	3	4	3	2	3	4	3
Scale 4 (6 is most serious)	Type	6	6	5	4	4	5	4	4	4	4	5	4	4	4	5	5
Size (3 is maximum)	Size	3	3	2	2	2	3	3	2	2	2	3	3	1	3	3	2
CONTROLS	-	-	-	-	-	-	-	-	-	-	-	-	-	-	-	-	-
Access control system in place,	Best		4	4	4	4		4	3	3				4			3	
1 features User-ID & password.	Test	?	?	?	?	?		?	?	?				?			?	
Access is mapped across systems	Both																	
-	-	-	-	-	-	-	-	-	-	-	-	-	-	-	-	-	-
Access rights agreed with the	Best		4	4		4	4	4						4				
2 system owners & reflected in	Test	?	?	?		?	?	?						?				
the access control system	Both																	
-	-	-	-	-	-	-	-	-	-	-	-	-	-	-	-	-	-
System ownership established -	Best		4	4		3	4	4						4				
3 owners define access rights &	Test	?	?	?		?	?	?						?				
grant appropriate permissions	Both																	
-	-	-	-	-	-	-	-	-	-	-	-	-	-	-	-	-	-
Access policy/procedures are in	Best					4												
4 place - define requirements	Test	?				?												
and responsibilities	Both																	
-	-	-	-	-	-	-	-	-	-	-	-	-	-	-	-	-	-
Only authorised users can gain	Best		4	4	4			4										
5 access to systems/data on	Test	?	?	?	?			?										
agreed basis	Both																	
-	-	-	-	-	-	-	-	-	-	-	-	-	-	-	-	-	-
Security Administrator manages	Best		4	4	4	3	4	4			4							
6 the set-up, amendment & deletion	Test	?	?	?	?	?	?	?			?							
of users per advice from owners	Both																	
-	-	-	-	-	-	-	-	-	-	-	-	-	-	-	-	-	-
Register of users & relevant	Best						4	4			4		4					
7 rights is reviewed and agreed	Test	?					?	?			?		?					
by system owners	Both																	
-	-	-	-	-	-	-	-	-	-	-	-	-	-	-	-	-	-

Table 17   continued

			A	B	C	D	E	F	G	H	I	J	K	L	M	N	O	P
8	System enforces password changes every 6 weeks, and prevents the re-use of previous passwords	Best							4				4					
		Test	?						?				?					
		Both																
-		-	-	-	-	-	-	-	-	-	-	-	-	-	-	-	-	-
9	System enforces minimum length for passwords and rejects blank passwords	Best							4				4					
		Test	?						?				?					
		Both																
-		-	-	-	-	-	-	-	-	-	-	-	-	-	-	-	-	-
10	Procedures define action required if user suspects breach of password confidentiality	Best							4				4					
		Test	?						?				?					
		Both																
-		-	-	-	-	-	-	-	-	-	-	-	-	-	-	-	-	-
11	Access system only allows three unsuccessful log-on attempts before reporting to controller	Best								4								
		Test	?							?								
		Both																
-		-	-	-	-	-	-	-	-	-	-	-	-	-	-	-	-	-
12	All attempted violations are reported by extracting data from systems journal	Best								4								
		Test	?							?								
		Both																
-		-	-	-	-	-	-	-	-	-	-	-	-	-	-	-	-	-
13	All attempted violations are investigated by the relevant manager	Best								4								
		Test	?							?								
		Both																
-		-	-	-	-	-	-	-	-	-	-	-	-	-	-	-	-	-
14	Unattended/inactive terminals are automatically logged-off after fixed time period	Best										4						
		Test	?									?						
		Both																
-		-	-	-	-	-	-	-	-	-	-	-	-	-	-	-	-	-
15	Users who are permitted access to sensitive systems are limited to use of specified terminals	Best												4				
		Test	?											?				
		Both																
-		-	-	-	-	-	-	-	-	-	-	-	-	-	-	-	-	-
16	Users are not permitted to log-on to more than one terminal at the same time	Best		3	3	3		4										
		Test	?	?	?	?		?										
		Both																
-		-	-	-	-	-	-	-	-	-	-	-	-	-	-	-	-	-
17	Initial passwords are delivered in sealed envelopes by the Security Administrator	Best													5			
		Test	?												?			
		Both																
-		-	-	-	-	-	-	-	-	-	-	-	-	-	-	-	-	-
18	All activity is recorded on systems journal, noting terminal, date, time, user-ID, etc.	Best														4		
		Test	?													?		
		Both																
-		-	-	-	-	-	-	-	-	-	-	-	-	-	-	-	-	-
19	Journal data is used to support usage charges for subsequent agreement by users	Best								3						4		
		Test	?							?						?		
		Both																
-		-	-	-	-	-	-	-	-	-	-	-	-	-	-	-	-	-

Table 17 continued

			A	B	C	D	E	F	G	H	I	J	K	L	M	N	O	P
20	Key users maintain manual records of system usage for comparison to journal charges	Best								3						3		
		Test	?							?						?		
		Both																
-		-	-	-	-	-	-	-	-	-	-	-	-	-	-	-	-	-
21	Journal data is interrogated for 'abnormal' situations, etc.	Best								3						3		
		Test	?							?						?		
		Both																
-		-	-	-	-	-	-	-	-	-	-	-	-	-	-	-	-	-
22	Use of 'high-level' facilities is protected by two levels of access control and two passwords	Best															4	
		Test	?														?	
		Both																
-		-	-	-	-	-	-	-	-	-	-	-	-	-	-	-	-	-
23	All 'high-level' access is reported (ex. Journal) to management for review	Best															4	
		Test	?														?	
		Both																
-		-	-	-	-	-	-	-	-	-	-	-	-	-	-	-	-	-
24	Production versions of programs held in separate Library with no direct on-line access	Best																4
		Test	?															?
		Both																
-		-	-	-	-	-	-	-	-	-	-	-	-	-	-	-	-	-

A Unauthorised access to systems - error, disruption, delay
B Unauthorised access to/amendment of data - disruption, etc.
C Unauthorised use of computing facilities - costs, disruption
D Absence of access policy/procedures - haphazard approach
E Failure to establish system ownership & agree access rights
F Users not restricted in their access and actions - disruption
G Inadequate password standards - ineffective access controls
H Failure to detect attempted violations & security breaches

I Failure to maintain up-to-date & accurate access records
J Unauthorised use of 'logged-on' terminals left unattended
K Failure to maintain effectiveness of access measures
L Failure to adequately protect confidential data - leakage
M Insecure dispatch of initial password - interception & use
N Failure to account for and record system activity - misuse
O Failure to control access to 'high-level' facilities
P Unauthorised access to production program library

18

BACK-UP AND MEDIA HANDLING

Scope

This chapter discusses the interconnected subjects of Back-up and Media Handling. In the context of the text and the matrix example provided as Table 18.1, the use of the term back-up is intended to relate to both data and software, and the term media infers all types (i.e. tape, disk, cartridge, exchangeable disk packs, CD, etc.).

There is intentional overlap with the detailed contents of other chapters, such as Personal Computers (Chapter 11) and IT Sites (Chapter 15).

BACK-UP

The back-up of data and software is a fundamental aspect of any type of computer operation from desktop PC to mainframe installation. There are three elements to back-up, namely copying, storing and retrieving. All three aspects are linked to media handling, which is explored in subsequent paragraphs. The overall process provides the ability to revert to a previous situation in either data or software version terms in the event of, for example, an operational failure.

In relation to *data*, back-up can provide for:

- disaster recovery

- retention of transactions for regulatory compliance purposes

- maintaining ongoing computer operations

- subsequent data analysis or interrogation

- resetting the point of processing in case of error.

For *software* (of all types), the main uses of back-up will be:

- disaster recovery (to rebuild the operational environment)

- Supporting the production (or 'live') versions of applications and operating software

- retaining earlier versions of programs, enabling the reversion to previous proven software

- maintaining (and supporting) the system development environment and software version control.

In summary terms, back-up, if correctly pitched and operated, can provide partial assurance for an organisation that its business activities can continue in the event of accidental or deliberate disruption to the underlying computer processing and operations. However, it is only one ingredient in providing total assurance. (See also Chapter 6 – Contingency Planning). Back-up routines should aim to adequately protect the business and operational interests of the organisation.

Back-up normally relates to the transfer of data/software to another form or unit of magnetic storage media (i.e. tape, disk, cartridge, etc.). However, back-up can also be achieved by the simultaneous writing of data, etc. to mass storage devices held on another site; these may be connected to duplicated processing facilities which can, in effect, 'take over' processing in the event of the prime or source site suffering a failure or significant disruption. Back-up can either be 'selective' (i.e. a particular data file or program) or 'full media' (i.e. the entire contents of a source disk or magnetic device). The nature of the back-up requirements for each organisation will be dependent on a wide range of variables. The contents of this chapter are general in nature and not all the points raised may be relevant to your own company situation.

The optimum point of time to take a back-up copy (and the frequency of same) will vary across systems and situations, and be dependent upon the frequency of data update, the criticality of the data to the organisation, the processing dependencies, data volumes, number of users, likelihood of failure, etc.

In order that the back-up processes in a company are directly relevant to the nature of the systems in use and the requirements of the business, a formal policy or procedure should be in place which specifies, for each logical grouping of data, the following criteria:

- when the back-up should take place (i.e. the point of processing and/or the frequency)

- the number of copies required (e.g. one retained in computer site library and the other stored off-site)

- the number of generations of the back-up files required

- the retention period (taking into account any statutory obligations)

- the appropriate media format

- the structure of the data (in order that the data can be reloaded without reformatting).

These factors, which should be determined with the consent of the data owner, will usually apply irrespective of the type of computer involved. However, additional guidelines and instructions should be provided for users of personal computers, so that their own localised activity is adequately protected.

MEDIA HANDLING

Media handling, in the context of this chapter, includes the following:

- the safe and secure physical handling and movement of the relevant media

- the adequacy of media identification labelling (i.e. physical and magnetic)

- the provision of adequate and secure media storage facilities

- providing a system for recording and trailing the whereabouts of media and the data/systems recorded upon them

- accounting for media sent to/received from third parties

- provision of the appropriate environmental conditions (humidity, etc.) to ensure that media remains useable

- establishing methods for preventing the premature, unauthorised or inadvertent re-use of media

- enabling the detection and removal of faulty media

- the preparation of media for initial use or subsequent re-use

- the secure disposal of damaged or unwanted media.

Again, these conditions will generally apply to all varieties of site, system type, etc., albeit that the methods employed will vary with scale. The responsibility for media control in medium and large scale installations should be allocated to a named individual and the role supported by relevant procedures and policies. Safe handling is primarily a matter of common sense (i.e. not touching magnetic surfaces) linked to established disciplines, such as ensuring that media awaiting transfer to the off-site storage facility is secure and protected from theft or damage. New media received into the library will have to be appropriately prepared for use (i.e. formatted, labelled and checked for faults).

Labelling will range from physical labels identifying the serial number of the media itself and its contents, to magnetic identification contained in the header information on the file, etc. contained on the media. Media library systems used in the larger installations will hold a range of supporting information related to a unique reference number attached to the media; this information can also be used in relation to the appropriate application systems so as to avoid the incorrect loading of data files, etc. The operating instructions (or JCL) associated with a system can specify the media or file identification number required and confirm whether the correct version has been loaded on the tape or cartridge deck. The maintenance of accurate records of media usage and status can therefore support the general integrity of processing operations.

Correct use of magnetic tapes for processing can be aided by the use of write permit rings, which have to be fitted to the reel to enable overwriting to take place. There are equivalent features on tape cartridges, etc.

Media library systems should provide facilities for the verification of the items held, and the physical layout of storage facilities should enable the contents to be efficiently traced. In practice an organisation's back-up media may be held at a number of different sites (i.e. remote store, bank vault for critical data, etc.), therefore the media library system should record the holding location; it may also record more precise storage details such as the row and shelf reference within the relevant library facility. In order to confirm the contents of the media library and thereby provide continued assurance of the ability to react to processing disruption, it is necessary for management to regularly check and reconcile the contents against the supporting control records. During this process all the media volumes should ideally be accounted for, but the contents of larger libraries may be checked in rotation with a bias towards confirming the presence of the most significant items.

The physical storage conditions provided should be suitable and avoid damaging the media or affecting the magnetic contents. Humidity, temperature, static and dust levels, proximity of magnetic fields, and strong sunlight can all have detrimental effects on media. Physical security is a key factor, as the data contained in the library represents the lifeblood of the organisation and if, for example, key items were mislaid this could severely affect operations.

Particular attention should be given to remote facilities, which may be unmanned for the most part. Remote facilities obviously offer greater assurance than libraries situated in the main computing complex as they would escape simultaneous damage in the event of major disaster, however this advantage can be eroded if the security at the remote facility is poor.

The movement of media between company sites or to/from third parties should be under secure conditions, and with suitable transport devices to prevent handling damage. All movements should be authorised and supported by relevant documents; signatures should ideally be obtained if custody moves between functional areas or outwith the company. Although media libraries and off-site storage are obvious precautions for larger installations, they do not normally cater for the needs of the PC user, albeit that the relevant PC system data may have a significant value to the organisation. There needs to be a specific procedure governing the regular back-up of PC systems and sensible arrangements in place for the storage of the related media (e.g. in the Legal Department safe). Very often, PC users will meticulously take back-up copies, only to store them in unsecured containers next to the source computer.

If the backed-up items have a long-term significance, it is necessary to ensure that the media containing the items remains readable. There can be deterioration over time which may render the media unusable. Any critical files retained for prolonged timescales should be periodically checked and/or transferred to other media. Files can be run through verification utilities which are capable of confirming that the recorded data is still in a readable form. In addition, the older contents of the media library should be considered when and if back-up facilities are replaced or upgraded, in order to ensure that the means to access the data is, if necessary, also retained.

The tape library tracking or recording system will often contain details of when the media can be released for re-use, and indeed may direct the librarian to recover the media and prepare it accordingly. This usually means cleaning and erasing (or degaussing) the tape or disk. Erasure will prevent any residue data corrupting future use and avoid unauthorised access to sensitive/confidential data which might otherwise remain on the media. The performance of media should be monitored, and any faults recorded so that 'rogue' media can be identified, erased and securely disposed of.

A final note of warning. Providing and maintaining a back-up facility can incur considerable cost, and a sensible and pragmatic balance should be established between the relevant risks and the cost of such provision.

Control matrix example

This subject has a natural affinity with the containment of risks and therefore Table 18 is *Exposure* oriented. *Scale* 4 has been applied in this example and this is fully described in Appendix 5. Back-up and Media Handling activities play an important role in the controlled continuity of IT operations, therefore the example values reflect a high level of significance.

Table 18   Back-up and Media - Exposures

Overall Inherent Risk (Size) Score [5 is worst risk; 1 is best] = 2.80

A Disruption, etc. due to inability to rebuild systems/data
B Inadequate procedures for back-up requirements - disruption
C Inadequate procedures for media handling/ storage - disruption
D Failure to identify key data & provide adequate back-up
E Insufficient back-up frequency, number of copies, etc.
F Failure to comply with current data retention legislation
G Failure to address PC back-up requirements - loss of data
H Inappropriate/insecure media handling & transport-data loss
I Failure to control/record data transfer to/from 3rd parties

J Inadequate, insecure or unsuitable media storage facilities
K Failure to record, track & account for main media - disruption
L Failure to detect virus infection on new or returned media
M Inadequate physical/magnetic labelling of media - error
N Failure to prevent unauthorised use or misuse of media/data
O Failure to erase/clean media before re-use - error, delay
P Failure to detect/remove faulty media - error, delay, costs
Q Failure to erase and securely dispose of unwanted media
R Failure to confirm that long-term back-up remains readable
S Failure to revise back-up/media arrangements per risks
T Excessive costs due to inappropriate back-up methods

Back-up & Media		EXPOSURES																			
		A	B	C	D	E	F	G	H	I	J	K	L	M	N	O	P	Q	R	S	T
Calculated Risk Score	Risk	4	4	4	4	4	3	2	3	3	3	3	3	3	3	2	2	2	2	3	2
Scale 4 (6 is most serious)	Type	6	5	5	6	5	3	4	4	3	5	5	4	3	4	3	5	2	3	6	2
Size (3 is maximum)	Size	3	3	3	3	3	3	1	2	3	2	2	2	3	3	2	1	1	2	2	2
CONTROLS																					
1 Back-up Policy & Procedures in place. Defining basis for effective back-up protection	Best		4	5		4	4														
	Test	?	?	?		?	?														
	Both																				
2 Each system has agreed data back-up schedule. Agreed with system owners and users	Best		4	4		5	4														
	Test	?	?	?		?	?														
	Both																				
3 Disaster Contingency & Recovery Plan establishes requirements for key system rebuilds	Best		5	4		4															
	Test	?	?	?		?															
	Both																				
4 Rebuilds for key systems are periodically tested	Best		4			3															
	Test	?	?			?															
	Both																				
5 Separate PC back-up procedures are in place. Agreed with IAD	Best			3				4													
	Test	?		?				?													
	Both																				
6 Media handling and storage procedures define correct and secure handling of all media	Best				5			4													
	Test	?			?			?													
	Both																				
7 Media is transported to the remote storage facility in suitable protected containers	Best				3			3													
	Test	?			?			?													
	Both																				

Table 18   continued

			A	B	C	D	E	F	G	H	I	J	K	L	M	N	O	P	Q	R	S	T
8	Specially designed off-site media storage facility used - temperature/humidity controlled	Best				5						5										
		Test	?			?						?										
		Both																				
-		-	-	-	-	-	-	-	-	-	-	-	-	-	-	-	-	-	-	-	-
9	Off-site store is adequately protected by alarms, security patrol, etc.	Best				4						4										
		Test	?			?						?										
		Both																				
-		-	-	-	-	-	-	-	-	-	-	-	-	-	-	-	-	-	-	-	-
10	Temporary media library is available adjacent to data centre - for media in transit	Best				3						3										
		Test	?			?						?										
		Both																				
-		-	-	-	-	-	-	-	-	-	-	-	-	-	-	-	-	-	-	-	-
11	Legal retention compliance is addressed as part of 2 above	Best						5														
		Test	?					?														
		Both																				
-		-	-	-	-	-	-	-	-	-	-	-	-	-	-	-	-	-	-	-	-
12	Most departments have access to safe for storing PC back-up and system dumps	Best							4													
		Test	?						?													
		Both																				
-		-	-	-	-	-	-	-	-	-	-	-	-	-	-	-	-	-	-	-	-
13	Main installation has media library & tracking system - provides data for each item	Best								4			4									
		Test	?							?			?									
		Both																				
-		-	-	-	-	-	-	-	-	-	-	-	-	-	-	-	-	-	-	-	-
14	All 3rd party movements are recorded, and receipts are exchanged	Best									4											
		Test	?								?											
		Both																				
-		-	-	-	-	-	-	-	-	-	-	-	-	-	-	-	-	-	-	-	-
15	Monthly reconcilation of system (at 13) with physical holding of media at all sites	Best											4									
		Test	?										?									
		Both																				
-		-	-	-	-	-	-	-	-	-	-	-	-	-	-	-	-	-	-	-	-
16	Quality control checks applied to all media before use to detect virus infections	Best												4								
		Test	?											?								
		Both																				
-		-	-	-	-	-	-	-	-	-	-	-	-	-	-	-	-	-	-	-	-
17	All corporate PCs have resident virus detection software	Best												4								
		Test	?											?								
		Both																				
-		-	-	-	-	-	-	-	-	-	-	-	-	-	-	-	-	-	-	-	-
18	All external media is checked for virus infection before use	Best												4								
		Test	?											?								
		Both																				
-		-	-	-	-	-	-	-	-	-	-	-	-	-	-	-	-	-	-	-	-
19	Physical & magnetic labelling applied to all main media - Allocated upon receipt	Best													5	4						
		Test	?												?	?						
		Both																				
-		-	-	-	-	-	-	-	-	-	-	-	-	-	-	-	-	-	-	-	-

Table 18   continued

			A	B	C	D	E	F	G	H	I	J	K	L	M	N	O	P	Q	R	S	T
	Magnetic labels used & checked	Best													4							
20	by application JCL to confirm	Test	?												?							
	use of correct files	Both																				
-		-	-	-	-	-	-	-	-	-	-	-	-	-	-	-	-	-	-	-	-	-
	All non-standard jobs are	Best														3						
21	authorised by users to allow	Test	?													?						
	use of relevant media/files	Both																				
-		-	-	-	-	-	-	-	-	-	-	-	-	-	-	-	-	-	-	-	-	-
	All media is cleaned and	Best															5					
22	degaussed before re-use	Test	?														?					
		Both																				
-		-	-	-	-	-	-	-	-	-	-	-	-	-	-	-	-	-	-	-	-	-
	Media performance is monitored	Best																4				
23	and faulty items identified for	Test	?															?				
	removal and disposal	Both																				
-		-	-	-	-	-	-	-	-	-	-	-	-	-	-	-	-	-	-	-	-	-
	All damaged media is degaussed	Best																4	5			
24	and disposed of via specialist	Test	?															?	?			
	waste company	Both																				
-		-	-	-	-	-	-	-	-	-	-	-	-	-	-	-	-	-	-	-	-	-
	Long term media is checked	Best																		3		
25	periodically for ability to	Test	?																	?		
	read data	Both																				
-		-	-	-	-	-	-	-	-	-	-	-	-	-	-	-	-	-	-	-	-	-
	Key system back-up requirements	Best																			4	
26	are reviewed annually to balance	Test	?																		?	
	risks with optimum security	Both																				
-		-	-	-	-	-	-	-	-	-	-	-	-	-	-	-	-	-	-	-	-	-
	Separate cost centre for media	Best																				4
27	handling - monitored within	Test	?																			?
	budgetary controls	Both																				
-		-	-	-	-	-	-	-	-	-	-	-	-	-	-	-	-	-	-	-	-	-
	Back-up is examined for	Best																			4	3
28	frequency of use to determine	Test	?																		?	?
	if necessary/justified	Both																				
-		-	-	-	-	-	-	-	-	-	-	-	-	-	-	-	-	-	-	-	-	-

A Disruption, etc. due to inability to rebuild systems/data
B Inadequate procedures for back-up requirements - disruption
C Inadequate procedures for media handling/ storage - disruption
D Failure to identify key data & provide adequate back-up
E Insufficient back-up frequency, number of copies, etc.
F Failure to comply with current data retention legislation
G Failure to address PC back-up requirements - loss of data
H Inappropriate/insecure media handling & transport-data loss
I Failure to control/record data transfer to/from 3rd parties

J Inadequate, insecure or unsuitable media storage facilities
K Failure to record, track & account for main media - disruption
L Failure to detect virus infection on new or returned media
M Inadequate physical/magnetic labelling of media - error
N Failure to prevent unauthorised use or misuse of media/data
O Failure to erase/clean media before re-use - error, delay
P Failure to detect/remove faulty media - error, delay, costs
Q Failure to erase and securely dispose of unwanted media
R Failure to confirm that long-term back-up remains readable
S Failure to revise back-up/media arrangements per risks
T Excessive costs due to inappropriate back-up methods

19

PROCESSING OPERATIONS

Scope

The objective of the processes covered in this chapter is to ensure that correct, accurate, complete and authorised data are correctly processed in accordance with current business needs, using authorised programs, and in the most efficient and controlled way. In a traditional mainframe data processing environment such requirements would have been addressed by all or some of the following discrete functions, the application of which would have ideally been handled by suitably segregated staff in order to further ensure the integrity of processing:

- *data preparation and control (input of data, accuracy, completeness, etc.)*

- *job scheduling (submission of authorised jobs and planning the loading of facilities)*

- *job assembly (bringing together all the requirements to run a job, i.e. media, data files, JCL or SCL requirements, operating instructions, etc.)*

- *production control (monitoring the progress of jobs, and confirming successful completion of same)*

- *computer operations (calling and executing authorised jobs, responding to file and media requirements, reacting to machine problems, etc.)*

- *output control (ensuring that all expected output is received, checked for accuracy and completeness, and distributed accordingly).*

However, in the current climate of distributed processing, on-line systems, direct entry of data by users, etc. some of these functions are no longer applicable in their original context (i.e. data preparation), or are catered for within application systems (i.e. the accuracy of data can be verified by embedded data validation processes). The following text aims to reflect the widest interpretation of the ideal requirements, and therefore it is likely that you will have to be selective in order to match the operations applicable in your specific installation. In striving to achieve the joint objectives of optimum machine performance and achieving the required service level, it is also necessary to take account of machine capacity planning.

Please note that related implications for media handling and the media library are addressed in Chapter 18. Reference should also be made to System Access Control (Chapter 17) and Software Maintenance (Chapter 21).

There are two prime, but interactive, elements in Processing Operations, namely data and programs. The principal and simple aim is to ensure the correct and accurate processing of the former by the latter. The essential factors in achieving this basic objective are:

- The accurate and complete preparation/input of prime data

- ensuring that use of data is authorised by the system and data owner(s)

- the use of current, tested, proven and authorised versions of programs

- use of the correct versions of necessary main data files for updating purposes, etc.

- the correct setting of key parameters, such as date, tax week, due date, etc.

- ensuring that each and every stage of processing has been correctly applied

- preventing the corruption or unauthorised amendment of data and programs

- ensuring that computer operators cannot in any way influence the validity of processing

- ensuring that semi-automated and automated processing is conducted accurately in the appropriate manner

- ensuring that all the expected output is accurately produced.

The actual methods applied to cater for the above-noted requirements will vary considerably between organisations, and be fundamentally dependent upon the nature of computer operations employed (i.e. mainframe, distributed processing, batch preparation and processing, on-line, etc.). With the increasing inclination towards users handling their own data input, perhaps by utilising personal computers acting as input terminals, greater reliance can be placed upon data input, validation, and reconciliation controls built into the relevant application systems. An equally important consideration is the requirement that all the appropriate processing is suitably co-ordinated so as to conform to both business and operational deadlines.

Many of the concerns held about the continuing integrity and reliability of corporate systems and data, hinge upon the efficacy (or otherwise) of a broad range of access controls that limit access to transaction data, standing data, official versions of programs and the configuration of systems. Using the traditional functional divisions as headings, the following sections provide guidance as to some of the key issues in each activity area. Co-ordination between these discrete functions is essential if the overall process is to run smoothly. However the actual processes should be effectively segregated to prevent unauthorised processing and to further ensure the integrity of both data and systems.

Data preparation and control

In order to ensure the completeness of subsequent processing, all the relevant input documents should be accounted for upon receipt and throughout the data input stage. Upon input, data can be subject to validation for accuracy and completeness, with suitable reporting of rejections and errors. The subsequent correction and re-submission of input rejections needs to be controlled to again confirm that all the expected data has indeed been accounted for.

The end-user may wish to conduct independent reviews of the data processed on his/her behalf and sign-off the relevant input reports as part of a wider concern for data quality. Additionally, source documents should be evidenced with the input action taken and returned to the user.

Input documents will require secure storage before and after processing as they may subsequently form part of either a vital management/audit trail or need to be retained for legal purposes. If documents are held overnight in the data input section, they should be securely stored to prevent tampering or unauthorised amendment. In a traditional environment, where data is entered by the staff of a dedicated input section, a process of double-keying may be employed, whereby the data is keyed twice by two different operators as a means of verifying the accuracy of data input. In order to be truly effective, this form of dual input needs to be undertaken by two different individuals. Any discrepancies between the two versions of the input should be reported for examination and subsequent correction.

Input processes utilising any form of Optical Character Recognition will need to cater for the rejection of documents as unreadable or damaged, and make allowance for the relevant resubmission of same.

It is of paramount importance that data input operators be prevented from amending the nature and context of user data; any queries about the data should be referred back to the originating user for amendment before being applied to the system. Beyond the fallibility of all humans in interpreting data, on no account should operators cross the line of their objectivity and amend, delete or add data.

Data input sections benefit from being located in secure areas, where physical access to the appropriate input terminals can be controlled and unauthorised use of the systems prevented. Where data is entered by users, perhaps via the use of personal computers acting as data input terminals, such considerations of physical access are more difficult to address in that the equipment is normally located on the user's desk and its very accessibility is part of the ethos of convenient, direct and open end-user driven computing. However, there are precautions that can be taken to minimise the risks associated with the use of personal computers and these are fully explored in Chapter 11.

In batch data input scenarios, it is usual to operate the section in accordance with the operational demands and timescales of the relevant business activities. Therefore, one would expect to encounter processing timetables with defined deadlines for the preparation of data, and it is important that there are methods in place to enable the detection of the status of data input and to prove that all the expected ranges of data have been received and duly keyed. Furthermore, in consideration of data completeness, the correction and re-input of initial rejections also requires to be taken into account.

If the data input is off-line (for example to either disk or tape) the media containing the data should be adequately identified and kept secure until required for use. The physical transfer of data from the Data Preparation area to the computer room needs to be securely handled, perhaps with signatures being obtained on a delivery document when custody is exchanged.

Job scheduling

This process should enable the effective and timely planning for processing requirements to meet the business and related information needs. In order to be effective, clear communication between all affected parties (i.e. end-users, operators, data input section, etc.) should be established so as to avoid failure to meet deadlines or prevent potential processing overloads or conflicts. Additionally, data preparation and submission timetables should be established for all mainstream jobs so as to further support inter-department co-ordination.

In consideration of overall machine loading, all regular and ad-hoc jobs alike will need to be prioritised and account taken of the need for any necessary maintenance. Historical records and general experience will support the estimation of the relevant process run-times and an element of contingency can also be accommodated. It is likely that the mainframe manufacturer will have defined optimum loads and capacities and these, together with potential processing and peripheral usage conflicts will have to be borne in mind when constructing the job schedules. More complex operations can be broken down into more manageable units and the exact sequence of processing for these elements may be critical; the review of the schedule before acceptance should identify any such out of sequence activities, abnormal runs, etc.

Non-standard runs, correction routines or other individual jobs will require to be authorised before being accepted for processing. Such special authorisation may be applied by the system owner or principal data user signing the relevant job sheet(s). However, in any event, all job schedules should be reviewed and authorised as a matter of course by operations management before processing commences. Job scheduling for a mainframe can be a fully automated process, but should still be subject to suitable approval before running. Known forward processing events (such as year-end accounting runs) should be identified well in advance and recorded on projected processing schedules to enable effective advance planning.

Job control and system control language

Operating systems allow for the prior entry of jobs into the system, which can be called to run at the appropriate time. These job control instructions normally contain all the relevant factors for the use of the required programs, files, etc., and are normally in the form of a Job Control Language or System Control Language (JCL or SCL). Such instructions can have far-reaching effects on the efficiency of operations, and therefore should be independently prepared by experienced staff.

The correct and effective use of either JCL or SCL requires the possession of specific knowledge and skills, therefore its use should be limited to suitably qualified and authorised personnel. Operators should neither have access to JCL nor be able to amend same once placed into the operating environment. In similar vein to system programs, JCL should be tested and authorised before production use and all subsequent amendments should only be undertaken by the appropriate staff acting upon management authority. Controls over the versions of specific job JCL will need to be established so that management are assured that only current and authorised versions are being applied by the operations department.

The inclusion of either JCL or SCL instructions may form part of the Job Assembly process described below, and measures should be in place to ensure that the correct versions are called.

Job assembly

This process basically brings together all the elements required to run particular processing jobs, i.e. data, run instructions, master file details, etc. There is a need to ensure that all the elements necessary to support effective and timely production are brought together at the appropriate time. Clear procedures should be in place to govern this area of activity and evidence of the necessary authority to proceed should be obtained and confirmed as part of the routine approach to job assembly.

Set-up and run instructions should be established for all jobs. Specific factors, such as run time parameters, may need to be recorded and these should be verified by an appropriate supervisor before submission and usage. Details concerning the actions required following the run will need to be recorded, for example, the generation of back-up copies of data, the production of output and management control reports, etc. Information recorded will hopefully include instructions for the operators in the event of, for example, a run restart. These guidelines may be critical if data is to be protected and resources economically used.

Any special requirements (for example the type of output stationery) should also be recorded to enable the operators to fully prepare for the job in good time. Control information governing the media files to be called during processing should be accurately recorded to further minimise the incorrect application of processing.

Production control

This function monitors the progress of all production jobs and independently confirms the correct and complete processing of same. The progress and completion of the various stages of all jobs are normally reported and electronically logged by the operating system. Any abnormal events (such as failures or restarts) will also normally be detected and reported. Surrounding mechanisms (perhaps manually administered) should enable the confirmation that such problems have been resolved in a controlled manner. Output controls should be examined and reconciled to confirm correct and complete processing (this action may augment any such process carried out independently by the users or owners of the system).

All machine activity should be recorded on the system log, which should be examined for any unauthorised or abnormal activity. (It is also possible that the log may be used to charge out for machine usage – see Chapter 16 IT Accounting). Mainframe operating systems normally permit the establishment of a number of layers of event logging, with some being optional and capable of suppression. Management should be satisfied that the chosen degree of system logging is appropriate for their control, trailing and review requirements.

Computer operations

This area should be governed by specific written procedures, responsibilities and standards, the application of which should be capable of being monitored by management. Access to the computer room and associated areas should be restricted to operations staff only and on no account should programming staff be permitted entry to such areas. As a general rule operators should not have direct access to data and/or programs, and should not be able to interfere with established processing routines. If these two principles are upheld by the application of suitable physical and logical access controls, there can be greater assurance that systems and data retain their integrity and remain accurate.

Computer runs and processing should be conducted in accordance with established and tested instructions and the system will need to be capable of detecting and reporting any deviations from these authorised routes. Only current and authorised versions of programs should be used for production purposes, and the introduction of either revised or updated programs into the production arena should require appropriate authorisation evidence.

Operations staff need to be suitably trained in respect of the use of all the equipment in their charge and their responsibilities in respect of processing procedures. Particular emphasis should be placed upon the correct application and practice of emergency procedures, system power down routines and computer room evacuation procedures. The computer and peripheral equip-ment should be correctly used and protected from damage or misuse. Due consideration needs to be given to the establishment and application of appropriate safety and security instructions. It is important to ensure that the computer room is appropriately manned at each shift so that production can be maintained and effective safety criteria observed.

Operator intervention in processing should be minimised by the approp-riate use of JCL, and the relevant processing runs can be made more secure by the incorporation of automatic checks that ensure the correct file or media item has been called and made available for processing. Additionally, the movement of media to and from the library should be controlled with only the relevant items being removed for authorised purposes and the guidelines defining correct handling of magnetic media being suitably observed.

Appropriate standards need to be in place for dealing with system or machine failures, accounting for media, stationery and print runs, etc. Any special stationery requirements (i.e. company cheques or payment warrants) will need to be securely handled and accounted for. In the event of systems failure or other major problems, operations staff require access to up-to-date details of relevant staff and management contacts including out of hours telephone numbers. Regular equipment maintenance can contribute to the prevention of disruptions caused by failure or malfunction.

Access to, and the use of, powerful utility programs should be controlled in order to prevent deliberate or indeed unintentional disruption caused by their inappropriate usage. System activity logs should be maintained and extracts of specific events can be reviewed by management, especially for program failures, run restarts, file recoveries, use of unauthorised programs or JCL, etc. so as to ensure that such usage was justified and authorised.

Output control

Records should be maintained which detail the expected output for each regular processing run and which can be used to confirm that all the correct output has been generated. The type of stationery (and the numbers of copies required) should have been specified as an element of the relevant job instructions. It is important to ensure that output reports are complete and that all the required pages are present before dispatch to users; additionally any confidential or sensitive output may require special handling. It will be necessary to check with Production Control that the related processing run has been confirmed and agreed as correct before the related output is released for use.

Where, given the sensitive nature of the output, appropriate and secure forms of distribution are utilised, evidence of successful delivery and acceptance should be obtained and retained. Ensure that any subsequent handling (i.e. the removal of carbon paper and copy separation of multi-copy output) prevents damage.

Performance monitoring and capacity planning

Data should either be gathered or accessible so as to enable the monitoring and assessment of mainframe performance, and particular attention should be paid to non-production events such as down-time caused by system or hardware failures, maintenance, and re-runs caused by errors. If Service Level agreements are in place, the monitoring should be more interactive and enable prompt management response to potential problems, bottlenecks or overloads.

Mainframes normally have optimum workload levels, above which performance and response times can start to noticeably deteriorate. These and other conditions can be monitored by built-in facilities which report on potential loading problems. Capacity management systems can provide useful reports (and graphical representations) of loadings and throughput, and these should be used to enable corrective action to be taken to suitably protect production facilities and priority processing.

Historical performance data can be used to support forward planning or job scheduling during abnormal processing periods (e.g. accounting year-end).

General

Where data is entered directly by users, the relevant applications should incorporate controls over the accuracy and completeness of input, for example by applying validation checks and/or input batch value control totals. The segregation of key duties apparent in more formal processing environments can be mirrored, to a certain extent, in user-driven systems by the application of authorisation over input, strong system access controls, back-end control reporting and appropriate reconciliations. Such features should be built into application systems and be effectively applied in order to provide the appropriate level of assurance.

In respect of all the functions featured throughout this chapter, it is important to stress the significance and influence of up-to-date and comprehensive departmental operational procedures in maintaining controlled and accurate processing for the organisation. The existence of such procedures should engender a positive attitude towards the reliability of systems, support the concept of systems and data ownership and enable employees to take responsibility for data and system accuracy.

In on-line system situations, it is obviously important that the master file and standing data made available to users is correct, and procedures will need to be in place within the Operations arena to ensure the loading and use of correct file and media versions. Access to such key data will also have to be restricted and any amendments suitably authorised and trailed. The Operations function is the natural focus of attention in large mainframe installations, and its success (or otherwise) can partly be a cumulative reflection of the effectiveness of a wide range of control and preventative mechanisms in place throughout the IT organisation.

Control matrix example

The example matrix provided in Table 19 is *Exposures* oriented, and as the correct performance of computer operations is vital to the ongoing existence and support of most businesses, the example data reflects this key significance. The relevant descriptions supporting the use of *Scale* 4 in this example are provided in Appendix 5.

Table 19   Processing Operations - Exposures

Overall Inherent Risk (Size) Score [5 is worst risk; 1 is best] = 3.55

A Unauthorised or invalid processing - disruption, cost, delay
B Use of inaccurate, incomplete, out-of-date data - error, delay
C Unauthorised access to/processing of data - error, cost,
D Data loss or corruption due to unauthorised amendments
E Use of unauthorised/untested programs - error, disruption
F Failure to provide required level of service - disruption
G Processing delays or incorrect processing sequence
H Fraud, disruption, damage due to non-segregation of duties
I Failure to detect unusual/abnormal mainframe activity
J Unauthorised access to JCL/SCL - error, disruption, delay

K Unauthorised use of utility programs - error, delay, etc.
L Mainframe overloaded - disruption, service degradation, etc.
M Inadequate procedures or insufficient/inexperienced staff
N Inadequate protection of main computer room - damage, etc.
O Programs subject to unauthorised amendments - error, delay
P Use of invalid/incorrect on-line data - error, disruption
Q Machine failure due to inadequate preventive maintenance
R Failure to restrict access to confidential data - leakage
S Inaccurate or incomplete output - delay, error, costs
T Lack of co-ordination in preparing/running jobs - delay, etc

Processing Operations	EXPOSURES	A	B	C	D	E	F	G	H	I	J	K	L	M	N	O	P	Q	R	S	T
Calculated Risk Score	Risk	4	3	4	4	4	4	3	4	3	3	3	4	3	4	4	3	4	2	3	3
Scale 4 (6 is most serious)	Type	5	4	5	6	5	6	4	5	4	3	5	6	5	6	5	4	5	4	3	3
Size (3 is maximum)	Size	3	3	3	3	3	3	3	3	3	3	2	3	2	3	3	2	3	1	3	3
CONTROLS	-																				
1 Only valid, tested & authorised program versions are available in the production environment	Best	4		4	3	4															
	Test	?	?		?	?	?														
	Both																				
2 All runs are authorised prior to operation	Best		3		3																
	Test	?	?		?																
	Both																				
3 JCL ensures that correct files, data and programs are called during processing	Best		4	4	4	3															
	Test	?	?	?	?	?															
	Both																				
4 Runs are reconciled & agreed before data/output is released	Best		2						3												
	Test	?	?						?												
	Both																				
5 System access controls prevent unauthorised access to data and mainframe facilities	Best		4		4	4															
	Test	?	?		?	?															
	Both																				
6 Data is only subject to amendment via authorised methods	Best			3	4																
	Test	?			?	?															
	Both																				
7 Data preparation (where applicable) is reconciled to source documents	Best			4																	
	Test	?		?																	
	Both																				

Table 19   continued

			A	B	C	D	E	F	G	H	I	J	K	L	M	N	O	P	Q	R	S	T
8	Data is validated for errors, etc., rejections are re-input and authorised	Best		4																			
		Test	?	?																			
		Both																					
		-	-	-	-	-	-	-	-	-	-	-	-	-	-	-	-	-	-	-	-	-
9	Users authorise the use of data once input is reconciled - evidenced by signature	Best		4													4					
		Test	?	?													?					
		Both																					
		-	-	-	-	-	-	-	-	-	-	-	-	-	-	-	-	-	-	-	-	-
10	Production program library only contains current/approved versions - regularly verified	Best		4			4															
		Test	?	?			?															
		Both																					
		-	-	-	-	-	-	-	-	-	-	-	-	-	-	-	-	-	-	-	-	-
11	It is not possible to amend programs held in the production library	Best		3			4										5					
		Test	?	?			?										?					
		Both																					
		-	-	-	-	-	-	-	-	-	-	-	-	-	-	-	-	-	-	-	-	-
12	Transfers of programs to the production library are subject to authority & access controls	Best					4										4					
		Test	?				?										?					
		Both																					
		-	-	-	-	-	-	-	-	-	-	-	-	-	-	-	-	-	-	-	-	-
13	Job Scheduling is planned in advance for mainstream production tasks	Best						4	4													
		Test	?					?	?													
		Both																					
		-	-	-	-	-	-	-	-	-	-	-	-	-	-	-	-	-	-	-	-	-
14	Jobs are prioritised during scheduling and their progress is monitored	Best						4	4													
		Test	?					?	?													
		Both																					
		-	-	-	-	-	-	-	-	-	-	-	-	-	-	-	-	-	-	-	-	-
15	Job progress is monitored and delays or problems are actioned	Best						4														
		Test	?					?														
		Both																					
		-	-	-	-	-	-	-	-	-	-	-	-	-	-	-	-	-	-	-	-	-
16	All activity is logged and reviewed - all non-standard jobs are authorised in advance	Best							3		4		4									
		Test	?						?		?		?									
		Both																					
		-	-	-	-	-	-	-	-	-	-	-	-	-	-	-	-	-	-	-	-	-
17	Sequence, program calls, etc. are controlled by authorised JCL	Best						4														
		Test	?					?														
		Both																					
		-	-	-	-	-	-	-	-	-	-	-	-	-	-	-	-	-	-	-	-	-
18	Key duties (i.e. data prep., job assembly, JCL maintenance, etc.) are adequately segregated	Best							5													
		Test	?						?													
		Both																					
		-	-	-	-	-	-	-	-	-	-	-	-	-	-	-	-	-	-	-	-	-
19	Abnormal jobs/actions are fully investigated	Best							4													
		Test	?						?													
		Both																					
		-	-	-	-	-	-	-	-	-	-	-	-	-	-	-	-	-	-	-	-	-

Table 19   continued

				A	B	C	D	E	F	G	H	I	J	K	L	M	N	O	P	Q	R	S	T
	Access to JCL facilities is	Best											5										
20	restricted - all JCL is tested	Test	?										?										
	prior to use	Both																						
-		-	-	-	-	-	-	-	-	-	-	-	-	-	-	-	-	-	-	-	-	-	-	-
	Utilities not held on-line -	Best											5										
21	use has to be authorised	Test	?										?										
		Both																						
-		-	-	-	-	-	-	-	-	-	-	-	-	-	-	-	-	-	-	-	-	-	-	-
	Machine performance & loading is	Best												4									
22	monitored. Potential overloads	Test	?											?									
	are avoided	Both																						
-		-	-	-	-	-	-	-	-	-	-	-	-	-	-	-	-	-	-	-	-	-	-	-
	Low priority jobs abandoned	Best												4									
23	if response time deteriorates	Test	?											?									
	beyond required level	Both																						
-		-	-	-	-	-	-	-	-	-	-	-	-	-	-	-	-	-	-	-	-	-	-	-
	Operations staff are suitably	Best													4								
24	experienced and/or fully trained	Test	?												?								
	where necessary	Both																						
-		-	-	-	-	-	-	-	-	-	-	-	-	-	-	-	-	-	-	-	-	-	-	-
	JCL & SCL is produced by	Best													4								
25	experienced personnel outwith	Test	?												?								
	the operating department	Both																						
-		-	-	-	-	-	-	-	-	-	-	-	-	-	-	-	-	-	-	-	-	-	-	-
	All functional areas have their	Best													4								
26	own procedures/disciplines in	Test	?												?								
	place; Managers check compliance	Both																						
-		-	-	-	-	-	-	-	-	-	-	-	-	-	-	-	-	-	-	-	-	-	-	-
	Access to computer room is	Best														5							
27	controlled by key-card and	Test	?													?							
	password - Key staff only	Both																						
-		-	-	-	-	-	-	-	-	-	-	-	-	-	-	-	-	-	-	-	-	-	-	-
	Job instructions define action	Best						3		3					3								
28	required in the event of failure	Test	?					?		?					?								
	& note points of contact	Both																						
-		-	-	-	-	-	-	-	-	-	-	-	-	-	-	-	-	-	-	-	-	-	-	-
	System controls ensure the	Best																4					
29	loading of correct data files	Test	?															?					
	and media	Both																						
-		-	-	-	-	-	-	-	-	-	-	-	-	-	-	-	-	-	-	-	-	-	-	-
	Regular maintenance programme	Best																		5			
30	applied to all computer room	Test	?																	?			
	equipment on cyclic basis	Both																						
-		-	-	-	-	-	-	-	-	-	-	-	-	-	-	-	-	-	-	-	-	-	-	-
	All confidential output is	Best																		4			
31	routed to laser printer and	Test	?																	?			
	shrink-wrapped	Both																						
-		-	-	-	-	-	-	-	-	-	-	-	-	-	-	-	-	-	-	-	-	-	-	-

Table 19   continued

			A	B	C	D	E	F	G	H	I	J	K	L	M	N	O	P	Q	R	S	T
	All output is checked for	Best																		4	4	
32	completeness and accuracy	Test	?																	?	?	
	before release to users	Both																				
-		-	-	-	-	-	-	-	-	-	-	-	-	-	-	-	-	-	-	-	-	-
	All output is logged via the	Best																		4		
33	post room and signed for upon	Test	?																	?		
	receipt	Both																				
-		-	-	-	-	-	-	-	-	-	-	-	-	-	-	-	-	-	-	-	-	-
	Minimum shift staffing levels	Best													4							
34	are established. At least two	Test	?												?							
	operators must be present	Both																				
-		-	-	-	-	-	-	-	-	-	-	-	-	-	-	-	-	-	-	-	-	-
	Job schedule data circulated to	Best																				4
35	affected parties in advance	Test	?																			?
		Both																				
-		-	-	-	-	-	-	-	-	-	-	-	-	-	-	-	-	-	-	-	-	-
	Lines of communication are	Best																				4
36	established in the event of	Test	?																			?
	faults, problems, etc.	Both																				
-		-	-	-	-	-	-	-	-	-	-	-	-	-	-	-	-	-	-	-	-	-

A Unauthorised or invalid processing - disruption, cost, delay
B Use of inaccurate,incomplete,out-of-date data - error, delay
C Unauthorised access to/processing of data - error, cost,
D Data loss or corruption due to unauthorised amendments
E Use of unauthorised/untested programs - error, disruption
F Failure to provide required level of service - disruption
G Processing delays or incorrect processing sequence
H Fraud, disruption, damage due to non-segregation of duties
I Failure to detect unusual/abnormal mainframe activity
J Unauthorised access to JCL/SCL - error, disruption, delay

K Unauthorised use of utility programs - error, delay, etc.
L Mainframe overloaded - disruption, service degradation, etc.
M Inadequate procedures or insufficient/inexperienced staff
N Inadequate protection of main computer room - damage, etc.
O Programs subject to unauthorised amendments - error, delay
P Use of invalid/incorrect on-line data - error, disruption
Q Machine failure due to inadequate preventive maintenance
R Failure to restrict access to confidential data - leakage
S Inaccurate or incomplete output - delay, error, costs
T Lack of co-ordination in preparing/running jobs - delay, etc

20

SYSTEMS/OPERATING SOFTWARE

Scope

This chapter addresses systems and operating software for all types of computer, although greater emphasis is intentionally placed upon mainframe installations. The aspects covered include choice of appropriate system, initial installation, configuration, subsequent software updates, fixes and amendments, access to facilities and utilities, the adequacy of internal experience, restart and recovery processes, the establishment and use of journals, control of privileged facilities, and diagnostic software.

The role of Technical Support staff in the maintenance of Systems and Operating Software is normally crucial, and their technical power is often seen as being disproportionate in relation to other specialist staff. It is apparent that, as a discrete group, they have the ability to severely enhance or disrupt operations if so inclined.

Although Access Control facilities can be incorporated in Operating Systems, the related issues are discussed in detail in Chapter 17.

The Operating System controls the elemental operation of a computer system and the use of associated peripheral equipment. It handles the running of all other software, manages all related tasks, controls the use of memory and other facilities, detects and reports upon errors in operations, and provides an interface with the operator(s). Systems software, which is often co-resident with the Operating System, handles particular processes, such as transaction processing, remote job entry, compiling programs, etc. This chapter mainly relates to mainframe operating and systems software, however some specific comments are provided in respect of Personal Computer operating systems.

The selection, correct installation and configuration of the operating system is crucial to all the computing activity that follows, as it literally governs all the actions of programs and human interfacing with the computer. All operating and systems software should only be acquired from reputable suppliers with the capability to provide ongoing support and expertise. Operating systems are, by their very nature, extremely complex, and our text does not intend to address all the precise technical issues and features, which will of course, vary between systems and hardware platforms.

Most operating systems are relative to a particular structure or type of computer, and most large mainframe manufacturers will have their own specific versions for their range of machines. Alternatively, some systems are available from third party suppliers, and they should be thoroughly checked out before any arrangement is finalised. In any event, it is necessary to ensure that systems are only acquired from reputable suppliers, who are capable of providing support and upgrades into the future. There has been progress towards the development and availability of 'transportable' operating systems which theoretically allow users to migrate between hardware platforms produced by participating manufacturers.

Given the complex nature of mainframe operating systems, it is necessary to have access to skilled technical support staff in order to install, configure, monitor, update and maintain the system. By virtue of a combination of their levels of skill and the fundamental nature of the operating system, these staff occupy positions of great trust; additionally the organisation could be vulnerable if all the required skills are held by a relatively few employees. It should not be possible for such staff to independently alter the fundamental functionality of operating systems. Due to the low-level languages used to construct such systems, lack of the relevant knowledge can act as a prime barrier to this variety of potential misuse.

In order to remain effective, Technical Support staff with responsibility for operating systems should be suitably trained and given access to the appropriate update courses and technical publications. The technical support function should be subject to procedures defining the relevant responsibilities and standards to be applied, and the work of technical support staff must be suitably authorised and capable of being monitored by management.

Prior to the initial loading of operating or systems software updates, the relevant media should be scanned for virus infection. New or updated versions of the software should be kept separate from live or production systems until they have been appropriately tested and approved for live use. Particular attention should be paid to assessing the performance impact of changes and software revisions.

The appropriate configuration of the operating system is crucial, because if the incorrect installation details (i.e. attached devices) or parameters are established, the day-to-day operation of the installation can be jeopardised. Supporting documentation detailing the configuration should also be provided, and updated with subsequent amendments; this will provide a trail for use if any problems are subsequently encountered. Where applicable the definition and application of the standard 'workmix' should be agreed and tested so that optimum performance is achieved. Amendments to this site standard should be suitably authorised by management and only applied by qualified staff.

Access to facilities, systems and data may either be controlled by mechanisms integrated within the operating system or augmented by separate packages (e.g. IBM's RACF) that are linked to the relevant operating system. The subject of access control is addressed in detail in Chapter 17.

Systems can provide relatively powerful privilege user facilities. Such facilities should be adequately protected by effective access controls and journal reporting for independent management review. Operating systems can contain catalogues of users, files, related permissions, and details of the installation configuration. These details are critical for the ongoing secure and controlled operation of the facilities and should be adequately protected and backed up.

An important feature of operating systems is the ability to restart and recover from a failure. This involves the maintenance of records of activity at a very detailed level as well as making copies of data, etc in the normal course of processing. These elements can then be brought together to recommence processing from the point of the failure. As part of proving the ability to recover from an IT-related disaster, the rebuilding of the operating environment should be periodically tested outwith the normal production service timetable.

Operating systems are capable of generating and recording vast amounts of data about activities, usage of facilities, etc. Such details are normally written to electronic journals or logs that can be subsequently printed out or transferred to microfiche. Journals can either be standard or have their contents tailored to the needs of management, for example to report upon instances of attempted access violation. Some journals are necessary for monitoring by management to determine the optimum system performance, whereas others can be tailored to specific needs, for example, use by either internal or external auditors. The usage of machine facilities is monitored and recorded by the operating system and can be used as the basis for usage accounting and client charging purposes.

Any errors reported either by or about the operating system will require to be logged, reported to the technical support staff or supplier and promptly rectified. There may also be the necessity to promptly confirm that processing has not been adversely affected and that data and systems retain their integrity.

In addition to the central operating system, a manufacturer or supplier will also provide a set of utility programs which normally handle basic or housekeeping activities, such as sorting files, copying files, and format conversions. These utility programs can be called during normal processing by the JCL which should have been previously authorised for use. However, some utilities (i.e. those enabling file editing facilities) could, if misused, cause considerable disruption, especially as they tend to operate at a high status level which can circumvent normal processing controls and restrictions. It is essential that the use of such facilities is controlled, restricted and monitored.

Most large operating systems provide diagnostic facilities for use by technical support staff or service engineers, etc. In some cases, this software can be accessed remotely by the manufacturer (by prior agreement) using communication lines. Operating systems are also capable of detecting faults and, where appropriate, routing functions via replicated components to avoid disruption.

PERSONAL COMPUTERS

Personal Computers offer users a much more direct way of handling their business data requirements, but this approachability does have its downside in that access and operating mechanisms on personal computers are not normally as secure as those found in mainframe situations. There are products available which provide facilities such as access control and basic journalising facilities for personal computers, and these can be considered for use on the more critical machines.

Operating systems for personal computers are normally supplied on diskettes and can be loaded via the on-board floppy disk drive. This same drive can be used to either reload the operating software or allow the re-booting of the machine from the software contained on the diskette. If the integrity of data and processing is to be maintained, it is essential that the operation of the PC is conducted on a known and approved basis using the appropriate operating software. To prevent the use of alternative or outdated versions of the operating system being applied, the source diskettes should not be readily accessible, alternatively the floppy drive can be disabled or locked to prevent unauthorised use.

As with mainframe systems, the loading, updating and configuring of PC operating systems should only be undertaken by experienced and authorised personnel and users should be discouraged from experimenting. Personal Computer matters are discussed more fully in Chapter 11.

Control matrix example

The example matrix provided as Table 20 is *Exposure* oriented and its contents address both mainframe and personal computer matters, albeit that there is an intentional bias towards mainframe issues.

In mainframe installations, the correct and efficient functioning of operating system software is crucial and therefore the example data is set to high values. A minor reduction in significance is recorded for the example data relative to the Personal Computer's considerations. *Scale* 4 has been used in the example and details of this and all the other *Scales* can be found in Appendix 5. The '*Best*' score data provided represents a middle range of expectation that the relevant controls will counteract the noted exposures.

Table 20   Systems/Operating Software - Exposures

Overall Inherent Risk (Size) Score [5 is worst risk; 1 is best] = 3.39

A Failed to achieve objectives due to incorrect configuration
B Errors, delay, etc. due to inexperienced technical staff
C Absence of adequate procedures - delay, error, disruption
D Inadequate documentation of environment - unable to recover
E Unauthorised amendment of operating configuration - delay
F Inadequate support of operating environment - disruption
G Inadequate assessment & testing of software upgrades, fixes
H Corruption of data/systems due to unauthorised access

I Inadequate segregation of duties - misuse of facilities
J Unauthorised use of privileged facilities - major disruption
K Inability to promptly recover following failure, etc.
L Failure to monitor/react to system performance - disruption
M Failure to detect and correct errors, faults, etc. - delay
N Unauthorised use of utility & diagnostic software
O Inadequate journals or inability to detect abnormal events
P Use of unauthorised PC operating system - affects integrity
Q Unauthorised access to/amendment of PC configuration files
R Ability to re-boot PCs from floppy disks - affects integrity

System/Operating Software		EXPOSURES																	
		A	B	C	D	E	F	G	H	I	J	K	L	M	N	O	P	Q	R
Calculated Risk Score	Risk	4	4	4	3	3	4	3	4	4	3	3	3	3	3	2	3	3	3
Scale 4 (6 is most serious)	Type	6	5	5	5	6	5	4	6	5	4	6	6	5	4	5	4	4	4
Size (3 is maximum)	Size	3	3	3	2	2	3	3	3	3	3	2	2	2	3	1	3	3	3
CONTROLS																				
1 Operating system reflects hardware configuration and all current systems	Best	4																		
	Test	?	?																	
	Both																			
2 Work scheduling software is utilised for mainstream processing	Best	4																		
	Test	?	?																	
	Both																			
3 System performance is monitored and necessary amendments are tested, approved & applied	Best	4																		
	Test	?	?																	
	Both																			
4 Experienced technical Support staff are employed - subject to fidelity bonding	Best		4				4													
	Test	?		?				?												
	Both																			
5 Relevant/current training is provided	Best		4				3													
	Test	?		?				?												
	Both																			
6 Procedures and standards are applied & monitored in relation to Tech.Support activities	Best			5																
	Test	?			?															
	Both																			
7 Access controls applied in accord with the system owner's objectives	Best		3						4											
	Test	?	?						?											
	Both																			

Table 20   continued

			A	B	C	D	E	F	G	H	I	J	K	L	M	N	O	P	Q	R
8	Configuration and amendments are documented. Recovery processes are recorded	Best				4														
		Test	?			?														
		Both																		
-		-	-	-	-	-	-	-	-	-	-	-	-	-	-	-	-	-	-	-
9	Only authorised/tested JCL is used in the production environment	Best		4					3											
		Test	?	?					?											
		Both																		
-		-	-	-	-	-	-	-	-	-	-	-	-	-	-	-	-	-	-	-
10	Access to operating system is restricted to Technical Support staff only	Best					4													
		Test	?				?													
		Both																		
-		-	-	-	-	-	-	-	-	-	-	-	-	-	-	-	-	-	-	-
11	Access to privileged user facilities is protected by access controls	Best					4					4								
		Test	?				?					?								
		Both																		
-		-	-	-	-	-	-	-	-	-	-	-	-	-	-	-	-	-	-	-
12	Use of privileged facilities is recorded on management journal for review and sign-off	Best					4					4					4			
		Test	?				?					?					?			
		Both																		
-		-	-	-	-	-	-	-	-	-	-	-	-	-	-	-	-	-	-	-
13	Unauthorised access is prevented by access controls defined in the Data Dictionary	Best					4			4										
		Test	?				?			?										
		Both																		
-		-	-	-	-	-	-	-	-	-	-	-	-	-	-	-	-	-	-	-
14	All technical support activity is journalised for management review	Best		4	4		4					4								
		Test	?	?	?		?					?								
		Both																		
-		-	-	-	-	-	-	-	-	-	-	-	-	-	-	-	-	-	-	-
15	Only tested & approved operating software is utilised. Configured to maximise performance	Best						3	3											
		Test	?					?	?											
		Both																		
-		-	-	-	-	-	-	-	-	-	-	-	-	-	-	-	-	-	-	-
16	Operating system is supplied by well-established and reputable mainframe supplier	Best						4												
		Test	?					?												
		Both																		
-		-	-	-	-	-	-	-	-	-	-	-	-	-	-	-	-	-	-	-
17	Supplier provides product upgrades, fixes, and telephone support for system	Best						4												
		Test	?					?												
		Both																		
-		-	-	-	-	-	-	-	-	-	-	-	-	-	-	-	-	-	-	-
18	All required amendments are assessed, tested, documented & authorised before live use	Best						4												
		Test	?					?												
		Both																		
-		-	-	-	-	-	-	-	-	-	-	-	-	-	-	-	-	-	-	-
19	All upgrades, etc. are assessed for impact, tested & authorised prior to live usage	Best						4												
		Test	?					?												
		Both																		
-		-	-	-	-	-	-	-	-	-	-	-	-	-	-	-	-	-	-	-

Table 20   continued

			A	B	C	D	E	F	G	H	I	J	K	L	M	N	O	P	Q	R
20	Strict segregation of duties is applied to programming, technical support, operations, etc.	Best								4	5									
		Test	?							?	?									
		Both																		
-		-	-	-	-	-	-	-	-	-	-	-	-	-	-	-	-	-	-	-
21	All events are logged, to enable recovery process	Best											4			4				
		Test	?										?			?				
		Both																		
-		-	-	-	-	-	-	-	-	-	-	-	-	-	-	-	-	-	-	-
22	All necessary recovery journals are maintained. Recovery is regularly tested	Best											4			4				
		Test	?										?			?				
		Both																		
-		-	-	-	-	-	-	-	-	-	-	-	-	-	-	-	-	-	-	-
23	Rebuilding of the operating environment is tested as part of Disaster Recovery Plan tests	Best											4							
		Test	?										?							
		Both																		
-		-	-	-	-	-	-	-	-	-	-	-	-	-	-	-	-	-	-	-
24	System performance is monitored - management approval is required to amend the 'workmix'	Best		4										4						
		Test	?	?										?						
		Both																		
-		-	-	-	-	-	-	-	-	-	-	-	-	-	-	-	-	-	-	-
25	All errors reported by the operating system are logged, documented, and actioned	Best												5						
		Test	?											?						
		Both																		
-		-	-	-	-	-	-	-	-	-	-	-	-	-	-	-	-	-	-	-
26	Utilities are called by tested and authorised JCL	Best													4					
		Test	?												?					
		Both																		
-		-	-	-	-	-	-	-	-	-	-	-	-	-	-	-	-	-	-	-
27	Use of utilities (other than at 26 above) is prevented by access controls	Best													4					
		Test	?												?					
		Both																		
-		-	-	-	-	-	-	-	-	-	-	-	-	-	-	-	-	-	-	-
28	Access to diagnostic software is restricted by access controls. Use is journalised	Best													4					
		Test	?												?					
		Both																		
-		-	-	-	-	-	-	-	-	-	-	-	-	-	-	-	-	-	-	-
29	Attempted access violations are recorded on specific journal & reviewed by management	Best														4				
		Test	?													?				
		Both																		
-		-	-	-	-	-	-	-	-	-	-	-	-	-	-	-	-	-	-	-
30	Single standard PC operating system is in use - disks held by User Support staff	Best																4		4
		Test	?															?		?
		Both																		
-		-	-	-	-	-	-	-	-	-	-	-	-	-	-	-	-	-	-	-
31	PC operating system files and configuration only loaded and updated by User Support staff	Best																4	4	
		Test	?															?	?	
		Both																		
-		-	-	-	-	-	-	-	-	-	-	-	-	-	-	-	-	-	-	-

Table 20   continued

			A	B	C	D	E	F	G	H	I	J	K	L	M	N	O	P	Q	R
	Disk drive locks prevent	Best																		4
32	unauthorised re-booting from	Test	?																	?
	floppy disks	Both																		
-		-	-	-	-	-	-	-	-	-	-	-	-	-	-	-	-	-	-	-

A Failed to achieve objectives due to incorrect configuration

B Errors, delay, etc. due to inexperienced technical staff

C Absence of adequate procedures - delay, error, disruption

D Inadequate documentation of environment - unable to recover

E Unauthorised amendment of operating configuration - delay

F Inadequate support of operating environment - disruption

G Inadequate assessment & testing of software upgrades, fixes

H Corruption of data/systems due to unauthorised access

I Inadequate segregation of duties - misuse of facilities

J Unauthorised use of privileged facilities - major disruption

K Inability to promptly recover following failure, etc.

L Failure to monitor/react to system performance - disruption

M Failure to detect and correct errors, faults, etc. - delay

N Unauthorised use of utility & diagnostic software

O Inadequate journals or inability to detect abnormal events

P Use of unauthorised PC operating system - affects integrity

Q Unauthorised access to/amendment of PC configuration files

R Ability to re-boot PCs from floppy disks - affects integrity

21

SOFTWARE MAINTENANCE

Scope

This chapter addresses the issues affecting the ongoing maintenance and amendment of application software, including the segregation of production and development program libraries, authorisation of amendments, change and version controls, and the verification of current production program versions.

The issues contained in the example data can relate to any type of computer, albeit that the terminology is naturally more relevant to mainframe installations. In appropriate circumstances, significant modifications should follow the same structured methods as for the development of new system; such requirements are fully explored in Chapter 9 (System Development).

The necessity to modify existing software can be due to a number of reasons, including:

- the detection of a programming error during live operation, which may require urgent correction

- an alteration to the business operation which requires amended software functionality

- changes required to feeder system when the target system has itself been amended, updated or redeveloped

- amendments to relative legislation affecting business systems

- hardware changes which require re-configuration or re-engineering of the software, etc.

Whatever the reason for modifying live programs, the changes need to be determined and applied in a controlled way so as to avoid any undue disruption and safeguard both IT and business operations. It is important that live or production versions of software are protected from unauthorised, untested, possibly malicious amendments. In mainframe installations it is usual to separate live and development (or test) versions of programs by utilising completely segregated libraries. The movement of amended software from the development library to the production (or live) library should then be subject to suitable control and authorisation.

As a further precaution, access to the libraries is restricted so that programmers have no access to the production versions of programs, and operators are barred from accessing the development versions. Such precautions can prevent both accidental and malicious use of incorrect or unproven software and thereby avoid the resultant operational disruptions. Additionally, this barring of access to the relevant program libraries reinforces the required segregation of operating and programming duties.

Requests for program amendments should be made in writing and provide all the relevant supporting facts. Significant or extensive amendments should be subject to a full appraisal of impacts, alternatives, justification, etc. as for new developments, and follow a structured development method so as to ensure that all the prevailing standards and documentary requirements are applied. Where necessary the amendment project should be examined and approved at a strategic level such as an Information Technology Steering Group representing users, the IT function and senior management.

In any event, all modifications should be extensively reviewed and tested before being applied in the live production environment. Such review and testing should not be undertaken by the programmer responsible for the modification, in case the modification contains code designed to deliberately disrupt processing. Users should be encouraged to participate in the testing of significant amendments as their practical knowledge of the business context will augment and support the technically-oriented approach of the systems development team.

The ability to introduce new program versions to the production library should be restricted and subject to effective access controls. All affected parties (users, operations staff, etc.) should signify, in writing, their acceptance of the applied amendment before its transfer to the production library. The relevant transfer process should be handled by staff outwith the programming function and be supported by duly authorised transfer documentation. There may be the necessity to apply amendments to job control processes, so that the new program versions are recognised and accepted. As discussed elsewhere in this book, such changes to JCL should also be fully tested before introduction into live usage.

In order that subsequent work on the relevant programs can proceed efficiently, the relevant parts of the systems and programming documentation should be updated with the effects of all maintenance amendments. Software faults or shortcomings can occur during production operations and a degree of urgency may apply to their correction if, for example, the business operations may be adversely affected. Procedures should be in place to enable the application of emergency fixes to software, and cater for effective testing and documentation. Additionally, the condition of the system and data prior to the error should be secured, so that if the problem is not satisfactorily resolved, the system can be accordingly restarted at the appropriate point.

In order to obtain assurance that the production library contains only previously authorised and correct versions of programs, management can instigate periodic comparisons of the production library version with that of a known secure copy of the program (i.e. the off-site contingency copy). File comparison utility programs are available which support this action, and they report any differences between the two versions. Full reviews of the contents of production libraries should aim to identify any outdated or redundant programs which require removal to archive.

Updating software on personal computers is more straightforward but potentially not so secure as the mainframe scenario described above, as the very ease of use provided by such machines can work against the application of effective levels of control to counteract their misuse. Amendments can be created on a dedicated machine, and they should be extensively tested before introduction into current use by authorised and experienced personnel. User Support staff should ideally undertake regular examination of the directory contents of personal computers, so as to ensure that only authorised and current types and versions of software are in evidence. Chapter 23 examines all the issues relative to User Support facilities.

Control matrix example

The example provided in Table 21 is *Exposure* oriented and the *Scale* and *Size* data used reflects a low to medium risk significance. The *Type* scores provided are related to *Scale* 4, which is described in Appendix 5.

Table 21   Software Maintenance - Exposures

Overall Inherent Risk (Size) Score [5 is worst risk; 1 is best] = 2.24

A Application of unauthorised software amendments - error,etc.
B Failure to adequately assess, document & justify amendments
C Failure to identify all implications of proposed amendments
D Program amendments handled in unstructured manner - error
E Failure to adequately test amendments prior to live use
F Testing applied by amending programmer-potential fraud, etc.
G Failure to develop amendments per prevailing standards, etc.
H Inadequate segregation of programming & operations - abuse
I Failure to apply version control & identify revised program

J Production programs subject to unauthorised amendments
K Inadequate segregation of development & 'live' libraries
L Unauthorised movement of files between program libraries
M Failure to obtain approval from all affected parties
N Failure to update all system documentation with amendments
O Absence of specific procedures for emergency program fixes
P Failure to confirm correct contents of production library
Q Unauthorised software versions & amendments applied
     to PCs

Software Maintenance		EXPOSURES																
		–	–	–	–	–	–	–	–	–	–	–	–	–	–	–	–	–
		A	B	C	D	E	F	G	H	I	J	K	L	M	N	O	P	Q
		=	=	=	=	=	=	=	=	=	=	=	=	=	=	=	=	=
Calculated Risk Score	Risk	3	2	2	3	3	3	3	2	2	3	3	3	3	2	2	3	2
		-	-	-	-	-	-	-	-	-	-	-	-	-	-	-	-	-
Scale 4 (6 is most serious)	Type	5	3	3	4	5	4	5	5	4	5	4	5	4	3	3	5	4
Size (3 is maximum)	Size	2	2	2	2	2	2	2	1	1	2	2	2	2	2	2	2	1
CONTROLS	-	-		-	-	-	-	-	-	-	-	-	-	-		-		-
1 Amendment requests are reviewed and authorised by the IT Steering Group	Best		4															
	Test	?	?															
	Both																	
-		-	-	-	-	-	-	-	-	-	-	-	-	-	-	-	-	-
2 Only authorised amendments can proceed through the official development channel	Best		4															
	Test	?	?															
	Both																	
-		-	-	-	-	-	-	-	-	-	-	-	-	-	-	-	-	-
3 Change Request Forms are raised, defining necessity for change, costs, implications, etc.	Best			4														
	Test	?		?														
	Both																	
-		-	-	-	-	-	-	-	-	-	-	-	-	-	-	-	-	-
4 Operational & other system implications are identified and reviewed for proposed changes	Best			4	5													
	Test	?		?	?													
	Both																	
-		-	-	-	-	-	-	-	-	-	-	-	-	-	-	-	-	-
5 Amendments applied using the facilities of a structured development framework	Best				5													
	Test	?			?													
	Both																	
-		-	-	-	-	-	-	-	-	-	-	-	-	-	-	-	-	-
6 Test plan developed for each modification project; approved before use	Best					5												
	Test	?				?												
	Both																	
-		-	-	-	-	-	-	-	-	-	-	-	-	-	-	-	-	-
7 Testing undertaken and reviewed by staff other than those programming the amendments	Best					5												
	Test	?				?												
	Both																	
-		-	-	-	-	-	-	-	-	-	-	-	-	-	-	-	-	-

Table 21   continued

			A	B	C	D	E	F	G	H	I	J	K	L	M	N	O	P	Q
8	Programming, documentation and project control standards are applied per current policies	Best							5										
		Test	?						?										
		Both																	
-		-	-	-	-	-	-	-	-	-	-	-	-	-	-	-	-	-	-
9	Segregation prevents programmers accessing production library, & operators accessing test library	Best								5									
		Test	?							?									
		Both																	
-		-	-	-	-	-	-	-	-	-	-	-	-	-	-	-	-	-	-
10	Version controls applied to all programs, and revised files are accordingly identified	Best									4								
		Test	?								?								
		Both																	
-		-	-	-	-	-	-	-	-	-	-	-	-	-	-	-	-	-	-
11	Access controls prevent programmers accessing the production library	Best									5	4							
		Test	?								?	?							
		Both																	
-		-	-	-	-	-	-	-	-	-	-	-	-	-	-	-	-	-	-
12	Separate development and production libraries in place - Protected by access controls	Best										4							
		Test	?									?							
		Both																	
-		-	-	-	-	-	-	-	-	-	-	-	-	-	-	-	-	-	-
13	Authorised Program Release form supports all file transfers between libraries	Best											4						
		Test	?										?						
		Both																	
-		-	-	-	-	-	-	-	-	-	-	-	-	-	-	-	-	-	-
14	Program transfers effected by staff outwith development and operations departments	Best											4						
		Test	?										?						
		Both																	
-		-	-	-	-	-	-	-	-	-	-	-	-	-	-	-	-	-	-
15	All affected parties confirm their acceptance of amendments by signing the release form	Best												5					
		Test	?											?					
		Both																	
-		-	-	-	-	-	-	-	-	-	-	-	-	-	-	-	-	-	-
16	Revised program listings & other supporting details placed in document library/off-site store	Best													4				
		Test	?												?				
		Both																	
-		-	-	-	-	-	-	-	-	-	-	-	-	-	-	-	-	-	-
17	Emergency fix procedures are in place defining requirements, authorities, trailing, etc.	Best														4			
		Test	?													?			
		Both																	
-		-	-	-	-	-	-	-	-	-	-	-	-	-	-	-	-	-	-
18	On-call arrangements established for contacting key development & user management in emergencies	Best														4			
		Test	?													?			
		Both																	
-		-	-	-	-	-	-	-	-	-	-	-	-	-	-	-	-	-	-
19	Key programs in production library are compared every six months to control versions	Best															4		
		Test	?														?		
		Both																	
-		-	-	-	-	-	-	-	-	-	-	-	-	-	-	-	-	-	-

Table 21 continued

			A	B	C	D	E	F	G	H	I	J	K	L	M	N	O	P	Q
20	Outdated versions or redundant programs are removed from the production library	Best																4	
		Test	?															?	
		Both																	
-		-	-	-	-	-	-	-	-	-	-	-	-	-	-	-	-	-	-
21	User Support Dept. undertakes the loading of all amended PC software	Best																	4
		Test	?																?
		Both																	
-		-	-	-	-	-	-	-	-	-	-	-	-	-	-	-	-	-	-
22	General staff are not permitted to update PC software - disk drives can be locked	Best																	4
		Test	?																?
		Both																	
-		-	-	-	-	-	-	-	-	-	-	-	-	-	-	-	-	-	-
23	User Support staff undertake periodic review of PC directory. Unofficial files are removed	Best																	4
		Test	?																?
		Both																	
-		-	-	-	-	-	-	-	-	-	-	-	-	-	-	-	-	-	-

A Application of unauthorised software amendments - error, etc.
B Failure to adequately assess, document & justify amendments
C Failure to identify all implications of proposed amendments
D Program amendments handled in unstructured manner - error
E Failure to adequately test amendments prior to live use
F Testing applied by amending programmer - potential fraud, etc.
G Failure to develop amendments per prevailing standards, etc.
H Inadequate segregation of programming & operations - abuse
I Failure to apply version control & identify revised program

J Production programs subject to unauthorised amendments
K Inadequate segregation of development & 'live' libraries
L Unauthorised movement of files between program libraries
M Failure to obtain approval from all affected parties
N Failure to update all system documentation with amendments
O Absence of specific procedures for emergency program fixes
P Failure to confirm correct contents of production library
Q Unauthorised software versions & amendments applied
    to PCs

22

SOFTWARE PACKAGE SELECTION

Scope

This section covers the establishment of a formal method of evaluating package software including the specification of requirements, researching the market for suitable solutions, assessing the technical requirements, assessing the suitability of available products, assessing the reliability and stability of suppliers, evaluating all the costs, making the final product selection, formalising the arrangements and monitoring supplier performance against expectation.

It is possible that some of the above noted elements, such as amending and implementing the software, will be controlled within the System Development process which is examined in Chapter 9.

In order to meet a relatively routine or standard business requirement (such as accounting ledgers), the use of an existing software package will usually be more practical and economic than developing an application in-house, which latter approach could be described as re-inventing the wheel.

The range of both general and sector-specific software packages is bewildering and the quality factors can vary enormously. Price can be a further distorting factor, especially given the pace of change and the upgrade policy adopted by the supplier. It is all too easy to fall behind the current version and functionality of a package product unless you are willing to subscribe to every upgrade modification. Additionally, failing to keep pace with the current software versions can leave users with limited functionality and systems which are no longer supported by the developers. Failing to choose the right package to meet the requirements from a reliable supplier could be a costly and time-wasting mistake and have direct consequences upon the dependent business operations.

A structured approach to package evaluation should be utilised to ensure that all possible packages are evaluated on the same basis, and to further ensure comprehensive examination of all the relevant factors, such as:

- identifying requirements (functional, hardware compatibility, scale, etc.)

- ensuring compatibility with any prevailing acquisition standards and the aims of the strategic plans

- researching the market for potentially suitable products

- attending demonstrations

- matching requirements to product features

- ensuring the software contains adequate controls and trailing facilities

- identifying the required operating environment and any technical limitations

- shortlisting apparently suitable products for more detailed evaluation

- determining the position in the market of the product (market share, age of product, reputation, etc.)

- appraising supplier reputation and/or track record

- seeking the opinion of existing users (a questionnaire can be used or a personal visit undertaken if practical)

- assessing the supplier's ability to support the product and/or apply any required modifications (written assurances should ideally be obtained)

- clearly establishing all costs (including those for future upgrades, customising, training, data conversion, etc.)

- analysing all the key factors identified and the replies received and making selection

- ensuring that critical factors, such as modifications, timescales, support expectations, etc. are formally agreed in writing with the supplier

- once the order is placed, monitoring progress on supply and/or modifications and managing against expectations

- planning and managing the delivery, installation and implementation of the software

- signifying the user's acceptance of the product before final settlement of accounts.

Packages fall basically into two categories, those that address a specialist requirement (for example a Fleet Management system), and those which address common business or functional requirements, such as accounting packages. In either situation, the user may not be able to satisfy all his/her requirements from the standard product, and will require some degree of modification to allow for this.

When considering a significant investment in package software, the available products should be extensively reviewed, in a disciplined way, against the established requirements of the users. The prime factor is to accurately identify the functionality, flexibility and features that the user requires, in order that adequate comparisons can be made with available products. If any product requires modification to more readily reflect the user's requirements, it is essential that the required changes are unambiguously specified in detail so as to form the basis for the action taken subsequently by the supplier/developer.

Some packaged software is specific to a particular hardware platform or configuration, therefore it is important, when evaluating potential software solutions, to ensure that you either have the current hardware capability to run the package, or are prepared to re-equip or upgrade if these are viable possibilities.

The reliability of the supplier is an important factor. The choice of software house/supplier for general packages can be bewildering, and it is important that they are stable so that future support and upgrading of the package is available. Additionally, assess the position of the product and supplier in the market and other obvious quality factors, including:

- how long the product been available

- is this the first version and are you going to be one of the guinea pig users?

- the number of sites currently using the software in live operations, not merely as reference or test sites

- existing users and their views about the product and the quality of support

- the public track record and general image of the supplier

- how long have they been in business, what scale of operation do they run and does this reaffirm the impressions of stability?

- what are the upgrade and maintenance costs likely to be during the lifetime of the package and are they justified in relation to the functionality provided?

- what are the warranty arrangements and do they include any user-specified modifications?

- is the documentation (including that for amendments) of an acceptable quality?

- what are the arrangements in respect of access to and ownership of source code?

- are the end user's needs for support and guidance going to be satisfactorily addressed?

- is there an established and effective user group?

Control matrix example

As this subject has a strong synergy with the provision of an effective method of product review, the example matrix provided as Table 22 is *Exposure* oriented. The supplied example value data relates to a low size impact situation, but where selected exposures could have potentially higher levels of inherent risk. The use of *Scale* 4 has been suggested in this example in the context of the exposures relationship to the achievement of corporate goals; details of the narrative for this *Scale* are contained in Appendix 5.

Table 22   Software Selection - Exposures

Overall Inherent Risk (Size) Score [5 is worst risk; 1 is best] = 1.31

A Failure to adequately assess package acquisition - costs
B Failure to accurately identify functional requirements
C Failure to adequately assess the technical implications
D Failure to comply with requirements of IT Strategic Plan
E Inadequate research of available solutions - additional cost
F Failure to identify/specify modifications - functionality
G Inadequate control & trailing facilities - error, etc.
H Failure to assess reliability of suppliers - no support

I Failure to assess market position & performance of product
J Inadequate support, upgrade path, etc. - business disruption
K Failure to identify and justify all related costs
L Failure to adequately test software and/or modifications
M Poor user documentation - delay, error, disruption
N Failure to adequately train users - error, delay, costs, etc.
O Failure to agree delivery, deadlines and other requirements
P Failure to adequately plan implementation process - delay

	Software Selection		EXPOSURES														
			—	—	—	—	—	—	—	—	—	—	—	—	—	—	—	—
			A	B	C	D	E	F	G	H	I	J	K	L	M	N	O	P
			=	=	=	=	=	=	=	=	=	=	=	=	=	=	=	=
	Calculated Risk Score	Risk	2	2	2	2	2	2	2	2	2	2	2	2	2	2	2	2
			-	-	-	-	-	-	-	-	-	-	-	-	-	-	-	-
	Scale 4 (6 is most serious)	Type	6	6	3	6	4	3	4	3	3	4	3	5	3	3	6	3
	Size (3 is maximum)	Size	1	1	1	1	1	1	1	1	1	1	1	1	1	1	1	1
	CONTROLS	-	-	-	-	-	-	-	-	-	-	-	-	-	-	-	-	-	-
	Software package evaluation	Best		5														
1	procedures established, define	Test	?	?														
	issues to address & methods	Both																
-		-	-	-	-	-	-	-	-	-	-	-	-	-	-	-	-	-
	Requirements specification is	Best			4													
2	produced to assess suitability	Test	?		?													
	& functionality of products	Both																
-		-	-	-	-	-	-	-	-	-	-	-	-	-	-	-	-	-
	Requirements include definition	Best				4	3											
3	of ideal hardware platform per	Test	?			?	?											
	IT Strategic Plan	Both																
-		-	-	-	-	-	-	-	-	-	-	-	-	-	-	-	-	-
	New / additional hardware needs	Best			4						4							
4	have to be cost justified to	Test	?		?						?							
	IT Steering Committee	Both																
-		-	-	-	-	-	-	-	-	-	-	-	-	-	-	-	-	-
	All purchases & developments are	Best				5					4							
5	checked for compliance with IT	Test	?			?					?							
	strategic direction per plan	Both																
-		-	-	-	-	-	-	-	-	-	-	-	-	-	-	-	-	-
	Data is gathered on potential	Best					2											
6	solutions for subsequent	Test	?				?											
	analysis and comparison	Both																
-		-	-	-	-	-	-	-	-	-	-	-	-	-	-	-	-	-
	Process in place to obtain data	Best					4		3									
7	about supplier. Existing users	Test	?				?		?									
	are contacted for opinions	Both																
-		-	-	-	-	-	-	-	-	-	-	-	-	-	-	-	-	-

Table 22   continued

			A	B	C	D	E	F	G	H	I	J	K	L	M	N	O	P
	Product assessed on time in	Best					4											
8	market, level of support, ease	Test	?				?											
	of modification, price, etc.	Both																
-		-	-	-	-	-	-	-	-	-	-	-	-	-	-	-	-	-
	Formal questionnaire used to	Best					4			3								
9	record supplier and product	Test	?				?			?								
	information	Both																
-		-	-	-	-	-	-	-	-	-	-	-	-	-	-	-	-	-
	Existing users are visited or	Best					4			4								
10	sent a questionnaire	Test	?				?			?								
		Both																
-		-	-	-	-	-	-	-	-	-	-	-	-	-	-	-	-	-
	Users and IT staff attend	Best					4											
11	demonstrations	Test	?				?											
		Both																
-		-	-	-	-	-	-	-	-	-	-	-	-	-	-	-	-	-
	Any required modifications are	Best						5										
12	documented, justified and costed	Test	?					?										
		Both																
-		-	-	-	-	-	-	-	-	-	-	-	-	-	-	-	-	-
	Specification for modifications	Best					4											
13	sent to supplier for agreement	Test	?				?											
		Both																
-		-	-	-	-	-	-	-	-	-	-	-	-	-	-	-	-	-
	Details of controls & trailing	Best							4									
14	are requested as part of	Test	?						?									
	matching with requirements	Both																
-		-	-	-	-	-	-	-	-	-	-	-	-	-	-	-	-	-
	Support services are assessed -	Best										3						
15	frequency & costs of upgrades	Test	?									?						
	are reviewed for reasonableness	Both																
-		-	-	-	-	-	-	-	-	-	-	-	-	-	-	-	-	-
	Products have to conform to	Best										4			5			
16	company documentation standards	Test	?									?			?			
		Both																
-		-	-	-	-	-	-	-	-	-	-	-	-	-	-	-	-	-
	All costs are identified (i.e.	Best											4					
17	customising, maintenance,	Test	?										?					
	training, implementation, etc.)	Both																
-		-	-	-	-	-	-	-	-	-	-	-	-	-	-	-	-	-
	All project costs are justified	Best											5					
18	and approved by systems	Test	?										?					
	committee	Both																
-		-	-	-	-	-	-	-	-	-	-	-	-	-	-	-	-	-
	Test programs are created and	Best												5				
19	applied (per development	Test	?											?				
	method) - results recorded	Both																
-		-	-	-	-	-	-	-	-	-	-	-	-	-	-	-	-	-

Table 22   continued

			A	B	C	D	E	F	G	H	I	J	K	L	M	N	O	P
20	User documentation (of the required standard) to be supplied per methodology	Best													4			
		Test	?												?			
		Both																
-		-	-	-	-	-	-	-	-	-	-	-	-	-	-	-	-	-
21	Training is provided (either in-house or by supplier) if required by users	Best														3		
		Test	?													?		
		Both																
-		-	-	-	-	-	-	-	-	-	-	-	-	-	-	-	-	-
22	All critical factors confirmed in writing to suppliers - confirmation is sought	Best															4	
		Test	?														?	
		Both																
-		-	-	-	-	-	-	-	-	-	-	-	-	-	-	-	-	-
23	All implementation impacts are identified and addressed. Plan produced and agreed	Best																4
		Test	?															?
		Both																
-		-	-	-	-	-	-	-	-	-	-	-	-	-	-	-	-	-
24	Implementation procedures (as per development methodology) are applied to software packages	Best																4
		Test	?															?
		Both																
-		-	-	-	-	-	-	-	-	-	-	-	-	-	-	-	-	-

A Failure to adequately assess package acquisition - costs
B Failure to accurately identify functional requirements
C Failure to adequately assess the technical implications
D Failure to comply with requirements of IT Strategic Plan
E Inadequate research of available solutions - additional cost
F Failure to identify/specify modifications - functionality
G Inadequate control & trailing facilities - error, etc.
H Failure to assess reliability of suppliers - no support

I Failure to assess market position & performance of product
J Inadequate support, upgrade path, etc. - business disruption
K Failure to identify and justify all related costs
L Failure to adequately test software and/or modifications
M Poor user documentation - delay, error, disruption
N Failure to adequately train users - error, delay, costs, etc.
O Failure to agree delivery, deadlines and other requirements
P Failure to adequately plan implementation process - delay

23

USER SUPPORT

Scope

This chapter explores the provision of services designed to support users of corporate computing facilities of all kinds in order to ensure efficient usage, continuity of service, security of systems, adequacy of guidance, and effective response to problems. The contents address the day-to-day needs of users, and although mention is made of preventing unauthorised amendments to software, the establishment of (and compliance with) corporate-wide Personal Computer operating standards is specifically addressed in Chapter 11.

The proliferation of end-user computing facilities and the related increase in dependence upon all the forms of Information Technology has, among other factors, resulted in the general de-mystification of computing and the opening up of learning opportunities for non-IT employees. Although it may be the accepted company culture to promote systems ownership and end-user computing in a positive context, these approaches should be adequately supported so that there is consistent and secure usage of facilities throughout the organisation as means of protecting the interests of the company through the assured security of systems and data. A little knowledge can be a dangerous thing, and measures should be in place to, at best, prevent users from amending company software and data or, at least, enable the prompt detection of such alterations.

The support functions can be broken down as follows, although perhaps not all the items listed will apply in every case:

- 'Help Desk' facility to respond to hardware, software or communications problems or failures

- point of contact for advice on use of specific applications or PC facilities

- ensuring that levels of service are maintained and problems are quickly and effectively resolved

- providing guidance on matters of security, data back-up, etc. and the promotion of IT best practice.

Before embarking upon the establishment of User Support facilities, it will be necessary to identify the nature and extent of systems and applications in use throughout the organisation. This process may already have been undertaken as part of a strategic planning process. Having obtained an accurate view of the current IT scene, consideration should be given to the level of expertise required to successfully operate this environment; again this type of review information may already exist as a by-product of a staffing and skills planning process. The aim is then to assess how well the existing skills levels (in both the IT and user communities) match with the prevailing demands of the environment. Shortfalls in the IT sphere can be addressed by, for example, targeted training. The accurate determination of the currency and effectiveness of user capabilities is more difficult to assess, but there are normally coarser indications of problems available, such as disruptions caused by incorrect system usage, interruption of production tasks due to heavy demands from on-line interrogation systems caused by inefficient use, etc.

One must take account of the potential effects of lack of knowledge on a scale ranging from mild irritation to major disruption of services. Time wastage is perhaps the most common outcome with time representing cost and lost productivity. It is difficult to measure user frustration in quite the same terms, but this can in itself lead to the adoption of alternative and potentially unsound practices. The root problem may lie with inadequate procedural guidance or inappropriate system structure and these shortcomings will need to resolved by other means.

In companies with a high dependence upon distributed systems and networks, the establishment of a central Help Desk facility may provide the answer. However it is essential to ensure that the staffing levels for this service are sufficient both in number and knowledge in terms of the equipment and systems in use. The Help Desk should be able to promptly respond to hardware, software and communications problems. All reported faults should be logged and classified according to inherent type, etc. Help Desk staff should be obligated to keep users informed about the progress of their enquiry if it has been referred elsewhere for rectification. The logging system will need to record the date and time of reports and all subsequent action stages, and ideally provide suitable triggers for the escalation of outstanding problems to the next level of action. There may be a service level agreement in place affecting the provision of help desk services, therefore data summarising the performance of same may be useful for management in determining whether these standards are being suitably maintained.

Although the Help Desk may also act as the focus for initial enquiries about corporate software, these may be referred to individuals who are registered as having the appropriate degree of knowledge. The existence of established company standards and procedures with regard to the consistent and controlled use of software products will be an advantage to both user and IT staff.

End-users should be generally discouraged and prevented from applying unofficial amendments to either software or system configurations. In this respect it may be necessary for the help desk and other IT support staff to visit users and apply any necessary changes themselves in accordance with any company instructions. In approaching the user computing facilities, it is important to ensure that the support arrangements do not infringe upon the security surrounding user applications, and that support staff are prevented from breaching access, data entry or confidentiality related controls. Users should be advised to change passwords as a precaution immediately after support staff involvement.

In larger organisations, it may be useful and productive to establish points of reference for staff to enquire upon matters of security, back-up and other matters of good practice where there are standard company policies and procedures available. If standards are in place which define such factors as basic PC configuration, these can be regularly checked by user support staff undertaking reviews of equipment; such a process would also enable the detection of unauthorised versions of software. An alternative is to devolve support activities out into the user community, although it is, in such situations, essential to ensure the adequacy and quality of the staff involved. However, this approach may still require a degree of centralised expertise, albeit on a reduced scale.

Control matrix example

The example matrix that follows in Table 23 is *Exposure* oriented and aims to represent a scenario with a medium level of IT dependency. The example *Controls* primarily relate to the personal computing environment with the potential to connect to central systems. The *Exposure* type scores are related, in this example, to *Scale* 4 (see Appendix 5 for supporting narratives for this *Scale*).

Table 23   User Support - Exposures

Overall Inherent Risk (Size) Score [5 is worst risk; 1 is best] = 2.33

A Inadequate/inaccurate assessment of support requirements

B Failure to provide adequate resources - delay, costs, error

C Support action fails to uphold IT policies - integrity, etc

D Failure to record/action hardware, software & comms. faults

E Inadequate action, progressing, escalation of faults - delay

F Absence of clear support/Help Desk procedures - error, delay

G Failure to obtain user opinion & agreement on procedures

H Failure to monitor time lost, support team preformance, etc.

I Failure to achieve required system availability targets

J Failure to provide adequate/experienced support staff

K Support staff have access to user data, etc. - fraud, error

L Failure to detect unofficial amendments to software, etc.

	User Support		EXPOSURES												
				A	B	C	D	E	F	G	H	I	J	K	L
	Calculated Risk Score	Risk		3	2	3	3	3	2	2	2	2	2	3	3
	Scale 4 (6 is most serious)	Type		5	6	5	5	5	3	3	6	6	3	4	4
	Size (3 is maximum)	Size		2	1	2	2	2	2	2	1	1	2	2	2
	CONTROLS														
1	Full review of active systems & user opinions/requirements was undertaken and results assessed	Best		5						4					
		Test	?	?						?					
		Both													
2	Support facility proposals were documented, discussed and agreed with all users	Best			5					4					
		Test	?		?					?					
		Both													
3	Help Desk & Support procedures documented	Best			2	3			4	3					
		Test	?		?	?			?	?					
		Both													
4	Procedures conform with all prevailing policies on security, service level, approved s/w, etc.	Best				5						4			
		Test	?			?						?			
		Both													
5	Help Desk logging & reporting system acquired - all calls are logged and progressed	Best					4	4			3				
		Test	?				?	?			?				
		Both													
6	System at 5 above produces daily weekly and monthly statistics on performance, etc.	Best									5	3			
		Test	?								?	?			
		Both													
7	Help Desk procedures provide for progressive escalation of serious faults or delays	Best					4	4	4						
		Test	?				?	?	?						
		Both													

Table 23   continued

			A	B	C	D	E	F	G	H	I	J	K	L
	Dedicated User Support staff	Best										5		
8	are provided, with the relevant	Test	?									?		
	knowledge of hardware/software	Both												
-		-	-	-	-	-	-	-	-	-	-	-	-	-
	Procedures define limits of	Best											3	
9	support activity, e.g. not	Test	?										?	
	entering data into live systems	Both												
-		-	-	-	-	-	-	-	-	-	-	-	-	-
	Users advised to change access	Best											4	
10	passwords, etc. immediately	Test	?										?	
	following Support team visit	Both												
-		-	-	-	-	-	-	-	-	-	-	-	-	-
	Support staff undertake PC file	Best												2
11	& configuration checks to detect	Test	?											?
	unauthorised amendments, etc.	Both												
-		-	-	-	-	-	-	-	-	-	-	-	-	-

24

BACS

Scope

BACS Ltd. was created in 1968 to facilitate an inter-bank automated clearing service. It is now widely used to deal with payroll, other payments, and direct debits. BACS transactions can either be made by a transfer of magnetic media (tape, cartridge or diskette) or via the BACSTEL telecommunications facility. This chapter contains references to both of these methods and also considers the accurate creation of data and the preparation of acceptable BACS files, the transmission of those files, and the reconciliation of the relevant transactions (including any rejections or queries).

It is not our intention to delve into the underlying technical aspects of BACS facilities but to address the general principles and key issues. Registered BACS users will have access to the official manuals which expand considerably upon the points raised here.

Before an organisation is permitted to use BACS facilities, it has to be sponsored by one of the member banks (or building societies); all communication with BACS is normally conducted via the BACS Liaison section of the user's sponsoring bank. Users have to satisfy the BACS requirements for the format and structure of data and the relevant protocols for BACSTEL transmissions. Users also have to be authorised by their sponsors and have satisfactory system test results before being allowed to use the BACSTEL system.

It is usual to nominate individuals to act as a 'Control Point' for BACS matters and to be responsible for holding the BACSAFE device and Authentication Key; these staff should not, for matters of added security, be involved in development of BACS conversion programs or related computer operations.

Although there is a natural inclination to place greater emphasis upon the BACS processing of payments, the incorrect or delayed processing of collections can also have significant effects on a business (i.e. customer dissatisfaction, impact on cashflow, cost of correction, image and reputation).

Although BACS will accept responsibility for the processing of data once it has entered their arena and been validated, the provision of accurate and complete data is clearly the responsibility of the user. BACS processing is conducted on a three day cycle, thus:

- *First Day* (Input day) The latest day for the receipt of files at BACS to allow for processing on the following bank working day

- *Second Day* (Processing day) All records accepted on input day are passed to destination banks

- *Third Day* (Entry day) All debits and credits reach their destination bank accounts.

The BACS systems offer a number of control mechanisms including:

- Each file submitted should be self-balancing

- Identity Labels (checked against data on the tape file header and details of the user held by BACS)

- BACSAFE Device – used to generate passwords for use to gain access to the BACSTEL system

- Transaction Authenticating Number (TAN) generated by the BACSAFE device (as an option) which can be compared to one generated by BACS as confirmation that transmission has been accurately received

- validation to confirm the general acceptability of data

- Overall Limit Checks (which compares the total value of transactions in a specified period to a pre-determined limit parameter)

- Item Limit Check (as above but for each transaction, only reported as a warning on the daily input report sent back to the user, the item will be applied to the account unless the user contacts their sponsoring bank before entry day)

- File Authentication (an algorithm which generates a check total from sort-code, bank account number, transaction value, and a private key supplied by BACS. This total is included in the file trailer record and compared to an equivalent calculated during the BACS validation process; if the two values disagree, the file is rejected in the belief that the data has been subject to alteration)

- Acceptance and Input Reports detailing items processed and any rejections.

It should be noted that BACSTEL users will be able to access their transmission control reports on-line and that it is also possible to arrange that reports are sent via such services as Telecom Gold.

Remember that the above noted measures only affect data from the point when files are passed over to BACS; they do not remove the need to address matters of data accuracy and validity in the processes leading up to the creation of data for BACS purposes. In addition to ensuring that the day-to-day processing environment surrounding all feeder applications is secure, all data converted for BACS purposes should be reconciled to source and its release should be appropriately authorised. Clear and comprehensive BACS procedures should be established and the various key responsibilities allocated.

Access to the use of all BACS facilities should be suitably limited to nominated and experienced individuals who will then be accountable for all subsequent actions. In order to further enhance the security, integrity and fraud prevention factors, suitable segregation of key duties will need to be established; these duties will include the preparation of BACS data, the authority to release data to BACS, the creation and amendment of in-house BACS process-related software.

It is vital to ensure that data submitted via the BACS processes is accurate and complete so as to avoid any subsequent disruptions, impact upon corporate image or reputation, etc. Suitable reconciliation of data back to source files or systems will contribute to the accuracy of transmitted data if applied prior to the release of such data. All data rejections will need to be promptly dealt with, corrected, re-submitted and confirmed as processed.

The release of all BACS transmissions or transfers should be subject to authorisation from the systems owner or their nominated representative. It is important that the release of data is correctly timed to be co-ordinated with the BACS three-day processing cycle and the availability of the requisite funds in the source bank account. Where transfer is effected by magnetic media, they should be securely stored prior to release in order to counter the possibility of tampering or interference.

All BACS processing will need to be confirmed, accounted for and reconciled to the appropriate feeder or target systems. All the constituent systems should provide a complete transaction trail.

Developers involved in the creation of data conversion programs will have to address the relevant data format and transmission protocol requirements of the BACS systems. All such programs will have to be tested to the satisfaction of BACS prior to live use. The integrity of the in-house BACS data conversion programs can be further ensured by the application of effective change control procedures and the regular verification of the current production versions to a known control version.

If there are concerns about abnormal transactions percolating through the existing controls, a further precaution would be the use of the Item Limit Check and the Overall Limit Check. However, management may wish to incorporate additional control checks into the data preparation programs which seek out and report data items for the same bank account.

Control matrix example

This subject has a more natural affinity with the *Exposures* orientation and the example matrix provided as Table 24 is accordingly structured. In actual usage the *Type* and *Size* data values would obviously be dependent upon the nature and scale of business; the example values provided for these factors reflect a low to middle range level of dependency (see *Scale* 4 in Appendix 5 for details in support of the *Type* scores applied). A range of *Best* score data is provided thus reflecting a variation in the anticipated degree of effectiveness of the prescribed *Controls*.

Table 24   BACS - Exposures

Overall Inherent Risk (Size) Score [5 is worst risk; 1 is best] = 1.63

A Inadequate procedures and/or allocation of responsibilities
B Unauthorised access to BACS facilities - error, fraud, etc.
C BACS transfer/transmission not accounted for - error, fraud
D Inadequate segregation of key duties - fraud, loss, disruption
E Unauthorised access to identity labels or BACSAFE device
F Failure to account for all tapes - incorrect tape sent
G Submission of inaccurate, incorrect data - image, delay, cost
H Failure to effect entries at the correct time - cashflow
I Submission of duplicate tapes - image, error, cost, etc.
J Unauthorised release of BACS data - error, fraud, etc.

K Access allowed to on-line BACS data before release - fraud
L Failure to detect abnormal transactions - error, fraud, etc.
M Failure to detect multiple postings to same bank account
N Submission of data in unsuitable format - delay, image, etc.
O Out of date or unrealistic overall and item limits
P Failure to receive or agree BACS reports - error, delay
Q Failure to react to or correct rejections and errors
R Failure to retain records, reports, etc.- lack of audit trail
S Unauthorised amendment of BACS conversion programs - fraud

BACS		A	B	C	D	E	F	G	H	I	J	K	L	M	N	O	P	Q	R	S
EXPOSURES		=	=	=	=	=	=	=	=	=	=	=	=	=	=	=	=	=	=	=
Calculated Risk Score	Risk	2	3	3	3	2	3	3	3	2	3	2	2	2	2	2	3	3	2	2
Scale 4 (6 is most serious)	Type	5	4	4	4	4	4	4	4	3	4	4	4	4	3	3	5	4	4	5
Size (3 is maximum)	Size	1	2	2	2	1	2	2	2	1	2	1	1	1	1	1	1	2	2	1	1
CONTROLS																				
1 BACS Procedure Manual, control point and release authorities established and applied	Best		5																	
	Test	?	?																	
	Both																			
2 Key duties (programming, operation, authorisation, etc.) are adequately segregated	Best		3		5															
	Test	?	?		?															
	Both																			
3 Use of identity labels & BACSAFE device is restricted to nominated individuals	Best		3			4														
	Test	?	?			?														
	Both																			
4 All data transfers/transmissions to BACS are authorised (in writing) by senior officer	Best		2					4		4										
	Test	?	?					?		?										
	Both																			
5 All tapes dispatched/returned are controlled via library system - holding checked monthly	Best		2				4													
	Test	?	?				?													
	Both																			
6 Tapes held in secure tape library prior to dispatch via security couriers	Best		2	2			4													
	Test	?	?	?			?													
	Both																			
7 Register of all BACS files is maintained & updated with detail of confirmations, errors, etc.	Best		3	4																
	Test	?	?	?																
	Both																			

Table 24 continued

#	Item		A	B	C	D	E	F	G	H	I	J	K	L	M	N	O	P	Q	R	S
8	All BACS receipts, acceptance and input reports are retained on file	Best			3															4	
		Test	?		?															?	
		Both																			
-		-		-	-	-	-	-	-	-	-	-	-	-	-	-	-	-	-	-	-
9	Labels, BACSAFE & keys are all held in safe; only accessible to nominated 'control' staff	Best			3		4														
		Test	?		?		?														
		Both																			
-		-		-	-	-	-	-	-	-	-	-	-	-	-	-	-	-	-	-	-
10	BACSTEL activity is confirmed via on-line reporting system	Best				4															
		Test	?			?															
		Both																			
-		-		-	-	-	-	-	-	-	-	-	-	-	-	-	-	-	-	-	-
11	Stocks of identity labels are agreed by user management	Best					3														
		Test	?				?														
		Both																			
-		-		-	-	-	-	-	-	-	-	-	-	-	-	-	-	-	-	-	-
12	BACS data is fully reconciled to source (i.e. value & number of transactions, cash totals)	Best							4				3								
		Test	?						?				?								
		Both																			
-		-		-	-	-	-	-	-	-	-	-	-	-	-	-	-	-	-	-	-
13	All tapes/transmission files are validated for format, etc. prior to release	Best							3						5						
		Test	?						?						?						
		Both																			
-		-		-	-	-	-	-	-	-	-	-	-	-	-	-	-	-	-	-	-
14	Application processing triggers BACS data production in good time for 3 day cycle	Best								4											
		Test	?							?											
		Both																			
-		-		-	-	-	-	-	-	-	-	-	-	-	-	-	-	-	-	-	-
15	BACS validation of file headers and password would reveal duplicate tapes	Best									5										
		Test	?								?										
		Both																			
-		-		-	-	-	-	-	-	-	-	-	-	-	-	-	-	-	-	-	-
16	Disk packs containing BACS files are removed from drive until time of transmission	Best											3								
		Test	?										?								
		Both																			
-		-		-	-	-	-	-	-	-	-	-	-	-	-	-	-	-	-	-	-
17	All BACS files transferred to tape a.s.a.p. following creation	Best											3								
		Test	?										?								
		Both																			
-		-		-	-	-	-	-	-	-	-	-	-	-	-	-	-	-	-	-	-
18	Any BACS files held (briefly) on-line are protected by user-ID and password access system	Best											3								
		Test	?										?								
		Both																			
-		-		-	-	?	-	-	-	-	-	-	-	-	-	-	-	-	-	?	-
19	Overall & item limits are set and reported prior to processing day - independently examined	Best												4							
		Test	?											?							
		Both																			
-		-		-	-	-	-	-	-	-	-	-	-	-	-	-	-	-	-	-	-

Table 24 continued

			A	B	C	D	E	F	G	H	I	J	K	L	M	N	O	P	Q	R	S
20	Overall & item limits are regularly reviewed for relevance, etc.	Best												4			4				
		Test	?											?			?				
		Both																			
-		-	-	-	-	-	-	-	-	-	-	-	-	-	-	-	-	-	-	-	-
21	Total transmission value is checked for prevailing overall limit before release of file	Best												4							
		Test	?											?							
		Both																			
-		-	-	-	-	-	-	-	-	-	-	-	-	-	-	-	-	-	-	-	-
22	In-house interrogation applied to BACS file data to highlight X number of postings to account	Best													4						
		Test	?												?						
		Both																			
-		-	-	-	-	-	-	-	-	-	-	-	-	-	-	-	-	-	-	-	-
23	Transaction data is recorded on multi-processing day files	Best								3											
		Test	?							?											
		Both																			
-		-	-	-	-	-	-	-	-	-	-	-	-	-	-	-	-	-	-	-	-
24	If input report for tapes is not received by processing day, requested via Telecom Gold	Best																4			
		Test	?															?			
		Both																			
-		-	-	-	-	-	-	-	-	-	-	-	-	-	-	-	-	-	-	-	-
25	Acceptance and input reports are examined for errors, etc. and recorded on control sheet	Best																4			
		Test	?															?			
		Both																			
-		-	-	-	-	-	-	-	-	-	-	-	-	-	-	-	-	-	-	-	-
26	All item rejections are actioned on the day of reporting	Best																	4		
		Test	?																?		
		Both																			
-		-	-	-	-	-	-	-	-	-	-	-	-	-	-	-	-	-	-	-	-
27	BACS file creation program is subject to change control procedures	Best																			4
		Test	?																		?
		Both																			
-		-	-	-	-	-	-	-	-	-	-	-	-	-	-	-	-	-	-	-	-
28	Source/object code for file at 27 above is subject to comparison with control version	Best																			4
		Test	?																		?
		Both																			
-		-	-	-	-	-	-	-	-	-	-	-	-	-	-	-	-	-	-	-	-

A Inadequate procedures and/or allocation of responsibilities
B Unauthorised access to BACS facilities - error, fraud, etc.
C BACS transfer/transmission not accounted for - error, fraud
D Inadequate segregation of key duties - fraud, loss, disruption
E Unauthorised access to identity labels or BACSAFE device
F Failure to account for all tapes - incorrect tape sent
G Submission of inaccurate, incorrect data - image, delay, cost
H Failure to effect entries at the correct time - cashflow
I Submission of duplicate tapes - image, error, cost, etc.
J Unauthorised release of BACS data - error, fraud, etc.

K Access allowed to on-line BACS data before release - fraud
L Failure to detect abnormal transactions - error fraud, etc.
M Failure to detect multiple postings to same bank account
N Submission of data in unsuitable format - delay, image, etc.
O Out of date or unrealistic overall and item limits
P Failure to receive or agree BACS reports - error, delay
Q Failure to react to or correct rejections and errors
R Failure to retain records, reports, etc. - lack of audit trail
S Unauthorised amendment of BACS conversion programs - fraud

25

VIRUSES

Scope

This chapter examines the prevention, detection and removal of computer viral infections and attempts to put the subject in perspective. In the context of the contents of this section, infection is intended to relate to all types of computer installations (PC, network systems, mini-computer and mainframe) and this range is reflected in the example matrix file.

In order to set the scene, the following definitions of the principal types of infectious device are provided.

- *a **Virus** is a program that can replicate itself inside other programs; each affected program can then place further executable copies of the original within yet further programs. This process is referred to as infection. With this capability, a virus can spread from computer to computer and from network to network, corrupting programs and data as it progresses*

- *a **Worm** replicates itself without the need to use a host program*

- *a **Time Bomb** is a delayed action program triggered into action at a pre-determined time and date*

- *a **Logic Bomb** is also a delayed action mechanism but may be activated by another machine related event, such as a certain limit of disk capacity having been reached or the use of a particular command sequence*

- *a **Trojan Horse** pretends to achieve one purpose while, in practice, undertaking some other, more destructive task.*

The list of known named viruses is considerable, and yet more are being developed and introduced. We do not intend to go into the various technical details of how viruses are constructed for obvious reasons and because there are publications, some of a somewhat dubious nature, that already cater for this niche market. More serious enquirers will find a number of general guidance sources available, but a side effect of the currency of this subject is that lists of viruses soon become out of date.

There has recently been considerable media interest in the subject of computer viruses and although this may have generally overstated the extent of the situation, the threats and effects are real enough. An infected system may be unreliable and data will be corrupted; the current trend for networking personal computers and connecting same to mini-computers and mainframes can aid the speedy transfer of the infection throughout an organisation. Considerable amounts of time may have to be spent in eradicating the problem, and in the meantime the ability to continue normal processing and trading may have been severely disrupted.

How do you know when you have been infected by a computer virus? Some of the more obvious initial indicators of the presence of a virus are noted below.

- strange graphics or text

- problems retrieving files

- unexpected sound effects

- unusual screen activities and prompts

- software failure or slow program execution

- unknown files or directories appearing

- alterations to the date and clock

- appearance of Bad Sectors on disks

- data being corrupted or destroyed

- unexpected responses to commands.

The following checklist notes some straightforward measures which can help in the process of avoiding and dealing with infections:

- prevent the introduction of unauthorised software

- never allow staff to transfer files onto the company machines from other sources, e.g. their home computer

- run all external disks through a virus checking program on a dedicated stand-alone machine before general use

- do not download software from bulletin boards which offer the more anti-social creators of viruses the perfect launching pad into the wider world

- equipment should only be acquired and installed by authorised members of the IT Department

- any demonstration software received from external sources should arrive shrink-wrapped and with a written certification that it has been successfully checked for infections, albeit that you still need to subject it to your own form of virus checking before use

- install and regularly run virus checking programs on critical machines

- increase the awareness of the problem through the user community and provide clear guidance on the preventative requirements and the action to take if an infection is suspected

- ensure that portable machines or those used regularly outside the main office are scanned upon return and before re-connection to a network

- lock your PC/Terminal when not in use and securely store the keys

- prevent unauthorised introduction of software by providing floppy disk drive locks

- introduce mechanisms whereby the system cannot be routinely re-booted from the floppy drive

- regularly back-up data, etc. so that you would be able to recover from an infection

- format disks/diskettes in-house

- write-protect disks

- only allow authorised company staff access to your machine(s)

- control access to personal computers and workstations by using user-ID and passwords

- prevent visiting engineers from using their own disks

- don't lend company disks to friends or other staff members

- if infection is suspected, immediately isolate the affected machine and clearly label it so as to avoid further use

- immediately contact your Help Desk or User Support facility and provide as much detail as possible regarding effects, etc. Take screen prints if possible and note any error messages

- identify and isolate all floppy disks used recently on the machine

- create (and document) a procedure for effectively dealing with potential infections

- undertake random, but regular, checks on machines to test for the presence of unauthorised software.

As can be seen, the necessary measures are straightforward, and in some cases just plain common sense and very easy to incorporate into general data security procedures and user awareness training materials. Independent checks on machines by managers may assist in the detection of infections caused by disgruntled employees set on deliberate sabotage.

With the proliferation of inter-company data communications and the application of Electronic Data Interchange to provide commercial advantages, there is the added concern over the export of virus infections to customer or supplier systems. Considerable damage could be done to the organisation's commercial reputation with potentially serious effects on trading relationships if it were the source of passing on an infection. Additional precautions need to be applied in such cases to ensure that media transported between trading partners is suitably screened for possible infection before release. Any such media received should be subject to the measures prescribed for all software arriving from external sources.

Where there is major infection of an organisation's equipment, it may be necessary to call in external specialist consultants who should not only fully identify the type and extent of infection, but provide a planned approach to cleansing and eradicating the problem. The marketplace now features a number of virus detection and clearing programs for personal computers and some include an update service which, in return for an annual service charge, provides necessary amendments to detect and deal with recently developed viruses. Users of the MS DOS 6 operating system will also be aware that this includes a virus detection and clearance application which can be updated.

Control matrix example

This subject has a more natural affinity to the *Exposure* orientation of the methodology. Management are not likely to establish complex objectives in relation to the virus menace other than to basically avoid and eradicate, therefore the example matrix provided as Table 25 accordingly features the *Exposures* versus *Controls* approach.

The example *Scale* and *Size* data are set to middle/high values representing a significant dependence upon IT facilities. *Scale* 3 has been used in this example because it takes account of the effects of the disruption and distortion of data that could follow from a serious virus infection (see Appendix 5 for narrative in support of the values applied).

Table 25   Viruses - Exposures
Overall Inherent Risk (Size) Score [5 is worst risk; 1 is best] = 2.53

A Loss of business, data, control, etc. due to infection
B Disruption, costs, etc. due to infection of data
   & systems
C Inability to operate normal processing/service levels
D Failure to promptly detect and/or isolate infections
E Inadequate response to, or resolution of infections
F Absence of effective procedures - incorrect action,
   delay
G Inadequate level of general awareness of subject -
   error

H Infection due to introduction of unauthorised software
I Infection due to unauthorised access to Personal
   Computers
J Failure to recover due to lack of adequate data back-up
K Infection due to ability to circumvent anti-virus software
L Transfer of infection to customers/suppliers - image,
   costs
M Failure to promptly isolate/contain infection
N Failure to keep pace with ongoing virus developments
O Inadequate in-house expertise - failure to prevent/contain

Viruses			1	A	B	C	D	E	F	G	H	I	J	K	L	M	N	O
Calculated Risk Score		Risk		3	3	3	2	3	3	2	3	3	3	2	3	3	3	3
Scale 3 (6 is most serious)		Type		6	6	5	5	5	4	4	6	6	6	6	4	6	4	4
Size (3 is maximum)		Size		2	2	2	1	2	2	1	2	2	2	1	3	2	2	2
	CONTROLS	----------																
1	All hardware & software is purchased and installed by central IT department	Best		3	3	3					3							
		Test		?	?	?	?				?							
		Both																
2	All incoming software/data is scanned for infection before use	Best		4	4	4					4							
		Test		?	?	?	?				?							
		Both																
3	Only approved software from recognised and approved sources is utilised or introduced	Best		3	3	3					3							
		Test		?	?	?	?				?							
		Both																
4	Disks are scanned on dedicated stand-alone machine	Best		3	3	3					3							
		Test		?	?	?	?				?							
		Both																
5	Regular (and random) checks are undertaken to detect unauthorised software	Best		2	2	2					2							
		Test		?	?	?	?				?							
		Both																
6	Anti-virus scanning software is installed on all personal computers. Runs on boot up	Best		4	4	4	4				4	3						
		Test		?	?	?	?	?			?	?						
		Both																
7	Staff are aware that introduction of unauthorised software is a disciplinary matter	Best		2	2	2				2	2							
		Test		?	?	?	?			?	?							
		Both																

Table 25 continued

#			1	A	B	C	D	E	F	G	H	I	J	K	L	M	N	O
8	Visiting engineers are not permitted to use their own disks	Best		2	2	2					2	2						
		Test	?	?	?	?					?	?						
		Both																
-		---------	-	-	-	-	-	-	-	-	-	-	-	-	-	-	-	-
9	Selected machines have disk drive locks fitted, preventing loading /re-booting from floppy	Best		3	3	3					3	3						
		Test	?	?	?	?					?	?						
		Both																
-		---------	-	-	-	-	-	-	-	-	-	-	-	-	-	-	-	-
10	Personal Computers are locked when not in use - keys should be securely stored	Best		3	3	3					2	3						
		Test	?	?	?	?					?	?						
		Both																
-		---------	-	-	-	-	-	-	-	-	-	-	-	-	-	-	-	-
11	It is not possible to connect machines to bulletin boards	Best		2	2	2					2							
		Test	?	?	?	?					?							
		Both																
-		---------	-	-	-	-	-	-	-	-	-	-	-	-	-	-	-	-
12	Staff are required to report potential infections, & isolate the machine and related disks	Best					3	3	3							3		
		Test	?				?	?	?							?		
		Both																
-		---------	-	-	-	-	-	-	-	-	-	-	-	-	-	-	-	-
13	Procedures are in place covering the required actions and responsibilities	Best		3	3	3	3	3	4	3								
		Test	?	?	?	?	?	?	?	?								
		Both																
-		---------	-	-	-	-	-	-	-	-	-	-	-	-	-	-	-	-
14	All users are made aware of the implications of infection and the relevant precautions	Best		2	2	2	2			2								
		Test	?	?	?	?	?			?								
		Both																
-		---------	-	-	-	-	-	-	-	-	-	-	-	-	-	-	-	-
15	All potential infections are logged, and immediately followed up by User Support team	Best					4	4						4				
		Test	?				?	?						?				
		Both																
-		---------	-	-	-	-	-	-	-	-	-	-	-	-	-	-	-	-
16	Data is regularly backed-up	Best		2	2	3												
		Test	?	?	?	?												
		Both																
-		---------	-	-	-	-	-	-	-	-	-	-	-	-	-	-	-	-
17	Media is write-protected whenever possible	Best		2	2	2												
		Test	?	?	?	?												
		Both																
-		---------	-	-	-	-	-	-	-	-	-	-	-	-	-	-	-	-
18	User Support team isolate, scan and examine all potentially infected devices and media	Best					4	4								4		
		Test	?				?	?								?		
		Both																
-		---------	-	-	-	-	-	-	-	-	-	-	-	-	-	-	-	-
19	PC system alerts users if scan program has been previously interrupted & forces execution	Best												4				
		Test	?											?				
		Both																
-		---------	-	-	-	-	-	-	-	-	-	-	-	-	-	-	-	-

Table 25   continued

			1	A	B	C	D	E	F	G	H	I	J	K	L	M	N	O
20	All data files created for export to customers or suppliers are scanned before release	Best													5			
		Test	?												?			
		Both																
-		---------		-	-	-	-	-	-	-	-	-	-	-	-	-	-	-
21	Company subscribes to update service from anti-virus software supplier	Best															4	
		Test	?														?	
		Both																
-		---------		-	-	-	-	-	-	-	-	-	-	-	-	-	-	-
22	Nominated user support staff maintain subject awareness / knowledge	Best															3	3
		Test	?														?	?
		Both																
-		---------		-	-	-	-	-	-	-	-	-	-	-	-	-	-	-

A Loss of business, data, control, etc. due to infection
B Disruption, costs, etc. due to infection of data & systems
C Inability to operate normal processing/service levels
D Failure to promptly detect and/or isolate infections
E Inadequate response to, or resolution of infections
F Absence of effective procedures - incorrect action, delay
G Inadequate level of general awareness of subject - error

H Infection due to introduction of unauthorised software
I Infection due to unauthorised access to Personal Computers
J Failure to recover due to lack of adequate data back-up
K Infection due to ability to circumvent anti-virus software
L Transfer of infection to customers/suppliers - image, costs
M Failure to promptly isolate/contain infection
N Failure to keep pace with ongoing virus developments
O Inadequate in-house expertise - failure to prevent/contain

26

SPREADSHEET DESIGN

Scope

This chapter considers all aspects of Spreadsheet usage including the processes of risk assessment of the requirements, specification, design, construction, testing, documentation, and implementation of spreadsheet models.

Whether the above-noted stages are applied to the development of a model will obviously be relative to the importance and scale of the model, but it is generally suggested that all significant spreadsheets should be subject to some form of objective appraisal or review to ensure the application of the appropriate best practice techniques. The contents are not relevant to any one spreadsheet product, but are intended to relate to all generically. However, some of the examples given relate to features which may not be universally available, for example spreadsheet auditor facilities.

The use of personal computer-based applications such as Spreadsheets has burgeoned in recent years and companies have become both intentionally and accidentally more dependent upon them for supporting day-to-day management and decision taking.

Although, by their very nature, their use lends itself to providing quick and cheaply developed solutions to business requirements/problems, without necessarily having to resort to the previous formal system development route, there are attendant dangers in not controlling their use and thereby ensuring the quality of the results. Some of these apparent benefits may be illusionary if too much staff time is spent grappling with the mechanics of spreadsheet systems and the result is likely to mislead management. Management may view the use of spreadsheets as a stopgap or throwaway solution bridging a period until a more stable system can either be justified or created.

The primary aims of applying forms of control over the development and use of spreadsheets are to ensure that they are accurate, reliable, capable of future support, serve the best interests of the company, are consistently developed throughout the organisation, and built in accord with the simple requirements of best practice.

Some form of initial risk analysis of the requirements should indicate whether the use of a spreadsheet is the best option for the circumstances; for example, a complex model which has many branches and alternative data routes may not be easily accommodated within a spreadsheet and might be better suited to a bespoke application using a program language. There also needs to be an assessment of the level of dependency for the relevant data and greater attention paid to ensuring that the model mechanisms and structure are suitable and robust enough to cope with the present and foreseeable data and functional demands. In determining the optimum solution to the problem, the consideration for using spreadsheets should include the importance of the model to the company, the knowledge and spreadsheet skills of the developer, the likely need for future amendments, and an assessment of all the alternative solutions.

The end users will need to accurately identify and document all the aspects of functionality required to address the problem. This process should include the recording of the required inputs, formulae, logic, calculations, the use of variables and the degrees of arithmetic tolerance with respect to number of decimal places. Other factors, such as the reporting and presentation requirements, will also have to be included in the form of a user requirements specification to be used as the basis for the subsequent construction and testing of the model.

Some may consider that the requirement to specify, test and document a spreadsheet is somewhat excessive and counteracts some (or all) of the advantages offered by these flexible and comparatively friendly applications. However, these requirements are directly relative to the significance of the model being developed. If, for example, the model will play an important role in the management decision-making process, there is a very strong case for ensuring that its development follows the same disciplined path as for a mainframe system development. The accuracy and reliability of the model will need to be actively demonstrated before live use.

The use of macro facilities and customised menus of options can render the final product more user friendly and assist in navigating around the model. Cell protection facilities can prevent the amendment of critical formulae and data. Additionally, password protection on the file(s) can provide further assurance.

Having established all the requirements, the construction can begin with the application of the identified design criteria. In the appropriate circumstances (i.e. where the model will play a significant role in management planning) a full test plan will need to be created and applied, with the test results being documented. Users can be encouraged to take an active part in the testing phase as a means of satisfying themselves of the functionality of the model and its ease of use. It is possible that during either the construction or testing phases, necessary changes and enhancements may be highlighted and these should be agreed with the end-user(s) and documented, applied and themselves tested.

Organisations do not remain conveniently static, and therefore the future use and amendment of the model also has to be considered; for example if the model developer leaves the organisation, will there be sufficient information available to support the continued use of the model? This type of situation and the need to successfully apply amendments to the original model will be greatly aided by the existence of comprehensive and coherent documentation. Furthermore, by structuring the spreadsheet accordingly, amendments can be more easily accommodated.

Separate areas of the spreadsheet can be set aside to accommodate descriptions of its overall structure and aspects of its use. Additionally, some spreadsheet software incorporates a Spreadsheet Auditor facility which aids the testing and documentation by, for example, identifying redundant cells and trailing the effects of calculations.

Each organisation will approach the use of spreadsheets differently, one of the prime considerations being the expertise (or otherwise) of the staff involved in the use of such applications. Much depends on the culture of the company, and whether it promotes a user 'hands on' approach to the use and development of applications/solutions. Although this can be a direct way of enabling staff to quickly create their own solutions to everyday problems and thereby encourage self-reliance, the adoption of such an approach should not be at the cost of inconsistent or unreliable data used to support corporate decision making and management activities. In the case of complex or critical models, there may justification for producing a user guide and instructions for effective and secure use. Consideration may also have to be given to the provision of initial user training and support.

Finally, but not least, there is the matter of security of the model and the information it contains; aspects such as access to models, amendments to formulae, circulation of reports, etc. will need to be considered in relation to the significance of the model subject and the characteristics of its usage.

Control matrix example

An *Exposure*-oriented example matrix is provided as Table 26 which summarises the key risks. The example *Type* and *Size* data relates to middle range levels of usage of and/or dependence upon spreadsheets. The *Best* scores used in the illustration are set at low to middle levels of optimism that the relative *Controls* will be effective. Appendix 5 contains full details of *Scale* 4 which has been applied to the example matrix in Table 26.

Table 26   Spreadsheet Design - Exposures
Overall Inherent Risk (size) Score [5 is worst risk; 1 is best] = 2.00

A Inappropriate use of speadsheets - error, cost, delay, etc.

B Haphazard/uncontrolled use of spreadsheets - error, etc.

C Development of inaccurate/unreliable spreadsheets
- error

D Best Practice methods not applied - affects decision
making

E Absence of guidance & support on spreadsheet
developments

F Inadequate model security - leakage of data, error, etc.

G Absence of adequate documentation - unable to maintain
model

H Unsuitable structure of model - affects maintenance ability

I Users not involved in specification of model - error, delay

J Failure to adequately specify requirements - cost, delay

K Failure to adequately test models - decision errors, costs

L Absence of user documentation - error in use, time
wastage

M Unauthorised/un-documented amendments to models
- errors

N Unauthorised access to model data - sensitive data
leaked

O Insufficient training for users - delay, error, time waste

P Spreadsheets difficult to use in practice - error, costs

Spreadsheet Design		EXPOSURES															
		_	_	_	_	_	_	_	_	_	_	_	_	_	_	_	_
		A	B	C	D	E	F	G	H	I	J	K	L	M	N	O	P
		=	=	=	=	=	=	=	=	=	=	=	=	=	=	=	=
Calculated Risk Score	Risk	3	3	3	2	2	3	2	3	2	2	2	2	2	3	2	2
		-	-	-	-	-	-	-	-	-	-	-	-	-	-	-	-
Scale 4 (6 is most serious)	Type	5	4	4	3	4	5	3	4	5	5	5	3	5	5	3	3
Size (3 is maximum)	Size	2	2	2	2	1	2	2	2	1	1	1	2	1	2	1	1
CONTROLS	---------	-	-	-	-	-	-	-	-	-	-	-	-	-	-	-	-
1 Risk assessment is applied to problem, requirements, and suitability of spreadsheet use	Best	4	3														
	Test	?	?	?													
	Both																
-	---------	-	-	-	-	-	-	-	-	-	-	-	-	-	-	-	-
2 Guidelines issued on the use & construction of spreadsheets	Best		3	2	3		3										
	Test	?	?	?	?		?										
	Both																
-	---------	-	-	-	-	-	-	-	-	-	-	-	-	-	-	-	-
3 Best Practice guidance is applied to all key spreadsheet model developments	Best		3	3		4											
	Test	?	?	?		?											
	Both																
-	---------	-	-	-	-	-	-	-	-	-	-	-	-	-	-	-	-
4 Users are involved in the model specification processes	Best				2					5	4						
	Test	?			?					?	?						
	Both																
-	---------	-	-	-	-	-	-	-	-	-	-	-	-	-	-	-	-
5 The various stages of model development are documented and agreed	Best		2	3			3										
	Test	?		?	?			?									
	Both																
-	---------	-	-	-	-	-	-	-	-	-	-	-	-	-	-	-	-
6 Consideration is given to the model size, memory usage, layout, use of range names, etc.	Best		2	2			2										
	Test	?		?	?			?									
	Both																
-	---------	-	-	-	-	-	-	-	-	-	-	-	-	-	-	-	-
7 IT Department provides support on the use of spreadsheets, tools, etc.	Best				4												
	Test	?			?												
	Both																
-	---------	-	-	-	-	-	-	-	-	-	-	-	-	-	-	-	-

Table 26   Continued

			A	B	C	D	E	F	G	H	I	J	K	L	M	N	O	P
8	Cell protection is applied to key cells	Best						4								3		
		Test	?					?								?		
		Both																
-		---------	-	-	-	-	-	-	-	-	-	-	-	-	-	-	-	-
9	Access controls present on key corporate personal computers	Best						4								4		
		Test	?					?								?		
		Both																
-		---------	-	-	-	-	-	-	-	-	-	-	-	-	-	-	-	-
10	Technical & user documentation is included in a separate area of the spreadsheet	Best							4					4				3
		Test	?						?					?				?
		Both																
-		---------	-	-	-	-	-	-	-	-	-	-	-	-	-	-	-	-
11	Training is provided to support the development and use of significant models	Best					4											
		Test	?				?											
		Both																
-		---------	-	-	-	-	-	-	-	-	-	-	-	-	-	-	-	-
12	Macros are used to aid use, and text is included alongside the macro to assist maintenance	Best							3									
		Test	?						?									
		Both																
-		---------	-	-	-	-	-	-	-	-	-	-	-	-	-	-	-	-
13	Diagonal structure is adopted as preferred method, to enable ease of update, etc.	Best							4									
		Test	?						?									
		Both																
-		---------	-	-	-	-	-	-	-	-	-	-	-	-	-	-	-	-
14	Comprehensive testing is applied as per agreed test plan	Best											4					
		Test	?										?					
		Both																
-		---------	-	-	-	-	-	-	-	-	-	-	-	-	-	-	-	-
15	'Spreadsheet Auditor' facilities are used to identify ranges, potential cell conflicts, etc.	Best			2								3					
		Test	?		?								?					
		Both																
-		---------	-	-	-	-	-	-	-	-	-	-	-	-	-	-	-	-
16	All problems encountered in testing are documented and amendment forms are raised	Best											3	3				
		Test	?										?	?				
		Both																
-		---------	-	-	-	-	-	-	-	-	-	-	-	-	-	-	-	-
17	End-users are actively involved in testing, and sign-off the results	Best											2			4		
		Test	?										?			?		
		Both																
-		---------	-	-	-	-	-	-	-	-	-	-	-	-	-	-	-	-
18	All amendments are subject to change and version controls - also subject to testing	Best												4				
		Test	?											?				
		Both																
-		---------	-	-	-	-	-	-	-	-	-	-	-	-	-	-	-	-
19	Data validation techniques are applied (i.e. the use of 'IF' command)	Best			3													
		Test	?		?													
		Both																
-		---------	-	-	-	-	-	-	-	-	-	-	-	-	-	-	-	-

Table 26 Continued

			A	B	C	D	E	F	G	H	I	J	K	L	M	N	O	P
	Preferred design approach uses	Best																3
20	Menu structures	Test	?															?
		Both																
-		----------	-	-	-	-	-	-	-	-	-	-	-	-	-	-	-	-
	Separate text areas on the model	Best																3
21	provide help and support	Test	?															?
		Both																
-		----------	-	-	-	-	-	-	-	-	-	-	-	-	-	-	-	-

A Inappropriate use of speadsheets - error, cost, delay, etc.

B Haphazard/uncontrolled use of spreadsheets - error, etc.

C Development of inaccurate/unreliable spreadsheets - error

D Best Practice methods not applied - affects decision making

E Absence of guidance & support on spreadsheet developments

F Inadequate model security - leakage of data, error, etc.

G Absence of adequate documentation - unable to maintain model

H Unsuitable structure of model - affects maintenance ability

I Users not involved in specification of model - error, delay

J Failure to adequately specify requirements - cost, delay

K Failure to adequately test models - decision errors, costs

L Absence of user documentation - error in use, time wastage

M Unauthorised/un-documented amendments to models - errors

N Unauthorised access to model data - sensitive data leaked

O Insufficient training for users - delay, error, time waste

P Spreadsheets difficult to use in practice - error, costs

27

DATA PROTECTION ACT

Scope

This chapter examines the issues relative to the correct registration for Data Protection, ongoing compliance with all the requirements of the Data Protection Act (1984), and dealing with data subject enquiries.

The principles of the Act can, for the most part, be adequately observed with the definition and consistent application of a range of controls which will also coincidentally benefit the organisation as a whole. The more significant of these measures are the subjects of separate chapters in this volume; for example Chapter 17 – System Access Control and Chapter 18 – Back-up and Media Handling.

The Data Protection Act (1984) (also referred to as DPA in this chapter) covers the use of personal data, and requires 'Data Users' to register all appropriate details on the acquisition, use, and disposal of such data with the office of the Data Protection Registrar. In addition to working within the confines of the details they have registered, data users must comply with eight principles defined in the Act, as noted below.

First Principle: 'The information to be contained in personal data shall be obtained, and personal data shall be processed, fairly and lawfully'

Second Principle: 'Personal data shall be held only for one or more specified and lawful purpose'

Third Principle: 'Personal data held for any purpose or purposes shall not be used or disclosed in any manner incompatible with that purpose or those purposes'

Fourth Principle: 'Personal data held for any purpose or purposes shall be adequate, relevant and not excessive in relation to that purpose or those purposes'

Fifth Principle: 'Personal data shall be accurate and, where necessary, kept up-to-date'

Sixth Principle: 'Personal data held for any purpose or purposes shall not be kept for longer than is necessary for that purpose or those purposes'

Seventh Principle: 'An Individual shall be entitled –

(a) at reasonable intervals and without undue delay or expense:

  (i) to be informed by any data user whether he holds personal data of which that individual is the subject; and

  (ii) to access any such data held by a data user; and

(b)
  where appropriate to have such data corrected or erased'

Eighth Principle: 'Appropriate security measures shall be taken against unauthorised access to, or alteration, disclosure or destruction of, personal data and against accidental loss or damage'.

Since the implementation of the Act, there have been few significant penalties applied. However, there could be greater impact upon the reputation or public image of an organisation that was not complying with the spirit of the Act. One point of view is that the Act represents legalised common sense, as the structures engendered by the Act can have general beneficial effects, although the measures taken should primarily be cost-effective and in relation to the added value of the data concerned.

A company should establish a simple and clear Data Protection Policy and someone should be made responsible for addressing the DPA requirements, ensuring that all affected staff are made aware of their responsibilities, and handling any enquiries from data subjects. If the company has established policies or standards on IT security, access to data, etc., the relevant Co-ordinator should also be satisfied as to their effectiveness in relation to DPA considerations. The registration details need to be accurate and keep pace with any changes of use that may come about as a result of new business ventures or amendments to trading activities.

A Data Dictionary system (or the relevant facility in a Database Management System) can be used to keep track of those data items which have specific Data Protection Act implications, and be used to identify those systems/applications which use such data. This information can be used, when updating applications or specifying new uses of the database, to pinpoint any DPA implications in order to ensure that they are suitably addressed. In any case, such implications should be automatically considered as part of any relevant systems development project.

Particular care must be taken with data security, including data in printed or microfilm form. The presence of effective access control mechanisms can cover the requirements of the eighth principle. Disposal of personal data also requires consideration, especially the destruction of reports and microfiche records. Validation at point of data entry can obviously help with the accuracy of data, albeit that access restrictions and exception reporting can provide further assurance that the data remains essentially accurate.

Control matrix example

An *Exposure*-oriented matrix is provided in Table 27 as this approach best supports the general requirement to comply with the defined legal requirements and implications of the Data Protection Act (1984).

The example data values relate to an organisation with mid-range levels of personal data, and a significant dependence upon IT systems. *Scale 3*, which has been applied to this example, is described in Appendix 5.

Table 27 Data Protection Act - Exposures

Overall Inherent Risk (Size) Score [5 is worst risk; 1 is best] = 2.06

A Failure to comply with DPA/Lack of preparedness
B Failure to allocate specific responsibility for DPA matters
C Inadequate general awareness or knowledge of DPA
D Inaccurate/out of date DPA registration
E DPA implications not addressed in systems developments
F Failure to obtain personal data fairly or lawfully
G Personal data held for non-registered purposes
H Personal data disseminated for non-registered purposes
I Inaccurate or out-of-date personal data held

J Unwanted, surplus or obsolete personal data held
K Unauthorised access to personal data
L Personal data subject to invalid or unauthorised amendment
M Personal data accidently destroyed or lost
N Insecure or partial disposal of printed/filmed data
O Absence of facilities for handling data subject enquiries
P Data subject enquiries not actioned within legal period
Q Failure to correct or erase defective data

Data Protection Act	EXPOSURES	A	B	C	D	E	F	G	H	I	J	K	L	M	N	O	P	Q
Calculated Risk Score	Risk	3	3	3	3	3	3	3	3	3	3	3	3	3	3	2	2	2
Scale 3 (6 is most serious)	Type	4	4	4	4	4	4	4	4	4	4	4	4	4	4	4	4	4
Size (3 is maximum)	Size	2	2	3	3	2	2	2	2	2	2	3	3	2	2	1	1	1
CONTROLS																		
1 Data Protection Co-ordinator appointed. Review procedures, forms, etc. for compliance	Best	4	5															
	Test	?	?	?														
	Both																	
2 DPA information packs provided as part of new employee induction process	Best			3														
	Test	?		?														
	Both																	
3 DPA training sessions held for relevant staff	Best			4														
	Test	?		?														
	Both																	
4 Co-ordinator is made aware of all relevant amendments to systems for DPA implications	Best					4												
	Test	?				?												
	Both																	
5 Co-ordinator updates DPA registration for subsidiaries as required	Best					4												
	Test	?				?												
	Both																	
6 DPA implication process is defined in development procedures	Best					5												
	Test	?				?												
	Both																	
7 Corporate data protection policy established	Best	4	3	4	3	3	4	4	4	4	4	4	4	4	4	4	4	4
	Test	?	?	?	?	?	?	?	?	?	?	?	?	?	?	?	?	?
	Both																	

Table 27 continued

#	Description		A	B	C	D	E	F	G	H	I	J	K	L	M	N	O	P	Q
8	Relevant company forms reflect notice to data subjects as regards their rights under DPA	Best						4											
		Test	?					?											
		Both																	
-		---------	-	-	-	-	-	-	-	-	-	-	-	-	-	-	-	-	-
9	Data recorded in Data Dictionary with user access rights - used to restrict/control access	Best				3		3	3				3	3					
		Test	?			?		?	?				?	?					
		Both																	
-		---------	-	-	-	-	-	-	-	-	-	-	-	-	-	-	-	-	-
10	Data validation applied at data input	Best								4									
		Test	?							?									
		Both																	
-		---------	-	-	-	-	-	-	-	-	-	-	-	-	-	-	-	-	-
11	Access to systems and data is granted on a 'Need to Know' basis - via user-ID & password	Best								4			4	4	3				
		Test	?							?			?	?	?				
		Both																	
-		---------	-	-	-	-	-	-	-	-	-	-	-	-	-	-	-	-	-
12	Reports reflecting personal data are distributed in sealed packets to addressee	Best								4									
		Test	?							?									
		Both																	
-		---------	-	-	-	-	-	-	-	-	-	-	-	-	-	-	-	-	-
13	Mail-outs, etc. request that recipients advise company of any data errors	Best								3									3
		Test	?							?									?
		Both																	
-		---------	-	-	-	-	-	-	-	-	-	-	-	-	-	-	-	-	-
14	Out-of-date personal data is archived to secure store	Best								4									
		Test	?							?									
		Both																	
-		---------	-	-	-	-	-	-	-	-	-	-	-	-	-	-	-	-	-
15	Access to data amendments & deletions is further restricted by access controls	Best											4	4	4				
		Test	?										?	?	?				
		Both																	
-		---------	-	-	-	-	-	-	-	-	-	-	-	-	-	-	-	-	-
16	Regular data back-ups are taken and securely stored	Best													3				
		Test	?												?				
		Both																	
-		---------	-	-	-	-	-	-	-	-	-	-	-	-	-	-	-	-	-
17	All unwanted printouts and micro-film containing personal data are shredded or burnt	Best														4			
		Test	?													?			
		Both																	
-		---------	-	-	-	-	-	-	-	-	-	-	-	-	-	-	-	-	-
18	All data subject enquiries are logged by the Co-ordinator and passed to senior manager	Best															4		
		Test	?														?		
		Both																	
-		---------	-	-	-	-	-	-	-	-	-	-	-	-	-	-	-	-	-
19	Each enquiry is investigated and assessed - decision reached and enquirer informed of action, etc.	Best															4		
		Test	?														?		
		Both																	
-		---------	-	-	-	-	-	-	-	-	-	-	-	-	-	-	-	-	-

Table 27 continued

			A	B	C	D	E	F	G	H	I	J	K	L	M	N	O	P	Q
	All enquiries responded to in	Best																4	
20	five days	Test	?															?	
		Both																	
-		---------	-	-	-	-	-	-	-	-	-	-	-	-	-	-	-	-	-
	Incorrect data is corrected	Best																	4
21	or erased as appropriate	Test	?																?
		Both																	
-		---------	-	-	-	-	-	-	-	-	-	-	-	-	-	-	-	-	-
	Enquiry log updated with	Best																	2
22	action and limited fee is	Test	?																?
	charged	Both																	
-		---------	-	-	-	-	-	-	-	-	-	-	-	-	-	-	-	-	-

A Failure to comply with DPA/Lack of preparedness
B Failure to allocate specific responsibility for DPA matters
C Inadequate general awareness or knowledge of DPA
D Inaccurate/out of date DPA registration
E DPA implications not addressed in systems developments
F Failure to obtain personal data fairly or lawfully
G Personal data held for non-registered purposes
H Personal data disseminated for non-registered purposes
I Inaccurate or out-of-date personal data held

J Unwanted, surplus or obsolete personal data held
K Unauthorised access to personal data
L Personal data subject to invalid or unauthorised amendment
M Personal data accidently destroyed or lost
N Insecure or partial disposal of printed/filmed data
O Absence of facilities for handling data subject enquiries
P Data subject enquiries not actioned within legal period
Q Failure to correct or erase defective data

Appendices

APPENDIX 1

Glossary of Terms

Noted below are explanations for the abbreviations and terms used both throughout this book and generally in the IT context. Given the ongoing proliferation of acronyms and terminology in the IT world, this list is not intended to be comprehensive, but is supplied as an aid to readers.

4GL	Fourth Generation Language
ASCII	American National Standard Code for Information Interchange
BACS	Bankers Automated Clearing Services (Ltd)
BASIC	Beginner's All-purpose Symbolic Instruction Code
BPS	Bits Per Second
CAAT	Computer Aided Audit Techniques
CAD	Computer Aided Design
CAE	Computer Aided Engineering
CAM	Computer Aided Manufacturing
CASE	Computer Assisted Systems Engineering
CCITT	The International Telegraph & Telephone Consultative Committee
CCTV	Closed Circuit Television
CEFIC	The European Chemical Industry Federation
CPM	Critical Path Method – A method of predicting which steps in a complex job control the overall speed of job completion
CPU	Central Processing Unit
CRC	A method of validating blocks of data bits to insure against destruction or modification during reading, writing or transmission
DBA	Database Administrator
DBMS	Database Management System
DD	Data Dictionary
DDP	Distributed Data Processing
DES	Data Encryption Standard (National Bureau of Standards, USA)
DOS	Disk Operating System
DP	Data Processing
DPA	Data Protection Act
DTP	Desktop Publishing
EDI	Electronic Data Interchange
EDIA	Electronic Data Interchange Association
EDICON	Electronic Data Interchange in Construction

EDIFACT	Electronic Data Interchange for Administration, Commerce & Trade
EDIFICE	Electronic Data Interchange Forum for Companies Interested in Computers and Electronics
EDP	Electronic Data Processing
EDPAA	EDP Auditors Association
EFT	Electronic Funds Transfer
EFTPOS	Electronic Funds Transfer at Point of Sale
FM	Facilities Management
GB	Gigabyte – Refers to memory storage capacity; two to the thirtieth power, 1,073,741,824 in decimal notation
HDR	Header – An internal label or data set label immediately preceding the first record of a file, that identifies the file and contains data used in file control
Hz	Hertz – A unit of frequency equal to one cycle per second; used to denote processor speed, e.g. 33Mhz (33,000 cycles per second)
IAD	Internal Audit Department
IIA	Institute of Internal Auditors
IPSE	Integrated Project Support Environment
ISDN	Integrated Services Digital Network
IT	Information Technology
JCL	Job Control Language
KB	Kilobyte
LAN	Local Area Network
MB	Megabyte – Refers to memory storage capacity; two to the twentieth power, 1,048,576 in decimal notation
MICR	Magnetic Ink Character Recognition
MIPS	Millions of Instructions Per Second – A relative measure of machine speed
MIS	Management Information System
MODEM	Modulator-Demodulator – A device that converts digital signals to analogue signals and vice versa for transmission over data communications facilities
MS-DOS	Microsoft Disk Operating System
NCC	National Computing Centre
OA	Office Automation
OCR	Optical Character Recognition
ODETTE	Organisation for Data Exchange by Teletransmission in Europe
OSI	Open Standards Interconnection
PC	Personal Computer
PDN	Public Data Network
PIN	Personal Identification Number
PSS	Packet Switchstream
PSTN	Public Switched Telephone Network
QA	Quality Assurance

QBE	Query By Example
RACF	Resource Access Control Facility – A program product that provides access control by identifying and verifying users to the system
RJE	Remote Job Entry
SCL	Systems Control Language
SQL	Structured Query Language
SSADM	Structured Systems Analysis and Design Method
SWIFT	Society for Worldwide Interbank Financial Telecommunications
TRADACOMS	Trading Data Communications Standard
UNICORN	United National Interactive (Message) Concept Over Reservation Networks (EDI ferry/holiday industry project)
UPS	Uninterruptible Power Supply
VADS	Value-Added & Data Services (alternative for VAN)
VAN	Value-Added Network
WAN	Wide Area Network

APPENDIX 2

Bibliography

R A Barden, *DP Back-Up Procedures*, NCC Publications, 1987

J Baston, A Brown, *Spreadsheet Modelling Best Practice, Accountants Digest 273*, The Institute of Chartered Accountants in England & Wales, 1991

K Bhaskar and Computer Industry Research Unit, *Computer Security: Threats and Countermeasures,* NCC Blackwell, 1992

A D Chambers, *Effective Internal Audits,* Pitman, 1992

A D Chambers, J M Court, *Computer Auditing,* 3rd Edition, Pitman, 1991

A D Chambers, G M Selim, G Vinten, *Internal Auditing,* 2nd Edition, Pitman, 1987

Chartered Institute of Public Finance and Accountancy, *BACS Guidance Note*, 3rd Edition, 1992

J M Court (Editor), *Audit and Control in a Complex Computer Environment*, The Institute of Chartered Accountants in England & Wales, 1984

J M Court (Editor), *Audit and Control in a Microcomputer Environment,* The Institute of Chartered Accountants in England & Wales, 1988

M Devargas, *Local Area Networks*, 2nd Edition, NCC Blackwell, 1992

M Devargas, *Network Security,* NCC Blackwell, 1993

R Doswell, G L Simons, *Fraud and Abuse of IT Systems*, NCC Publications, 1986

I J Douglas, *Audit and Control of Minicomputers,* NCC Publications, 1982

R A Elbra, *A Practical Guide to the Computer Misuse Act 1990,* NCC Blackwell, 1990

R A Elbra, *Security Review Manual,* NCC Publications, 1986

J R Ellison, J A T Pritchard, *Security in Office Systems,* NCC Blackwell, 1987

W A Freyenfield, *Decision Support Systems*, NCC Publications, 1984

R R Garcia, *Human Factors In Systems Development*, NCC Publications, 1988

C Hook, *Data Protection Implications for Systems Design*, NCC Publications, 1989

Institute of Chartered Accountants in England & Wales, *Countering Computer Fraud,* 1987

B Jenkins, R C L Perry, P J Cooke, *An Audit Approach to Computers,* The Institute of Chartered Accountants in England & Wales, revised edition, 1986

W C Mair, D R Wood and K W Davis, *Computer Control and Audit*, Institute of Internal Auditors Inc., revised edition, 1978.

S Nugus, S Harris, *PC Data Recovery and Disaster Prevention,* NCC Blackwell, 1992

G O'Shea, *Security in Computer Operating Systems*, NCC Blackwell, 1991

M Parfett, *What is EDI?*, NCC Blackwell, 1992

J Parkinson, *Making CASE Work,* NCC Blackwell, 1991

D S J Remenyi, A Money, A Twite, *A Guide to Measuring and Managing I T Benefits,* NCC Blackwell, 1991

D S J Remenyi, *Increase Profits with Strategic Information Systems*, NCC Publications,1988

D S J Remenyi, *Introducing Strategic Information Systems Planning (SISP),* NCC Blackwell, 1991

D S J Remenyi, *Strategic Information Systems,* NCC Blackwell, 1990

A F Robb, *The Management Guide to the Selection and Implementation of Computer Systems,* NCC Blackwell, 1992

D W Roberts, *Computer Security: Policy Planning and Practice,* NCC Blackwell, 1990

I Walden, A Braganza (Editors), *EDI: Audit and Control,* NCC Blackwell, 1993

APPENDIX 3

Index of Subjects to Chapter Numbers

Entries marked * are the subject of a separate chapter

APPENDIX 4

Table of Related Subjects

Chapter	Subject	Related chapters
	THE STRATEGIC DIRECTION	
4	IT Strategic Planning	All
5	IT Organisation	4, 6, 9, 10, 15, 16, 17, 18, 19, 21, 23, 27
6	Contingency Planning	4, 5, 7, 8, 10, 11, 12, 13, 15, 18, 19, 20, 21, 23, 24
7	Databases	4, 6, 9, 17, 18, 19, 20, 22, 27
8	Electronic Data Interchange	4, 6, 9, 17, 18, 19, 22, 25
9	System Development	4, 5, 7, 8, 11, 15, 16, 17, 18, 19, 21, 22, 23, 27
10	Facilities Management and Bureaux	4, 5, 6, 15, 16, 17, 18, 19, 23
11	Personal Computers/Workstations	4, 6, 9, 12, 13, 14, 17, 18, 20, 21, 22, 23, 25, 26, 27
12	Local Area Networks	4, 6, 11, 13, 17, 18, 20, 21, 22, 23, 25, 27
13	Electronic Office	4, 6, 11, 12, 16, 17, 18, 21, 22, 23, 25, 26, 27
14	Expert Systems	4, 14, 17, 22, 23
	THE OPERATIONAL FRAMEWORK	
15	IT Sites	4, 5, 6, 9, 10, 16, 17, 18, 19
16	IT Accounting	4, 5, 9, 10, 13, 15, 17, 19, 20, 26
17	System Access Control	4, 5, 7, 8, 9, 10, 11, 12, 13, 14, 15, 16, 19, 21, 23, 24, 26, 27
18	Back-up and Media Handling	4, 5, 6, 7, 8, 9, 10, 11, 12, 13, 15, 19, 20, 23, 24, 25, 26, 27
19	Processing Operations	4, 5, 6, 7, 8, 9, 10, 15, 16, 17, 18, 20, 21, 24, 27
20	Systems/Operating Software	4, 6, 7, 11, 12, 16, 18, 19, 21
21	Software Maintenance	4, 5, 6, 9, 11, 12, 13, 17, 19, 20, 27
22	Software Package Selection	4, 7, 8, 9, 11, 12, 13, 14, 26
23	User Support	4, 5, 6, 9, 10, 11, 12, 13, 14, 17, 18, 25, 26, 27
24	BACS	4, 6, 9, 17, 18, 19

Chapter	Subject	Related chapters
25	Viruses	4, 8, 11, 12, 13, 18, 23
26	Spreadsheet Design	4, 11, 13, 16, 17, 18, 22, 23
27	Data Protection Act	4, 5, 7, 8, 9, 11, 12, 13, 17, 18, 19, 21, 23

APPENDIX 5

Category scales used in control matrices

The control matrix technique used in this book, and explained in detail in Chapter 3, measures the inherent and control risks of each objective or of each exposure. The measurement of inherent risk has two dimensions – first, the category of the inherent risk and secondly, its likely size. The category of the inherent risk is shown in the 'Scale' (or 'Type') row near the top of the control matrix as a number in the range '1' to '6' for each objective or exposure. The scale used is also given as a number immediately after the word 'Scale' – such as 'Scale 4'. Each control matrix at the end of Chapters 4 to 27 makes use of Scale 1, 2, 3, 4 or 6 and Table 3.3 in Chapter 3 is a variant of Scale 4. Other scales are given in this Appendix as examples. Some scales are suitable for control matrices oriented to *Objectives* and others for matrices oriented to *Exposures*. Users should consider whether one or more of these sample scales are suitable for their purposes or whether they need to develop scales which are more relevant to their businesses.

Category Scale 1 (Objectives)

Point of Scale

6 (Most serious)	Management must understand what is happening to the business overall, and be able to adapt appropriately
5	Medium- to long-term corporate objectives must be achieved
4	Budgets and profit targets must be achieved
3	Management must be taking appropriate action to correct performance
2	Management must understand what is happening at operational levels
1 (Least serious)	Motivation must be high

Category Scale 2 (Objectives)

Point of Scale

6 (Most serious)	Strategically vital to the business
5	Contributes significantly to, or participates significantly in business analysis and decision taking

4	Contributes significantly to the reliability of data, records and management information
3	Contributes significantly to administrative and operational efficiency
2	Makes operational economies
1 (Least serious)	Makes administrative economies

Category Scale 3 (Exposures)

Point of Scale

6 (Most serious)	Loss of Information
5	Loss of cash or other asset, or increase in liability
4	Political sensitivity or loss of reputation
3	Loss or exaggeration of profit
2	Distortion of the balance sheet
1 (Least serious)	Accounting error without profit and loss or balance sheet effect

Category Scale 4 (Exposures)

Point of Scale

6 (Most serious)	Failure to achieve business objectives
5	Systems failure
4	Loss of control of the corporate database
3	Damaging delay
2	Unnecessary financial costs
1 (Least serious)	Delay of no commercial significance

Category Scale 5 (Objectives)

Point of Scale

6 (Most serious)	Strategically vital to the business
5	Vital for fully complying with the Data Protection Act
4	Makes an important contribution to data protection
3	Operationally important for business analysis and decision making
2	Makes administrative economies
1 (Least serious)	Makes operational economies

Category Scale 6 (Objectives)

Point of Scale

6 (Most serious)	Contributes significantly to business analysis and decision taking
5	Contributes significantly to management information
4	Contributes significantly to the reliability of data records
3	Contributes significantly to administrative and operational efficiency
2	Makes operational economies
1 (Least serious)	Makes administrative economies

Category Scale 7 (Objectives)

Point of Scale

6 (Most serious)	Loss of corporate reputation
5	Loss of competitive edge
4	Delay in processing data
3	Misunderstanding of what is happening
2	Contributes to operational efficiency and economy
1 (Least serious)	[not used]

Category Scale 8 (Exposures)

[Designed for Contract Auditing]

Point of Scale

6 (Most serious)	Incorrect identification of needs ('Should the business have embarked on the project in the first place?')
5	Need unfulfilled
4	Unnecessary financial cost
3	Delay
2	Ineffective accountability
1 (Least serious)	Inadequate information

INDEX